BLOOD, BONE, AND MARROW

BLOOD, BONE, AND MARROW
A Biography of Harry Crews

TED GELTNER

The University of Georgia Press   Athens

*This publication is made possible in part through
a grant from the Bradley Hale Fund for Southern Studies
and by the generous support of Donna Scott Reed.*

© 2016 by the University of Georgia Press
Athens, Georgia 30602
www.ugapress.org
Designed by Melissa Bugbee Buchanan
Set in Franklin Gothic and Sabon
Printed and bound by Thomson-Shore
The paper in this book meets the guidelines for
permanence and durability of the Committee on
Production Guidelines for Book Longevity of the
Council on Library Resources.

Most University of Georgia Press titles are
available from popular e-book vendors.

Printed in the United States of America
20 19 18 17 16 C 5 4 3 2 1

Library of Congress Cataloging-in-Publication Data
Geltner, Ted.
    Blood, bone, and marrow : a biography of Harry Crews / Ted Geltner.
        pages cm
    Includes bibliographical references.
    ISBN 978-0-8203-4923-7 (hardcover : alk. paper) —
ISBN 978-0-8203-4924-4 (ebook : alk. paper)
    1. Crews, Harry, 1935–2012. 2. Novelists, American—20th
century—Biography. I. Title.
    PS3553.R46Z64 2016
    813'.54—dc23
    [B]
                                    2015032701

To Dorny and Maz, my teammates in one of the most
memorable games of three-on-three of the twentieth century.
We lost, 50–12, but we had the momentum at the end.
At least, that's how I remember it. How about you?

How joyous I am now that I've learned that there is
no such thing as happiness.

INSCRIPTION, BUDDHIST TEMPLE

It was all pie-in-the-sky, it was impossible to start with.
There is nothing possible about this. So if you're going to
ask for it, you might as well ask for all of it.

HARRY CREWS, 1977

CONTENTS

FOREWORD

Where do storytellers come from? In this book, Ted Geltner relates that Harry Crews likened the difficult task and craft of writing to looking for gold in a coal mine. But what brings the writer into that dark and suffocating space in the first place? Why go into the coal mine when there are places in the sun to be instead? Every writer is different. Every writer has a cauldron—literal or figurative—from which the art boils to the surface. My own path is inextricably influenced and entwined with Harry Crews. It was Crews who lured me into the coal mine and the hunt for gold. For forty years I have been under the sway of a man I never really met.

Harry Crews was a uniquely gifted and haunted storyteller. Novel, journal, memoir—he made each form his own in a way like no one else before or since. The pages that follow in this absorbing biography detail this and reach into the guts of the experiences that formed him and gave him a voice that was sad, brutal, and funny. Harry said that when it came to writing the truth about himself—or anything for that matter—he was not as interested in facts as he was in memory and belief.

My memory and belief about Harry Crews begins in August 1974, when I stood as a freshman on the campus of the University of Florida. Three weeks earlier President Richard Nixon had resigned in disgrace, and we were at the tail end of what the new president called our long national nightmare. Three weeks before that I had registered for what would be the last military draft of the Vietnam War.

It was my first day of classes. I knew no one and was hovering around the outside entrance of an auditorium where I was on the schedule to be taught English lit, a freshman requirement. I didn't want to go in, I didn't want to be there, I didn't want to take the class. I was only in college to appease parents and have a deferment edge against the draft.

I heard a man's loud voice, turned and saw the instructor, Harry Crews, walking toward the auditorium door. Walking is a bad description. He was hobbled, limping. His shoulder swung a bit to balance a bad leg as he moved. I wouldn't know the reasons until later, but Harry Crews was a captivating storyteller in just the way he walked.

I want to say that he was wearing a sleeveless denim shirt and was leanly muscled and tattooed—a fresh hinge painted permanently on the crook of the elbow on his drinking arm. That's what I believe in memory, at least. But when I look now at my collection of books authored by Crews I see photos of him crouched in a creek bed in sleeveless denim, his face chiseled by life, but no tattoos. Maybe what I remember and believe is wrong. Maybe it's just the photo I believe.

I had never seen a real author before. Crews was pointed, opinionated, and profane when he lectured. He was larger than life and intimidating. In this book Ted Geltner describes professional journalists being intimidated by Crews, not wanting the assignment of interviewing him. Imagine how an auditorium full of college freshmen reacted when he posed a question about Flannery O'Connor. Nobody would raise a hand to answer. And Crews didn't want them to anyway. Crews answered his own questions, didn't seem to care for other opinion.

I was transfixed. It would be the only class that quarter—they weren't called semesters back then—that I didn't regularly cut. I started disregarding assignments in my other classes to read the handful of novels Crews had published and was soon mesmerized. I would compare what I was reading in these novels to the man I saw in English lit. On occasion I would go to a bar in downtown Gainesville where Crews was known to hold court, sometimes from a barber's chair that functioned as his throne. I would go and watch and listen. I never introduced myself or spoke to him there. Not once. I was just a literary stalker, and there were others there like me.

In the course of the quarter I ran out of Crews books to read. I started over. A couple months after Christmas break I bought a Playboy magazine. Yes, for the articles—or I should say, article—a Crews story on the Alaskan oil boom called "Going Down in Valdez." Oddly, or maybe ironically, the centerfold of that edition—yes, I did take a look—was named Laura Misch. She would years later become a writer and would compete with me daily on the crime beat in Fort Lauderdale—she working for the Miami Herald, me working for the Fort Lauderdale News. It was a small world.

I didn't go the distance as a student. The Vietnam War was no longer a threat on my life, and hiding out in college was not necessary. I quit going to class in the spring and was eventually asked—no, told—to leave. I spent most of the next two years as a dishwasher by day and a reader by night. I kept reading Crews novels and stories. I inhaled the work of other masters like Raymond Chandler, Hunter Thompson, Ken Kesey, and Kurt Vonnegut. Some of it was fiction, some journalism. It was all storytelling to me.

Somewhere in that time I decided I wanted to be a writer. I wanted to take a shot at it. I served my academic penance and went back to school. The first class I signed up for was creative writing with Harry Crews. I didn't care how intimidating it might be. I wanted to be inspired. I wanted to experiencethat larger than life personality and to hear about the cauldron from which true storytelling came. I wasn't sure I had what it would take and thought Crews would either convince or dissuade me.

He did neither. Harry didn't show up that semester—yes, now we were on semesters. About ten of us gathered in a small classroom that first day and a graduate assistant told us that Harry was late returning from an assignment for Playboy. He gave us our own writing assignments and said Crews would be back soon and would read and critique our work.

But he never did, and I never saw Harry Crews again.

I continued to know him through his writing. I continued to be inspired. I am sure my path would be different if not for Crews. Even though I never actually met him. That is my memory and belief.

Almost twenty years after that English lit class, Harry Crews was at a bookstore in Sarasota, Florida, talking about and signing his new novel, Scar Lover. A woman named Mary stepped up to Mr. Crews and asked him to sign a copy of his novel to her son Michael. She said her son's first novel had just been published and had been reviewed well in the Washington Post. She said her son had been one of Crews's students and had been greatly inspired by him. Crews asked the name for the inscription.

"Michael Connelly," Mary said.

"Never heard of him," Harry said.

My mother withheld the story from me, instead just sending me the book that Crews had warmly and generically inscribed to me. Several years later, when one of my novels cracked the New York Times bestseller list for the first time, she thought I was properly accomplished and steeled to hear the full story about the rebuke from my literary hero. I smiled when she told me and reported to her that Crews had spoken the truth. He could not possibly have ever heard of me. We had never actually met.

Several years later I watched a television interview with Crews. All these years after school, I still craved his writing, his personality, his take on the struggle to write something that was true. I continued to glean from him inspiration. He continued to bring light into my coal mine.

In the video he sat in a chair in his writing room in front of a wall of shelved books and spoke of his life and work. Over his right shoulder I saw one of my books on a shelf. I had never met the man and he had once professed to having never heard of me, but there was my book within easy reach of his writing spot.

I smiled. My mother was dead by then, so I couldn't tell her the kicker to her story. But I sure felt proud that day.

Michael Connelly
Los Angeles

BLOOD, BONE, AND MARROW

PART ONE

THERE IS NO ROAD UP, NO PATH

The features editor at the *Gainesville Sun* pivoted in his chair slightly and looked down the two short rows of cubicles that housed the *Sun*'s feature writing staff. The writers paused, put down their phones, swiveled away from their keyboards, and focused their attention on the editor.

"Who wants to call Harry Crews?" he asked.

The question hung in the air for a few seconds, and most of the writers swiveled back to their keyboards, picked up their phones, or just stared dully in the opposite direction, hoping to avoid eye contact.

His first effort thwarted, the editor began directly addressing his writers, one by one, this time adding a pleading quality to his query.

Still no takers.

Since much of the staff had been working at the *Sun* for years, and Crews had been one of Gainesville's most famous, or infamous, residents for three and a half decades, many had been assigned to write about him in the past. One young female writer politely turned down the assignment and recounted her last interview with Crews, which had involved perceived sexual harassment and far too much profanity to produce even a single usable quote for an article in the family-friendly *Gainesville Sun*. Another veteran writer said he wasn't paid anywhere near enough to subject himself to the likely verbal abuse. One by one, everyone listening bowed out. With regrets, one reporter said he was a real fan of Crews's books. But he had interviewed Crews once and would rather not relive the experience. "I felt like he was this close," the writer said, "to crumpling me up into a little ball and putting me into his back pocket."

I had joined the staff just a few weeks earlier. A severe case of journalism burnout had caused me to spend the previous nine months in a job where my main responsibility was proofreading phone directories and editing fascinating trade magazines with names like *Asphalt Today* and *Chicken & Egg Monthly*. So now I was back at a newspaper, ready for something a little more exciting. With more than a little trepidation, I consented to make the call.

Crews was back in the news that week because we had gotten word that a movie crew was coming to town to make a feature film based on his 1973 novel, *The Hawk Is Dying*. Ever since Crews published his first novel, *The*

Gospel Singer, in 1968, Hollywood had been buying up the options to his books. Crews had pocketed the money, written a few of the screenplays himself, but thanks in large part to the strangeness of the stories, not one reel of film had been shot. Now, finally, a crew had been hired, and real actors were prepared to bring Crews's work to life.

To ready myself for the interview, I went out looking for a copy of the book. It was listed as available in the University of Florida library, but when I found my way to its spot in the stacks, it wasn't there. Stolen, I was told. Same story at the Alachua County Library. A check on Amazon clued me in to the reason: the book had been out of print for years, and used copies started at two hundred dollars and went up quickly. Luckily, the library at Santa Fe Community College had managed to hang on to its copy (it looked like it had been gnawed on by a raccoon and probably wouldn't have netted much on eBay).

I started dutifully carrying the battered green volume with me to and from the office. A colleague noticed the book lying on my desk and asked me what I thought so far.

"A guy put a dead hawk down the garbage disposal," I said.

"Hence, the title," he said.

My awareness of Crews at that time was rather limited, especially for someone who had lived in Gainesville off and on for a decade. I had copyedited a few reviews of his recent novels, heard some horror stories about his ruthlessness with students, and by virtue of living in north central Florida, been schooled in the Harry Crews legend, CliffsNotes version.

Though Crews had lived the majority of his life in Gainesville, the epicenter of the legend lay in Bacon County, Georgia, where he was born and lived until he was about twelve. Thanks to the Great Depression; a drunken, violent stepfather; a series of physical ailments; and general bad luck, Crews packed a lifetime of suffering into those twelve years. Through the suffering, however, he was apparently compiling enough material to fill the thousands of pages he would write once he emerged from the desolate territory of his youth.

Along with material, he somehow acquired an unwavering drive to write, a pursuit that was about as common in Bacon County as nuclear engineering. All retellings of the Crews legend include the detail that Harry learned to read with the only two books at his disposal: the Sears catalog and the holy Bible. And while all the people around him, young and old, were enamored with the Bible, Harry was partial to the catalog, with its shiny, perfectly chiseled models, decked out in all the new fashions, fashions that never seemed to make it to south Georgia. Harry looked at the people in the catalog and then looked around at the characters in his life, with their scars and wounds and various disfigurements, and a narrative buried itself deep within his psyche. He became a literary sleeper agent, ready to be activated years later, when Bacon County was no longer his prison but only a backdrop for his scarred, wounded characters.

I looked him up in the phone book and was surprised to find him listed. I dialed the number, not sure what to expect. From the warnings I had received in the newsroom, nothing short of being physically assaulted through the phone line seemed out of the realm of possibility.

On the first ring, he picked up and bellowed "Harry Crews," with the same intonation that one might demand "What do you want?"

Once I explained the nature of my call, though, he seemed eager to talk. His voice was a low gravel. The patterns of his speech were an odd mixture of Georgia–North Florida drawl and late sixties hippie speak, with words like "man" and "jive" and "dig it" peppered throughout his sentences, outnumbered only by expletives.

He managed to seem both pleased and disturbed by the prospect of an interview. Nearly every utterance that came through the receiver seemed to be quote worthy (once the unprintable modifiers were removed). He talked and talked, and it was all gold. If you could get past the bluster, he seemed to be a reporter's dream.

Was he concerned with how the filmmakers would treat his novel?

"I don't care if they make a fucking musical out of it. My book's in the library."

Did he do research about hawks to write the book?

"I don't do research for my books. Robert Penn Warren told me, 'Doing research for a novel is obscene.' If you've got to do research, you're not ready to write the novel."

Was he glad that one of his books was finally going to be on the big screen?

"I'm glad they gave me all the fucking money, man. I just wish they'd given it to me a few years ago, when I could still use it to get into some shit."

I hung up the phone with a notebook full of material. Of course, he had said many of the things he told me to dozens of reporters for dozens of years, many of his answers rolling off his tongue before the question was even asked.

But I didn't know that then.

CHAPTER ONE BACON COUNTY

> The Lord sends me every misery He can think of just to try my
> soul. He must be aiming to do something powerful big for me,
> because He sure tests me hard. I reckon He figures if I can put up
> with my own people I can stand to fight back at the devil.
> —Erskine Caldwell, *Tobacco Road*

In the world of Harry Crews, both real and fictional, all roads lead back
to a 286-square-mile stretch of pine groves and sandy soil located a
few miles up the road from the Okefenokee Swamp.

He was born in Bacon County, Georgia, and he made it known that
when he died, his ashes should end up in that same sandy soil. Some of
his greatest fictional characters, clearly created from the same DNA that
was running through his own veins, were Bacon County natives as well.
It was part of his public persona, and, more importantly, it was part of
who he was, who he believed himself to be. Wherever he went, he was,
and would always be, a tenant-farmer's son from Bacon County. When he
left the people and place of his youth to pursue his dreams, he knew "it
would be forever impossible to leave completely. Wherever I might go in
the world, they would go with me."

The feeling did not seem to be reciprocal.

A pilgrimage to Crews's hometown can feel like a wasted trip. There
is no Harry Crews Park, no Harry Crews Highway, and the local event
calendar is entirely void of Harry Crews Day. In Appling County, which
borders Bacon, the author Caroline Miller is honored with a park in her

name. Carson McCullers, Flannery O'Connor, Erskine Caldwell, Crews's old friend James Dickey—writers of renown across Georgia—are honored by a state that seems to take seriously its literary heritage and mythologizes those who made their mark with the pen. But the same is not true in Bacon County and of Harry Crews. And it seems personal.

In Alma, the county seat of Bacon County and the population center of the region, the public library has four Harry Crews novels buried deep in the *C*'s on the fiction shelves and a couple files of clippings in a cabinet in the back room. That's it.

And it's not as if Bacon County has been turning out celebrities by the dozen. Ask for another famous homegrown Baconite at the local historical society, and the best they can muster is a current member of the Georgia Board of Regents, the body that makes the budget for Georgia universities. Not exactly the A-list.

Walk down Main Street in downtown Alma asking about Harry Crews, and you'll receive mostly blank stares. If you get a glint of recognition, chances are it will include mild distaste, possibly outright disgust. A fifty-ish receptionist at a downtown business: "Harry Crews? I read one of his books in my twenties, and it was raunchy then! To each his own, I guess." A cashier at the Food Mart: "That book? I got that book at my house— never did finish it, though." At the Alma Pharmacy on 12th Street: "His first book was all right, but then he went and got filthy."

Well, Crews was pretty filthy right from the beginning, but it's difficult to see why that disqualifies him from adulation in the place where he was raised, the place which he spent thousands of hours and thousands of pages paying homage to. It's as though Bacon County has placed an asterisk by his name: "Yes, Harry Crews is from here, but he's not really one of us."

In *The History of Alma & Bacon County, Georgia*, the one book dedicated solely to the history of the county, there is an entry about Crews and his memoir, *A Childhood*. The book describes Crews's masterpiece as a "brutal biography" in which he "recorded the hard way of living among his relatives and friends, which he describes most graphically." The short entry goes on to cast doubt on the book's accuracy and summarizes the local reaction thus: "Naturally, there persisted, even until today, resentment by Bacon countians who wish to have the publication banned. Some say it is evil, others describe it as the biography of a minority group, totally nonexistent today in Bacon County."

Tom Davis preaches at Big Creek Baptist Church, located in the community where Crews grew up, and owns Davis Floor Covering in downtown Alma. A devotee of Crews's writing, Davis has spoken to his congregation and his customers about the subject regularly over the years. He sees the prevailing attitude toward their lost son as one of mild embarrassment, verging on shame. "What I see from talking to people is that there has been, attached to Harry's name, a sort of negativity," he said. "What they will tell you is 'We really don't want Harry to stand for Bacon County, or we don't want to hold Harry up as an emblem of what we want to be.'" Those who can actually remember Harry the human being, not just Harry the idea, have little recollection of him as a young man, when he actually resided in Bacon County. Some can recount one or two drunken encounters on the rare occasion that Crews crossed back over the border into the county as an adult. "It's almost as if Harry was a whispered and unpleasant rumor that passed through these parts, rather than a real person," Davis said.

Today's Bacon County is difficult to distinguish from a thousand other similar counties that dominate the roadmap of Red State America. It lies eighty miles away from the interstate highway system in three directions, a twist of fate that costs the local economy millions of dollars annually. Instead, U.S. Highway 1, the gateway to Florida pre-1960, and a series of two-lane state roads snake through the miles upon miles of farmland and pines, interrupted by a lonely truck stop or convenience store every few minutes.

The county seat of Alma has taken on the veneer of most American small towns, seemingly rotting from within. The musty downtown is peppered with hundred-year-old buildings, only about half of which contain active businesses. The *Alma Times* office, Georgia Power, and a few other companies have offices downtown; the theater, closed for years, recently reopened; the farm supply office is for rent. The Alma Hotel was a marvel when it opened in the 1930s, sporting a center atrium that made it architecturally unique in its day. Today, it looks like it hasn't been renovated since Truman was in the White House. The hotel once served as a stopover for the wealthy tobacco executives and big-game hunters on their way to and from Florida, but it stopped taking in guests years ago and now is home to low-rent apartments.

Most of the commerce now lies on the outskirts of town, on U.S. 1 and

Pierce Street. Here, you'll find McDonald's, KFC, Dairy Queen, Flash Foods, the Huddle House, and several other options for cheap goods and services. Aside from retail businesses, the county today has a small manufacturing base, headlined by the Milliken Carpet company and D. L. Lee and Sons, producers of bacon, sausage, ham, and other fine meats. "There's not all that much here," said Ann Harvey, director of the historical society. "We're not booming like Douglas [twenty-five miles to the west]. They've got the Walmart Distribution Center."

Crews painted a portrait of the region as one steeped in both religion and violence, and that ethos has lived on to this day, according to Davis. In the early 1930s, when prohibition was still on the books, moonshining was a way of life. Today, it's marijuana. Over the years, pot worked its way to the top of the agricultural pyramid, thanks to generous profits and the subsistence-level living of most farmers who stick to legal crops.

One of Bacon County's least proud moments was when ABC News sent a reporter to the area as part of a Peter Jennings 20/20 special broadcast called "Pot of Gold," about the rise of marijuana in America. The story centered on a sheriff, Larry Tanner, who had the brilliant idea of enforcing the drug laws on the local pot growers. Bad idea. As recounted in the 20/20 program, the locals rose up and elected a new sheriff, Bucky Hayes, whose little brother, Timer Hayes, had recently been caught by Tanner with 1,700 marijuana plants. Bucky, as one would expect, brought the marijuana enforcement to a complete halt. Of course, ABC News asked him about what was behind this strategy. The results weren't pretty.

"He was a real Bubba-type," Davis said. "I mean, he was just dumb. Peter Jennings got him on camera and just let him be his dumb self. It was embarrassing. We're not all like this in Bacon County, but this guy, he was a caricature of a bumbling, dumb southern sheriff."

The outlaw posture might be strongest in the aptly named community of Scuffletown, famous for moonshining and violence in the 1930s and still hanging onto some of that reputation today. Crews said it was called Scuffletown "not because it was a town or even a crossroads with a store in it, but because as everyone said, 'They always scuffling up there.'" "He [Crews] wrote about people being expected to take care of their own grievances and mete out their own justice without the help of the law," Davis said. "Now, that was certainly accurate in Bacon County during that time. Over the years, I guess you can say it got more civilized. . . . But there's still some of whatever that is, hanging around in the DNA, or in the mind-set, of Scuffletown, and of Bacon County."

Bacon County lies in the southeastern section of the state of Georgia, about forty miles north of the Okefenokee Swamp. To the west is Douglas, thirty miles south is Waycross, and thirty miles east is the equally underwhelming town of Jesup. The county is cut from west to east by two parallel creeks, Big Hurricane and Little Hurricane, which meander toward the Alapaha River in Pierce County to the east, and eventually into the Satilla River, which empties into the St. Mary River and then the Atlantic Ocean. This is wiregrass country, named for a type of grass that carpeted the ground in the South Georgia pinelands. The terrain—gray, sandy dirt and trees as far as the eye could see—has never really been enticing to humans in the area, Indians or Europeans. Prior to 1800, southern Georgia was inhabited mostly by the Creek Indians, but it appears they had little interest in putting down roots in Bacon County. There are very few records of prehistoric artifacts being discovered in the area, only the occasional arrowhead turning up in a farmer's plow, showing that Indians ventured in, at least for hunting purposes. (One deterrent might have been the overabundance of razorback hogs, who roamed the woods in great numbers, subsisting on the roots of wiregrass.)

The British came in the early part of the eighteenth century, fended off the Spanish intrusion from the south, and colonized the state of Georgia, the thirteenth of the original thirteen colonies. Until a few years after the Revolutionary War, the British mostly stayed on the coast, in and around Savannah, where they had first made land. After the war for independence was concluded, there were about 50,000 English settlers in Georgia and perhaps 35,000 Indians. Settlers showed up in droves in the first four decades of the nineteenth century. By 1840, Georgia's population had grown to nearly 700,000, and the Indians were gradually and brutally forced westward. By the end of 1838, the U.S. Army had marched the last of the Indians out of Georgia.

Bacon County wouldn't become Bacon County for another hundred years, but the end of the Revolutionary War and the eviction of the Creeks led to the early population growth in the area. When the land was acquired from the Creeks, the State of Georgia divided it into plots and offered it to veterans of the Revolutionary War. Many current Bacon countians can trace their roots to these land grants. The war veterans were descendants of English, Scotch, Irish, and other nationalities who made their way down from the more populous states of Virginia and the Carolinas, or from North Georgia. Most had been farmers before the war, and they began to use their newfound land for agriculture; first cotton, and then tobacco. Later, the wiregrass would prove to be ideal for raising cattle. They were slave owners, many of them, but they did not live in antebellum plantations and oversee dozens or hundreds of slaves. That was a lifestyle that never made it to Bacon County.

The area remained strictly agricultural for most of the century, but toward the end the inhabitants began to squeeze some value from the pine forests that dominated the landscape. Northern interests had decimated the pine forests through logging, but it was not a complete decimation. And now there was money to be made in turpentine. Across the state, Georgians were tapping pines to satisfy the growing need for the product. Within a few years, Georgia would lead the nation in turpentine production.

Two industrious fellows named A. M. McLaughlin and C. W. Deen opened a commercial turpentine distilling operation, which became the genesis of the town of Alma. In 1906 the Alma Land and Improvement Company was founded by A. M. and C. W., and the company laid out a street map, sold plots, and planned themselves a nice little town. It got its name from either the first letters of the first four state capitals of Georgia (Augusta, Louisville, Macon, Atlanta), an orphaned child who was related to the founders, or the wife of a visiting salesman. Nobody seems to be quite sure. About eight years later, the State of Georgia saw fit to make Alma the seat of a new county, carved out of Appling, Ware, Pierce, and Coffee counties, and named for a distinguished and recently deceased U.S. senator from Georgia, Augustus O. Bacon.

Crews's grandfather, Henry Theodore Haselden, would eventually get into the turpentine business that had stimulated the growth of Bacon County. Henry was born on September 8, 1860, in Georgetown, South Carolina. Family lore has it that Henry's father joined the Confederacy and went off to fight in the Civil War, never to return. Henry, his mother, and sister came down to Blackshear, Georgia, where Henry would join the ranks of the turpentine men. He also met and married Lilly Elizabeth Davis, the daughter of a successful Pierce County landowner named Harley Davis. Harley and his wife, Susan Aspenwall Davis, had nine children, and enough money to provide all nine with some land of their own. Henry and Lilly raised a family, and in 1916, when their youngest daughter, Myrtice, was four years old, they sold off some of their land, moved to Bacon County, bought themselves a twenty-five-acre farm, and built a house on it.

The Haseldens had a comfortable existence for the time and place in which they lived. In 1926 Henry bought the family a brand new Ford Roadster. Instead of learning to drive it himself, he handed off the driving responsibilities to Myrtice and her older brother, Alton.

Around this time, a twenty-one-year-old Bacon countian named Ray Hoyett Crews was about five hundred miles to the south, battling mud, mosquitoes, and members of his work crew in the Florida Everglades. In 1916 a businessman who owned most of the Everglades came up with the idea of building a road to connect the Gulf and Atlantic coasts, and word of the need for labor had leaked up to South Georgia. Ray Crews was ready to venture out on his own at the age of seventeen, so he went south and joined an advance crew, charged with the job of clearing virgin swampland ahead of the main construction teams. Work crews on the Tamiami Trail, as it came to be called, earned between twenty and sixty dollars a month, good pay for manual labor at the time. For their wages, they braved the elements, slogged through waist-deep, bug-infested water, and spent months at a time away from civilization. Violence was rampant among the work gangs, and young Ray became a target but survived thanks to his best friend and fellow Bacon countian, Cecil, who had traveled south with him and happened to be six foot, seven inches tall and 275 pounds. Cecil couldn't save Ray from a Seminole prostitute, however, who gave him the clap and cost him a testicle.

The job took twelve years, 2,584,000 sticks of dynamite, and several million dollars to blast through 273 miles of swamp, and Ray was there for the last six. He was a dredge operator by age nineteen and eventually worked his way up to foreman, earning himself enough money to come home to Bacon County in 1927 with a Model T Ford, a white linen suit, and a good bit of cash left over.

Ray enjoyed the bachelor life for a short while upon his return, spending his winnings and introducing the young women of Bacon County to his Model T, but in fairly short order he met Myrtice, the pretty young sister of his friend Alton. After a four-month courtship, the couple married on November 7, 1928, in a simple ceremony with just a few relatives at the Ten Mile Missionary Baptist Church. Ray was twenty-three, Myrtice sixteen. Shortly thereafter, Ray traded in his Model T for a mule and traded the bachelor life for that of a farmer and a family man.

Ray and his brother-in-law, John Carter, rented a two-horse farm from a local landowner named Luther Carter, and Ray settled into the life of a sharecropper. The living was hard. Ray worked from sunup to sundown to tend to his thirty acres of tobacco. And despite all the hours under the hot sun, the crop failed, as many did across the county.

The following year, Ray and Myrtice tried farming for Myrtice's parents. Again, failure. Ray and Henry feuded, and eventually Ray boiled over, packed up his family, and stormed out in the middle of the night. A crop-swap was arranged between Ray's family and Alton's family. Ray never set foot in the Haselden house again.

Ray had thought himself sterile after the incident with the Seminole prostitute, but Myrtice got pregnant, and the couple lost their first child, who died shortly after birth. On July 9, 1931, they had a son and named him Ray Hoyett. Ray Sr. worked endless hours plowing the field with his mule while Myrtice tended to the baby and the household.

In 1932 Lilly, Myrtice's mother, who was still fairly wealthy, gave Ray and Myrtice a farm of 120 acres of land, and Ray hired some friends to help him build a three-room house on the grounds. The land wasn't farmable, so Ray went to work clearing it while hiring out to plow fields for other farmers.

Life was harsh, but despite the constant setbacks, the couple maintained a positive outlook. They had plans. They had a little land now, and they would clear it, make a little profit, and buy a better piece of land nearby. They even bought a radio.

Pretty soon, Myrtice was pregnant again. Still, she helped Ray in the field, doing what she could, pulling roots and hacking palmetto with the hoe, until, in her seventh month, she finally pulled herself out of the sun and retired to the little wood hut they called home to wait out the last few weeks of summer before the new baby was to arrive.

CHAPTER TWO

DREAMS AND NIGHTMARES

Anybody who has survived his childhood has enough information
about life to last him the rest of his days.
—Flannery O'Connor, *Mystery and Manners*

The cloudless blue Georgia sky that canopied Bacon County on June
7, 1935, belied an encroaching darkness that would envelop the
early years of Harry Eugene Crews and shape the way he viewed
the world and the human condition for his entire life. The unique vision
that would appear on the pages in the fictional environments he would
eventually create—filled with violence and pain and hideously damaged
people—was born out of an introduction to life replete with disease and
alienation and indescribable suffering. Harry was hit with a trifecta of bad
luck—time, place, and circumstance. He would be raised in a community
and a region thrown into the depths of poverty and isolation. When barely
a boy, he would be touched by both devastating disease and unthinkable
tragedy. And he was to be the product of a broken family, marred by loss
and abuse. It was, very often, childhood as a house of horrors, and survival
would simultaneously warp him and imbue him with an incredible strength
and resilience. And the nadir of Harry's life was to occur just five years in,
when he would find himself looking up into the faces of a dozen shrieking
children while floating in a pot of scalding water, next to the simmering
corpse of a freshly killed hog.

When the sun peaked on the afternoon of Harry's birth, Ray Crews,
for once, cut short his workday. He climbed onto his plow horse, Daisy,

and rode off the farm to track down Emily Ahl, Bacon County's resident midwife. Miss Emily served the white folks who couldn't afford to go to Alma to give birth in a hospital; another midwife attended to the black families. Ray and the midwife hurried back to the Crews home, Miss Emily outfitted in the black bonnet and long black dress of her profession. They made it to the house in time to find Myrtice deep into labor, and Miss Emily performed her craft admirably, guiding her patient through a quick and uneventful birth. The baby arrived ahead of the doctor, who made it to the scene shortly thereafter to find the healthy baby in the arms of his mother, with his father observing from nearby.

America in 1935 had been in the grips of the Great Depression for half a decade. It had been going on long enough for the conditions of life to become the new reality throughout the land, and in parts of Georgia and the South, the reality had taken poverty to previously unimaginable depths. In Washington, D.C., Franklin Delano Roosevelt, his popularity near its peak, was experimenting with the powers of the federal government to save those in poverty's wake, but circumstances often kept aid from reaching its targets. The year saw the advent of the Works Progress Administration and the Rural Electrification Act, following on the heels of the Civil Works Administration, the Tennessee Valley Authority, the Civilian Conservation Corps, and a bevy of other efforts, all with the goal of making life livable for those hit hardest by the economic downturn.

The hardships of the southern farmer were by now clearly on the radar of politicians and commentators. Henry Wallace, FDR's secretary of agriculture, publicly toured Georgia and Arkansas and found farmers and their families living in "hundreds of thousands of miserable, unpainted shacks, constructed more than 50 years ago, some of them without glass in the windows or doors in the openings." FDR had recently set the goal of creating a society in which "people lived as Americans should live." FDR's declaration placed a spotlight on the way of life found in much of the South, where, according to the *Macon Telegraph*, the majority of the citizenry would be "delighted to live as well as a Negro's mangy coon dog lived just a few years ago."

No level of despair could completely extinguish the defiance of a certain element of the southern population. The farmers of Georgia had elected a country lawyer named Eugene Talmadge from Forsyth, Georgia, as governor. Talmadge became the loudest and most strident critic of FDR and the New Deal relief programs. He declared that the president was a communist, and said that recipients of relief money were "bums and loafers," and generally took it upon himself to frustrate the efforts of the federal government to ease the conditions of his poorest constituents. He did his best to prevent the Civil Works Administration, created to bring government jobs to the unemployed, from operating in the state. Government programs, he told his followers, were just tricks by city folk to lure the weak away from an honest day's work, never mind the fact that the wages paid to tenant farmers for a day in the sun were well below the level of subsistence. It was a view held by many of those working the fields of southern Georgia, across all income levels. Eventually, FDR was forced to federalize the CWA to allow the relief efforts to proceed.

To "live how Americans should live" was not an easy task, with or without the means to attempt it. In Bacon County, residents were still living as Americans had lived in the mid-nineteenth century. The methods of survival that were now failing them had been abandoned decades before by their brethren in other parts of the country, and not just in those big cities that their governor used to scare them. Tractors had become prevalent on American farms nearly twenty years earlier, relieving farmers in the North and Midwest of much of the backbreaking labor and increasing production at the same time. In the South, it was still horses, mules, and men doing all the work.

The mechanized farms of the North no longer required the entire family in the fields. In Georgia, every able-bodied family member—man, woman and capable child—was still told to pick up a hoe. Electricity, running water, telephones—these were everyday conveniences, not given a second thought anymore in 1930s America. In Bacon County, they were still many years in the future.

Buck Nall, born in 1939, was raised less than a mile from the plot of land where Harry Crews spent his first years. The region, Nall said, didn't get electricity until 1947, the same year Nall's father, an ice-truck driver, got the community's first tractor. In the 1930s, modern life, which could have been found a couple hundred miles to the south or the north, was still years away in the land that Erskine Caldwell named "Tobacco Road."

"You lived off the land, whatever you could catch or kill. That's what you had, that was it. Just a lot of poor people," Nall recalled. "Most these people, they didn't have a damned thing. They had no damned income . . .

no electricity, no running water. There'd be one room in the house heated, if that. I remember lying in the bed and finding a star in the crack of the shingles up yonder. I lived that way, we all did."

That was the life they knew, however, and even under those conditions would occasionally come a glimmer of hope. Harry was six months old when Ray Crews saw such a glimmer—an offer on his land for much more than he believed it was worth. He accepted the offer and with the proceeds bought a two-hundred-acre plot of land down the road, forty acres of it farmable. The family moved in December 1935, and in the spring of 1936 began farming the new plot. Ray worked sunup to sundown, built a barn, a corral for the horse, and took in a family of tenants, a widow with three sons, to help with the cultivated land and readying the rest of the acreage. The work was never-ending, but occasionally Ray would come within range of the house and hear Harry crying while Myrtice was cleaning and hanging clothes. He would patiently hitch the horse, come in the house, and quiet Harry, caring for the baby until Myrtice finished her chores.

There were signs, however, that Ray's health was not good. Heart problems caused him to fall regularly in the field. Often, it was an hour or more before he was back on his feet. Once he was, though, he went right back to work. He lost his two front teeth to pyorrhea, his weight dropped precipitously, yet he refused to see a doctor. The family couldn't afford the cost, he told Myrtice. But the work was paying off; the glimmer was expanding. The crop was strong enough in 1936 that with the money he made, along with the turpentine rights to the timber, Ray was able to completely pay off the mortgage to the two hundred acres. And there was even enough money left to start next year's crop. As in a Steinbeck tale, there appeared, just over the horizon, the possibility of a better life. Ray Crews would begin 1937 free and clear, ready to pump more money and sweat into a farming enterprise that might support and even improve the lives of his family.

"Daddy won't wake up and his nose is cold."

It was the morning of April 17, 1937, and a chill had come over the farm. The family had slept together in the same bed for warmth. Myrtice woke up first, a rarity, and built a fire and started the grits. On Sundays, when Ray slept late, Hoyett, the older son, would wake him by twisting his nose, a joke between father and son. After the four-year-old got no response, he reported it to his mother, who went back into the room and, as she already knew she would, found her husband's lifeless body, eighteen-month-old Harry sleeping peacefully at his side.

Hoyett's words, which Harry never heard spoken and wouldn't have remembered if he had, echoed through his psyche for the rest of his life. "I have come to manhood with that sentence. It never seemed particularly sad or tragic or even unfortunate. It was simply there. It was part of who I was. Like the color of my hair or the shape of my nose," he wrote in 1973.

Ray Crews was buried two days later at Corinth Freewill Baptist Church, ten miles from the family farm. Blood drained from the body was buried in a deep hole behind the house. A day before the burial, the family's supply of food, meat that Ray had cured and hung in the family's smokehouse in the days before his death, was stolen. Only a small slab of pork, the size of a man's hand, was left behind.

Harry would not learn of his father's death, or the existence of Ray Crews, until years later.

By the time he reached the age of awareness, another Daddy was already in place, and had been for some time.

His new father figure was, in reality, his uncle. At Ray's funeral, Ray's brother Paschal was in attendance, with his bride, Dinah, the daughter of the preacher who had married Ray and Myrtice, at his side. Six months later, Paschal had divorced Dinah, married Myrtice, and had taken the patriarchal role in Harry's family.

How and why Paschal came to take on that role were questions that haunted Harry throughout his life. He never truly believed the story he was told—that Ray Crews was his biological father. There were too many holes in the story. How was it possible that Paschal had gotten divorced and married in six short months? Divorce was not common in a small, Bible-belt community like Bacon County, and for a man to marry his brother's widow so soon was sure to attract attention. Why was it that Paschal cared for and protected Harry like a son, but treated Hoyett worse than the family dog?

To compound the issue, Paschal was the polar opposite of his brother. Ray was steady, reliable, and driven to work. Paschal was unpredictable, regularly disappearing for days at a time. Ray was rarely seen with a drink. Paschal was a drunkard who would spend what little money the family had on whiskey to fuel his binges. Ray was a dedicated family man. Paschal was violent to the core. He wore the imprint of a man's teeth on his left cheek from one of his more vicious brawls and, when he was on the bottle, was always prowling for a fight, and usually found one. So why was it that Hoyett was a teetotaling family man, like Ray, and he, Harry, grew up to be weak for the bottle and prone to fighting, like Paschal?

The questions did not evaporate, no matter how many years passed, probably because he could not know the answer. In 1996, years after Myrtice had died, Harry traveled back to Bacon County to interview, on tape, for several hours, his aunt Eva Haselden, who was the widow of Myrtice's brother Alton. Eva was nearing ninety at the time. Harry, at age sixty, was still investigating the events surrounding his birth and the tale of two Daddies, grasping for truth before the last members of the generation who might know the answers went into the ground. "Whose blood I got in my veins? I mean, it's a question that'll keep you awake at night," Harry told Eva.

Sometime after Ray's death, Myrtice acquired a plot of land directly adjacent to her brother Alton's farm, in an area of Bacon County called the Junior High Community, because of its proximity to the local grammar school. Alton Haselden, and his wife, Eva, had seven children, all living in a two-bedroom farmhouse, along with Grandma Haselden. Myrtice and Paschal settled a quarter mile down the road, in view of Uncle Alton's house. The two families farmed tobacco, corn, and cotton, raised hogs and cattle, and generally lived at the mercy of the crop. Most of Harry's early years, which he would later chronicle in his memoir, *A Childhood*, were spent in this setting.

Between his fifth and sixth birthdays, Harry escaped death not once but twice. The first occurred three months after he turned five. He woke up one night in August 1940 with a high fever, and shortly thereafter his legs began to draw up, to the point that his heels were touching the backs of his thighs. This was the beginning of a nearly year-long bout with polio, though neither he nor the doctors who treated him knew it at the time.

In the 1940s, polio, also known as infantile paralysis, was still one of the most dangerous and prevalent diseases in the world. An infection that can move from person to person orally, it attacks the spinal cord and can lead to paralysis, most often of the legs, and to death. In the first half of the twentieth century, polio epidemics were common, and treatment was limited. Indeed, the sitting president was himself a victim of the disease. Annually, thousands of people, mostly children, were killed by polio, and tens of thousands left with some level of paralysis.

The iron lung, which allowed polio victims suffering from respiratory infections to breathe while they recovered, was invented to combat the disease and became widely available in cities. For those in rural areas, however, little could be done. In victims where the virus reached the spinal cord, 50 percent recovered fully, 25 percent suffered minor paralysis, and 25 percent were left severely paralyzed. The mortality rate for polio when the virus becomes a disease is 5–10 percent. In the United States, the incidences of the disease peaked in 1952 with 58,000 reported cases. By the end of that decade, vaccines had been created that would eventually eliminate polio as a threat to the general population. By the end of the century, less than 2,000 cases were reported worldwide each year.

Harry's fever would not abate, and the pain in his legs was nearly unbearable. In the first days of the disease, two doctors examined Harry; both declared that he would never walk again. Neither was able to diagnose the disease or offer anything other than medications to ease the pain, which had little effect. A faith healer was brought in and recited Bible verse. The leader of a band of gypsies examined Harry and prescribed herbs, which Harry took for ten days, to no avail. And all the while, aunts, uncles, cousins, friends, acquaintances, people from nearby farms, strangers from distant counties, all paraded through the family's shack to get a look at the little boy with his feet stuck to his rear end. The pain, combined with the humiliation, would have a lasting effect. "Right there, as a child, I got to the bottom of what it meant to be lost," he wrote later, "what it means to be rejected by everybody (if they had not rejected me, why was I smothered in shame every time they looked at me?) and everything you ever thought would save you. And there were long days when I wondered why I did not die, how I could go on mindlessly living like a mule or a cow when God had obviously forsaken me."

After six weeks, his legs began to loosen up, and he was able to be taken from the bed to the porch for a few hours a day. Soon, he was well enough to be carried around the farm, and deposited by Paschal under an old oak tree, so he could spend the day sitting with his dog, Sam, and watching the goats graze in the sun. By October, he had progressed to the point that he could be pulled around the farm in a goat cart by Old Black Bill, the most dependable of the goat herd, with his friend Willalee T. Bookatee, a quiet black boy who was about a year older than Harry, ambling alongside. When the weather turned, Harry was remanded back to the house, where his bed had been set up in front of the fireplace. But by then his legs, though still paralyzed, were no longer drawn tightly to his thighs, and he could pull himself around the floor with his arms. While Paschal worked in the field, Harry would while away the day listening to Myrtice and the other women of the Junior High Community spin yarns of death and disease, treachery and deceit.

As the calendar turned to 1941, Harry finally regained the ability to straighten his legs completely. He was put on a home-grown rehabilitation regimen, pulling himself along the fence line to restore strength and help him relearn the ability to walk. Soon, the pain began to fade, but the shame of his disease remained firmly in his conscience.

Harry was still limping noticeably from his bout with polio when he found himself at the center of yet another tragedy and was once again plunged into the depths of pain and suffering. This time, there was no mystery to what felled him—nearly his entire extended family was watching as they witnessed what they believed to be a child being boiled to death in front of their eyes.

It was February 1941, time for the annual butchering of the hogs, a ritual celebration in the community. Paschal was on one of his increasingly frequent binges and hadn't been heard from in four days, but Myrtice, Hoyett, and Harry and their current tenant farmers walked up the road to Uncle Alton's house to take part in the communal operation. While the children played and the women worked to prepare the hogs that had already been killed, the men went about the business of dispatching the live hogs, straddling them and crushing their skulls with an axe. Then they would prepare the hog corpses to be lowered into a pot of scalding water, so the hog's hair could be easily scraped. The vats of water were just above ground level, sitting on staves in holes that had been dug out, large enough so a wood fire could be made beneath them to heat the water to the correct temperature, which was just slightly below boiling.

Nearby, Harry, Hoyett, Willalee, and several other cousins were playing a game of Pop-the-Whip. The kids would line up holding hands, and the lead child would start running, pulling the rest behind. The leader would then begin to turn sharply, right, then left, causing the other kids to have to run faster to keep up. The round would eventually come to a conclusion when the child on the end was popped loose and sent catapulting off behind. When it was Harry's turn to be in the end position, the whip edged over toward the vat of water, and when Harry was popped loose, he flew directly into the steaming vat and found himself floating next to a dead, blistering hog with a newly crushed skull.

The closest adult, a farmer named John Pace, reached in, pulled Harry from the pot, set him down next to it on his feet, and slowly backed away. "I did not fall, but stood looking at John and seeing in his face that I was dead," Crews wrote later. "The children's faces, including my brother's, showed I was dead, too. And I knew it must be so, because I knew where I had fallen and I felt no pain—not at that moment—and I knew with the bone-chilling certainty most people are spared, that, yes, death does come and mine had just touched me."

The children screamed and ran in all directions, but at first Harry remained silent. Relatives alerted Myrtice, and she ran toward her son. As Harry saw her approaching from across the yard, the first wave of pain set in. Harry, beginning to scream now, touched his hand, and the skin came loose and fell to the ground, fingernails and all. The pain grew much, much worse as his mother removed his clothes, taking most of his skin with them.

There was an old, worn-out Model T on the farm that day, and Myrtice wrapped Harry in a sheet and climbed into the backseat for the sixteen-mile ride to town. (The decision to use the sheet would cost Harry more skin and more anguish in the coming days.) The Model T moved so slowly that Alton, sitting in the front seat, would periodically jump out of the vehicle and run alongside, urging the driver to speed up. For the entire interminable ride, Harry screamed and pleaded to his mother that he didn't want to die.

He had burns over two-thirds of his body, but Harry's head had not gone under the water, a fact that, according to the doctor who finally examined him in Alma, had saved his life. Scabs formed over the majority of his body, and a balm was applied constantly to ease the pain. Harry was now condemned to his bed twenty-four hours a day, once again an invalid for the second time in a year. He was not yet six years old.

The closest hospital was thirty miles away and unaffordable, so Harry was taken back to the farm, where, on doctor's orders, Alton built a wood frame over his bed. Since nothing could touch his skin, the frame was covered with a sheet, and Harry spent the next few months suffering in his makeshift buggy tent, black scab crumbs littering the floor beneath.

At least in terms of physical agony, Harry's life had bottomed out early. The scabs from the burn would take months to heal, but the scars would eventually recede. By the time he was in high school, the scars were barely visible. His bout with polio rendered him a clumsy child, prone to accident, but left few other physical traces.

The traumas he had experienced did little to dampen the thirst for ad-

venture in him. He was a chubby kid until he matured, and his mother remembered him as quick to cry, but he was considered the most courageous
of the cousins, and he would often lead the other children into mischief.
He was always the first to take a dare. On one occasion, he was the test
case when Hoyett and their cousin Theron decided it was a good idea to
jump off the smokehouse using an umbrella as a makeshift parachute. Only
minor injuries resulted. Another time, the group was seeking a volunteer
to bite the head off of a hornworm—a large green insect common on the
farm, but not for consumption. Harry again was the willing participant.
He downed the worm head, and his reputation for bravery was once again
enhanced.

Life on the farm, though spare and unforgiving, allowed for many forms
of rural adventure. Goats, chickens, dogs, and other farm creatures were at
his disposal for entertainment much of the time. In the summer, hours could
be spent at the watering hole on the Little Hurricane River, a short walk
from the house. His brother, though he was Harry's main tormenter, was
often up for some mischief. And school was much less of an imposition
on his time than might be the case if he had lived in a more populated area.

Many of the memories Harry would later choose to recount in his memoir of his early life on the farm revolve around Willalee Bookatee. About
a year older than Harry, Willalee lived just past the tenant house on the
family's farm. Harry and Willalee, while both were still too young to work
but old enough to explore the environs without constant adult supervision,
were inseparable.

Among the poor, lives intermingled, and Harry and Willalee spent much
time in the belly of each other's families. A good portion of their fun involved playing tricks on each other. Often, Hoyett was involved, helping
either Willalee or Harry bamboozle whichever one wasn't in on the ruse.
On one occasion, Hoyett and Harry convinced Willalee, who was deathly
afraid of bulls after being trampled by one at age three, that he had to
carry a twenty-pound citron fruit across the length of the farm. The fruit,
they told him, would ward off charging bulls. Harry and Hoyett walked
alongside Willalee as he struggled mightily to lug the fruit, which was a
third of his body weight.

"How come it is you ain't got no citron," asked Willalee.

"We already carried ourn," Harry answered. "That bull don't make you
tote but one. After you tote one citron, you can come out here in the field
anytime you want and that bull don't pay no more mind than if you was

a goat." Willalee carried the citron until the Crews brothers finally let him in on the joke.

Willalee soon returned the favor. He hollowed out an apple, filled it with a generous portion of cow manure, and covered it with blueberry jam.

"Bes' thing you ever put in your mouth," he told Harry.

Harry bit, literally and figuratively, and two bites in, the smell reached his nose.

"I believe this thing is ruint," he said. "It smells just like, like . . ." And with that realization, the two boys were exchanging blows in the dirt, until Hoyett stepped in and ended the bloodshed. Whatever hurt feelings resulted from the trickery, however, would never last more than an hour or two.

One particular diversion that occupied many hours of Harry and Willalee's time turned out to be an early indicator that Harry had a mind for fiction. Though storytelling was the social fabric in the community, the written word was as scarce a commodity as electricity or gasoline in the Junior High area of Bacon County. In the Crews home, there were only two books: the Sears Roebuck catalog and the Bible. Harry preferred the catalog. It had been around since the 1890s, beginning as a sales tool for farm equipment, but eventually morphing into what America's rural class termed the "wish book," filled with all types of merchandise to order that they couldn't possibly hope to afford. In the hands of Harry and Willalee, however, it was the ultimate story prompt. It was filled with attractive people, wearing sharp, big-city clothing, and lacking the scars and wounds that marked the people of Bacon County.

In Harry's mind, since all the people were perfect, they must all know one another. And they must be engaged in the kind of dastardly dealings that he knew the adults of Bacon County traded in. So he and Willalee would turn the pages and concoct stories of treachery and deceit like the ones they listened to their mothers and grandmothers spin around the fire.

"See this man here in the red coat?" Harry would ask. "Well, if you turn back here where these ladies are wearing nothing but under-drawers, you'll see his wife, that's her with the lacy drawers, except nobody don't know it's his wife cause her daddy's got a whiskey still. That's him there in front leaning on the shovel. Her daddy don't like the feller in the red coat cause he don't make a living just by wearing the coat. He's a sheriff on the side and busts up stills, so they keep it a secret they was married, see."

To them, it was of no consequence that the subject of the stories was wearing a coat and tie, or an evening gown. They could be easily tied to a hog-theft ring, or a moonshine operation, or any of the other forms of regional chicanery. The stories would get progressively more complicated and violent, as the storytellers marked pages and brought more and more of the clothing models into the intricate webs of deceit. Much later, Crews would remember these afternoons as seminal in his life as a writer: "Since where we lived and how we lived was almost hermetically sealed from everything and everybody else, fabrication became a way of life. Making up stories, it seems to me now, was not only a way for us to understand the way we lived but a defense against it. It was no doubt the first step in a life devoted primarily to men and women who never lived anywhere but in my imagination. I have found in them infinitely more order and beauty and satisfaction than I ever have in people who move about me in the real world."

Harry didn't need the catalog to create fiction. Sometimes all he needed was a few minutes alone. Jeannie Gaskins was one of Uncle Alton and Aunt Eva's seven children, born just three months after Harry. The Haselden clan spent a lot of time with Harry and Hoyett, and Eva and Alton served as second parents to the Crews boys. Gaskins remembered Harry as a dreamer with an active imagination. With Paschal usually unavailable, Uncle Alton gave Harry a lot of attention. "They'd go squirrel hunting, or something like that. And when they were done, they would start back to the house. Harry would come up on a log, and he'd say, 'Uncle Alton, just let me set here a while. I'll be on to the house directly.' And of course, Daddy would say, 'Don't do this and this and this.' Then Daddy would go on to the house and leave him. So Harry would sit there on that log and just daydream. And whenever he'd finally come back to the house, he'd have some of the wildest stories to tell, and he'd tell them as if they were real."

If his daydreaming was the work of a future artist's imagination, night brought with it dreams originating in a much darker place. Life in the Crews home was getting more desperate and violent. Myrtice and Paschal fought constantly over Paschal's drinking and spending, and over his disappearances. Harry began to have episodes of sleepwalking. Often he would be discovered shivering out in the fields near the house. The arguments in the home became progressively more confrontational, and more physical. Harry and Hoyett would huddle together in a single bed and wait out the conflicts.

The dysfunction in the Crews home was accentuated by the seemingly peaceful existence of Alton and Eva's house just up the road. Both families lived under the weight of poverty, but the Haseldens did not have the added burdens of mistrust and abuse. "The house we lived in, there's big cracks in the floor," Gaskins, Harry's cousin, remembered. "You could see the chickens underneath the house. At one point, the roof was leaking so bad, it was hard to find a dry corner to be in when it was raining. But the thing about it, there was always food, and there was always love, and we didn't go cold."

Harry and Hoyett often used the Haselden house as an escape, but at night they could not avoid their own home. The situation boiled over just a few months after Harry's dip in the hog pot, as his scabs were beginning to heal. Paschal returned to the house one spring night, fueled with whiskey and once again ready for a fight. Paschal and Myrtice argued, pots and pans banged off the walls, the children heard the distinctive thump of flesh on flesh. The brothers shook silently in their beds. Paschal left the room and returned with a twelve-gauge shotgun. The one and only shot he fired went just over Myrtice's head, blowing the mantelshelf off the wall. Then there was silence.

Myrtice gathered what belongings she could in the middle of the night, roused the children, and, in the darkness, walked them down the road to Alton and Eva's house. The marriage was over, and the next day Myrtice and the children were on a sweaty bus to Jacksonville, Florida, with two suitcases and barely enough money to pay the fare. Paschal stewed in the abandoned home, his anger growing. He never again lived with Harry and his family, but he would hang around their lives a little longer to provide a few more moments of terror.

CHAPTER THREE   JACKSONVILLE

> The world smelled deeply of shit. Always had. Always would. At
> only 10 years old, I'd known that fact for a long time. I cannot
> remember a time when I did not know it.
> —Harry Crews, "Leaving Home for Home"

To Bacon County residents, the Springfield section of Jacksonville was synonymous with failure. Broken families with no other recourse would give up whatever plans for survival they had been pursuing, pack up, and prepare to do their time until they could make it back. A bad crop, a missed payment, an absent husband, an injured mule—any minor misfortune could result in a sentence of a term in the city, the majority of which to be served on the line in the factory. In Bacon County, no matter how poor they were, people at least had their space. In Springfield, they were on top of one another, stuck in tiny shotgun row houses, each divided room by tiny room to accommodate as many renters as possible. The narrow streets were littered with junk, from glass to tires to old car parts, along with a generous helping of general domestic trash, which would be picked through by the bony cats and dogs that roamed the streets day and night. Children, school age and below, shared the streets with the junk and the animals, as their parents drank or slept in preparation for the next twelve-hour shift.

Myrtice found work at the King Edward Cigar factory, where many of the single mothers from Bacon County ended up. (Men often found work in the shipyards, in high production due to the war effort, or the pulp mill, or the Jacksonville Paper Company, or a variety of other forms of labor that required minimal training beyond physical endurance.) King Edward Cigars was, at that time, the largest cigar producer in the world. Hundreds of women were stationed along the line, preparing the leaves and filler to be rolled, or packaging the cigars, paid by the number of cigars they could produce in a day. Myrtice spent much of the next ten years of her life on that line, producing six thousand cigars a day, which was still never enough to provide for herself and her two boys.

For the remaining years of Crews's childhood—until he graduated from high school—the family shuttled between the Springfield section and Bacon County. Poverty was the normal state of affairs. More than once they came home to find their belongings on the sidewalk and wooden planks nailed over the door. They would be forced to go without heat for days in the winter, to steal water from the neighbor's spigot because theirs had been turned off. During holidays, and whenever else they were available, the family accepted charity food baskets from a nearby Baptist church. Harry remembered a single Christmas present from his entire childhood, a Baby Ruth candy bar, made memorable only because he wasn't forced to share it with his brother.

With money tight, anybody who could earn a dime to further the cause was expected to do just that. When Harry was eight years old, he took a job delivering newspapers for the *Jacksonville Journal*, the afternoon newspaper in town. Hoyett already had a morning route for the *Florida Times-Union* for which he had to wake up at four a.m. seven days a week, and another job bagging groceries at the A&P store. The *Journal* job required Harry to take a city bus to downtown Jacksonville, pick up the papers and sell them to commuters, and then return to Springfield on the bus after dark. The process scared Harry, and after one day on the job, he told Myrtice he wasn't going back.

"Why is that?" she asked.

"You wouldn't want me to, Mama. Down there when we was getting them papers, it was just the awfulest cussing and carrying on you ever seen. You wouldn't want me to sell no papers in such mess as that."

"Them that cuss and carry on, that's their business. You sell papers without doing what they do," Myrtice told him. "It's cussing and carrying on all over the world."

Harry kept the job. He could get the papers for two and a half cents each and then sell them for a nickel. Many of the boys his age in the neighborhood had routes for the *Journal*, and a week of sales would net a paperboy about fifty cents. Harry could make more by purchasing bundles and selling them on street corners downtown. One cold afternoon in the winter of that year, Harry was selling papers near the St. John's River as the wind whipped off the water. A well-dressed woman took pity on him, handed him a five-dollar bill, and said, "This will pay off the rest of your papers. Go home; you'll freeze to death here." Harry thanked her, walked half a block and stood behind a building until she had left, then returned to the street to sell the rest of his stock. His mother's voice in his head told him they needed every two and a half cents they could get.

But often, Harry would play to his role as the baby of the family. His sickness early in life had given him a taste for the sympathy of others. He still cried regularly even though he was of school age, and would tearfully beg Myrtice not to go to work. She would scold her youngest son but be in tears herself at the factory when she left him by himself.

A rare treat for the boys was a Saturday trip to Jacksonville's Capitol Theater, at the intersection of 8th and Main. The cost to enter was nine cents, and for that price theatergoers could take in cartoons, serials, feature films, and news, and since the theater was never cleared after showings, they could do it all again until the theater closed. Occasionally Harry would tag along with Hoyett, but more often, he preferred to stay home with his mother. After spending a few hours with his mother on her day off from the factory, he would venture out, and she would see him out the window, regaling the younger children on the block with more of his concocted stories.

Charles Loyless met Harry while the two were both paperboys, and both would run in the same Springfield circles through their adolescence. Loyless's family was in a slightly better economic position—his father, though a heavy drinker, lived with their mother and four children and held down a regular job—but both boys, and their friends, developed street sense at a young age. When they weren't selling papers or going to school, they found ways to entertain themselves.

"Harry was a good friend," Loyless said. "He would laugh, cut up, and participate in things that we did. If we were down in the woods building a tree swing, or something, he would be right in the middle of it." Loyless lived a few blocks away, and Harry would often come over to his side of the neighborhood with their mutual friend, Gary Jones. "They would come down the railroad tracks and meet us over in the woods, and we would all play around over there. There was a black man who had a big cane patch, and we would sneak up there and get a stalk of cane every once in a while. He knew us from seeing us out there on the railroad track. He would yell at us, that he was going to shoot us. The next thing you know, a shotgun would go off, and, in a little bit, you would hear the pellets rain down on you in the cane field."

But Harry never became too attached to his friends in Springfield because he knew, and they knew, he was always just a day away from pulling up stakes and heading back to the farm. "At times, we didn't know where Harry and his family were, and they had moved. You would find out, later, that they had moved back to Georgia because they weren't making it."

When Harry was ten, it was disease that sent him back to Bacon County. This time, the ailment struck Myrtice. Cancer was found in her thigh and hip, and after an operation to remove it, she was to be placed in a body cast, from the shoulders to the knees, for six months. Because she couldn't work and couldn't care for Harry, obviously, he was to be sent back to live with Alton and Eva until Myrtice was back on her feet. Hoyett, fourteen at the time, would quit school and take a job at Getters Box Factory, catching boxes off a conveyor belt and loading them onto trucks.

By that time, Hoyett had been hardened by their life of deprivation and stoically accepted the decision. He was sullen and harsh by nature, often taking his frustrations out on his younger brother. Now, at fourteen, he would be working a twelve-hour night shift alongside grown men. The first night, he went to the factory with a pair of thick cotton gloves Myrtice had gotten for him. He returned with his hands in his pockets, the gloves torn to shreds, hands bright red and covered with scabs. Most of the men had leather welding gloves; Hoyett would have to face the boxes bare-handed. "The men on the job say you hands'll callous up. If you can stand it long enough and soak you hands in salt water for an hour ever night," he told them.

Harry was scheduled to leave the following afternoon, so that morning he went to the box factory, seeking one last look at his brother before he got on the bus. After a few trips up and down the aisles, he spotted Hoyett, shirt and pants dark with sweat, hair matted down on his forehead. Hoyett hit a button and the conveyor belt grinded to a halt.

"What the hell you doin' here," he demanded.

Harry said nothing.

"I cain't keep this thing stopped. I'll lose this job."

Harry saw blood dripping off the ends of his fingers, and could not speak.

Hoyett grew angrier. "You get on out of here and go home. You ain't nothing but a kid."

The moment was burned into Harry's memory.

"As old as I was," he remembered many years later, "what he had said nearly made me cry. What a terrible thing for a bloody handed boy working a twelve-hour shift at a man's job to have to say to his ten-year-old brother. You ain't nothing but a kid."

In the summers, and occasionally at other times during the year, Harry would be sent back to Bacon County, where he would take up residence under Uncle Alton and Aunt Eva's roof and assimilate into the Haselden family. His uncle and aunt were like a "second momma and daddy," according to Don Haselden, one of the siblings and a summer roommate of Harry's. The living quarters were tight, but Harry would find a spot in the brothers' room and quickly become one of the boys. "He was just like another one of the family," Don recalled. "Whatever us boys got up and did, he got up and did." Sometimes that meant work, such as harvesting tobacco, sometimes it meant fun: bull riding, squirrel hunting, corncob wars. Harry was comfortable among his cousins and found a family life he'd rarely known during these excursions.

When the children weren't working on the farm or engaged in a group activity, Harry would often find his young cousin Don and invite him to come along on a squirrel hunt. Harry was a crack shot with a .22 rifle and loved to show off. Don would jump on his back, and the two cousins would head off into the woods. Sometimes, however, Don would find out that there wasn't going to be as much squirrel hunting as he thought. Instead, Harry would put his rifle down and be lost in his thoughts for what, to a seven-year-old, seemed like an eternity. "We'd go down there and he'd just sit up against one of those trees," Don said. "There'd be squirrels running all around the woods, and Harry wouldn't fire a shot. It was like he was in a daydream."

By the time he reached high school, the independent streak was becoming more developed in Harry. His constant moves between Georgia and Jacksonville had made it difficult for him to form lasting friendships outside his family. And as he grew older and became more aware of the hierarchies of class and that, even among the working-class environs of Springfield, he was at the very bottom, a greater level of shame developed within him.

"In the summertime, none of us could wait until it got warm enough so that we could take our shoes off, and play barefooted all summer," Loyless recalled. "When we were younger, and he was with the rest of us, he was barefooted, too, and we were barefooted with him. Nobody thought anything about him not having a pair of shoes. I think after he got older, and it got harder to do things, maybe that had a lot to do with him being as reclusive as he was."

Hoyett had dropped out to work, but Harry, though a below-average student, was determined to graduate. After attending Kirby Smith Junior High School through ninth grade, he went to Andrew Jackson High School, where students could take college-preparatory, business, or general classes. Harry took the general path—nothing advanced, nothing specialized, just taking what he needed to stay on course to graduation.

"He did enough just to get by. I do remember that much," said Loyless. "He never really made any effort to excel. He just, basically, did what it took to get by, as I would say, to get through school and get out."

By then his penchant for self-education, which would become his process through the rest of his schooling, had begun. He had now discovered books, and the dream of becoming a writer himself one day had begun to ferment. He would often stay up all night reading. At age fourteen, he composed his first attempt at fiction, about a child detective armed with firecrackers, on a hunt for a gang of crooks.

Hoyett had joined the Marines and gone to Korea, and Myrtice was still pulling the six a.m. shift at the cigar factory, so there was often nobody there to tell Harry to go to school. He missed class regularly and withdrew from most of the social aspects of high school. His 1956 yearbook picture, surrounded by his classmates' photos and all their engagements and accomplishments, lists only "funny and friendly." He received his fair share of D's but managed to avoid any failing grades.

Among the material covered in his all-night reading binges were a number of novels by a Jacksonville writer named Frank Slaughter. Slaughter was a physician who used his knowledge of medicine and his work experience as the basis for most of his books. When Harry was sixteen, he was compelled to contact Slaughter, wanting to speak to a real writer face to face. This was during one of the family's stints back in Bacon County, so Harry hitchhiked the 110 miles to Jacksonville and looked up Slaughter in the phone book. He made his way to Slaughter's neighborhood, found a pay phone, and called him up. Slaughter's wife answered the phone and informed Harry that the author/doctor had gone out to get his haircut, and invited Harry to come back in a few hours.

"I never did go to see him," Crews recalled later. "I went back in the street and put my thumb in the air. Because the notion that a writer had to get a haircut! I mean, writers don't get haircuts. They don't have to deal with everything the rest of us do, do they? Really? I just couldn't put together my own love of literature—the mystery, the overwhelming, profound grandness of literature—with going to the barbershop and getting your hair cut. I thought, if the man's getting his hair cut, he can't be the man I want to talk to."

CHAPTER FOUR

THE MARINES

> When the war broke out . . . Bubba and almost every other
> southern boy, black or white, went down and joined up, because
> the service was at least three hots and a cot and there were no
> jobs at home and, besides that, some gook motherfuckers were
> trying to do violence to the U.S. of A., and the southern boys
> were going to go show them whose ass was the blackest.
> —Harry Crews, *Celebration*

Less than four weeks after he became the first member of his extended family to earn a high school degree, Harry walked into the post office in Jacksonville looking for a ticket to Korea. Since receiving his diploma from Andrew Jackson High in Jacksonville, he had been back on the farm in Bacon County, searching for a way to earn some money. But there was no work to be had, at least none beyond the level he had been performing on the farm since he was old enough to lift a hoe. And there were just too many mouths to feed, he felt, to make those who had been responsible for him all these years continue to provide for his well-being.

In the summer of 1953, American troops had been fighting in Korea for nearly three years. Hoyett had joined the Marines a few years earlier and was on the front lines. Harry had yet to set foot beyond southern Georgia and northern Florida. In the South, the military was viewed as both an honorable choice and a way out. And at seventeen, he wanted to test himself, to prove his manhood. "Going to the Marine Corps was the only way I knew to get out, to leave the state, leave everybody whom I knew, and see if I could do it alone," he said later. "I'd been so damn isolated and knew it, simply because I'd gone to some trouble to get books. I knew the bigger world was out there, and I wanted to see it."

At the post office, Harry found a U.S. Army recruiter and made his wishes clear. He wanted to join the army and go to Korea. "It was a good simple time when young men wanted to go out and kill a gook for Democracy," he said. The recruiter was a paratrooper who had served in the Korean theater. He told Harry some war stories, pitched his branch of the service, and sent Harry on to the doctor for observation. Once the doctor took a look at Harry's right calf, which still bore the marks from his bout with polio, Harry's brief tenure with the U.S. Army came to a swift conclusion.

He came back to the post office the next day and tried it all over again, this time with the Marines. The Marine doctor was much less interested in Harry's leg, or in examining him at all. And Harry, on first glance, seemed to be the perfect Marine specimen. He was six foot, two inches tall, over two hundred pounds, and all muscle and sinew from the on-again-off-again duties he was expected to perform in the fields whenever he was back in Bacon County. Before the day was through, the doctor had signed on the dotted lines, and Harry was booked on a train to South Carolina.

The U.S. Marine Corps has been training enlisted men at Parris Island, South Carolina, since 1915, before World War I. During the Korean War, the Marine Corps Recruit Depot reached its peak, training more than 138,000 during the course of the war and supplying a large portion of the U.S. fighting force in Asia.

By 1953, the culture of the U.S. Marines was well known to ordinary Americans. Officially, it was a branch of the U.S. Navy with the stated mission of assisting the navy by providing amphibious support in attacking enemy-held bases and protecting U.S. forward bases. But through heroic efforts during World War II and through some masterly public relations, the Marines had assumed the mantle as the toughest, bravest branch of the service. Marines were known, by civilians as well as servicemen in other branches, for their physical toughness, their buzz haircuts (high and tight), their over-the-top arrogance and dismissiveness toward non-Marines, and their constant self-promotion.

Harry said his goodbyes to his mother that night at their little apartment on Iona Street, and the next day he boarded the train for Parris Island with the other recent recruits. The mood was subdued on the train, and Harry talked to the other recruits, mostly southern boys like him, looking for a respectable way into adulthood. As the train crossed out of Georgia and into South Carolina, Harry noted that he had made it beyond Georgia's northern border for the first time.

As the train pulled into the station at Port Royal, South Carolina, civilian life ended for the recruits. A swarm of drill instructors climbed aboard and began screaming at the newbies, demanding they spit out their gum and put out their cigarettes. The recruits knew what they had signed up for and were ready for the treatment. They were loaded onto buses and driven to the Parris Island facility. The recruits, amid constant barking from their new superiors, were led off the buses and told to stand next to a giant statue of the Marines' crowning moment: the iconic flag-raising at Iwo Jima. "It was when we got off the bus that I first knew for certain we had all truly stepped in shit," Harry remembered.

The drill instructors hollered and slapped everybody, but one sergeant fixated on a pale, skinny boy with red hair and a bemused smile etched across his face. The recruit had sat near Harry on the train. "You goddamn civilian turd, wipe that smile off your face!" the DI spat. The sergeant had been screaming at the red-haired boy on the bus earlier, and by the time the kid climbed down the stairs, the sergeant was frothing. As the amazed recruits looked on from beneath the statue, the sergeant beat the smiling boy over the head until blood ran down his face. He knocked him down and kicked him, all the while raining verbal abuse down on him. The other drill instructors ordered the rest of the recruits to run across the field toward the center of the camp. As they would now do twenty-four hours a day, they followed orders, sneaking glances at their first fallen comrade, whom they would never see again.

Marine Corps boot camp is unlike any other training in the U.S. military. And it's that way for a reason. Those who join the army and the other branches of the service must undergo grueling training regimens as well, but the physical training is offset by skills training associated with the specific job they will undertake upon completion. A Marine's first contact with the corps aims not for orientation, but for shock and disorientation. Their new overlords aim to break them down, to remove any trace of individuality or ego. They are stripped naked for physical examination, bathed together, their hair is shorn (each haircut is exactly the same: a half dozen swipes with an electric clipper: twenty-three seconds), their pockets emptied and all remnants of civilian life are removed, and they are dressed in the same drab training garb as all their brethren. The goal is to strip them down to nothing, and then begin the process of building them into Marines.

Harry wasn't the first of his group to ignite the temper of his instructor, but it didn't take long. The drill instructors liked to focus on any superficial weakness they could find on a particular recruit. The recruit next to Harry happened to be black. "You goddamn black bastard!" the instructor screamed. "You think I give a shit if you're a nigger? I don't give a shit if your skin is green or blue or black!" While he was slapping the recruit across the face, Harry's head turned ever so slightly. He noticed that the tormenter had "the biggest, most brutal wrists I'd ever seen on a human being."

When the drill instructor noticed Harry looking and popped him in the ear, Harry's bladder gave way.

"You degenerate turd, look what you've done! You've pissed on yourself!"

Physical punishment was now a part of life for Harry and his fellow recruits. Any misstep, in which a recruit forgot to follow one of the many instructions concerning Marine life, would result in a slap, a kick, or an order to perform some ungodly number of push-ups or some other exercise. Say the word "floor" instead of "deck" or mishandle a rifle, and a recruit could earn himself yet another beating. The boot-camp regimen also included a healthy dose of recruit-on-recruit violence, including hand-to-hand unarmed combat, judo, and wrestling.

Physical combat was old hat for Harry, who'd been fighting with his brother as long as he could remember and had fought often with strangers just for the sake of fighting. And he had learned some boxing skills by training with his brother over the years. His willingness to engage in fisticuffs quickly and eagerly earned him the respect of his superiors.

Another aspect of boot camp involves the subjection of recruits to physical pain and suffering. Those that submit to the violence and pain often are filling a deeper need to move from childhood to manhood, and for Harry it was a ritual that hit home. "I joined the Marine Corps for two reasons," he wrote later. "I thought if you were going to go, that you might as well try yourself. And the other reason, I frankly admit, was to see if I could do it."

His best friend in the barracks was a recruit named Buddy, who had been raised in Alabama. Harry was naturally anxious and, for the first month, felt like he was only one slap away from breaking under the pressure. During particularly tough training exercises, Buddy would tell Harry stories about his Alabama upbringing to get Harry's mind off the proceedings.

Failure was unacceptable. For the recruits, it could result in a trip to the Psychological Observation Unit, which served as a way to shame those who couldn't, or wouldn't, maintain the schedule of being built into a Marine. More than a few recruits folded under the stress and became mentally unstable. Those who ended up in the POU would be paraded, walking backward, in front of the rest of the recruits, while instructors hurled verbal abuse at them. Eventually, if they couldn't prove themselves well enough to return to their platoon, they would be dressed in mismatched civilian clothing and put on a bus back to civilian life.

After about three weeks, Buddy began to withdraw. He spent most of his time reading the Bible, stopped speaking, and walked around in a daze. Eventually, two military police officers removed him from the barracks, and he was taken to the POU. Harry suspected Buddy of ulterior motives—he was looking for the easiest way out of the Marines. A week later his suspicions were confirmed. The POU sergeant prepared Buddy for dismissal by dressing him in red pants, an electric purple shirt, and a long blue tie. Patent-leather yellow shoes completed the outfit. Buddy was marching, by himself, toward the gate that would lead him to the bus home. "Five yards from the gate, with nobody around to make him do it, he suddenly whipped around and started walking backward, and as he did the solid gold tooth he wore on the right side of his mouth caught and winked the sun directly at me," Harry recalled later.

About forty-five of the sixty men that had started boot camp with Harry made it to the end of the eight-week process. Upon graduation from Parris Island, the recruits were expected to make a donation to their drill instructor. The recruits were paid a small wage by the month and had recently received their payment. Harry had been given the position of second platoon leader. He assisted the leader in collecting from the recruits, and the platoon leader was sent upstairs to give the gift to the drill instructor. A minute later, the platoon leader ran back into the squad bay, with the drill instructor screaming insults behind him. The instructor threw the money on the ground and cursed the entire platoon. "So we collected one more time and took him the money again," Harry remembered. "Took every fuckin' penny out of the squad bay. Then it was enough. He knew what we had, and he wanted it all. It was that kind of place."

Three weeks into Harry's Parris Island training, the Korean War ended. Instead of Asia, he would spend the next three years stationed mostly in Florida, rising to the level of temporary sergeant near the end of his tour.

Since there was no war in which to see combat, he had completed the most difficult part of his service when he left Parris Island.

After graduating from Parris, the newly crowned Marines boarded another train and rode the rails back to Jacksonville, where the Naval Air Technical Training Center was located. There, Harry and trainees received introductory courses in photography, hydraulics, mechanics, and a variety of other subjects germane to their new roles. At the end, they were asked to choose a preferred specialty and sent on to their next assignment.

After training, Harry wound up at the Marine Air Corps Station in Miami, as part of Marine Wing Service Group 37. Located in the town of Opa-Locka, the station had served as an air base during World War II and had been reopened during the most recent engagement. The large base was known as the Marine's first flying field and housed all manner of aircraft related to combat, along with a cache of nuclear weapons. Marines stationed at the base worked on the planes, monitored towers, controlled test flights, and stayed on alert for the next threat. "Cuba was starting to act funny," said Tom Lavin, a veteran who had been injured in Korea and was stationed in Miami during that time.

While stationed in Opa-Locka, Harry lived with his squadron in a large open barracks with other enlisted men. His squad was charged with maintaining a portion of the aircraft on the base. Now that it was peacetime once again, the tension was ramped down, and Harry's life improved significantly from his time in South Carolina. "The weather was nice, the chow was superb—our lives were good," Lavin recalled.

Once a month, the commanding officer for the base would bring in a truck with canned and draft beer, and the men would lounge around, play softball, and socialize. Melvin Harrelson remembers getting to know Harry at these base-wide get-togethers. Harrelson was part of the maintenance squadron during much of the time Harry was stationed in Miami. He remembers Harry as talkative and at ease among his fellow Marines. "He was a very outgoing guy," Harrelson said. "He was always very jovial, very happy. He had lots of friends. Everyone who knew him liked him." For a while, Harry took over the job of running the coffee mess, collecting contributions from base java-drinkers, and mixing coffee in a huge fifty-cup container, getting to know more of his fellow Marines as he handed out the drinks.

Not all of Harry's time was spent drinking coffee and babysitting planes in South Florida, however. For three months of each year, the base went on a float, escorted by the Navy through the Caribbean to Puerto Rico. With no war on, the Marines needed a beach to storm. Marines would drop into the water and climb the beach as planes dropped dummy bombs from above. "It was plain war," Lavin remembered.

The Marines lived in tents and conducted bombing exercises and other combat activities by day. At night, they often would be given "Cinderella liberty" and be set loose on the streets of San Juan, with orders to be back in the bunk by midnight. "We'd go to port, and mess around like young men do," Lavin said. These nighttime adventures would eventually become the source for Harry's first published story, a decade later. "The Unattached Smile" would relate an incident between two off-duty soldiers and two prostitutes at the end of one such evening.

North Korea may not have been shooting at U.S. Marines, but on one tension-filled night the Puerto Rican police almost did. A group of officers on liberty in San Juan was stopped by the local authorities. One of the officers did not have sufficient paperwork to satisfy the local cop and was told he would be taken to jail until it could be provided. The Marine officers had spent time at the bars that evening and, in their condition, felt the affront warranted an international incident. If you don't let him through, one of the officers told the police, we'll get every man on the island and come back to tear this place down.

Calls were made to Puerto Rican police headquarters, and word filtered back to the Marine encampment. Harry and his fellow squad-mates were rousted after midnight and told to grab their guns and ammunition and wait. Though it strained credulity, they were told the Puerto Rican police were planning to storm the base and start making arrests. So there they stood, locked and loaded, and ready to go to war with Puerto Rico.

Soon, somebody did some quick checking and found that the incident was actually minor and had already been resolved. News of the incident reached the commanding officers, who, noticeably perturbed by the situation, came down and demanded the Marines involved turn in their ammunition and stand down.

No actual blood was shed that night. In fact, only once during his service did Harry witness action that resulted in the death of an active-duty Marine. Harry's squad was again involved in war simulations in Puerto Rico. When the activities had been completed, the squad boarded a transport plane headed for St. Thomas. The plane was halfway between the two islands when one of the engines went out. The crew chief determined that the squad would have to jump out of the plane. The squad members had jumped off towers but were not trained as paratroopers. The doors opened, and the crew chief ordered the men to jump. Most opened their chutes too early, and one of the men was never found. The rest were left paddling in the middle of the Caribbean Sea as the plane went on to St. Thomas. "They picked us up later with a Coast Guard cutter, and then flew us back on the same plane," Harry remembered.

While he was being educated about life outside Georgia, Harry was continuing his literary self-education. "When I went to my first duty station, I found out there was a library, there was a library at every station," he said. "And if they didn't have a book, they'd get it for you. So I spent my time in the Marine Corps with a rifle in one hand and a book in the other." He started with the crime novels of Mickey Spillane, and compulsively read every one on base. And when he wasn't reading, he was writing, often staying up late at night scratching away at a tablet long after his platoon-mates had drifted off to sleep.

His education went beyond books. He was exposed to people and things and attitudes he hadn't encountered before. He heard a New York accent for the first time. He was introduced to the joys of pizza. Once while on leave, Harry brought a friend of Latino heritage home with him to Jacksonville. Myrtice was hospitable and prepared a meal for the two hungry Marines, but when Harry's friend was out of the room, she pulled Harry aside.

"He ain't our kind of people, is he?" she asked.

"No ma'am, he's not," Harry said.

When the three years he had committed to were complete, Harry took his leave of the Marine Corps. He had been, by all accounts, an honorable Marine. He was promoted to corporal on May 28, 1956, just a few months before his discharge. At the time, he was performing the duties of a parts clerk at the air base in Miami. He had earned the National Defense Service Medal and the Marine Good Conduct Medal. And he had won several base boxing championships, competing as a light heavyweight and racking up thirty-three victories against only two defeats.

In later years, Harry was of divided mind concerning his time in the Marines. On the one hand, he despised the tyrannical tactics his superiors used on him and felt they contributed to his problems with authority. He felt the military took advantage of poor farm kids who had few other options, and that those same farm kids bought into the lore of patriotism and honor. But he also saw how the experience helped build his own character. "What it put into me is what a writer has to have: discipline," he said. "When I went into the Marine Corps, I was a sorry S.O.B. There wasn't nothing too low for me to do, including stealing old ladies' purses. But 14 months later when they let me off the island, I 'sirred' everything that moved, and I spoke kindly to little old ladies with purses."

CHAPTER FIVE **KING OF THE ROAD**

As we crossed the Colorado–Utah border I saw God in the sky
in the form of huge gold sunburning clouds above the desert that
seemed to point a finger at me and say, "Pass here and go on,
you're on the road to heaven."
— Jack Kerouac, *On the Road*

Corporal Harry Crews of the U.S. Marine Corps Reserves was quite a different person from the teenager who had left Jacksonville three years before. He had no intention of taking his place back in the fields of South Georgia for good, but he returned for a visit a few weeks after his discharge. It was summer and tobacco harvesting season, so Harry joined several of his cousins for a day of cropping. He was in the field on a normal July day in Bacon County—unbearably hot. Three years away from the farm had left Harry susceptible to the sun, much more so than his cousins, who had never left. After a few hours in the heat, the cousins noticed Harry struggling. The good-natured ribbing began. After a few comments, Harry was beginning to think it wasn't all that funny.

His head turned to the sky. "Goddamn sun," he said under his breath.

His cousins flinched, and the smiles left their faces. They looked at him with a mixture of surprise and disgust. Harry tried to apologize, but the tone of the day was forever changed. "I had done what, in Bacon County, was unthinkable," he wrote later. "I had cursed the sun. And in Bacon County, you don't curse the sun or the rain or the land or God. To curse any of them is an ultimate blasphemy. I had known that three years ago, but somehow managed to forget it. I stood there feeling how much I had left this place and these people, and at the same time knowing that it would be forever impossible to leave them completely."

His years in the Marines, filled with reading and different accents and new attitudes, had alienated him from the home and people of his youth. At the same time, he was emboldened with his newfound knowledge, both experiential and literary, to proceed on his quest to become a writer. He spent the summer of 1956 working at a pulp mill in Jacksonville. It was backbreaking work, loading timber into machines and carting around wood of various types and sizes from one area of the factory to another. But he was able to save some money and prepare for another venture that had never been undertaken by any of his family members. He was going to college.

Along with his diploma from Andrew Jackson High, what made Harry's matriculation possible was the Korean War GI Bill, which had been signed into law in 1952. In the later stages of World War II, Congress had passed the Servicemen's Readjustment Act, known as the original GI Bill. In the hopes of easing the transition for soldiers returning from the war, the bill offered significant government benefits, mostly in the form of training and education. The 1944 law allowed returning servicemen up to four years of funding for education, and allowed tens of thousands of GIs to take a shot at college. Though Harry never made it to Korea, he was in uniform during the war, which was enough to qualify him, under the newest GI Bill, to four years of higher education, courtesy of the U.S. government.

He arrived in Gainesville in the fall of 1956 with a plan: he would live off his GI Bill funding while he taught himself how to be a writer. Classes, grades, tests: those were an afterthought—the price of doing business. His high school grades were subpar, but his status as a veteran got his foot in the door at the University of Florida.

The first week on campus, he was called down to an administration building and asked to take an aptitude test. After it had been graded, an administrator called him aside.

"Look," the administrator told Harry, "on the basis of these scores on these tests, what you ought to do is drop out and apprentice yourself to a cabinetmaker or a plumber or something, because you're going to fail here. Then you're going to think of yourself as a failure."

"Does that mean I have to leave?" Harry asked.

"No, you can stay if you want to."

"Then I think I'll stay and give it a shot," Harry told him.

Despite the GI Bill funding, money was tight. He moved into an apartment near campus that was so small, if a second person entered the room, the first person had to climb onto the bed. He secured a job as a student assistant to Frances Apperson, the librarian in charge of government documents at UF's Library East. The job did not last long. After a few weeks, Apperson discovered Harry's "creative" methods of document organization and told him he should seek employment elsewhere.

Harry fared better in the classroom. Despite the advice of the friendly administrator, he made the dean's list his first semester. He had been reading voraciously for years, and had already read most of the books he was assigned. He studied geology, history, and read Shakespeare for the first time.

Still, the goal was not a college degree. The goal was to become a writer. And gradually Harry began to feel that those two objectives were incompatible. The university, he wrote, "was full of granite men riding granite horses." His professors had become, in Harry's eyes, just another version of his drill instructors in the Marines. "Both men's worlds were carefully prescribed; both men knew exactly what you ought to do and say, and where you ought to squeeze your juice."

What he decided he needed was yet another quest for self-discovery. This one would largely take place on the back of a motorcycle. And so, in the late spring of 1958, with less than a hundred dollars and no real plan, he put down his textbooks and charted a path west.

It started out as a solo journey. He camped under the stars, using a rolled-up sleeping bag and a tent and a traveling coffee pot. He took jobs for a few days here and there tending bar or flipping burgers to earn a few dollars, just enough to keep gas in his tank and food in his stomach. Then he'd move on. He spent the first few weeks in Wyoming, then went north through Montana, "a state so ruggedly beautiful that to look at it was enough to make me feel my own insignificance."

A few months into the trip, he was driving north on the Going-to-the-Sun road, which cuts through the middle of Glacier National Park and runs right over the Continental Divide. A little past sundown he came upon a restaurant and decided to take a break from the road. The place was packed tightly and filled with the noise of drunken banter and the smell of grease. Harry found a table, sat down, and lit a cigarette. Pretty soon, a one-legged man using a crutch approached Harry's table.

"What you want?" the man asked.

"Oh, you taking my order?" Harry replied.

"Yeah," he said. "I'm taking your order."

"Four scrambled eggs," Harry said. "And bacon and any kind of beer in a bottle."

The man grabbed a half-eaten plate of eggs off an abandoned table and slammed it down in front of Harry.

"You ordered eggs, you got eggs. Eat 'em."

Harry looked around and began to understand his surroundings and the quickly escalating danger. He was on a Blackfoot Indian Reservation and everybody, except him, was a Blackfoot Indian. And they were all looking at him, in silence.

"I don't know what your problem is, friend—" Harry started.

"I'm not your friend. Eat the goddamn eggs."

Harry took one final stab at halting the proceedings.

"I've been on a motorcycle all day. Does it have to be this way?"

Apparently, it did. The one-legged Indian tossed his crutch, grabbed Harry by the thick denim coat he was wearing, and started slamming Harry into walls and tables as the assembled crowd removed obstacles to the fight. The Indian performed the entire beating while hopping on his one leg. When he was through, his friends courteously tossed Harry out of the restaurant, sans eggs, in the general direction of his motorcycle. He felt the cold air against his blood-covered face. The Indian had left him with a broken nose and a bruised rib. But he had also given him a gift—relieving Harry of the last remnants of anxiety from the university. The beating was "the ultimate refreshment," and set the course for his journey.

Trading college for a vagabond life on the highways of the West was an act of rebellion during a period in America when mass rebellion was just over the horizon. America was on the tail end of the buttoned-down, conservative Eisenhower era, dominated by the Cold War and the threat of big bad Communism. It was a time for fitting in, and the reasonable backlash, for those with an anti-authority bent, was to drop out.

The fall before Harry set off on his journey, the seminal dropout masterpiece, Jack Kerouac's *On the Road*, appeared on the best-seller lists. The book, one of the sparks that would help light the coming countercultural revolution, arose from the same instincts that were now driving Harry off the cloistered confines of a college campus and out into the wilderness. Kerouac had traveled some of the same highways and mountain passes less than a decade before. He had his epiphany in Miles City, Montana, in 1949, across the state from where Harry received his introductory beat-down courtesy of the one-legged Indian. Kerouac saw a copy of a book called *Yellowstone Red* in a bookstore window. He turned the pages and discovered a version of *The Odyssey*, set in the Wild West. His generation needed its own *Odyssey*, this one set among the hobos, horn players, and lost artists that populated America's final, untainted frontier.

Kerouac's *Odyssey* delivered the perfect antidote to American conformity, at the perfect time. On the back of the 1957 Viking Press edition, readers were promised the "odyssey of the Beat Generation, the frenetic young men and their women restlessly racing from New York to San Francisco, from Mexico to New Orleans in a frantic search—for Kicks and Truth." The book was a cultural phenomenon, and Kerouac was crowned the King of the Beats, now called on to serve as the voice of discontented American youth.

It was a generous helping of discontent that put Harry on the highway. After his bout with the Blackfoot, he continued on into Canada, then made his way back down to Yellowstone National Park, where he would come off the road and settle down for the first time in the trip. "They've got these little places around the park where you can stop and get a beer or a hot dog," Harry remembered. "I was 21, just over 21, just two or three months older, and so I could work tending bar. . . . So I served beer, tended bar, and cleaned dishes."

In Yellowstone, Harry met up with a pair of fellow travelers slightly younger than he. Ben Roark had come to the park from Warren, Arkansas, holding a recommendation from a local politician that secured him work on the grounds. He was on his second summer traveling the U.S. in a search for adventure and an attempt to make money for college; the previous summer he had spent time in Alaska and California. Keith Shaver had come from the other direction, making his way down from Clearlake, North Dakota. Females outnumbered males ten to one among the summer staff at Yellowstone, so Harry, Roark, and Shaver quickly formed a companionship.

Thanks to the ten-to-one ratio, life in Yellowstone was exceedingly pleasant. The boys lived in a dorm behind the restaurant, just a few steps away from the building that housed the waitresses. Harry and friends handled the bar while the girls waited tables, sold souvenirs, or cleaned up.

One of the boys' favorite responsibilities was the loading of the beer coolers. The restaurant shut down from two till five, and the cooks would go off duty. The boys would open the boxes and put enough beer in the coolers for the dinner crowd, making sure to place a case in the garbage room for their own personal use later in the evening. Then, when the restaurant closed for the night, they would retrieve the case of beer, along with some boxed meals the cooks had prepared for them. Then they'd find some willing waitresses, pack up the refreshments and some blankets, and enjoy a night under the star-specked western sky, waiting for Old Faithful or another one of the geysers to provide some extra atmosphere.

On off days, the group would pack picnics and go to Mammoth Springs to fish among the geysers or just explore the park on foot. Harry didn't particularly like to fish, Roark remembered. His interests tended more toward girls and arguing.

"Harry held himself a little above a lot of people. He was a little bit aloof," Roark recalled. "He would argue about anything. He really felt like he had knowledge of the world, and that he could beat you on any argument. He loved to spar with you. It didn't make any difference if it was politics, or women, or geography, or what."

But above women and debate was Harry's devotion to his writing, Roark said. Harry kept a spiral notebook, and he would finish each night sitting on his bed, deep in concentration, entering the days' experiences, sentence by sentence, into the book. "We all slept in one room, and old Harry would leave the light on, for writing," he said. "I always thought, goddamn, tonight he would finally skip a night. He just wasn't made that way. It didn't make any difference how late or how much we drank, he would still do those two pages a day."

Life was good, but the pay was not. Their contracts called for them to pocket eighty-eight dollars a month, after room and board. Both Roark and Harry wanted to earn money. Roark had spent part of the previous summer working for Hunt's Foods in California, and knew it to be very lucrative. He made contact with his former boss to find out when the harvest season, which was dependent on the weather, would begin. Shaver, the only one of the three with a car, needed some convincing, but soon he was on board too.

The three left Wyoming in midsummer, traveled into Utah and spent some time in Salt Lake City, then to Redwood City, California, where they got temporary jobs mining salt, waiting for the tomato season to begin. Harry was a gym rat, Roark said, and when they moved on to Heyward, home of Hunt's Foods, he went downtown and joined a health club. He could earn free club time by signing up other members, so he convinced his traveling partners they needed some exercise as well. Soon, the group was passing much of their free time pushing up weights. Harry was thin and lanky and always looking for a fight, Roark said, but did not look or act to his companions like a recently discharged Marine.

To add intrigue during their travels, Harry liked to bet—on anything that would lend itself to wagering. The price of entry was usually a dollar, and Harry took the majority of the dollars from his friends. On trips to the health club, Harry would park in a no-parking zone in front of the building and bet his friends that he wouldn't get a parking ticket. He won several dollars on that particular bet.

One day Roark decided to change his own luck. He made the parking bet with Harry, and then while Harry was inside the health club, he went out to a pay phone and called the police. He impersonated the health club owner and told the officer that someone had parked illegally in front of his place. The police arrived shortly thereafter and wrote Harry a ticket. The bet cost Harry a dollar to pay off Roark and another twenty dollars to the Heyward Police Department.

Once the tomato season was under way, the money and tomato sauce began to flow. Roark talked his boss into hiring him and his friends. The work was hard labor. Harry landed in a two-story room where the ketchup was mixed in huge vats. His job was to lift hundred-pound sacks of salt and sugar and put them on the second level, six feet up, so the cooks could mix the contents into the vats. The lifting, along with the intense heat from the cooking, made for physically draining, backbreaking work. Instead of complaining, Harry reveled in it.

"The [boss] said, 'That damn boy, I've never seen anything like it,'" Roark remembered. "'I have never had a man that would stand it over a week.' It was just really, really not a good job, and [the boss] told him he would give him another job. Harry said, 'No, I want this one.' So the boss said, 'I'll tell you what, I'll give you a raise, then.'"

The Hunt Foods factory operated seven days a week during peak production. The boys worked twelve hours a day, earning overtime, and on holidays, triple time. With barely any time to spend their earnings, they accumulated ample savings. Occasionally, they would venture across the Golden Gate Bridge and try to fit in an evening in San Francisco. They didn't get off work until six o'clock and had to be back at the factory by six the following morning, so the best they could hope for was a few quick beers. Shaver, the quieter and more introverted member of the group, did not like to drive in the city, so Roark would pilot the car into town.

"Right about that time, the damned beatniks had come in, and we would go over there and hang around on [Haight-Ashbury]," Roark said. The beatniks favored berets and spent most of their time smoking dope and arguing about how "the system wasn't working." Rebellion was in the air. Roark and Shaver hung back, hoping a rebellious young girl would seek them out, but mostly they drank beer and watched. Roark, who was sporting a beard at the time, picked up a beret himself to gild his approach to the beatnik girls, but his Arkansas drawl outed him as a country boy a few syllables in. Harry, however, blended right in. He was clean-shaven and beret-less but as well read as anyone there and not intimidated. On occasion, there were poetry contests, and Harry would engage in verbal battle, reciting long poems from memory. "They would stand up in these bars and they'd rattle off a dissertation about something, or poem about something. And Harry was right there with 'em. He was as smooth as glass," Roark said.

On a few occasions, Roark recalled, the great Kerouac would be spotted in one of the bars. A buzz would rise among the beatniks. Neither Shaver nor Roark had any idea who he was, so Harry filled them in, and then the three approached the king of the beats. "I shook his hand a few times. It didn't mean anything to me." But Harry would approach him and try to engage him in writing talk. "That made Harry's day whenever he was there," he said.

The tomato season was profitable but short, and once their services were no longer needed, the traveling crew said their goodbyes and headed in different directions. Shaver went back to North Dakota. Roark spent some of his money on a '48 Plymouth coupe and went back to Yellowstone looking for one of the girls he had dated. Harry purchased a brand new 650 CC Triumph motorcycle, rented a room, and spent some of his cash racing his new toy on a dirt track east of Heyward.

He also continued to make trips into San Francisco to listen to tunes and look for women. He found one of the latter in a club—a "spectacular black dancer." The relationship was short and passionate, and Harry would later say that he had fallen in love with her and even asked her to marry him.

"She told me I had Georgia in my mouth. I thought it was a beautiful and true thing to say," he wrote. As abruptly as she had entered his life, she was gone, to exist from then on as another story from the road.

After several months in California, Harry was ready to move on, and he had Mexico on his mind. He set out on the Triumph headed east.

Harry's own transformation, begun when he left Gainesville, was now fully realized. Gone was the high and tight buzz cut from the Marines. He stopped cutting his hair and rarely shaved. He had a single pair of Levi's that would be replaced only when they were rendered unwearable from the battery acid coming off his motorcycle. Somewhere along the way, he acquired a sheepskin-lined leather flight jacket at a secondhand store. (The price was right because the zipper didn't work, so he used four large safety pins to clasp the jacket in the front.) He wore no helmet but did use a pair of World War II goggles to keep the road detritus out of his eyes. And he wore a pair of engineering boots, with a quarter inch of lead in the sole for when he scraped pavement while piloting the Triumph. The boots would often give off sparks when Harry ambled down the sidewalk.

He crossed Monarch Pass, which crosses the Rocky Mountains at 11,000 feet in central Colorado. It was early fall, and the temperature had dropped precipitously. The side of the highway was coated with snow, and more snow was falling. Harry was freezing. Every few miles he would stop, dismount his bike, and hold his gloved hands in front of the exhaust pipes to regain some feeling. He found the nearest town, came in out of the snow, and secured a spot in the dormitory at the local YMCA. Here, he would have an encounter that would, a decade later, result in one of the most memorable characters in his fiction.

He went into the dormitory, a small, dark room with a dozen beds, and immediately fell asleep. Sometime during the night, he was awoken by another guest making strange noises, grunts, and howls. The two began arguing in the dark. At first Harry was aggressive, but something about the stranger's voice, and the claustrophobic room, and the haze of recent sleep, struck fear in him. The fear grew into desperate paranoia.

"What do you want?" Harry demanded, trembling.

"What I want, you cannot give," said the disembodied voice.

The cold and the strange surroundings and the ghostly pronouncements were affecting Harry's nervous system. He was in the midst of a good old-fashioned freak-out.

"You've come for the wrong man!" he cried. "You've got the wrong man!"

"No," the voice responded. "It is you for whom I've come. You and all your kind."

This sent Harry sprinting for the door. He ran to the lobby in his underwear, accosted the clerk, and demanded he come into the room to see the man who was threatening to kill him. When they got to the dormitory, the lights were on. The room's only occupant was Billy, a regular at the YMCA who, according to the clerk, believed himself to be Jesus Christ. He was, Harry wrote, "a man about the size of a jockey. His legs, skinny as a child's and marked with blue veins, were hardly long enough to let his toes brush the floor."

Harry did not spend the night with Billy. The incident sent him back out into the Colorado night. But it also remained in his memory bank. The memory of Billy would eventually become Didymus, a deranged and violent music manager in Harry's first published novel, *The Gospel Singer*. "The little man in the YMCA sat up in his bed and up in my head as alive and immediate as he had ever been," Harry would write later. "Out of his skinny legs and maniacal voice I made the character of Didymus, and it was in the person of Didymus that I first felt the miracle that keeps fiction writers writing fiction, the miracle of the alphabet turning into blood."

The trip still had a few adventures left, but Harry was now "purified and holy," ready to rejoin society, return to the University of Florida, and get back to the task at hand. He brought with him the journal he had kept throughout the trip, which he titled "Something About Being a Straddle of a Thing." He traveled from Colorado down through Raton Pass to New Mexico, then Texas, then the town of Chihuahua in Mexico, where he spent significant time among the sand and cactus. Then he crossed the border back into the U.S. and started the final trek through the South back to Gainesville. On one of the final days on the highway, a large woman wearing a leather jacket pulled up next to him on an impressive Harley-Davidson chopper. Harry made eye contact.

"Wow, that's a hot bike," he remarked.

"Baby," responded the woman, "if you'd been between these legs as long as this bike has, you'd be hot too."

By August 1959, Harry was back in Gainesville. The trip had left some marks, but, miraculously, no long-term physical damage had been done.

His only major motorcycle accident had occurred around Christmas of the previous year, when he and his Triumph slid under an eighteen-wheel mail truck and came out the other side. Again, both bike and rider emerged with minor scrapes.

Whatever spiritual force had been protecting him throughout his trip abandoned him once the journey ended. On his first day back in Gainesville, he was idling on his Triumph in front of the Gainesville police station. He saw the light turn green, gave the bike some gas, and eased into the intersection. Out of the corner of his eye he saw a vehicle approaching at a much higher rate of speed than he expected. He saw a young coed behind the wheel, eyes focused toward her left, unconcerned with the red light, and unlikely to be aware of the motorcycle passing in front of her car. Harry tried to accelerate, but this time the Triumph failed him. The car collided with the back end of the motorcycle, knocked bike and rider into the air, and drove Harry's left knee right through the bike's gas tank. In a split second, Harry's journey had come to a sudden and painful end.

CHAPTER SIX

MR. LYTLE

Life is melodrama. Only art is real.
　—Andrew Lytle

T he crash put him in the hospital and added to the defined limp
that he already carried from childhood. But good fortune and bad
fortune often walk hand in hand. The pain in his leg was still sharp
when Harry, sporting a full leg cast and new pair of crutches, attempted
to navigate the steps of the large auditorium that housed the Spanish class
that he had enrolled in for the fall semester. It was the first day of classes
at the University of Florida. He noticed an attractive young blonde girl
sitting by herself in the front row and decided he should try to walk a little
further down the steps and find out who she was.

The girl was Sally Ellis, an eighteen-year-old freshman who had just
arrived in Gainesville from Dayton, Ohio. Just a few days prior, she had
unpacked her trunk at her dorm room in Mallory Hall, after spending the
summer labeling her clothes in preparation for her first extended time away
from home. The Ellis family lived in an enormous, Spanish-style home in
the wealthy Dayton suburb of Oakwood. Sally's father, Roy Ellis, was the
president and founder of the Rubber Seal Product Company, a successful
firm that had made him a rich man. Sally had developed a love of Spanish
in high school and came to Gainesville with the idea of majoring in the
language. Harry needed to fulfill a language requirement to graduate, and
before long Sally, happily, was doing homework for two.

Once the cast came off, Harry was back on the motorcycle, and soon

Sally was accompanying him on rides. "I was really attracted to him and to his outlook on life," she remembered. "We spent so much time together. We used to go everywhere on that motorcycle. He used to get on, and I'd be behind him, and he'd start singing 'C'mon Baby, Let the Good Times Roll.' It was our theme song."

Prior to his trip west, Harry had fallen in with a group of veterans and aspiring artists who would form the supporting cast in his life for the majority of his time as an undergraduate at the University of Florida. The group lived in a large two-story clapboard house in the student residential area near campus. The house had a large dining room and living room downstairs and several small bedrooms on the second floor. The residents of the house sardonically christened it the Twelve Oak Bath and Tennis Club. "There was no tennis and there was no club," Pat Waters, a regular guest at the house, remembered. "There was a lot of play going on, but it wasn't tennis."

Ed Nagel was Harry's first roommate at Twelve Oak. Nagel had grown up in Melbourne, Florida, and had joined the navy around the same time Harry entered the Marines. They arrived at the University of Florida as freshmen in 1957 and quickly developed an affinity for each other. At first, they lived together in a small room and shared a double bed that sagged in the middle. Many a night, they would awaken to find themselves far too close for comfort in the dead center of the bed.

The leader of Twelve Oak was Don Lewis, another navy veteran whose girth and cheerful attitude had earned him the nickname Buddha in the house. Lewis, who was pursuing a PhD in French, had a skill for organization and ran the house with the precision of a naval unit. The residents would fork over half of their stipend from the GI Bill at the first of the month, and Lewis would cover the grocery bill and other household expenses. Out of those expenses would come the salary for Pigmy, the house cook. Pigmy was a petite black woman with a penchant for adding a generous portion of grease to all her recipes.

Pigmy would arrive at the Twelve Oak house at noon, find the evening's menu taped to the icebox, where Lewis had left it for her, and have a full meal on the table at six p.m. The residents would bring guests—girlfriends, visiting friends or relatives, even professors—to share the meal and camaraderie. After dinner, they would play rounds of poker to determine who would have the honor of cleaning the mountain of pots and pans and plates left over from the meal.

Along with Harry, Lewis, and Nagel, Twelve Oaks residents included Roger Coles, another creative writing student; Piers Wright, an aspiring artist; and Don Mateen, who majored in partying. Mateen was the least dedicated to his studies of the group, and the most dedicated to the bottle. On one occasion, he organized a day trip to the beach at St. Augustine. The planned one-day excursion evolved into four days, and while he was away he missed an important exam in one of his classes. Always on the edge of failing out, Mateen believed a failing grade on this test would end his university career.

At the dinner table back at Twelve Oak, the group came up with a plan. Mateen, they decided, would say he had been in a terrible accident and suffered a head wound. Harry was seeing a nurse named Mitzi at the time, who was a guest at dinner. Mitzi offered to soak a bandage in plaster of Paris, creating a head wrap that Mateen could take on and off like a hat. She would even provide a wig stand for him to store the bandage on.

The plan worked well, but too well. The professor in question not only believed the story, he was near tears with sympathy. He agreed to allow Mateen to retake the test and granted him as much time as he needed. Mateen, the professor said, was "on his honor." Mateen brought the test back to the Twelve Oak house and sipped whiskey while his roommates completed the test for him. After Mateen had safely passed the exam, the professor invited himself to dinner at Twelve Oak to congratulate Mateen. When the professor walked into the house, his eyes immediately locked in on the wig stand. He picked it up and then looked at Mateen's bandaged head. "Interesting," he said, and the assembled housemates silently tried to interpret what he meant.

Mitzi saved the day once again. She grabbed the wig stand out of the professor's hand and said, "Yes, quite interesting. And useful, too. I sometimes use it to keep a hair piece fresh when I stay overnight. Otherwise, Crews would probably tear the wig off my head and eat it, barbarian that he is." Mateen's education, for now, was safe once again.

Harry's education, however, was in a bit of a rut. He still firmly believed that his writing could not be improved in a classroom, but only by practice, and by reading other great writers. "Harry was intent on writing but not having anyone help him," Nagel said. Instead, he aimed to learn through the masters and to widen his intellectual scope on his own. In one determined stretch, he read everything Sigmund Freud had ever written.

Nagel and Harry signed up for a Shakespeare course together, and Harry excelled, earning an A. (Nagel ended up with a D.) The Shakespeare course led to an increasing interest in poetry, and Harry began competing in poetry jams at a bar near campus. One participant would offer a line of verse, and another would pick it up. "It was like 'Dueling Banjos,' only with poets," Nagel remembered.

Harry's prose, however, was lagging behind. Nagel and Coles had both begun taking classes in the creative writing program, which was still run by the man who had created it a decade prior: Andrew Nelson Lytle. "I fell into Lytle's class," Nagel said. He was hooked. "Mr. Lytle gave me *A Good Man Is Hard to Find*, by Flannery O'Connor, which sort of got me going in Southern writing. Harry was slugging away, writing on his own. So, one night, I said, 'Harry, this shit is really terrible.' He was just writing stories about people on campus. It had no territory, it had no soul. I told him, 'I'm not that good either; why don't you come to Lytle's class? You might like it.'"

Although Harry Crews and Andrew Lytle were both children of the South, they may as well have come from two different planets. Lytle, born in 1902, was the son of a patrician farmer from an old, established family in Murfreesboro, Tennessee. His parents sent him to Sewanee Military Academy for his secondary education, where he excelled as a student. He was offered, and turned down, an appointment to West Point, and instead traveled in France with his mother and sister. From there the plan was to study at Oxford, but a death in the family brought him to the U.S. to study instead at Vanderbilt, where he excelled once again. From Vanderbilt it was off to Yale, to learn drama at the foot of famed educator George Pierce Baker, then to New York City, where he dabbled in stage acting (and crossed paths with a young actor named Humphrey Bogart) before being called back to the South by his father to manage a large plantation called Cornsilk near Guntersville, Alabama.

As an undergraduate at Vanderbilt, Lytle had become associated with a group of poets who dubbed themselves the Fugitives. The group was made up of men who would fill out the southern literary lineup for the first half of the twentieth century: Robert Penn Warren, Donald Davidson, Allen Tate, and John Crowe Ransom, their young professor, a poet who had been an artillery officer in World War I. The Fugitives met late at night to critique each other's work, philosophize, and feed off the collective intellectual power they created. In 1922 the group began publishing a magazine call *The Fugitive: A Magazine of Poetry*. (Poetry was not Lytle's strong suit; Ransom suggested it was like an expert fiddle player who had only mastered one string.)

By 1930, the Fugitives had morphed into the Agrarians, a society of writers who took it upon themselves to defend the way of life in the South. They contributed essays to a 1930 manifesto called *I'll Take My Stand: The South and the Agrarian Tradition*, in which they lauded the virtues of their beloved South while laying the blame on industrialism, urbanization, and the North for the ruination of American society. The book was celebrated in some circles and denigrated in others, and each member of the Agrarians would spend the rest of their lives either defending their position or attempting to disassociate themselves from it.

Lytle remained a firm defender of the Agrarian view of the South. It would infuse his writing for the rest of his life. After *I'll Take My Stand*, he managed the plantation for a while but gradually moved toward a life of writing and teaching of literature. He published short stories, literary criticism, and a pair of novels, *The Long Night* and *A Name for Evil*, and taught at several stops along the way, most notably at the Iowa Writers' Workshop, where spending time north of the Mason-Dixon Line reinforced his view that the South was where he belonged.

It was in Iowa that he met his most famous student and refined his teaching methods. Flannery O'Connor was twenty-two and, like Lytle, a southerner venturing north for the first time. Lytle understood O'Connor to be a rare talent, and their status as southerners deep in Yankee territory formed the emotional foundation for a strong, lasting master-apprentice relationship. Lytle's teaching and revisions wrenched the vagueness from O'Connor's student writing, and her work became more pictorial, more compressed, more vivid in detail.

In Lytle's Iowa workshops, he developed the process for teaching creative writing that he would take with him through his academic career. When he arrived, workshop students would read their own work, which would lead to supportive comments from friends and negative reaction from enemies. "I knew that wouldn't do, so . . . I did the reading. I would read the manuscripts anonymously to the class and then they could speak. That's the way to do it, because then the questions you ask can be very searching. If they say something, you ask them why, what made them think that. Of course, at that point, they're not prepared to do it, but they learn," he said.

In the fall of 1948, he came to the University of Florida, and for the first time the UF English Department offered undergraduate and graduate courses in creative writing. The university now had on its faculty a distinguished writer who was recognized as a champion of southern literature. He had by that time published a well-received biography, three novels, and numerous essays and short stories. For the next decade, Lytle simultaneously created a legion of disciples to his monklike devotion to the craft of literature and worked on his masterpiece, *The Velvet Horn*, which was published in 1958. His critical yet paternal style continued to yield success, and through the years he continued to mentor writers to literary acclaim, among them Jesse Hill Ford, Merrill Joan Gerber, and Madison Jones.

One notable exception was Lytle's relationship with the poet James Dickey, whom he brought to Gainesville in 1954 when Dickey was an unknown poet teaching unhappily at Rice University. At first Dickey soaked up Lytle's commentary, but soon Dickey became discouraged with the drudgery of teaching composition to college freshmen, began to see Lytle's criticism as heavy-handed, and acted out against his mentor. Dickey was invited to deliver a poetry reading to an organization called "the Pen Women," which was comprised of wives of faculty members and elderly amateur writers. Dickey chose to entertain the staid group with a poem about a young boy admiring his father's sexual organ in the shower, which he spiced up with several ad-libbed four-letter words. The subsequent uproar led to a demand for apology from the president of the University of Florida, backed up by Lytle, which Dickey declined, choosing instead to pack his bags and leave town, midsemester, never to speak a word to Mr. Lytle again.

One night in Lytle's workshop was enough for Harry to know it was where he needed to be. "That was the first glimmer, the first notion I had of how truly ignorant I was of what I was trying to do and how much I had to learn if I was ever to write," he said later. For the next two years he was a regular in Lytle's class. The creative writing classes and faculty were housed in a structure known only as Building D. It had been built in the 1930s as a temporary barracks at Camp Blanding and shipped to the University of Florida after World War II as a temporary location for the department. It would last into the 1980s. It had no air-conditioning and could become a steam room when the Florida sun drove up the temperature. The graduate classes, since Lytle's days, were held in a small classroom filled with wooden chairs situated around a long oak table. The room had a single gold chair, the only cushioned chair in the room, which Lytle had reserved for the best critic in the class. The students called the chair Old Sparky.

When Harry began attending his classes, Lytle had been in Gainesville over a decade and had become more confident and more eccentric. He dressed like a "Southern gentleman from the early 1900s." He wore a black suit and skinny black tie, and a fat gold watch on a black ribbon around his neck, the watch deposited in his vest pocket. To officially begin class, he would remove the watch from his pocket and place it on the table in front of him. Class was over when the watch was deposited back in the pocket, often when the hour hand was approaching midnight. He eschewed the university's class schedule and instead made his own agrarian-based schedule, moving the starting time up and back with the sunset.

His thespian background seeped into his behavior in class and out. His intense, dramatic readings of student writing and of published stories of his choosing would turn each one into a performance. His passion for the craft inspired devotion; the converts would plan their lives around his weekly orations and always address their leader as "Mr. Lytle." He polished his acting outside class, walking the paths of campus between buildings. Each day he would take on a persona, perhaps an eighteenth-century French nobleman, or a southern backwoodsman, and inhabit the character completely as he mingled with students in the courtyards under the campus's canopy of magnolias.

Many of the characters would be drawn from the time in history when Lytle believed civilization had reached its pinnacle, when Christendom ruled western Europe, and society had firmly drawn class lines. Nobility, clergy, peasantry; each understood that they had been put in their respective circumstances by the Anglo-Saxon god. This perfect society had been achieved in North America, Lytle believed, in the pre–Civil War South and had been ruined by the sinister Democratic commonwealth.

Those students in whom he saw promise would be invited to his home, a pale brick ranch-style house on North Sixth Avenue. There, they would meet his wife, Miss Edna, and be invited to share some Rebel Yell bourbon with their professor. Mr. Lytle would always drink his out of "The Lytle Cup," a silver goblet used only for this purpose. Some would be asked to babysit his three daughters, Pamela, Katherine Anne, and Lily Langdon.

In his younger days, he had written fairly quickly, finishing his early novels in a matter of a few years. Over time, however, he had developed the theory that writing must be nurtured and cultivated over a long period of time. Anything less was an insult to the craft. He spent the entire decade of the 1950s writing *The Velvet Horn*, a time-shifting Civil War epic that would be nominated for the National Book Award. He would wake at four a.m. and bleed for hours over each sentence. He would emerge later and tell his students, "I got one line today," or "It just won't come today, boys."

Lytle was in his early fifties, with daughters around the age of his students, and fit nicely into the role of father figure to Harry, who was, unknowingly at that point, on a lifelong quest to find his own father. Lytle quickly took a liking to Harry. He saw the rough outline of genuine talent in his writing and the determination to learn the craft. And he offered Harry lessons in life as well.

One night after Harry had gone to sleep at Twelve Oak, he awoke to find Mr. Lytle standing at the foot of his bed in the dark.

"Son," he said, "let's go to the Lion and get a drink. I feel poorly tonight."

Harry flipped on the light, sure that he was still dreaming. But, even in the light, his professor was there in the flesh. They climbed into Lytle's 1957 yellow Cadillac convertible and drove across the county line (Alachua County, where Gainesville is located, was a dry county at the time), to the Lion, one of Lytle's favorite watering holes. Together they spent the next few hours at a scarred wooden table drinking whiskey and discussing craft. Lytle took Harry back to Twelve Oak, and Harry went directly to the typewriter, flush with pride and excitement after Lytle's act of acceptance.

Soon thereafter, Lytle invited Harry out to dinner at an elegant downtown restaurant. Harry was far more comfortable in establishments with ashtrays and stools than with chandeliers and tablecloths. The two took a table in the center of the dining room. Harry fiddled with his tie and tried to hide his discomfort as Gainesville's upper crust sipped their chardonnay at the surrounding tables. Lytle sensed Harry's unease.

The waiter arrived at the table and placed bowls of soup in front of the men. Harry looked down in complete confusion at the multiple pieces of silverware in his table setting. Before he could make a choice, Lytle picked up his bowl with two hands, brought it to his mouth, and commenced loudly slurping. Heads around the room turned to their table, followed by audible gasps. Lytle consumed half the bowl, set it back down, and then smiled at Harry. "Remember, son, we're better than they are," he said. "We're writers."

Lytle became an occasional guest at Twelve Oak and a drinking companion for Harry, Waters (whom Harry brought into Lytle's circle), and other members of the group. Harry began to spend time at Lytle's house, discussing his writing in his mentor's study. "The game was, I wrote and he read, and sometimes he talked to me about what I wrote, sometimes he didn't, which was precisely right. Much of what I wrote wasn't worth talking about," Harry said.

Often, he and Nagel would go to the Lytle house and sit with the man they dubbed "the Marster," discussing writing and life. Nagel remembered one night when Pamela, Lytle's youngest daughter and a high school student at the time, came out to the porch in a skimpy nightgown to say goodnight to her father. "Go put some clothes on," Lytle demanded. Pamela scampered away. Sometimes, Harry would come by himself and sit quietly, observing while Lytle struggled at the typewriter with his own work.

Harry's own work was still extremely rough, and he knew it. He said to fellow students that he was interested in finding the energy in his writing and unconcerned with details like grammar. He liked to include southern Cracker dialect in his stories and, oddly, would write in the third person using an omniscient narrator who also spoke in Cracker dialect. Lytle was patient with him and understood that it would take more time to coax brilliance out of his new protégé.

"There wasn't any question of Harry revolting against the master," remembered Lawrence Hetrick, another student in those workshops. "There were other people who did that and just made total fools of themselves in that class . . . but not Harry. On the other hand, Harry always kept something in reserve, which I think was very wise on Harry's part. He said, 'I'm going to do something different, and [Lytle] doesn't have the final say on my work.'" Only later would Harry outwardly rebel against the harsher aspects of Mr. Lytle's criticism.

The methods and style Harry observed in the classroom with Lytle would become the basis for his own teaching years later. Many of the mantras Harry would recite for the rest of his life came out of those workshops. "Fire is the great refiner," Mr. Lytle told his students, urging them to have the courage to discard inferior work, no matter how much time and sweat had gone into it, and start over. Harry took it literally and regularly set pages afire. "There are only two subjects: love and the absence of love," Mr. Lytle liked to say. To Harry, this meant that all characters in all stories are searching for the same things. And above all, Lytle tried to teach his disciples that, be they masters or apprentices, they would all eternally be students of the craft, struggling to achieve something that went beyond the individual, something that was transcendent. Mr. Lytle, for Harry, attached a value to writing that he himself had felt since he was a boy but, before he found his way into the small classroom in Building D, he had not been able to truly understand.

The Twelve Oak residents had their own little vacation house for when they wanted an escape from campus. It was the former home of the writer Marjorie Kinnan Rawlings, Pulitzer Prize–winning author of *The Yearling* and a celebrated writer in the late 1930s and early 1940s. Rawlings had purchased property and built a house in a rural area called Cross Creek, about twenty-five miles south of Gainesville, in the 1920s, and written most of her classic works there. Upon her death in 1953, she had donated the home and land to the University of Florida, which turned it into a retreat for creative writing students. (It eventually became a state park.)

Charlie Rose, another friend of the Twelve Oak group, was a doctoral student who served as an assistant to Lytle and lived in the Cross Creek house. The house was built in traditional Florida Cracker style and pre-served as Rawlings had left it, complete with chicken coops and tractors and rocking chairs. To get around the dry-county issue, the group would climb in Lewis's four-door Plymouth, which they dubbed "The Green Beast," and go over the border to Marion County, buy enough Heaven Hill bourbon and other refreshments for the weekend, and head to the Rawlings home for a night or two of partying and revelry.

"We'd party all night," remembered Nagel. "A lot of us would be sleep-ing around on the house on various couches and on the floor. Sunday morning, we'd sometimes hear a knock on the door, and these people, tourists, fans of Rawlings, would come in, look at us, and shyly ask, 'Can we come in and see the Marjorie Kinnan Rawlings House?' And we'd be all hung-over, and we'd say, 'OK, come on in,' and show them around." Harry grew attached to Cross Creek. Many years later, he would buy a cabin of his own in the area and, once again, use the little town as an escape from the university and Gainesville.

The Twelve Oak group had their share of girlfriends and conquests, but

Harry's took the house title in that area. "He was voracious," Nagel said. Whether or not he had a current girlfriend, Harry seemed to be making a move on whatever female guest was brought to the house. One evening, Nagel invited his girlfriend, Sarah Broward, over to study. "We're working and doing our studies, and she disappeared," he said. "Now, Don Lewis watched out for Sarah—he really liked her. . . . So he went looking for her. He found her up in Harry's room. Harry had said to her, 'Come up and see my poetry,' or something like that. So, Lewis went over there with a broom and went into the room and started beating Harry over the back with the broom. He yelled at Harry, 'Get your ass out of there, stop screwing around with that girl!'"

On another occasion, Nagel had agreed to drive Mr. Lytle and Pamela up to Vanderbilt where she was to enroll as a freshman. Harry was not going on the trip but drove Nagel to Lytle's house, since Nagel would be driving Lytle's car. (Lytle did not like to drive and regularly arranged to be chauffeured by one of his students.) Pamela came downstairs and got in the car to wait for her father, who was still inside getting his luggage together. When Nagel came out, Harry had climbed in beside Pamela and the two were locked in an embrace. "I said, 'Harry, get the fuck out of there,'" Nagel said. Harry would eventually "deflower" Pamela under a tree, Nagel said.

By late 1959, however, Sally Ellis was occupying most of Harry's time. The relationship, at least on Harry's side, was by no means exclusive. Nagel was in his room one evening and heard a loud moan coming from Harry's room, one that he said "sounded like a stuck pig." He went over and found Harry, still groaning, rereading a letter. It was from Mitzi, the nurse and another of Harry's on-again, off-again girlfriends, informing Harry that she was pregnant. Harry read Nagel the letter. Nagel consoled him and began to offer advice. Before he could finish the thought, Harry dropped the other shoe: Sally was also pregnant. The world had instantly become complicated, and the easy life at the Twelve Oak Bath and Tennis Club was, sadly, soon to be a thing of the past.

CHAPTER SEVEN **MARRIED LIFE**

> A man doesn't have to be prepared with a plan of action for the
> unexpected, but he does have to be ready to accept it.
> —Smith Kirkpatrick, *The Aftermath*

The complication of two pregnant girlfriends was short-lived. Mitzi miscarried early in her pregnancy. She was soon out of the picture. Not so with Sally. The couple began planning for the future. There was a baby coming. Sally, they decided, would finish her classes for the year and then travel home to Dayton to have the baby. But it was 1960, Sally came from a respectable upper-class family, and it just would not do to have a child out of wedlock. It was out of the question. Harry took Sally to Bacon County to meet Myrtice, and mother-in-law and daughter-in-law got along nicely. Myrtice appreciated Sally's sweet countenance, and Sally was impressed with Myrtice's southern delicacies. "She was a little possessive of him," Sally recalled. "But that was alright. I mean, you could really tell how much she loved him."

With Sally receiving the Bacon County seal of approval, Harry was ready to take the next step. He walked over to Mallory Hall and together they strolled to the tunnel that runs under 13th Street, one of the main roads through campus. In the middle of the tunnel, with light filtering in from either end of the graffiti-covered tunnel, Harry stopped, got down on his knee, and offered his proposal. Sally said yes on the spot.

Wedding plans commenced rapidly. The quickest way to obtain a marriage license, they determined, was to drive across the Florida state line to Georgia. Sally found a white wedding dress, and the invitations went out around the Twelve Oak house. On January 20, 1960, Harry and Sally, along with Mateen, Lewis, Nagel, Coles, and a few girlfriends, climbed into the Green Beast and a few other vehicles and formed a caravan heading north, to the Lowndes County courthouse in Valdosta, Georgia, fifteen miles over the Georgia–Florida border. The group crowded into the courtroom for a short ceremony in front of the justice of the peace and then celebrated all night at a Valdosta tavern. Harry was now a married man.

Being married, however, did little to change his social behavior. While Sally was around, he spent the majority of his time with her, when he wasn't writing or studying. But soon the pregnancy progressed, Sally went back to Ohio to have the baby, and Harry went back to pursuing any available co-ed within his eyesight.

Pat Waters had become a close friend of Harry's by this time in his collegiate career. Waters had grown up in Montgomery, Alabama, child of a working-class family, and understood how life could be for farmers and the children of farmers in the South. Waters had earned a bachelor's degree at Auburn and then come to the University of Florida to study history. He enrolled in one of Lytle's writing seminars and quickly found himself in over his head. After two or three classes, Waters walked in early one evening, and only one other student was at the table. Waters did not notice the other student, but instead walked over to the window and said, to nobody in particular, "I have no business here."

"None of us do," Harry replied. "But we're all here, ain't we?"

Perhaps because of their backgrounds, the two developed an easy rapport and began serving as first readers for each other. "I remember his saying, very soon after we met, that he meant to write a lot of novels," Waters recalled. "Right from the beginning. Even before he was anywhere near publishing anything, it was his intention to write a lot of them."

Waters's degree track included a language requirement, and it gave him tremendous trouble. At one point, he had a German exam scheduled that he knew he had no chance of passing. Somehow, he arranged with his professor to be allowed to take the exam outside the classroom. He was to receive it in the afternoon and return it the following day. Waters knew a German student from his days at Auburn who had agreed to take the test for him. So after he got the test from his professor, he and Harry drove through the night to Auburn, Alabama. Harry slept while Waters and his friend worked on the test, then drove Waters back to Florida, arriving in Gainesville as the sun rose. "I had to do it," Harry remembered. "He was my friend, and he needed me, so I did it." Waters successfully passed German.

Harry took Sally's departure for Ohio as a pass to resume his premarried life. Waters saw the behavior as a sign of a side of Harry's personality that would become more prominent as he grew older: "He drank a lot. We drank a lot. And he had a lot of girlfriends. And I didn't realize it at the time, I've realized it since, but he may very well have an addictive temperament."

Meanwhile, Sally's pregnancy was moving along. The two made plans for Harry to come up to Dayton to meet the Ellis family and be present for the birth of the baby. He made the trip north on his motorcycle, and when he arrived in Oakwood, he began following the written directions Sally had recited to him over the phone. He found the upscale neighborhood where the Ellis family lived, arriving at their street and house number. There he sat, idling his motorcycle in front of a ten-foot gate that protected the largest mansion he'd ever seen. Since he was sure this couldn't possibly be the home of his wife, he drove on and found a pay phone to tell Sally about the mistake.

No, Sally told him, you've got the right place. Just ring the bell at the gate and we'll let you in. In Harry's mind, he was barely removed from the tenant farm, and now he was supposed to walk the steps up to the front door of the main house on the plantation. He didn't belong there, and he could feel it in his gut. It took all the coaxing Sally could muster to get him in to meet her family.

Harry soon conquered his anxiety, and the introductions went smoothly. Sally's parents and siblings were welcoming. They showed him around the home. Harry was astonished to see all the bedrooms, and that each bedroom had its own bathroom. The bedrooms had balconies as well. And downstairs, the enormous basement had been transformed into a shooting range where Roy Sr. could use a pellet gun to teach his children how to hit a target. Harry complimented his hosts, all the while counting the minutes until he could get out the door and back on his motorcycle.

Patrick Scott Crews was born on September 3, 1960, at Miami Valley Hospital in Dayton. Harry was in the waiting room and beamed as he held his son. Patrick was a healthy baby, and, as they had planned, Sally cared for him while Harry went back to Florida to resume his studies.

When Sally and Patrick rejoined Harry, however, Sally began to hear about Harry's women. It didn't take long for the truth to be exposed. Harry was clearly not ready to lead a life as the married father of a child. "I was obsessed to the point of desperation with becoming a writer, and, further, I lived with the conviction that I had gotten a late start toward that difficult goal," Harry wrote later. "Consequently, perhaps I was impatient, irritable, and inattentive toward Sally as a young woman and mother."

A rushed marriage based on an unplanned pregnancy was about to come to an abrupt conclusion. Sally wanted a divorce, and Harry was happy to oblige. He did not offer excuses for his behavior, nor had he made much of an effort to hide it. He accepted the blame for the failure of the marriage. Sally threw him out and told him it was time to make the divorce official.

Harry moved into Waters's tiny apartment above a garage, near campus. Waters remembered when Sally filed for divorce. "Harry asked me to do him a favor, and I said, 'What?' He said, 'I need you to go to the lawyer and say some bad things about me.' And I said that wasn't a problem. I could do that for him. I just asked him to tell me what bad things I need to say. So he did and I did." Waters made his statement under oath, and it was official. On December 16, 1961, less than four months after their first anniversary, Harry and Sally Crews were legally divorced.

The upheaval in Harry's personal life coincided with massive changes in the English Department. Mr. Lytle had announced that he was moving back to the land of his ancestry, for what would turn out to be the rest of his long life. His ongoing disputes within the English Department had reached a crescendo.[11] In late 1960, he had applied for a leave of absence from the University of Florida after negotiating a position as a lecturer at the University of the South in Sewanee, Tennessee, fifty miles from Nashville. Murfreesboro, the town founded by his ancestors, was only a few miles down the road from Sewanee. And more importantly, he would become the editor of the *Sewanee Review*, a position he had held for a short time in the 1940s. There, he planned to "change the course of American Literature."

Lytle would remain in contact with Harry and many of the advanced students in his writing program. But his authoritative presence was gone, and his disciples were now forced to move forward without his guiding hand. Lytle had run UF's creative writing program as a one-man show, and his departure created an immediate vacuum. Some within the English Department, most notably Dr. Aubrey Williams, a Shakespeare scholar with significant political power in the department, argued for the dissolution of the program.

Carrying the banner for the program, along with the students, was Smith Kirkpatrick, Lytle's much beloved assistant. Whereas Lytle was already anthologized in books about southern literature, Kirk, as his students called him, held little to no stature within the department. He did not hold a PhD, had only a master's in journalism, and had published just a few stories. He was, however, married to the daughter of J. Hooper Wise, the current chair of the Comprehensive English Department. The power struggle played out during the summer of 1961, and when classes began for the fall semester, the creative writing program was alive and Kirk was in charge.

Smith Kirkpatrick had grown up in Arkansas in the 1930s in a working-class family. During summers in his adolescence, he ferried travelers across the Arkansas River, charging a dime per ride. He came of age as World War II was at its peak and lied about his age to join the navy. He was trained as a fighter pilot and flew missions in the Pacific, including at the Battle of Midway. His aircraft carrier, *The Enterprise*, was nearly sunk at Guadalcanal.

He had come to the University of Florida after the war to study journalism and fallen into Lytle's circle, where he excelled and soon became Lytle's top assistant and disciple. He had a love of southern idiom, which united him with both Lytle and, later, Harry. *Moby-Dick* and *War and Peace* were "too much sugar for a dime"; too many writers were "all truck and no hogs."

In his mid-thirties, Kirk was much closer in age to his students than Lytle had been. Where Mr. Lytle was fatherly, almost grandfatherly, Kirk related often as a peer. His devotion to the craft, however, rivaled Lytle's. Students learned not to say they "wanted to become a writer"; that, in Kirk's view, was something far different than submitting to the lifelong, solitary struggle that would allow one to be a true student of the craft.

When classes resumed in the small room in Building D, the vibe had changed. The Master was no longer present. Discussions often became unruly. One night, Waters sensed another student wasn't paying attention to his story and lashed out, demanding he listen up or drop the course. Harry had regular conflicts with Hetrick. Hetrick gravitated toward poetry and often included a poetic element in his fiction. Harry hated it and said so. Hetrick, in turn, criticized the southern dialect in Harry's stories.

At another class meeting, tempers flared to a higher degree between Harry and a student named Tony Austin. The two moved past heated exchanges about writing and nearly came to an exchange of punches before they were pulled apart. The outbursts were infrequent, but the tenor had changed. For Harry, graduation was now on the horizon, and his apprenticeship was moving toward the solitary struggle that Kirk preached was essential to learning the craft.

Nothing can improve a relationship like not being married. Living apart eased the conflict between Harry and Sally, and pretty soon their contact was becoming more frequent. Harry missed Patrick more than he had imagined, with a deep longing he compared to the way he longed for his father. He called Sally in Dayton, using all of his powers of persuasion to convince her that their future was together, as a family. It worked. Shortly before Harry was to receive his degree, the young divorcees signed their names on the dotted line, and once again they were officially man and wife.

Harry achieved another Crews family first in the spring, earning his bachelor's degree from the University of Florida. Despite Lytle's departure, the graduate program in creative writing remained viable, and Harry wanted a spot for the fall of 1962, in order to pursue a graduate degree. The GI Bill wouldn't cover the cost. However, there was one fellowship available that would get him into the program and cover the costs. In the end, it came down to two applicants. For reasons Harry was never told, another student was given the fellowship. It was a slight that Harry never forgot. He would hold it against everyone associated with the University of Florida English Department and use it to motivate himself for years to come.

Without a fellowship, Harry was left to find an actual paying job. Yet again, he found himself following a family tradition and heading to Jacksonville in search of a paycheck. But there would be no cigar rolling, box catching, or paper stacking. For the first time, Harry would be doing the job that he would hold for the rest of his life: teaching English. He had secured a job at Lakeshore Junior High School in Duval County. He was to teach six classes of English, every day, to kids ages twelve through fourteen.

Harry had ditched the Triumph in favor of a more family-friendly Renault car. It had some miles on it and several quirks, one of which was that the driver had go around to the front of the vehicle and turn a crank to get it started. He and Sally packed up the Renault and drove to Jacksonville.

At first, they lived with Hoyett, who was working in a Jacksonville paper mill at the time. Harry and Hoyett still fought whenever they were together, and living under the same roof only exacerbated the situation. It quickly became untenable, so Harry and Sally found a little trailer in a remote area of Jacksonville. There wasn't much room to move in their new home, but it had a nice porch where Sally could sit and rock Patrick, and a small shed out back that Harry converted into a study. It had no electricity, so he would run an extension cord from the trailer to the shed to work. He also put a small stove in the shed, and each night, after junior high let out and he had eaten dinner with Sally and Patrick, Harry would go out to the shed and write. During the school year, he completed his first novel, *This World Uncommitted*, based on his experiences in the Marine Corps.

Junior high school teaching did not agree with Harry. He was in charge of thirty adolescents at a time, six hours a day, in six different classrooms. Discipline became his number-one problem. He found himself to be, at least with young kids, no Marine drill sergeant. Lakeshore Junior High had a dean known as "The Professor," whom everybody called "Fess." Fess was in charge of discipline, and Harry sent his biggest problems to Fess, who would beat them with a board and send them back to Harry's classroom. A short time into the school year, Fess called Harry down to his office.

"Crews," Fess said. "You can beat them just as easily as I can. Don't send them up to me anymore."

"Fess, I can't beat these children," Harry complained.

"The hell you can't."

"I'd really rather not," Harry replied. "Besides, it doesn't seem to help."

"It don't hurt," Fess said, showing Harry to the door.

Harry himself was looking for the door very early into his stint at Lakeshore Junior High. He knew early on he could only last a year, if that. During the fall semester, he applied to the master's program in English at Florida, the same program he'd wanted to attend on fellowship the year before. In the spring, he received word that his application had been rejected. It was another slight that would be added to the list.

Staying in Jacksonville and in junior high was not an option, however, and Harry found another way to get back to Gainesville. He applied to the graduate program in education and was admitted. He finished out the year at Lakeshore Junior High, and then he and Sally packed up their few belongings from the trailer and prepared for another move.

The trip to Gainesville did not go smoothly. They were still driving the Renault. Harry stuffed the car with their luggage and strapped the baby's crib and the remaining bags to the roof. Then they piled in, cranked it up, and left Jacksonville behind. Halfway to Gainesville, the skies opened up and unleashed the type of downpour that Floridians grow accustomed to in the summer. Bucket upon bucket of water lashed the car, soaking everything. In the midst of the storm, both windshield wipers flew off the car. Harry pulled the car over to the side of the highway, and they waited out the rain.

They finally arrived at the university late at night and made their way to the small upstairs apartment they were to live in, at the Flavet Student Living Quarters for veterans. Sally took one look around and decided it needed work. "I cleaned all night long, because the apartment was kind of dirty and I just cleaned and cleaned and cleaned," she said. In the morning, Harry met the building manager in the office. Soon, Sally heard him yelling, "Stop!" He appeared at the window and told her that they had moved into the wrong apartment.

All was corrected and the family began acclimating to their new surroundings. Harry resumed the writing schedule he had followed in Jacksonville. A room in the apartment became his writing studio, and when he was not studying or working (he took a job as a bartender to cover expenses), he was in the studio, writing.

The master's in education was an afterthought. He placed far more importance on his own writing than his studies in the College of Education. He did not buy any of the assigned books. He did little research and made up sources for the research papers he was assigned to write. The program was far less rigorous than the English Department—there was no thesis requirement and no language requirement. Harry was still acquainted with some of the students pursuing master's degrees in the creative writing track, and Kirk remained at the helm. Harry consulted with Kirk and stayed in touch with the students, but he felt a sharp sense of inferiority. He was again the outsider, stuck in the loser's den, and, in his eyes, looked down upon by his peers.

There was little satisfaction when he received his degree in the spring.

Harry did not want to don the robes and walk in the ceremony, but, on Sally's urging, he agreed to participate. On Saturday morning, June 9, 1962, he climbed onto the stage and accepted his graduate degree in education.

The degree paid immediate dividends. Late in the spring semester, he had interviewed with the dean of instruction at Broward Junior College in Fort Lauderdale. As luck would have it, the dean was from Georgia. Harry and he became fast friends, and a job offer quickly followed. Instead of junior high, Harry would now teach at the college level, as a lecturer in English. Harry and Sally began making plans for yet another move to yet another coastal Florida city.

CHAPTER EIGHT **A SELF-EDUCATION**

Artists are doomed to live in an atmosphere of perpetual failure.
—Graham Greene

W hen Harry arrived in South Florida to join the faculty of the Junior College of Broward County (JCBC), the college was in its infancy. In 1957 the State of Florida had undertaken a massive expansion of its junior college system. The state's high school graduates, it was decreed, needed more postsecondary options—schools that could serve both as a bridge to the state's four-year institutions and as training facilities for technical trades. At the time, there were five junior college institutions in the state; five years later, there were twenty-nine.

Broward County was one of the beneficiaries of the state plan. The first day of class at the brand-new school was September 6, 1960. Classes were taught in the former Naval Station Junior High School, a few miles south of the city of Fort Lauderdale. A faculty of 28 and a staff of 9 welcomed 701 students that year, while construction was being planned for a new campus in the nearby town of Davie. By the fall of 1962, when Harry arrived to unpack his boxes into his new office and get ready to teach his first college students, the school's enrollment was already growing at an extremely rapid pace and would reach 2,500 within a year.

The faculty, which had grown to sixty by the year of Harry's arrival, consisted mostly of highly credentialed professors from prestigious institutions. The administration was aiming high. Despite the stated goal of providing technical training for trades, Broward Junior College had begun with only liberal arts courses, and the makeup of the faculty reflected that fact. The dichotomy between the nature of the faculty and the objectives being communicated from Tallahassee was to lead to a war of wills in the very near future.

To Harry, however, Broward Junior College was an oasis. "The money was better, the hours were better, everything was better," Harry remembered. Instead of six classes of thirty students every day, he now carried a four-class load, large for a college professor, but next to nothing when compared to junior high school. He was to teach composition a few hours a day and grade student assignments, which left plenty of time to devote to his own writing. At first he and Sally rented a small house until they could afford to buy. Within a few years, they had purchased their first home, a three-bedroom ranch house right near the college. Patrick had his own room, and the remaining bedroom was converted into an office for Harry.

Grady Drake was both a neighbor of the Crews family and a coworker of Harry's at Broward Junior College. Drake was the fourth member of the administration hired in 1959, behind the president, the dean of students, and the director of counseling. He joined the group to run a library that at the time did not contain a single book. Drake had served in the military during World War II and had used his GI Bill money to earn a degree in library science. Degree in hand, he had worked at several institutions, in the U.S. and overseas. He was working in the library at the University of Florida when he heard the state was opening a new school in Fort Lauderdale. He would spend the next twenty-eight years overseeing the growth of the school and the library.

Drake tried to keep abreast of the new faculty members, and when he heard an English instructor was coming aboard from the University of Florida, he asked around. Drake remembered: "A friend of mine who taught at the university in Gainesville knew Harry and told me, 'You may want to look out for him. He might need some help.' I gathered that my friend thought that Harry might have a degree of, I won't say shyness, but possibly an inability to immediately mesh with the existing faculty."

Where Harry had wanted to run screaming from the junior high classroom, the junior college student body was much more to his liking. He had a natural ability to hold the attention of an audience. He began to incorporate the teachings of Mr. Lytle, as well as some of Lytle's style, into his own presentation. His reputation as raconteur extraordinaire grew across the fledgling campus. As would be the case throughout his teaching career, most who attended his lectures flocked back for more, while a few detested the performance and flocked in the other direction. One member of the second group came to complain to Drake during Harry's first year at the school. "He told me, 'I came to learn English, not to sit in the class and be an audience to a drama,'" Drake said. "It wasn't a surprise to me, because I'm sure Harry did sort of perform in the classroom. Harry did like to be noticed."

He integrated the Lytle message into his class, but some of the messages delivered were strictly his own. One of his classes operated similarly to the fiction workshops in Gainesville, with students turning in stories for critique. During one class, Harry read aloud a story submitted by a female student, who had included a scene with oral sex.

Harry stopped reading, paused, and looked at the student.

"Have you ever given a blow job?" he asked.

The student reddened and then answered, "No, sir."

Harry waited a second, then hammered home his point to his new disciples: "Never, NEVER, write about something you've never witnessed or done."

Still, writing remained the focus of Harry's life. He spent most of his time away from the classroom locked in the converted office in his home. For fifty dollars, he had purchased a typewriter from Sally's grandmother, who lived in Vero Beach. Patrick was three years old by this time and looking for attention from his father. Sally usually entertained Patrick while Harry was writing, but occasionally the toddler would wander over to the study, turn the knob, and interrupt his father. It was an old door, and after a while the screws loosened, and eventually the doorknob came off the door. Harry was in no hurry to fix it. "I didn't put it back on because I didn't want everybody opening the goddamned thing when I was working," he said. Patrick was deterred, but only for a while. "Pretty soon, I started hearing things," Harry said. "I'd turn and look over at the hole in the door every once in a while, and I'd hear some breathing, and I'd see this little blue eye, just staring at me."

Harry, through his own reading and via the recommendations of Lytle and Kirkpatrick, was now extremely well versed in literature. In his own teaching, he had a command of the recognized masters and regularly used the classics as teaching instruments. But his own most important literary influence did not emerge from the usual suspects of American literature—

Faulkner, Hemingway, Fitzgerald. Instead, he chose a writer from across the Atlantic, Graham Greene, and undertook an exhaustive examination of Greene's work that would last a full year.

In the early 1960s, Graham Greene was both a writer and a celebrity, in England and in the United States. He was born in Hertfordshire, England, a well-off county north of London, and educated at Berkhamsted School (where his father was the headmaster) and Oxford. He spent some time as a reporter for *The Times* of London before embarking on a prolific fiction career that would span half a century. Greene was the rare writer whose books were both best-sellers and "serious fiction." His genre was the thriller; his novels usually took place in a political hot spot somewhere on the international stage and involved espionage with a generous helping of melodrama. The books were elevated to the level of literature, however, by a religious subtext that was almost always present and in which he, and his characters, dealt with the distinction between faith and belief, and the related themes of guilt, treachery, and failure. Greene was prolific; he pumped out books at the pace of a romance novelist, along with screenplays, criticism, and even letters to the editor. His work usually had a cinematic feel to it, and nearly everything he wrote ended up on-screen. At the very core of his success, however, were his clarity and his mastery of the art of storytelling. And it was this element of his writing that drew Harry to his work.

In his ongoing self-education, Harry decided to completely deconstruct Greene's 1951 novel, *The End of the Affair*. Harry had long ago digested Lytle's characterization of writing as a technical craft. Now he created a project for himself in which he would take apart a novel as one would a car, then put it together again in order to discover, with his own senses, how it worked. Other apprentice writers tried various methods to get inside the work of their heroes—around the same time, Hunter Thompson was retyping, page by page, Hemingway's *A Farewell to Arms* and Fitzgerald's *The Great Gatsby*, just to get a feel for the rhythm and cadence of the words and sentences of the masters. But Harry, as was usually the case, took an exercise to its limit and beyond.

The End of the Affair takes place in London during and immediately after World War II. It is a story that encompasses all of Greene's trademark themes. It begins as a story of deceit and betrayal surrounding the affair between a nonbelieving novelist and a married woman. But in the second half of the book it evolves into an examination of faith and religious mystery, as Greene slowly reveals that the novelist is in a struggle for the woman's heart, not against her husband, but against God.

It wasn't the themes and the plot of the novel that were important to Harry's exercise so much as the nuts and bolts of it: sentences, word count, paragraph size, punctuation. In his home office, he began his deconstruction. He reduced the book to a series of numbers: How many characters were there? How many days, weeks, years did the action take? How many cities? How many children, adults, women, men? On what page were the climaxes, the twists in the story? He worked for weeks, then months, cataloging the answers to all the questions he could think of. He read and reread the book, forward and backward, until it was dog-eared and ready to fall apart. Then, building piece by piece on top of what he saw as the skeleton of the book, he began to construct his own novel, adhering exactly to Greene's specifications. He was under no illusion, he said later, that the exercise would produce a publishable book. It was "a desperate ploy by the rankest kind of amateur who could find no help, no reader, and was just thrashing about trying to learn something."

The months added up, and after a year the project was finally complete. It was, not surprisingly, terrible. "It was the bad novel I knew it would be . . . a mechanical, unreadable book," he said. "But by doing it I learned more about writing fiction and writing a novel and about the importance of time and place—Greene is a freak about time and place—than I had from any class or anything I'd done before." The strength of Greene's work, his constantly flowing narrative and a continually unspooling story, would eventually become signatures of Harry's writing as well. For a long time, however, he would not show his paint-by-numbers creation to anybody. Finally, he relented and sent it to Mr. Lytle. His mentor confirmed, without hesitation, what Harry already knew, and not long after receiving Lytle's response, the pages of Harry's Graham Greene simulation were quickly reduced to ash by the flames of the master's "great refiner."

The adjustment to teaching college students had gone smoothly, and Harry seemed to be taking to married life as well. With a little more money coming in, the creaky Renault was traded for a brand-new Volkswagen bug. And Sally was now pregnant again, with the baby expected in the summer of 1963. But the piles of failed efforts were piling up in Harry's study, and it was getting to him. Failure, and lust for success, began to creep into his dreams. "I used to dream that one of my novels had been published; and dream while I was asleep this tremendous joy and celebration and the rest of it and then wake up literally humiliated, crushed, depressed, stricken that I was still where I was."

Once he was established as a writer, Harry's regular refrain when discussing this period in his writing life was that he faced a wall of rejection without any support whatsoever. In reality, before he even left Gainesville, he had already written what would, after many, many rounds of revision, become his first published work of fiction. "The Shape of Terror" was conceived while Harry was still in graduate school. It tells the story of a Navy seaman who goes cruising for women with a shipmate in the dingy bars of Puerto Rico. The unnamed protagonist of the story reveals an incestuous relationship with his older sister from the recent past. He is consumed with guilt and finds himself on an unending quest to bed older, experienced whores, searching for the "unattached smile" that was burned into his mind during his forbidden trysts.

Harry first showed a draft of the story to Lytle and Kirkpatrick while he was still an undergraduate. Lytle's initial reaction was that it lacked meaning, but he offered a number of ideas and strongly encouraged Harry to revise. Harry worked on the story, off and on, for the next year and a half. Kirkpatrick saw many versions of the story, spending hours dissecting it for his student. Harry incorporated suggestions liberally. With Kirkpatrick's blessing, he sent a version to Lytle in Tennessee in June 1962, expecting another of the gentle rebukes to which he had become accustomed. Instead, he received from his mentor the most positive response yet to anything he had written and, more significantly, the promise of publication in *The Sewanee Review*.

It was the validation Harry had been seeking for as long as he could remember. Several of his contemporaries from the UF creative writing program had published in literary journals; now Harry would join the exclusive club of "real writers." Lytle's letter suggested another series of changes—removing the name of the narrator, a change to the title—but indicated that the story was very close to "done," Lytle's term from the classroom, which meant that it had reached an acceptable level of technical craftsmanship and was now of high enough quality that it could be taken off the table and allowed out of the workshop.

In his response to Lytle the following week, Harry still fully inhabited the role of the grateful novice:

I never want to say or do anything that would give the impression that I think I am anything but what I am—an apprentice. Particularly this is true where you are concerned. I feel very humble at the prospect of publishing in *The Sewanee Review*. At the same time, you have already given me more than publishing *anywhere* could ever give me. I have written a story about which you have said "I think it is pretty good." I have always told myself that someday I would write something that you could read and say "It isn't badly done." I never thought it would come this soon. I can't expect you to understand how I feel about this. I don't want to sound sophomoric or maudlin, and if I have conducted myself badly in saying what I've said, I apologize.

With a single exception, he agreed to incorporate all of Lytle's final suggestions. Lytle's title, "The Unattached Smile," would adorn the story when it was set to type. Lytle had suggested significant changes to the final paragraph, and here, Harry demurred. In an extended explanation in his letter, he made an argument to keep one particular phrase in that last paragraph. And, again, he added an apology: "God knows that I am not trying to sound like I know what I'm talking about."

Two weeks later, Harry received another letter from Lytle. The story had been accepted and was scheduled for publication in the winter issue of *The Sewanee Review*. "The Unattached Smile" contained vivid writing and some of the themes that Harry would revisit for the rest of his life—sexual deviance and obsession, compulsion to confront psychological demons. It lacked the dark humor that would become the Crews style. The central point, the act of incest, occurs off the page, as does all the sex in the story. The narrator's relationship with his sister is barely explained, and much is left to the reader to discern. But it has the polished feel of a realistic story told with a sure hand and containing insight into the human condition that is the signature of literature.

Even before "The Unattached Smile" appeared, however, Harry began to believe that he had lost ownership of the story. Though he saw how his apprenticeship had transported him miles down the road, he did not like the feel of outside influence on his writing. It was a conviction that would grow stronger over time. Kirk, who was dedicated to the workshop system, tried to assuage Harry's fears about the story: he wrote to Harry and said he had "a nagging feeling that perhaps I helped you too much on the incest story. Which was not so, the words were yours, I only helped get them more closely joined around your action." Harry was not convinced. He spoke little about it after it was in print, and later, once he had a few novels under his belt, he would say of his first publishing experience, "I didn't write that story. Mr. Lytle wrote that story."

"The Unattached Smile" was the only story of Harry's that Lytle would publish, despite that fact that he would remain the editor of *The Sewanee Review* for another eleven years. But Harry was now to be a published author, and, flush with success, he began submitting to literary journals more frequently. Before the first story was printed, he sent a story titled "You'll Like My Mother's Grave" to *The Georgia Review* and several other publications. The story was similar in tone to "The Unattached Smile" but took place on more familiar territory for Harry. An old farmer, dying of cancer and already grotesquely misshapen from treatment, must decide whether to have his tongue amputated to stem the tide of the disease. His daughter and a farmhand discuss, in veiled terms, the farmer's decision to end his life. The characters are drawn straight out of Bacon County and Harry's childhood, and the story exudes the despair of those who are used to being dealt a bad hand and don't have the means to fight it. The story gets closer to depicting the farm life of his youth than any of his subsequent fiction:

> The old man looked past Gaff to the door, and his vision was distant, stretching past the porch, past the field and even the night, down to the forest pines. "Since the first frost of November in this country, living on the land I growed out of as a boy, I been a stranger. Not eating with anybody, not talking with anybody, and follered by a scent that'ed sicken a hog." His eyes suddenly snapped back, and Gaff met them steadily, sucking at a front tooth, and wiping his mouth with the back of his hand. "Now I'm supposed to fix it so I cain't even holler when I hurt."

After the acceptance of "The Unattached Smile," Harry told Lytle of his plans to move forward with "You'll Like My Mother's Grave." Lytle had seen several previous versions of the story, initially titled "A Fool About Clabber," but before he reviewed the latest incarnation, he chastised Harry for what he saw as an unhealthy desire for recognition. "Naturally, you want to publish, and I'm sure you would not release anything you did not think was done," he wrote to Harry. "A young author is not always clear what is done, however. Don't send away everything you write. . . . It is very easy to feel a thing is done, simply because you want to publish it."

Once Lytle saw the version that had been submitted to *The Georgia Review*, he felt even more strongly that it was not ready for publication. It had many flaws, he felt, not the least of which was the title. "Don't you see you can't use this kind of a title unless in all its force it delivers an overwhelming irony? It is vaguely frivolous. This is so, because you don't know what makes any of your people move or act." On Lytle's advice, Harry changed the title to "A Long Wail," which, as in the title of his previous story, referred to a chilling detail in the story's last paragraph. The new title was not enough, however, to change Lytle's negative opinion of the piece.

The editors at *The Georgia Review* felt differently. The story was accepted for publication and would come out within a few months of "The Unattached Smile." Though Lytle saw *The Georgia Review* as a second-rate publication and let Harry know it, Harry could not help but be encouraged. In his mind, he had discounted the meaning of the publication of "The Unattached Smile"—it had been accepted by Lytle, his own teacher and the same person who had guided him in the writing of the story. But now Harry had outside confirmation of his talent. It was a different kind of endorsement, another step toward independence. Lytle had vociferously objected to elements in the latest story, but Harry had pushed on anyway, and now the story would be published.

Circumstances appeared to be improving. All the time alone in his office with his typewriter might actually pay off. Sally had given birth to the couple's second child, Byron Jason, on August 24, 1963. He was another healthy boy and quickly absorbed into the household operation. Another novel, which Harry had titled *A Delicate Wound* and had written concurrently with his short-story work, was now complete. His successes with his stories gave him the confidence to begin submitting his novel. The appearance of "The Unattached Smile" resulted in recognition, both from his friends from Florida and from the world of publishing.

Shortly after publication, he received a letter from an editor at Atheneum Publishers in New York: "I read your story, THE UNATTACHED SMILE, in the Spring Issue of *The Sewanee Review* and found it most interesting. Are you presently working on a novel? If so and if it is not yet committed, may I have a look?" A similar inquiry came from McGraw-Hill, another prominent publisher. The thrill of his name being discussed in New York, the publishing capital of America, motivated him to devote himself even more completely to his goal. Harry sent *A Delicate Wound* to both interested parties and to several others, then monitored the mailbox daily, hopeful for more good news.

The early seeds of success would take a much longer time to grow than Harry imagined at the time. He would not see another acceptance letter of any kind for four long years. And the rejections would begin to pile up in his study. He would shortly lose sight of the light that had flickered for a moment. To Lytle, however, Harry's reaction to his early success was a sign of a deficiency in Harry's character. Harry, Lytle felt, had not yet committed to his writing or developed the endurance to sweat over his work until it was truly done. "Your stories seem to me not quite finished, perhaps, not quite ready for sending around," Lytle wrote. "I wish I could see you; then I could tell you more explicitly my critical sense of these two stories. . . . The things that you burn will not be wasted. Anything that you have to say will come out sooner or later in a more refined form."

CHAPTER NINE **HOPE FADES**

A man does not expect to be the orphan of his son.
—Harry Crews

Tragic events often require a series of coincidences to occur. There was only one house in the 800 block of Southwest 17th Street in Fort Lauderdale that had a swimming pool. The home was two doors down from the Crews residence. The family that lived in the home with the pool, the Lees, was vigilant about closing the gate to the six-foot, basket-weave-type fence that surrounded the pool. The Lees had invited the Crews family to use the pool several times in the past. Harry and Sally had never known the gate to the Lees' pool to be open, and one of the Lees, usually the wife, was almost always home.

The Crews backyard was also fenced and gated. Patrick liked to play outside in the grass and would often do so while Sally worked inside in the kitchen. Sally always made sure to keep the gate closed. Patrick was only three years old and had never gotten out of the yard before. Harry and Sally were quite certain that, even if for some reason he became determined to leave the yard, he would not be able to climb the chain-link fence that surrounded their property.

On a Thursday morning in late July 1964, Harry, uncharacteristically, was sleeping late. The Lee house was vacant that morning; Frank Lee was at work, and Mrs. Lee had gone to visit a friend. And Sally was in the kitchen, confident that Patrick was playing by himself in the backyard.

A group of neighborhood kids, only a few years older than Patrick, were loose in the neighborhood, unsupervised, and noticed Patrick playing in his yard. A few of them came over and helped Patrick scale the fence, and, eventually, the group found their way down to the Lees' backyard. The gate was closed, but Patrick unlatched it and, alone at first, went inside. He did not know how to swim, but his parents had taken him wading many times before. He took off his shoes and socks, placed them neatly by the edge of the pool, and dipped his foot into the pool. As his playmate watched, he slipped and immediately fell below the surface of the water.

Harry was awoken by Sally's screaming. He jumped out of bed and found her at the front door, surrounded by little kids. Once he was able to determine what had happened, he sprinted out the front door, still in his underwear, leaped over the hedge leading to the yard with the pool, and entered the open gate. The moment he entered the pool area, he could see Patrick's blond hair waving in the water as the child lay face down in the deep end, beneath the diving board.

He dove in and retrieved Patrick and began the mouth-to-mouth re-suscitation techniques he had learned in the Marines. Sally had called an ambulance and then followed Harry down the block, still screaming. The two of them were hunched over their little boy, Harry pinching his nose and desperately blowing air into his lifeless body, when the rescue workers arrived. In the ambulance on the way to the hospital, Harry felt Patrick's carotid artery with his fingers and knew he had lost his son.

Outside the hospital, Harry and Sally desperately waited for word on Patrick's condition. A photographer named Minerva Wagner, of the *Miami Herald*, who had heard of the incident on her police scanner, pulled up to the hospital and snapped off a few frames. In one, Sally stares straight ahead, a look of blank despair on her face. Harry, his arm around his wife's shoulder, holds a cigarette and stares into the ground. It is a searing portrait of parents in the midst of their worst possible nightmare.

The photograph ran the next morning in the *Herald* under the headline "Hope Fades." The caption reads: "Grief-stricken parents of 3-year-old Patrick Scott Crews wait for word at Broward General Hospital, and it came too soon. Patrick was dead, the county's 21st drowning victim this year and the second in two days."

Harry's friends Larry Hetrick and John Morefield were living in South Florida at the time. Separately, they opened the paper on the morning of July 31 and were stunned by the image. "The photo was absolutely devastating," Hetrick said. "The look of absolute grief made you turn away." Morefield also was moved by the photo. "They had been caught in a terribly private moment," he remembered. Fifty years later, the image was still burned into both of their minds.

Patrick was pronounced dead later that morning. The doctors determined that in the struggle to breathe in the water, the boy had thrown up the cereal Sally had given him less than an hour before and had sucked it back into his throat, blocking his air passage. He was a little over a month shy of his fourth birthday.

Fort Lauderdale police were in the neighborhood later that day investigating Patrick's death. They found one of the neighborhood children, Brian Held, who gave them a version of the story similar to the one the children had told Sally and Harry. The boy told the officers that the gate indeed had been closed. Police worked the neighborhood further, spoke to neighbors, and determined that the Lees' pool gate was always closed. Police could find no fault in the matter of the death of Patrick Crews.

Grady Drake heard about what happened a day later from another employee of Broward Junior College who lived on the same street as Harry and Sally. The coworker told Drake that Harry "had gone berserk" and was moaning audibly. The sound could be heard through the neighborhood. In the first hours after Patrick's death, Harry was inconsolable, wracked with guilt, outwardly wishing for his own death. "In those nightmare days following Patrick's death, I inevitably thought long and hard, usually against my will, about the circumstances of his brief life and his death," Harry wrote later. "Much of it came as incriminations against myself."

An image now began to appear to Harry at night, one of "a monstrously high black wall of glass." He felt compelled to climb the wall, but to accomplish such a feat was impossible; there was no way to grasp onto the structure. Patrick, he knew in the dream, had passed over the wall. Harry was left to stare at it, with no explanation, no hope that he could follow his son.

The funeral for Patrick would be held the very next day, with a service at Fairchild Broward Funeral Home, followed by a gravesite ceremony. On August 1, 1964, Patrick Scott Crews was buried at Fort Lauderdale Memorial Park Cemetery. Family from both sides came to South Florida to help the family grieve. Hoyett, who was working in the paper mill in Jacksonville, was one of the pallbearers, along with Drake and several other colleagues of Harry's from Broward Junior College. Sally was numb with grief and mostly unable to speak with anybody, so friends and relatives brought food, organized the service, and handled all of the arrangements associated with the gathering and the funeral.

Sally called some of Harry's relatives in Bacon County and told them the news. Eva Haselden, Harry's aunt, received the call and informed her husband, Alton, of the tragedy. Alton, who was in the middle of harvesting that year's tobacco crop, dropped his tools and came out of the field. Within a few hours, Alton and Eva were on the highway to Fort Lauderdale.

Now Alton assumed the role of father to Harry once more. He, above all others, was able to provide comfort and soften Harry's grief. Harry later recalled confiding in Alton as he had been unable to confide in anyone else. Relatives, neighbors, and friends had gathered at the Crews home after the service. Harry pulled Alton aside and the two went out into the backyard, where Patrick had climbed the fence just a few days before. Alton had always been extremely reticent; what he had to say was always reduced to the smallest number of syllables possible. While Harry talked, Alton, as was his habit, picked up a stick and began drawing lines in the dirt.

"It feels like I'm going crazy," Harry said.

"You ain't gone crazy, son," Alton replied. He produced a long kitchen match and examined it for a while, then fired it up on the tree beside them and lit up.

"That's what it feels like," said Harry.

Alton dismissed the idea. "What you gone do is the next thing," he told his nephew.

Harry told him that he felt as if going crazy was the next thing.

"I reckon it might," Alton said. "But it's some of us that cain't afford to go crazy. The next thing is yonder in a crib." He waved in the direction of the house and Byron. "You ain't gone give up on blood, are you, boy?"

"No, sir," Harry replied. "I'm not."

Harry and Sally both would say that Byron was the reason they were eventually able to pull themselves out of deep depression and remain a family. "He was just a blessing," Sally remembered. "You know, he just sort of carried us through, and he was just the sweetest little baby. I mean, here's the mother talking, but he too had a great personality, and he helped us see our way back." Harry concurred. A few days after the funeral, he was still mourning, looking through Patrick's toys, when he heard Byron gurgling in his crib in the next room. He walked into the next room and examined his son for several moments. Harry had undergone a vasectomy after Byron's birth, so he ruminated on the fact that he was looking at the only remaining child he would bring into the world. He picked up his son and looked into the child's eyes. "It's you and I now, buckshot," he said, "just the two of us."

Alton's advice became Harry's mantra—do the next thing. He was back at the college in less than a week, interacting with his colleagues. He soon resumed his writing. Grief, he decided, must be faced immediately and then put away. Speaking about the subject many years later, he dispensed the wisdom he took from the loss of his son: "I think it's terribly important to really grieve. Really get down and gnash your teeth, pull your hair, beat your breast, claw your eyes, and get it all out. And then, straighten up, stand up, clean up, put that behind you, and go on with your life instead of dragging it out every Sunday." He resolved not to look back. After the funeral, he never again visited his son's grave.

Friends detected a change in Harry's character, however. His dark view of the world managed to get even darker. Kirkpatrick came for the funeral and saw in his protégé a transformation, both then and later. After the drowning, Kirk, said, Harry was never the same person. He held the guilt deep inside and was unable to rid himself of it. "That's the secret to Harry," Kirk would tell a friend years later. "That's why Harry never, ever really was able to believe in anything."

CHAPTER TEN BROWARD BLUES

> In Raiford, there was this old guy, an old newspaperman, an
> obvious drunk. And he said, "You'll write a million words before
> you publish your first thousand." That always stuck in my head.
> —Donn Pearce, "This Was a Man"

Following the publication of "A Long Wail" in the summer 1964 edition of *The Georgia Review*, Harry entered the bleakest period of his apprenticeship, a three-year stretch in which he toiled in utter anonymity and fought against the slow creep of doubt that can bring down even the most confident of writers. He was most definitely not that. He harbored, due to his upbringing, a well of insecurity that he had to battle against daily. He had begun regularly having painful migraine headaches, which could debilitate him for hours at a time. But his output did not slow; he continued to finish a novel every year, and short stories in between. Another novel, *Don't Sing My Name*, was finished in 1964. He began to submit it, along with *This World Uncommitted* and *A Delicate Wound*, to publishing houses and literary agencies.

Over and over, Sally sacrificed in order to allow Harry to throw himself into his work. Harry understood his own compulsion, but writing was the focus of his life nonetheless, and everything else remained secondary. Understandably, it was a strain on their marriage. In the summers, he would devote even more time to his writing. Sally took Byron to Ohio for most of July and August, allowing Harry even more freedom to concentrate on his novels.

It also opened doors to Harry's continued infidelity. And when Sally was in town, Harry looked for other locations in which to entertain women. He came to visit his friend John Morefield at Morefield's bayside cottage in South Grove. He looked around, nodded approvingly, and asked Morefield if he could use the cottage to entertain women. Morefield demurred, telling Harry he didn't feel he could allow it because he knew and liked Sally.

Grady Drake had become his closest friend at Broward Junior College; the two families spent time together socially whenever possible. Drake kept his eye on Harry when Sally and Byron were up north; he and his wife would regularly invite Harry to their home, invitations that were only occasionally accepted. "He didn't like to waste any time," Drake said. "He was very much interested in whatever particular novel he was writing at the time, and that was where his mind was."

His friends from the University of Florida worried about his isolation. Lytle wrote to Kirkpatrick to say he was concerned about Harry's mental state. Working in seclusion was unhealthy, Lytle believed, and he told Kirk that Harry needed to be closer to his peer group in order to continue to advance his writing. The back-and-forth of the workshops in Mr. Lytle and Kirk's classrooms was now reduced to a few letters from select friends whom Harry trusted enough to show his new writing: Waters, Lytle, Kirkpatrick, and a handful of others.

And the reactions he was receiving from Lytle were moving in the wrong direction. Lytle's feeling that Harry's pace was much too fast had now been cemented. He thought Harry's work was regressing, and told him so. After the acceptance of "The Long Wail," Harry sent three more stories to Lytle for comment; all three were judged harshly by his mentor. "You're too far away from the action in these stories. I suspect you've done them too fast," Lytle wrote. "I cannot understand, after that fine story I published, how you can back off this way and only half work at what you have to do. These stories give the sense of being worked off the top part of your head. You have one of the real gifts. I've been wondering what you are doing with it."

Against Lytle's wishes, Harry submitted the stories to multiple journals. Unlike the reaction to "A Long Wail," this time around editors agreed with Lytle's assessment. *Virginia Quarterly* rejected the stories without comment, followed by *The Literary Review* at Fairleigh Dickinson University. Several other publications followed suit; some offered encouragement and asked to see more of Harry's work; most did not. Undaunted, Harry continued to submit his work. *The Colorado Quarterly, The Kenyon Review, Prairie Schooner, The Texas Quarterly, The Partisan Review*, and many others sent form rejections, some with a few scribbled notes of negative reaction. He tried general-interest magazines as well—*Esquire, Playboy*, the *New Yorker*, others—but all had the same reaction. Harry dropped the notes in a folder filled with similar correspondence and moved on.

The glimmers of hope that had emerged following the publication of "The Unattached Smile" in *The Sewanee Review* soon vanished as well. The editors at McGraw-Hill who had asked for Harry's novel *A Delicate Wound* now delivered their verdict. The unrelenting doom that had worked in the short story was judged to be unsustainable over the course of an entire novel:

> Three of us have now read your novel, and while we were all impressed by your ability, we all feel that the novel is not successful. The primary reason, I think, is you have centered it so thoroughly on the neurotic symptoms of the protagonist that the book becomes much more of a case history than a novel and what is lost is any kind of sympathetic relationship between the reader and [the protagonist]. We don't see him doing anything else but agonizing, and this partial view is not enough. Also, the very good satirical elements are lost in the tone, which is heavy throughout.

The McGraw-Hill editor, again acknowledging Harry's talent, recommended a few agents, whom Harry dutifully presented with the novel. That glimmer was short-lived as well. None found *A Delicate Wound* worthy of representation. The editor from Harold Ober Associates made little attempt to cushion the blow when he delivered the news, which was mirrored by the others who read the novel: "I think the trouble is that the characters are insufficiently vivid to carry a story which is basically on the drab and unattractive side." It was a discouraging time, but Harry had developed a very high tolerance for discouragement. As his early success faded into the past, he tried his best to ignore the criticism, tamp down his uncontrollable desire to publish, and force himself back into his chair in the study, so he could roll yet another blank page into the typewriter.

While his writing success was far below his expectations, on campus he was proving to be an important part of the faculty. He had arrived fresh out of graduate school with only a year of junior high school teaching on his resume. But Broward Junior College was a small pond, and Harry took little time becoming a big fish. He was both respected and liked by most of his colleagues. Students who were exposed to him in the classroom more often than not signed up to have the experience again. He took on the role of adviser to *P'an Ku*, the student literary/arts magazine, as well as the college yearbook.[11] And since the college was growing at an astounding rate and hiring more faculty members each year, it didn't take long for Harry to acquire a level of seniority over his peers. The campus newspaper, the *Venetian Crier*, profiled him in his second year at the school, applauding the publication of "The Unattached Smile." The life of a professor, he told the student reporter, fit him nicely: "I really enjoy teaching. The wonderful freedom of mind a teacher has is priceless to me."

The dichotomy at the heart of the college remained, however, and it hung like a cloud over everything that took place on campus. Was Junior College of Broward County to be a liberal arts gateway to the university system, or was it to be a trade school? The faculty leaned to the former, while the administration, influenced by the politicians in Tallahassee, leaned toward the latter.

Harry wrestled with the question in his own teaching experience. The students he saw in his courses were usually from a different social class than those at the University of Florida, with working-class backgrounds and limited skills. Many were unprepared to learn on the college level—some shockingly so, barely able to read or write. Harry would work individually with these students, schooling them on the most rudimentary of tasks. More common than unprepared students, however, were students who Harry felt were enrolled at college not to learn but because some outside influence—parents, high school teachers, society—had convinced them that if they didn't go to college, they were somehow inadequate. The disinterested students angered him the most. Because he had spent the majority of his life striving with the very core of his being to educate himself, he could not abide students who looked on education as an unnecessary chore.

The coalescence of these feelings soon led to Harry's first paid writing job. He took a break from fiction and penned an editorial that espoused his views on the character of the junior college student and the state of junior college education. The increased availability of higher education, due to the growth of institutions such as JCBC, was cheapening education across the United States. "The very accessibility of college and America's laudable goal of universal education have collaborated to bring into the classroom students who have no interest in expression, debate, or reason," he wrote. "A high school graduate with the worst record imaginable can enroll in a junior college in the state of Florida. And the very fact that this is true has encouraged students to think of a college education as a Quantity instead of a Quality." Not everybody was suited to study literature; many were meant to work with their hands or their backs, and that type of work should be respected as well, he wrote: "The nation that humiliates its workmen, the nation that makes its craftsmen feel they are craftsmen not because they chose to be but because they could not become something better, that nation is in grave danger." The article ran in the *Fort Lauderdale News and Sun-Sentinel* and was later reprinted by *The Surplus Record*, a catalog for industrial machinery. For his trouble, Harry received a check for twenty-five dollars.

The conflict that Harry was witnessing in his classroom was also playing out on a larger stage and, around the time that his editorial appeared, was just beginning to reach critical mass. It would very shortly explode into a statewide political conflict that put JCBC on front pages across the state.

Under the college's first president, Joe B. Rushing, JCBC had developed a reputation as academically rigorous, well beyond the level of comparable institutions. There also arose the belief within the state education offices in Tallahassee that the school was not fulfilling its vocational responsibilities. A successor to Rushing with connections in the governor's office, Myron Blee, was brought in and given the task of redirecting the college's mission. Vocational aspects would be emphasized; liberal arts would be marginalized. And, to accomplish this, professorial heads would soon roll. At least, that was the rumor which permeated the halls and walkways across campus.

To add a little more drama to the impending crisis, in the midst of the change in leadership there was also a change in political power in Tallahassee. Out went Democratic governor W. Hayden Burns, supporter of Myron Blee (and husband of the college roommate of Blee's wife), in came Republican Claude Kirk Jr. And the Broward County School Board, which at the time could hire and fire the president of JCBC, went from a 5–0 Democratic majority to a 3–2 Republican majority. Now Blee himself was on shaky ground.

With Drake's guiding hand, Harry entered the fray. He took a leadership role in the faculty senate and soon emerged as the president of the college's faculty union, the American Association of University Professors. (Drake had held the same position prior to Harry.) The faculty was divided. The majority wanted no part of Blee and his plans. But the plans moved forward. In his first months in power, Blee fired nearly 15 percent of the faculty. The new president had a strong despotic streak. His handiwork was not done gently; victims were summoned to his office and dispatched without explanation. A list was circulated that purportedly named those who were next to go. Some faculty members stamped their feet, others ducked under their desks, wary of upsetting the new dictator. An emissary was sent from Tallahassee to interview faculty members and determine whether the state's push toward vocational education was being undermined, and by whom.

But the political power had shifted, and the faculty had the ear of the Republican school board. Harry and the most vocal elements within the faculty publicized the machinations of the new president and were able to garner public support. At faculty meetings, Harry took to the lectern to implore his colleagues to stand and fight. The faculty position began to be echoed on the editorial pages of state newspapers as well as the *Venetian Crier*. Though the new makeup of the school board gave the faculty some hope, Harry had little confidence the conflict would swing their way. His time at the school, he told Kirk, was now limited:

> I might as well tell you that things are not going well at this college. We have a new president who is probably insane. He has abolished all Division and Department Heads. He's cut the staff by 40 people. He refuses to give tenure to anybody that does not already have it. He is a cynical, sarcastic sonofabitch. But the worst is that I stood up in faculty meetings and told them in polite language that they were engorged with shit. They didn't like it. And if not this year, I shall almost certainly have to leave here next year.

Before Blee could clean house entirely, the board acted. With the new governor's support, he was summarily dumped. He sued and won an injunction that kept him in the president's office for a while, but the die had been cast. The matter landed in court, and the newspapers breathlessly reported Blee's undoing. The list of his transgressions included "the institution of a 'nocturnal gestapo' to spy on faculty members at evening classes," changing student records, botching faculty negotiations, firing professors indiscriminately, and generally ticking off anybody within earshot.

Blee lasted less than a year. In wake of the controversy, the governor formed a task force that eventually led to the transfer of power over state community colleges from local school boards to a state advisory board.

On campus in Broward, the smoke from the crisis soon cleared, and under the new administration, peace was restored and growth continued. Harry's leadership had not been lost on his colleagues. "We all thought we were going to be fired," Drake remembered. "But Harry was willing to stick his neck out. For the stand he took for the faculty and against the president, he was practically revered."

Up to this point, Harry's relationships with other writers existed within the confines of the classroom in Building D. Mr. Lytle had brought in ex-students who had become respected authors, and the occasional big name would show up to give a speech or a reading and then go on their way. The halls of Broward Community College, as it was now called under the new regime, were not bustling with published writers. There was, however, a writer who was in the process of achieving significant fame and success living right outside the ivy walls, and he would soon become a close confidant of Harry's.

Just as Harry was, Donn Pearce had been toiling in front of a typewriter for a decade with no success to speak of. A fast-talking Floridian with a wry sense of humor, he came with a backstory that almost made Harry's life seem ordinary. He was born in 1928, the son of a sign-maker who hadn't finished sixth grade. The family moved from state to state, job to job through the Depression, often reduced to begging for food at the Salvation Army. At fifteen, Pearce lied his way into the Army. World War II was in its final stages; Europe, and the front lines, beckoned. Army life didn't agree with him, though, and when he found out he was to be used as infantry replacement, which he interpreted as "expendable," he ran away, was recaptured, spent time in the stockade, and was eventually thrown out when, per his wishes, his mother revealed his age. Undeterred, he joined the U.S. Merchant Marine, a fleet of ships that transport goods around the world. This time, he hoped, he would finally make it overseas, but not as cannon fodder. Before he was twenty, he docked in ports across the globe, learned how to counterfeit, spent time in a French prison, and eventually made his way back to the United States.

Having acquired several criminal skills during his travels but no legal ones, he decided to go into the safe-cracking business. It was profitable for a while, and he found a partner with whom he robbed and stole his way across the eastern United States. But, eventually, he got caught, right in his home state, and wound up on a chain gang in Raiford Penitentiary, where he spent nearly two years. While incarcerated, he discovered a love of reading, started keeping a journal, and was soon hooked. He became a writer and, following his release, endured a lonely apprenticeship similar to Harry's through the 1950s. The majority of that time was spent writing, and rewriting, over and over, the manuscript that would eventually become *Cool Hand Luke*, the story of a charismatic chain-gang inmate with authority issues, and his merry gang of followers.

He eventually found a publisher, and the novel was released in 1965. It didn't sell all that well, but it was well reviewed and quickly optioned by Hollywood. Pearce wrote the screenplay, and once Paul Newman agreed to play the title role, the film got an immediate green light. The small-time-criminal-turned-author was on the fast track.

Pearce's Hollywood experience was underwhelming. He thought little of Paul Newman, was snubbed by Jack Lemmon during a visit to the set, and ignored by the director. But the film was a huge success. The role of Luke was perfect for Newman and became one of the seminal roles in the actor's career. Released in 1967, *Cool Hand Luke* was critically praised and earned several Academy Award nominations, including one for Newman and one for Pearce himself.

With the proceeds from the screenplay, Pearce bought himself a house in Fort Lauderdale, only a few city blocks from where Harry lived. The two had become acquainted after the publication of *Cool Hand Luke*. They shared an ironic sense of humor and a similar writing background, and soon Pearce was part of Harry's inner circle. "We got drunk a lot," said Pearce. "We did a lot of yelling all the time, had a generally good time. People around us seemed to enjoy themselves because we were always putting on such a carnival."

Because Pearce had *Cool Hand Luke* under his belt, Harry took his advice to heart. And his new friend offered a different perspective from Harry's earlier influences. Pearce wanted readers, recognition, and, above all, to be paid for his work. He already knew the life of a writer was a tremendously difficult road and was sufficiently jaded by the publishing process. But the insights he gave Harry would eventually prove exceedingly helpful in paving his path toward legitimacy as a writer.

While Pearce's misdeeds were in the past, in 1966 Harry would also encounter someone whose crimes were firmly in the future. And those crimes made Pearce's felonious past look like a couple of parking tickets. A student named Gerard John Schaefer Jr. enrolled in one of Harry's creative writing classes that year. Harry saw some of his younger self in Schaefer; specifically, Schaefer had no idea how to write grammatically or punctuate, but he had creative potential. Harry spent some time with him outside class, coaching him on writing and even playing racquetball with him. Eventually his writing became disturbing enough to Harry that he recommended his student see a counselor.

Schaefer soon left Broward Community College for Florida Atlantic, and Harry quickly forgot about him. Schaefer would continue writing, though, and when he was arrested on murder charges, police found fifty pages of such writing in a trunk that also contained teeth, women's clothing, and unspecified "souvenirs." Schaefer's writing took the form of "rambling, diary-like notes describing a long series of real or imagined acts of murder, necrophilia, dismemberment and burial," according to *Time*. Harry was destined to meet his former student one more time, behind glass, at the Florida State Prison in Starke, Florida.

Donn Pearce was a shining example that success was possible. But Harry's reality was unchanged. Very little positive news had arrived in the mailbox in months. The high drama at the college was at best an occasional distraction from the continuing disappointment. In early 1966, he managed to convince the Daniel S. Mead literary agency to pitch his novels to publishers, some of which had already turned them down. The agency was encouraging toward Harry's work, and they set about targeting editors at the major houses.

Again, what seemed like a breakthrough turned out to be one more soul-crushing defeat. In August, his new agent delivered her report. "We are returning under separate cover manuscripts titled THE DELICATE WOUND and DON'T SING MY NAME," the letter read. "The above manuscripts were declined by Viking; McGraw-Hill; New American Library; Farrar, Straus; Simon & Schuster; Harper & Row; Atlantic Mo. Press; Scribner's; Grove Press; Vanguard Press; Gold Medal Books. Sorry we were unable to place your work." If it was possible to write a more devastating rejection letter, Harry had not yet thought of it. Without a hint of irony, she signed off: "Best wishes from the staff." With that coda, he was once again without representation and, in his mind, without prospects.

Unbeknownst to him at the time, a chance encounter had already occurred that would change his present course. His mother had moved to a farm near Tifton, Georgia, and Harry paid her a visit during a break from classes. He was asleep in bed on a Sunday morning when Myrtice returned from church and excitedly roused her son. A famous singer who had grown up in the area had returned to town and was set to perform at her church, she told him. Myrtice loved church music and would regularly travel hundreds of miles to attend all-night religious concerts. To her, gospel singers were royalty. And now she had brought one back to the farmhouse to meet her son.

After some prodding, Harry put on his clothes and stepped out onto the porch, shielding his eyes from the blinding late-morning sun. There before him, wearing a five-hundred-dollar blue silk suit and rings of every shape and stone on his fingers, stood what seemed like an apparition. For a moment, Harry could not speak. He stared at the singer, as rays of sunlight flashed from the man's jewelry into Harry's eyes. He looked past the singer into the yard where several Indians, wearing full feathered headdresses and buckskins, peered up to the porch. Harry absorbed the scene for a few seconds longer, and as a wide grin grew across his face, he stuck out his hand and wished the man who would inspire the Gospel Singer a good morning.

CHAPTER ELEVEN   GOLD FROM A COAL MINE

> There is no way to be at the top of the mountain, except to be at
> the top of the mountain. There is no road up, no path.
> —Harry Crews, "Teaching and Learning Creative Writing"

It didn't take long after the encounter on the porch in Tifton for the ideas to begin percolating. And when they did, they came swiftly. A few days later, he bid Myrtice farewell, got in the car for the trip back to South Florida, and quickly got lost. He found himself in the town of Enigma, Georgia, just east of Tifton. Enigma wasn't really a town at all, just a few blocks of buildings surrounding a two-lane highway, but it had an old stately courthouse at its center and the dusty feel of a place that time had forgotten. And it was, after all, called Enigma. Harry parked and got out of the car. As the midday sun beat down upon him, he walked up and down the town's few streets. This is it, he decided. This is where it happened.

What had happened, as the story he planned to tell began to crystalize in his mind, was that a child had been born in Enigma who was marked with beauty and had the singing voice of an angel. Enigma, on the page, would take on the characteristics of Bacon County, as would its inhabitants. The world of his childhood, more so than in any of his previous writing, would be represented in this novel. The child would grow up and leave Enigma to find fame and fortune, only to return, a nonbeliever, alienated from the people of his youth—one of them, yet not one of them at the same time. It was a story that Harry knew, immediately, he was meant to tell.

He was back at the typewriter as soon as he could find the time. Though

Don't Sing My Name and *The Delicate Wound* were still circulating through the New York publishing houses, Harry now felt strongly that the work that would finally see its way to publication for him had not yet been written. The Enigma book came much quicker than his previous efforts too. Instead of heeding Lytle's advice and slowing down, Harry was going in the other direction. With each page, he felt more strongly that he was in the middle of his best novel yet. By the spring of 1966, he had another completed manuscript.

Since graduate school, Pat Waters had become Harry's most consistent reader. Waters had been teaching English at Mercer University in Macon, Georgia, unhappily. As he sought work elsewhere, he, too, was trying to produce a publishable novel and sending his work down to Fort Lauderdale for Harry to review. The two had an agreement that had been set years earlier—whoever published first would buy a bottle of Jack Daniels, and the two would celebrate together. Waters had a very unusual style in critiquing Harry's work. In fact, he offered almost no critique at all. And Harry would not ask for any reaction, either. "I don't think I ever offered any opinion, whatsoever," Waters said. "Certainly I don't recall ever offering any opinion. I always felt he really didn't want one. It is not in Harry's nature to say, 'Well, what do you think?'"

Waters received the first draft of the Enigma novel in early May of 1966, the first person to whom Harry showed the completed manuscript. (Sally read much of Harry's work in progress.) It was different from everything else Harry had sent him over the past seven years. And now, finally, he offered his friend a critique: "I think the first sentence I ever said to him about any of his work was 'Somebody will publish this.' And he said, 'I've heard that before.' Keep in mind . . . I was very young and very full of myself, I think, because only a young man who's full of himself could have said what I said: 'Not from me you haven't.' But that's a little confession of youthful arrogance."

Waters clarified his feelings in writing soon thereafter. The novel, he wrote, contained a voice that was heretofore absent. The tone was harsh and ominous, as with Harry's previous efforts, but it was also funny: "You said that you had no sense of humor, but that's simply not true. As a matter of fact, humor, of a rather dark sort, might be your salvation." There was no question in Waters's mind that this was finally the novel that Harry would publish: "I will be a frightened man if nobody takes it."

The response from Waters did contain some criticisms, however, and they were comments that Harry would hear again down the road. Waters disliked one scene in particular. It took place in a restaurant, between the Gospel Singer and some fans who expect him to perform a miracle. Waters strongly urged Harry to remove the scene. "I don't know exactly what words were exchanged, but we talked rather freely with one another, and it was clear that he didn't like that suggestion at all," Waters said. Some days later, however, Harry was sitting at the kitchen table in his house in Fort Lauderdale, going over the manuscript while Sally cooked breakfast. He found the scene that Waters did not like, and, with tears welling up in his eyes, he took his pencil and drew a line through the entire section. The restaurant scene was removed from the manuscript forever.

The positive response from Waters confirmed what Harry already believed about the quality of the Enigma novel. It was ready to be sent to New York and the gatekeepers of the publishing industry. Mr. Lytle, he decided, need not see it at this stage; there was too much positive energy, and Harry's psyche might not be able to handle his mentor's judgment. He titled it *The Gospel Singer* and began searching for agents he had not already approached.

The publishing industry is designed as a barricade against unpublished writers, and here, Harry made another misstep that grew out of his ignorance of the business. The price for his mistake would be another year of heartache. Instead of going back to the well of literary agents, all of whom so far had failed to sell any of his work, he tried another route. He saw an advertisement for Award Books, an entity of World Publishing. The company was holding a contest for first novels. The winner's manuscript would be published following the contest. And the competition was to be judged by Herbert Gold, a well-known member of the Beatnik writing community, a friend of Allen Ginsberg's, and a writer Harry respected. If Gold was associated with the contest, Harry thought, it must be legitimate.

For a few months, he heard nothing. Then in the summer, some good news. *The Gospel Singer* had survived the first reading. It wouldn't be much longer now, he was assured. And even better, his novel was of such high quality, Award Books wanted to publish it, no matter how the contest turned out. That was not something they wanted to put in writing at this juncture, however.

At first, Harry was overjoyed. What he'd been waiting for all these years had finally arrived. But there was no contract and no money. It was real, but somehow it wasn't. Still, he asked no questions. As summer turned to fall, Harry tired of waiting by the mailbox. But Award Books was still the only publisher that had actually said they would publish his work, so he treaded lightly. He wrote a letter gingerly inquiring about the state of the contest. In October, he heard back again: *The Gospel Singer* was in the final six. It would only be another month or two, at the most, he was told. And Harry's book was still slated for publication, kind of: "I will reiterate . . . the notion that your manuscript at the very least will be published as an Award original novel, although that must be taken as an off-the-record remark," the editor in charge of the contest wrote evasively.

The anticipation was almost impossible to bear. But life went on as it always had, and Harry was back in front of the typewriter as *The Gospel Singer* hovered in publishing purgatory. On another excursion on the back roads of Florida, Harry had driven into a central Florida town called Mulberry, also known as the phosphate capital of the world. As he had in Enigma, he looked around and felt he had discovered the setting for a novel. With some chemical assistance, his writing speed shifted into yet another gear. Harry discovered he could write faster, and longer, with the help of amphetamines. "I had a Mason fruit jar full of amphetamines and a bottle of Wild Turkey, and if you get too wired, just take a hit," he wrote later of this period. "I'd bubble the bottle a couple of times and be ready to work."

The result was *Naked in Garden Hills*. A draft was completed before the end of 1966. The plot revolved around a burned-out phosphate mine and the eccentric characters that lived around it. It was even more satirical than *The Gospel Singer*, and more technically ambitious as well. Harry believed he had again written his best novel and contemplated his next move.

Incredibly, there was still no word from Award Books. They had now held his manuscript for nearly a year. The promise of publication was eight months old. Contest deadlines had come and gone. Harry had been discussing his travails with *The Gospel Singer* with Pearce throughout, and Pearce had reached a slow boil. He thought publishers were thieves, every last one of them, and felt for sure that Harry was being taken advantage of.

"You're fucking crazy," Pearce told Harry. "You've got to write them and withdraw your book."

Harry could not be convinced. "No, no. They said they were going to publish it. I just can't do it."

Unable to change Harry's mind, Pearce decided to enlist some help. He recommended another literary agent. In early 1967, Harry sent *Naked in Garden Hills* to Bert Cochran of American Authors, Inc., on Pearce's recommendation. Cochran responded positively in a matter of days, and Harry had a new agent, one who, for once, seemed genuinely enthusiastic about Harry's work. "Write me about anything that's on your mind; your writing plans, and what have you." Cochran wrote to his new client. "I'm glad to note that you are 30 years old. It means you have a big career ahead of you."

The show of support boosted Harry's confidence. He wrote to Cochran and told him the story of the contest and the current state of *The Gospel Singer*. As Pearce had been, Cochran too was outraged. On Harry's wishes, he conducted an investigation into the contest that Harry had been frightened to do himself. The editor-in-chief of Award Books informed Cochran that there was still no firm deadline for the end of the contest, which had started nearly a year and a half earlier. The competition, he was told, had turned out to be more than the company could handle. Cochran found the judges and called them; they had indeed read and returned Harry's book to the editor but knew nothing else about the contest. Now Cochran echoed Pearce's advice: Harry should withdraw the book from the contest.

Still, Harry fought against the idea. "For God's sake, don't withdraw it," he wrote in response to Cochran. "They've said they were going to publish it. That's more than anybody else has ever said."

All those rejections sitting in the folder in his office were a weight on him that, despite all evidence to the contrary, caused him to hold on for dear life to a year-old promise backed with nothing. Finally, he relented. Cochran could act as he saw fit. The agent continued his investigation into the state of a book that he still had never read. A week later, he wrote to Harry: "I checked around some more, and spoke to the editor again, and decided that it would be criminal for you to be imposed on any longer. So I took THE GOSPEL SINGER from them." He had already read the manuscript, and was as enthusiastic as he had been upon reading *Naked in Garden Hills*. He planned to sell them, and, this time, it would be done quickly. "I have both books in the hands of editors, and insisted in both cases that I require an answer in the next several weeks."

Five days later, *The Gospel Singer* was under contract.

Throughout the long tortuous road for the book, Harry had withheld it from Lytle. He had barely been in touch with his mentor at all, the longest such stretch without communication since the two had met nearly a decade before. Now Harry called Lytle to tell him the news. Lytle had seen some difficult times in recent years. His wife had died of cancer, and he had been struck by the disease as well. He had recently had a colostomy after cancer had reached his lower intestine. He was thrilled for Harry's success, but melancholy over the fact that the two seemed to be drifting apart:

> I've thought of you many times and wondered how you were doing, hearing indirectly about you, some good, some bad. I mean that sometimes you forgot the ways of discipline in the craft for more immediate gains. But I believe you when you say you've done the best you could at the time on this book, and I'm looking forward to reading it. . . . You are certainly devoted in your art, and you have a gift. The two together, plus luck, will take you far. I find that it takes a lifetime to unfold your subject. Every artist has one, and it has to have something to do with the human predicament, which is forever true. . . . I would like to see you. If sometime you feel like it, come up to see me.

Lytle promised his comments and help with *The Gospel Singer*, and Harry dutifully sent the manuscript up to Tennessee, and sent a copy to Kirkpatrick in Gainesville as well. In September, Lytle offered his response. The book was clearly Harry's best work to date, he said; through the act of writing, he had truly learned his craft and had produced a work that was technically superior. The praise, however, lasted four lines; the next page and a half pointed out, in no uncertain terms, the large flaws in the manuscript. The biggest lapse was the ending of the book. Harry had concluded with a scene of chaotic mob violence, one that Lytle viewed as a refutation of the rest of the book. "You were doing fine until three quarters of the way through, and then you backed off," he wrote. "I cannot understand this, nor can I understand why Kirk did not speak to you about it."

Kirkpatrick weighed in with a similar response; *The Gospel Singer* was a fine novel, but a flawed novel. To his mentors, the obvious next step was to eliminate the flaws. Revise, revise, revise. Harry felt differently. In his years in isolation, his own views on art had diverged from his teachers'. And now, with publication a certainty, he was beginning to feel that he was no longer a student at all. He responded to Kirkpatrick's criticisms: "I never expected to do a perfect thing. Nor do I ever expect to. . . . Everybody who had read the book has had reservations. . . . I try not to think about it. If I had waited until everybody could have agreed on everything, the book would never be published. I'm going to write a lot in my lifetime and it's probably going to be second-rate shit—all of it. But then one does not expect gold to come from a coal mine."

The steady flow of rejection had now reversed course, and barely a week went by in the fall of 1967 that Harry did not learn of more good news about his career. In October, he received his advance check for $1,575 from William Morrow, a very respectable figure for a first-time fiction writer. It wasn't a fortune, but to somebody with an annual salary below $10,000, it was significant. Morrow had already sent the galleys out for review, and now real, live writers were reading Harry's work. Richard Kim, a popular writer whose book *The Martyred*, about the Korean War, had been nominated for the Nobel Prize in Literature just a few years prior, was the first to respond. *The Gospel Singer*, Kim wrote, "is a remarkable first novel and as such I hope it will be widely read."

Around the same time, Cochran wrote to inform Harry that Morrow had bought *Naked in Garden Hills*. It would be published one year after *The Gospel Singer*. Before he had even signed off on the galleys on his first book, Harry would be cashing another advance. And Cochran had received some interest from some of his Hollywood connections about both of Harry's books. He would soon be hearing from several executives in the motion-picture industry. Further, Cochran wrote, it would be a nice idea to arrange a "Harry Crews Day" in South Florida. His wife knew a restaurateur in Miami who ran a swanky joint, and, for a rising star like Harry, he could easily make it happen. Harry's trips to the mailbox had become an entirely different experience.

Among the strokes of luck that befell Harry during the year 1967, one of the most serendipitous was the hiring by William Morrow of an editor named Jim Landis. Landis had grown up in Springfield, Massachusetts, and studied at Yale, graduating with an English degree in 1964. While at Yale, coincidentally, he had studied under Robert Penn Warren, under whose tutelage he had formed the ambition to eventually become a writer. But first, he thought he'd give the publishing industry a shot.

Landis moved to New York after graduation, looked up publishing in the yellow pages, and went building to building handing out résumés until he was hired by the publisher Abelard-Schuman. After a few years as the second person in a two-person office, mostly working as a copyeditor and earning sixty dollars a week, he was hired by William Morrow in early 1967, just as Bert Cochran was beginning to shop *The Gospel Singer*. "I went to Morrow to interview, and [the interviewer] said, 'Well, let me tell you the kind of person we're looking for. We're looking for an editor who will buy fiction by young writers,'" Landis recalled. "It's hard to imagine anybody would say such a thing to an editor today. In other words, he was looking for someone who could do literary work, which is what I was interested in. And I said, 'That's me.'"

The new job came with new perks. At Abelard-Schuman, he was a line editor, charged with cleaning up manuscripts. His boss had told Landis that if he found out he was meeting with agents, he would be fired on the spot. Now at Morrow, Landis had joined a large-scale operation. His new company had a team of copyeditors to do the grunt work. Landis, instead, was expected to spend his time taking writers and agents to lunch, paying for rounds of drinks, and bringing some new blood into the fold. His role had been reversed: If you *don't* charm some agents, you're fired.

At the time, Morrow was known for publishing commercial fiction, much of it by established writers the company found in England or Australia, including Nicholas Monsarrat, Mary Stewart, Morris West, and others. What they needed, Morrow executives felt, were young writers. Landis, in his mid-twenties himself, set about to find them some. When Cochran brought him *The Gospel Singer*, he'd been at the hunt for less than a year. Cochran was not from one of the major literary agencies, and Landis had not heard of him, but he agreed to take a look at the manuscript. "I recognized something in it immediately," he remembered. "I asked if I could publish it, and my bosses said yes. There was no question. All you had to do was read a page of Harry's work, and you knew you were reading a *writer*-writer. It was not just simply distinctive, it was good."

Landis would become Harry's longest serving editor. The two began a relationship, through written correspondence, that would continue for several books before they would finally meet, years later. Harry was at first extremely deferential. Though he was working with a very green editor, one who was several years his junior, to Harry, Landis represented the unconquerable fortress that was publishing. Landis, for his part, took on the role of the champion of Harry's work. Harry was his first discovery, and he aimed to shepherd him to ultimate success. "I happen to feel quite close to you personally, through your writing, which may damn well be dangerous, yet it is a danger I am willing to face, and I do have an overwhelming trust in my instincts when it comes to you and to your work," he wrote to Harry. "I happen to think you are going to emerge as one of the finest writers this country has."

The publication date for *The Gospel Singer* was set for February 15, 1968. Publicity from Morrow had given Harry name recognition, and he began giving readings around Florida in advance of the book's release. His dramatic presentation, honed in the classroom, now began to earn him a reputation as a performer who could entertain a crowd. He traveled to Orlando, Tampa, Daytona Beach, at each stop feeling more like an author and less like the failure he felt he had been for so long.

The *Miami Herald* received some of the advance publicity and sent a reporter out to Broward Community College to meet the soon-to-be-published author. Harry laid on the redneck charm thick, "spreading humor like a Southern Smothers Brother." The article appeared at the top of the "For and About Women" section of the *Herald* in early November, under the headline "Just an Ole' Georgia Boy Tryin' to Write a Novel." Harry dressed up for the occasion and appeared in two photos, pictured deep in thought, wearing a blue sport coat and thin black tie and sporting a close-cropped haircut. The captions read "writes compulsively" and "rotten with pride."

In December, the first outside review came in from Kirkus Review Service, an industry publication aimed at bookstore owners. "This thoroughly modern macabre piece has the relentless fascination of a revival meeting," the reviewer wrote. "*The Gospel Singer* is one libretto you won't easily forget." The service also gave the book a "Q" rating, meaning the content was not suitable for public libraries. Landis was slightly perturbed by the ramifications of such a rating but put it in the best possible light when informing Harry: "While such a judgment is utterly ridiculous, there is nothing we can do about it. If I were you, however, I would feel at least somewhat flattered by it, because I think the reason they gave it a Q was not for what sex you put in the book but for the power with which you delivered it."

As publication approached, Harry began to explore the idea of using the book as a springboard to his next job. The Blee Affair, and his role in it, had instilled in him the feeling that his days at Broward Community College were numbered. And his marketability, he felt, would never be higher. He began working his connections in Gainesville. He mentioned his interest to Kirkpatrick, who passed it along to James Hodges, the chairman of the English Department. Kirkpatrick told Hodges about *The Gospel Singer* and gave him some press clippings, including the *Herald* piece. Hodges was impressed. He invited Harry up to meet the dean and promised to inform him of any openings.

Harry was pleased, but he wanted out of Broward immediately, whether he escaped to Gainesville or to somewhere else. "They know I'm available," he wrote to Kirkpatrick. "They know where I am." He contacted Lytle, who offered to set up a meeting with the University of Alabama. And he began pursuing a position at Universidad de las Américas in Mexico City. He had decided that his career as a community college teacher, for better or for worse, would not extend for another year.

In the midst of the positive upheaval, Harry made a call to Myrtice that he had been dreaming of for years. His mother was always supportive but had little understanding of Harry's literary ambitions. He called shortly after he signed on the dotted lines with Morrow.

"Ma, I've sold my book. It's going to be published."

"You mean one of them made-up books? Was it all made up?"

"Yes, ma'am," Harry replied. "It was a novel."

"Son, you didn't pass it off as the truth, did you?" Myrtice asked.

"No, Ma, they know it's made up."

Myrtice was incredulous. "You mean, you made it all up, and they taken it and give you real money for it?"

"Yes, Ma," Harry said. "Yes, they have."

PART TWO

TOP OF THE MOUNTAIN

The actors, the grips, the cameramen, the rented birds all made their way to Gainesville a few months after the announcement that *The Hawk Is Dying* was going into production. As the filming progressed, I called Harry each time the editors wanted a story, and he never failed to entertain. The director, he said, reminded him of a soda jerk. The lead in the film, the actor who would portray the fictional "Harry Crews" on screen, was Paul Giamatti. Harry said he couldn't pronounce his name, so he had taken to calling him Paul Spaghetti. No, Harry said, he would not be going to the set. A movie set is no place for a writer. It's just a lot of waiting around, and nobody wants to hear a writer's bullshit about his "vision."

More than anything, Harry was concerned about the treatment of the hawks. He heard they were feeding them dead rodents. Feed a hawk dead mice, and you'll have a dead hawk before you know it. A hawk needs live prey to thrive, he said.

It was six years since he had published a novel, and he seemed pleased to be in the news again. Still, each time I asked to interview him in person, he demurred. His health was bad, he said. His feet were in constant pain. The doctors botched a knee operation, fucked him up real nice, turned him into a goddamn cripple.

On several occasions, he agreed to schedule a visit, told me to call him the day of, only to cancel when I called to confirm.

Months went by. The final scenes of *Hawk* were shot and the wrap party was held. Paul Spaghetti and friends packed up their trailers and left town. Soon, the movie was on the schedule for the Sundance Film Festival in Park City, Utah. I called Harry to give him the good news.

"Tell the fucking editors at the *Gainesville Sun* to buy me a ticket to Utah," he said with just a hint of glee. "You, me, and Robert Redford will chase pussy all around the Rocky Mountains."

The movie version of *The Hawk Is Dying* was gone before you could say "straight to video." One morning a few months later, after another article about Harry had run in the *Sun*, a letter was dropped on my desk. The author was Ed Nagel. He'd seen the article, and it had brought back memories of his college days, when he'd shared a room with Harry Crews. The letter contained tales of a distant era of Gainesville, full of convertibles, cheap whiskey, drunken sunrises. To conclude, he quoted the Great Mr. Lytle: "Life is melodrama; only art is real."

Ed hadn't seen Harry in years and was glad to learn that he was still alive. (That, I would learn, was the initial response from anybody I called who had known Harry in his glory days. "He's still alive?!" they'd blurt. "You're kidding!") Ed was also a writer who'd had a roller coaster life himself since his days with Harry. He was a long-recovered alcoholic and recovered lawyer, now living and writing in town. He wanted to be put in contact with his old college buddy, and a few phone calls later, the room-mates were back in touch.

Ed called me a few weeks later. He'd been to see Harry and was helping him out now, driving him around, cleaning up the house. It was perfect, Ed said. They were on the same schedule, writing in the early morning, sleeping in the evening.

Ed asked Harry if he could bring me over to the house, and after a few near misses, a date and time were set. I picked Ed up one bright morning at his apartment. He bounded out, wearing an Adidas-style sweat suit, circa 1980, and sneakers. Ed is a beacon of light (a counter to the darkness of Harry, I would find out), radiating positivity at all times. He's got a head of unkempt reddish hair streaked through with gray, which, like his attitude, belies his age. He always, I would learn, has several projects in the works — plays, novels, articles — so if he runs dry on one, he can shift seamlessly to one of the others.

We picked up coffee and doughnuts and drove the few miles to Harry's house. The house is right off a main thoroughfare, a hidden gravel driveway marked by a plastic mailbox. Ed had warned that Harry was not at his best at this time of day. I parked, and Ed told me to wait by the car. From the driveway, I heard a voice growl, and Ed entered the house. After a minute or so, he reappeared and waved me over.

I entered the house, and there, sitting in a big tan recliner in his sunken living room, was Harry Crews, wearing a shirt, naked below the belt, working on the final drag of a cigarette. Ed did introductions, we shook hands, and I tried to find anything in the room above the equator on which to focus my gaze. There was a large picture of Muhammad Ali in the posi-tion of honor above the fireplace, posters from some of the documentaries that had been made about Harry, a framed picture of Harry and Charles

Bronson. Harry rose, with great difficulty, and announced he would go get dressed.

"Anybody who looks at my dick," he announced to no one in particular, "better be prepared to suck it."

The plan was for Ed and me to chauffer Harry around town, a few errands, some shopping. We climbed into Harry's Taurus, me at the wheel, Ed in the backseat. As we drove through the streets of Gainesville, Ed and Harry talked. The banter between them, it seemed, was just as it must have been fifty years before.

Ed is a deep thinker, usually in the middle of writing a play about Kant or Descartes. Sometime during the morning, he launched into an extended story, somehow related to their college years, about the philosophical implications of Zeno's Paradox. He went on for some time, getting deeper and deeper and more and more intellectual, when finally Harry broke in.

"Ed?"

"Yeah, Har?"

"What the fuck are you talking about?"

We took Harry to pick up his prescription at the drugstore and to the bank, and the two old roommates repeated oft-told college tales, one after the other, one of them taking the lead, the other filling in the details. They talked about Bob Graham, their classmate and later a U.S. senator from Florida, who was apparently much less talented as a writer than he would become as a politician. They talked about their struggles to get whiskey in a dry county in the late 1950s, and which direction and which highway was the shortest drive to obtain a drink.

Mostly, though, they spoke about Mr. Lytle. And they spoke not as septuagenarians who had been mentoring younger generations for a lifetime, but as young men, delivering the type of patter you would hear from graduate students swapping reverential stories about their committee chairmen, or young employees talking about their first boss.

They went back and forth with stories, each painting another brushstroke about the master. Each moment, no matter how small or insignificant, was a teaching opportunity to Mr. Lytle, they said. Ed was thoughtful: Mr. Lytle, he offered, had the ability to show his students what was between the lines of the words on the page. Harry was admiring yet crass: I did anything he asked me to, he said: Mowed his lawn, cleaned his floors, fucked his daughter. Well, he added, he didn't actually ask me to do that.

Then Harry grew serious. I didn't have a father, he said. Well, I had one but never knew one, never knew what it was like to have one, until I met Mr. Lytle.

We drove through the tree-lined streets as the sun gradually rose in the sky, the Florida heat radiating around us. As we passed through campus, we watched the latest batch of students inhabit the roles Ed and Harry played together in their youth. Eventually, we made it back to Harry's house, helped him up the steps, through the door, and back into his recliner.

"I can't remember when I've spent a more enjoyable morning, fellas," Harry said as we headed out the door. Before we could get to the car, he called us back in. He asked for my phone number, put his freshly lit cigarette into the ashtray, and scribbled the number in his address book.

CHAPTER TWELVE **ARRIVAL**

> It seemed a fact of the world that the Gospel Singer could save a
> soul. No matter how hard he argued against it, sinners at every
> turn accepted God on the strength of his voice. All his troubles,
> he told himself, stemmed from that.
> —Harry Crews, *The Gospel Singer*

On the cover of the book review section of the *New York Times* for February 18, 1968, Fyodor Dostoevsky is drawn, bearded and brooding, deep in shadowed contemplation. The first paragraph of a review of Konstantin Mochulsky's biography of the iconic Russian author quotes a young Dostoevsky, bursting with pride over the reviews of his first published novel. "Read and see for yourself," he wrote to his brother in 1846. "I have a most brilliant future before me!"

The front page of the *Times* that day pictured two American soldiers helping a comrade injured in combat in Vietnam, and the seriousness of the era was reflected on the best-seller list. William Styron's Pulitzer Prize–winning slavery novel, *The Confessions of Nat Turner*, held the top slot; thoughtful fiction by established writers such as Leon Uris, John O'Hara, and Chaim Potok round out much of the rest of the offerings. About forty pages deep in the book review section, in the third item in Martin Levin's weekly column, readers could find reference to another first-time author, who, like Dostoevsky, was in the process of seeing his lonely efforts finally validated. "Mr. Crews' novel," Levin wrote, "has a nice wild flavor and a dash of Grand Guignol strong enough to meet the severe standards of Southern decadence."

The published version of *The Gospel Singer* that Levin was responding to was very close to the manuscript that Harry had typed in his Fort Lauderdale office more than two years earlier. Landis had asked for only minor revisions, and Harry had ignored the advice he'd received from his other first readers. But what he'd produced in that room was a bizarre yet powerful tale bursting with sexual and racial tension, alienation, and violence.

The Gospel Singer opens in the jail cell in the courthouse in Enigma, where Willalee Bookatee Hull is being held, a suspect in the vicious rape and murder of MaryBell Carter, who had been stabbed sixty-one times with an ice pick. Willalee (Harry had chosen to use the name of his childhood best friend) has no recollection of the crime, but the population of the town is thirsty for his blood. "The most frightening aspect of his crime was that everyone in Enigma had apparently forgotten his name. He had suddenly become 'the' nigger or 'that' nigger, but never Willalee Bookatee Hull." Out the window, Willalee sees a sign for a Freak Fair, promising "the midget with the largest foot in the world." The Freak Fair is setting up in Enigma in anticipation of the return of the Gospel Singer, Harry's protagonist, who, as in Harry's first published short story, has been given no name. He is a product of Enigma, and now, years after he left to find fame, fortune, and an unquenchable sexual desire for nubile young girls, he is worshiped like a god by the poor, desperate townsfolk he left behind.

Though he is now repulsed by his family and the people of Enigma, he has returned because of his uncontrollable yearning for MaryBell, whom he deflowered years before, and who now appears nightly in his dreams. For his manager, the Gospel Singer has a Bible-quoting former monk named Didymus, a character Harry based on the ghostly hobo he'd met in the YMCA hostel in Wyoming ten years earlier. Didymus provides the Gospel Singer with opportunities for trysts with virginal young gospel fans of his, then forces him to sing his penance. Didymus, "the violent murderous lover of God," has killed the Gospel Singer's previous manager, which is all part of a twisted religious vision that is a mirror of actual Christendom:

> If evil gave the opportunity for good, it ceased to be evil; if evil set into motion a chain of events that caused an eventual good, larger than the original evil, then it ceased to be evil. He had seen the logic of that at once.

And from that logic he had concluded that pain and suffering was God's greatest gift to man. His mother, of course, had confirmed the reasoning. As she pointed out, without suffering there can be no martyrdom. All religious fervor should be the seeking of the greatest discomfort, a lusting for the greatest danger to life and limb. Go into strange lands where the people have never heard of you and tell them what they do not want to hear and cannot understand. If you are lucky, they will kill you and eat you. Oh! Great good fortune to be stripped of flesh, cooked in a pot, and flushed down some pagan's throat! Lucky man that flops about being hit over the head with clubs, bashed with bricks, and set upon by vicious dogs. That is the way to God, righteousness and the moral life.

Upon being told of MaryBell's murder, the Gospel Singer is relieved. Through his sexual demands, he has turned her from a virgin into a vixen, forcing upon her behavior he's learned from Atlanta prostitutes, but her reputation for virtue in Enigma has remained strong. Now, with her death, she will no longer beckon him to return. The town goes about preparing for both the funeral and the Gospel Singer's performance. The Gospel Singer's family is a mirror to the Freak Fair: they've brought pigs and chickens into the brand-new house he's built for them. His two youngest siblings, Mirst and Avel, have decided they want to be a rock 'n' roll duo, and his other brother, Gerd, is being recruited by the actual Freak Fair because of a disgusting skin condition.

The novel's original construct—the mystery of MaryBell's death—is broken two-thirds of the way through, when the Gospel Singer visits Willalee and learns why MaryBell was killed: she had tried to reveal the truth about the Gospel Singer, that he was not who they believed him to be. The Gospel Singer, upon learning that he is to blame for Willalee's predicament, unravels. As the tension builds under the revival tent before his concert, he explodes and blurts out that MaryBell was a whore and he had made her so. In the first of many chaotic, violent novel endings that Harry would publish, the crowd turns into an angry mob, grabs the Gospel Singer and Willalee, and hangs them both from an oak tree:

When he saw the rope, he fainted. The robe had been stripped from him when he regained consciousness. His hands were crushed and he was bleeding from cuts in his stomach. Directly above him, sitting straddle of a mule with a rope around his neck, was Willalee Bookatee Hull. He was naked too. Blood poured from a wound between his legs and ran down over the mule's shoulders. The Gospel Singer could feel nothing. He opened his mouth to tell them to leave him alone but he screamed instead. Somebody brought a second mule up and they threw the Gospel Singer straddle of it. He fell off. They threw him on again and steadied him this time with a rope around his neck. The Gospel Singer was close enough to Willalee now to hear him saying 'Lord forgive them.' His voice was as calm and soft as if he had been sitting in the woods alone watching the sun go down.

The closing of the novel was the sound and fury that Lytle and Kirkpatrick had detested. Harry's protagonist, instead of understanding his predicament and confronting his flaws, had died because of them. But it was a shocking, powerful conclusion that was foreshadowed by the epigraph that Harry had opened the novel with: "Men to whom God is dead worship each other." Below it, a dedication: "This book is for Smith Kirkpatrick, whose apprentice I am."

The reviews were nearly all positive. Newspaper writers lined up to form a cheering section for "the personable young English teacher from Broward Junior College," in the words of one local scribe. Some of it was beyond effusive. The *Nashville Banner* compared Harry to both Carson McCullers and Tennessee Williams. "Crews' . . . force is doubly potent when one realizes the overall grandeur of his design, his ability to make a small corner of rural Georgia take on the limitless areas of great space, as if the air itself was bearing witness to the madness of men," cooed reviewer Howell Pearre. "Harry Crews has written a masterful book of conscience and consequence, a testimony to the inescapability of man's actions—or his inaction," raved the *Richmond News-Leader*. The unequivocal high praise from the outside world was a bounce that Harry would ride emotionally and professionally for some time.

The critical reaction to *The Gospel Singer* only accelerated the transformations in Harry's life. His colleagues at Broward Community College, as it was now known—at least those of them who had been on his side through the Blee controversy—were complimentary about his success. Drake contacted the publisher and had a copy of the dust jacket mailed to him at the library. He gathered the signatures of nearly all the faculty, had the book jacket framed, and arranged a surprise party for Harry at his home. Harry and Sally arrived, unaware, and after the shock wore off, both turned their attention to the display that had been arranged on a table in the center of Drake's living room. Thirty copies of *The Gospel Singer* surrounded an enormous, yellow papier-mâché foot. Harry happily signed the books, genuinely touched by the acknowledgment of his peers.

They would not be his peers much longer. Negotiations with the University of Florida had taken a positive turn. The same day that *The Gospel Singer* was officially published, Kirkpatrick wrote to Harry to say that not only had a position opened up, but the dean was now considering bringing Harry in as an assistant professor, a level above the instructor position he had been seeking. *The Gospel Singer*, it seemed, had opened doors. Hodges, the chair of the department, had called Lytle for a recommendation, and all that was needed was a letter of support from Morrow, and Harry was in. Kirkpatrick was elated but chagrined that it took a few articles in newspapers to sway the UF administrators. "Oh, how devious life is," he wrote. "Ideally in this world one should do the work, and just value and treatment be its natural issue, but that's asking for justice, and, Lord help us, there isn't two cents worth of that loose in the world."

The official word came in a month later. Harry would be an assistant professor of English at the University of Florida, earning $9,500 a year, with the possibility of summer pay as well. The title was significant; it placed Harry on the tenure track and gave him a stature within the department usually reserved for those who had earned doctoral degrees. (Felicity Trueblood, a writer who had studied with Harry during his undergraduate days, had taught the courses Harry would assume the previous year. She had the title of instructor and earned a salary of $7,200.) Whether due to insecurity or experience, Harry had developed an animosity toward PhD's, dating back to his rejection by the department when he was a graduate-school applicant. He expressed his displeasure with the degree requirement to friends during his negotiations, and would view PhD-holding professors as the enemy throughout his years in academia.

But for now, it was time to celebrate another success. He was soon to be free of Broward and would be a professor at the premier university in the Florida State system. He wrote to his mother, including a copy of his offer letter from the University of Florida. He and Sally were ecstatic to be moving back to Gainesville where they had so many friends already, he told Myrtice. He would be closer to her in Georgia and would have fewer classes to teach, so more time to devote to his writing. Things couldn't be better, he wrote. "Well, the only way they could be better is if my agent sells THE GOSPEL SINGER to the movies for about a hundred thousand, but that probably won't happen. But I don't really care about that. The book is having wonderful success, more than I ever hoped it would."

The movie contract had not come through yet, but *The Gospel Singer* was continuing to pay dividends. In March, Morrow sold the paperback rights to the book to Dell for $10,000 plus royalties, a very good contract for a first-time author. Harry would receive half of the advance, a nice check to help pay for his impending move to Gainesville. *The Gospel Singer*, Landis wrote, had just the right amount of titillation to appeal to the paperback market: "It is a somewhat rare thing, a book not at all obscure on the surface, a rather violent and sexy book, and yet obviously a work of real literary distinction. Dell will be proud to publish it and won't hesitate for a moment to wrap it in a rather suggestive cover (which will probably make both of us laugh); so it's good on both sides for them." Indeed, the book from Dell appeared the following February, with a cover featuring a drawing worthy of any paperback romance bodice ripper: a shirtless lothario staring into the distance, defined abdominal and pectoral muscles glistening, with one scantily clad girl staring up at him from her knees, and another topless sexpot adoring him from behind. "A Torrid Novel by Harry Crews," read the subtitle. Undoubtedly, many of those purchasing *The Gospel Singer* in the grocery store expecting a romantic sex romp were surprised to find themselves reading about a midget with a giant foot and a geek who ate live chickens.

As summer approached, Harry and Sally began planning their move back to Gainesville. Lytle, whose support had helped Harry secure his job at UF, wrote with congratulations: "I'm awfully glad you're going to Florida next fall. They're glad to get you and they better be." He had closely followed the reviews of *The Gospel Singer* (a blurb from Lytle appeared in advertisements for the book) and acknowledged the praise, while holding firm to his earlier criticism. "The flaw is real, but the book is real, too, in spite of it," he wrote. "Don't look askance at the gifts of this world; just don't be taken in by them."

Before he settled in North Florida, however, Harry would reap another benefit from *The Gospel Singer*. Landis had recommended him for a fellowship to the Bread Loaf Writers' Conference in Vermont. The conference, which had originated during the 1920s, was a two-week session where aspiring writers gathered to learn from and mingle with established writers in a picturesque log-cabin setting in the woods of New England. In

August, just before classes got under way at UF, Harry would be feted by another group of new admirers and introduce himself to more members of the literary glitterati of the day.

The family made one last visit to the beach—so Byron, now five years old, could play in his beloved sand—packed up their belongings, and got on the road to Gainesville. For their new residence, they had found a shaded little complex, the Granada Apartments, which had a swimming pool and was right across the street from an elementary school. Byron would start kindergarten in the fall. Harry was well into his next novel. He unpacked his typewriter, and he and Sally set up yet another home office for him in the cramped space. They had not brought along Harry's desk, so they set up an old door on cement blocks on which he could type. On one of the first nights in the apartment, after they had put Byron to sleep and were settling down for the evening, they heard a sound they had not expected. One of their new neighbors, it seemed, played the organ. The walls at the Granada Apartments were not soundproof, and the melodious sounds of the instrument drifted easily into the Crews apartment. And along with the sound came vibrations that they could feel in their bones. It was a feeling that, over the next few years, they would become extremely familiar with.

CHAPTER THIRTEEN

SECOND TIME AROUND

> The sign said A-GO-GO and that was what she had come to
> do, go-go to the top, to the place where people had contracts,
> security, to the place where nobody was a virgin because
> nobody had any reason to save it.
> —Harry Crews, *Naked in Garden Hills*

The creative writing program at the University of Florida was at low ebb in the fall of 1968. Andrew Lytle was now a distant memory. Smith Kirkpatrick had been running the operation on his own for nearly a decade and had developed an extremely devoted following among the students who found their way into the program. But creative writing was the redheaded stepsister of the English Department, and many of the literature professors viewed it as an embarrassment. Kirkpatrick had weathered the attacks and the threats to dissolve the program. It was still alive and populated with would-be writers. And they still gathered on weekday evenings in Kirkpatrick's office in old Building D, as they had ten years earlier, when Harry had occupied a seat at the table.

The program-wide malaise made the anticipation for Harry's arrival all the more palpable. Faculty members remembered him from his undergraduate days, and students knew him as the rising star whose book had been slathered with praise in all the papers. He was a catch for UF, someone who could add a shot of adrenaline and get the blood pumping through the program once again. To announce his arrival, Kirkpatrick scheduled a reading early in the semester. The halls buzzed for days before the event.

When it arrived, Harry did not disappoint. He defied expectations. He looked unlike any other professor any of the students had seen. His confidence had gone through the roof thanks to his success, which only added to the power of his performance before a crowd. He exuded charisma.

His hair was still closely cropped, and he arrived in Gainesville thin, tan, and sinewy. He usually retained the outward markings of a college professor—tie, jacket, loafers—yet it was in his countenance and style that his dynamism shone through. He had maintained the devotion to weight training that he had developed as a teenager, and it showed, adding to his imposing presence. His face had taken on a new maturity. He had a jutting brow and extremely deep-set blue eyes that could produce a stare of shocking intensity, a stare that he liked to hold for several beats longer than was comfortable for anybody in the room with him. If the stare didn't produce the desired effect, he also had the ability to close one of his eyes and open the other one to absurd proportions, a feat that he used to express both surprise and disgust. All his facial expressions, in fact, were outsized, from his threatening scowl to his wide, toothy grin, both of which he displayed regularly, often within seconds of each other. On that fall night in Gainesville, he paced back and forth in front of the audience, gesticulating wildly as he delivered a dramatic oration of several passages from *The Gospel Singer* and *Naked in Garden Hills*. By the end of the evening, which concluded much later at a local bar, many of the assembled crowd were ready to grab a pen that moment and sign up to study under the university's newest attraction.

Ward Scott was a student of Kirkpatrick's who also coached football at Gainesville High School. He met Harry that fall, and the two developed a quick friendship thanks to football and weightlifting. Scott shared Harry's intensity and love of the gym. He regaled Harry with stories from the football field, and soon, on Harry's advice, Scott was working on a novel about those experiences. At the time, Harry was finishing up the next novel he planned to send to Landis, titled *This Thing Don't Lead to Heaven*, about the inhabitants of a nursing home in Georgia. The two decided to see if the communal experience they shared in the weightlifting room could transfer to their writing. They would find a spot in Building D and engage in dueling typewriters, both pecking away at their novels simultaneously. The building still lacked air-conditioning, and one afternoon the heat was unbearable. They stripped down to their underwear, wet some towels at the drinking fountain, wrapped them around their heads, and went right on typing. Harry, of course, was difficult to keep up with. "It was just so fucking hot, and I tried and tried, but I just couldn't keep my typewriter going as fast as his," Scott said.

Though he was beginning to develop a persona that set him apart from his colleagues, Harry had not adopted the late 1960s attitude or appearance. Early during his tenure at the University of Florida, he still wore a coat and tie to faculty meetings and into the classroom. When he did try to partake in the fashion of the times, he wasn't always successful—one friend remembered that when the bell-bottom pants which covered one's shoes were popular, Harry bought a pair that stopped six inches above the floor. He drank socially but had never touched marijuana or the other easily available hard drugs. And he was unsure of how his work would sit with the general public. Shortly after arriving in Gainesville, he and Sally went house hunting with a real estate agent who also happened to be the mother of one of his students.

"I understand you are a writer," the agent said.

"Yes, ma'am."

"Well, I am an avid reader," she said. "One of my sons says he wants to be a writer."

"That's neat," Harry said.

"I think I will read one of your books," the agent continued.

"Well, OK," Harry said tentatively. "They're really raunchy."

He knew he didn't quite fit in with the professor crowd and liked to use his outsider status for effect. One afternoon at the end of a semester, professors were arriving in groups at an office in Anderson Hall to turn in their grades. A few older faculty members were standing around chatting in one group, some younger professors in another, when Harry walked in.

"I just had a student tell me they would fuck me if I would give them an A," he announced.

He waited a few seconds for the shock to sink in.

"Can you believe that? HE wants to fuck me!" The story drew a big laugh, but from only a portion of the room.

Harry still felt like an apprentice to Kirkpatrick and, at the beginning of his UF career, operated as if he was still one of Kirkpatrick's students. Around that time, Kirkpatrick had purchased a new home in Gainesville. The house had been vacant for several months, and the pool was filled with stagnant, murky water that was crawling with frogs. Kirkpatrick asked Harry and Scott to come over and help clean up the pool. Upon examining the situation, they decided the best course of action was to fill it with chlorine, wait for the frogs to die, and then return and remove the corpses.

They returned a few days later, and, sure enough, all the frogs were dead. Their next move, they decided, was to form a bucket brigade. Somebody would dip the bucket into the slime, pull out a load of frogs, hand it up out of the pool, and it would be taken down and dumped in Hogtown Creek, which bordered the property. The group was getting ready to draw straws to see who had to climb into the sludge and extract the dead frogs. The straws, it turned out, weren't necessary. "Old Harry says, 'Hell, I'm a Georgia boy! Gimme that bucket, I'll get down in there!'" Ward remembered. "And he just rolls his damn pant legs up and goes right down into that damn slop, and starts going to town."

The brigade was running smoothly, and dead frogs were filling up the pond, when Scott heard Harry shouting from in the pool. Ward ran back into the yard and looked down at Harry in the deep end. "We came over there and he was standing in there, bent over, looking at a huge frog that hadn't died. He said, 'That son-of-a-bitch got big on the poison!' I couldn't believe it, it was too good. I said to him, 'Harry, you're looking at yourself.'"

The excitement surrounding Harry was only amplified by the run-up to the publication of his second novel. *Naked in Garden Hills* was in the galley stage and set to be published in the spring of 1969. The book featured even more bizarre and memorable characters than *The Gospel Singer*. The pseudo-protagonist of the story was Mayhugh Aaron, aka the Fat Man, a five-hundred-pound bookworm who drinks case after case of diet milkshakes and governs a dormant phosphate mine from a mansion overlooking the mining village. His driver and manservant is a four-foot, ninety-pound failed jockey named Jester, the book's representative midget, scarred by an incident in which the horse he was riding committed suicide. And the femme fatale of the story is the beautiful, virginal Dolly, who has left the mine to be a go-go dancer in New York City, only to return with the idea of seducing the Fat Man and turning the mine into a roadside dancing attraction.

Since he had first seen the manuscript, Landis had believed it to be better than *The Gospel Singer*, and now that he'd seen the positive reaction to the first book, he thought he had a masterpiece on his hands with the follow-up. The first outside reactions confirmed his suspicions. He sent the galleys to Jean Stafford, the Pulitzer Prize–winning fiction writer of much renown. The response from Stafford went well beyond a few complimentary sentences. She wrote to Landis to say that she had read the novel twice and was overwhelmed, and had not seen a work this exceptional in many years. Instead of providing a blurb for the book cover, she said she would review it upon publication. Landis sent the galleys to Harper Lee, also the recipient of a Pulitzer for *To Kill a Mockingbird*. Again, praise bordering on hyperbole. William Faulkner, Lee told Landis, has come back to life.

With writers of the magnitude of Stafford and Lee throwing around accolades and even invoking the name Faulkner, Harry felt certain he now had a book that could do the one thing he most wanted to accomplish with his writing: to please Mr. Lytle. He had Landis send the galleys to his mentor at *The Sewanee Review* and waited for the ultimate confirmation. Instead, he received the opposite, and worse. *Naked in Garden Hills*, though a work of technical quality, was less successful than his first book, and the consistency of the errors in the two novels had revealed a flaw in Harry's character, Lytle felt. "I will tell you what you have to think about," Lytle wrote. "The first novel ended in a lot of noise and violence; this one in a kind of moral despair and violence. The reason you can't end your fiction right is you have no basic belief in the nature of things, no sense of the divine."

The dichotomy between the outside reactions he was receiving and Lytle's comments hardened in Harry the feeling that he would never be able to please his mentor. Around the same time, Lytle visited Gainesville on Kirkpatrick's invitation. During his visit, Kirkpatrick invited Harry and Scott over for drinks and to spend some time with the master. The group went into the backyard, and as they sat at the table and sipped their whiskey, the conversation turned to Harry's writing. Lytle reiterated his criticisms and told Harry that he was writing too fast. You're just skimming the surface, he said. You've got to slow down and give your work meaning. While Lytle was speaking, Harry got up from the table and began pulling up grass from the yard, putting pieces of grass in his mouth and violently chewing on it. "I don't know how to give it meaning!" he blurted. "I don't know how!"

Harry was visibly hurt by the criticism, Scott remembered. "The only person he ever wanted to please was Mr. Lytle. He felt like he never got any of Lytle's approval." After Lytle went back to Tennessee, he continued to voice his concerns in his correspondence, deliberately spelling out the heart of his philosophy of writing, and where Harry was violating it:

> It may be you need to slow down at times your pace of writing. You may need to lie fallow a while, a hard thing to do, and let your unconscious, where it all is, work out things you can't do with the conscious mind. I say this, because I don't think you've ended those first two books. An end ought to bring everything together, purge the reader, as well as the author, of everything, so that we can feel clean and elated. The ending should fall off the tree like a ripe pear.

The disagreements over *Naked in Garden Hills* led Harry to believe that Lytle could not, and never would, be pleased. The two were programmed differently, Harry decided, and that would never change. Harry reflected on the differences many years later: "[Lytle] liked to sort of work on his books, and then he would quit whatever he was writing, and then he would . . . chew on it, and mull on it, and walk around the block on it. Well, I never walked around any blocks. And I never chewed, or mulled. I wanted the motherfucking thing finished and out of my house, and a contract, and some money, and on to the next thing." He would go his entire career without dedicating a book to Lytle, because, he said, he didn't think he ever wrote something that Lytle would want to have his name on. And after *Naked in Garden Hills*, he ceased the practice of sending his mentor manuscripts prior to publication.

The new novel appeared on the shelves of bookstores in early April 1969. The reviews mirrored the advance reaction Harry had received. They were far more celebratory than the notices he had received after *The Gospel Singer*. The first time around, most reviewers saw a debut effort that showed promise. The unasked question was: Is he for real? Now, Harry had bettered his first effort, and most reviewers were ready to crown him as the new voice in American fiction. Faulkner's name came up repeatedly, and he was joined by many of the other names from the Southern Lit Hall of Fame: O'Connor, Welty, McCullers. "A fine and furious morality play of a plot, full of suspense, imagination, surprise and delight," raved the *Los Angeles Times*. "'Naked in Garden Hills' lives up and beyond the shining promise of Mr. Crews' first novel," opined Stafford in the *New York Times*. The praise was overwhelming, and Harry reveled in it. But the reviewers had also, in almost every instance, categorized him as a southern writer, a label he did not like and would try to climb out from under for the rest of his life. Regardless, the passionate critical support of *Naked in Garden Hills,* along with the complicated plot structure, would lead Harry to call it the work he was most proud of for years to come.

Sally continued to slip into Harry's office occasionally and read bits and pieces of his latest work. One evening in the spring of 1969, Harry was at the typewriter, and Sally picked up a chapter, sat down, and began reading. After a few sentences, she looked up. "Harry," she asked, "you don't intend to make a career out of midgets, do you?"

Indeed, though Harry claimed he hadn't realized it at the time, she had a point. Third novel; third midget. Though he didn't want to be typecast as a writer of southern gothic fiction, he was now into another novel full of eccentric southern characters, another one populated with freaks. A question about "freaks" was now an essential part of any discussion of Harry's work. He eschewed the psychological analysis that said the freaks appeared because Harry saw a freak in himself. No, he said, it wasn't just him. It was everybody, every last one of us. Those of us without deformities are just able to hide our inner freakishness. "If you have a withered arm or a badly deformed back, or if you're a midget, all the facades that people maintain in their lives to keep people from knowing who they are and what they're doing, don't work for you," he said.

The manuscript of *This Thing Don't Lead to Heaven* arrived in Landis's office in New York in March. Within days of its arrival, Cochran had sold the book to Morrow. Publication was set for the following year. Landis, once again, thought he was holding in his hands a masterwork. "I have to say that this book is deeply satisfying, in a sense, perhaps perfect; that is, a perfect reflection of your aims, the consummate expression of your art at this time," he wrote to Harry. However, the book was similar in structure and tone to *Naked in Garden Hills*, and Landis hinted that the latest book was the last of a trilogy, and Harry's future work might (*read:* should) veer off in a new and exciting direction. The comment put Harry somewhat on the defensive, and he responded in kind. Landis backtracked a bit a few weeks later: "You have achieved something of the ultimate in this book, something so perfect it could not be surpassed," he wrote. "I don't mean for you to change anything at all, I'm only trying to tell you to have the courage to move on; and you've suffered enough in your writing, I think, to know just what sort of courage it takes." Both, it seemed, agreed that they had reached a turning point in Harry's work; where it would lead, neither was sure.

A year later, when *This Thing Don't Lead to Heaven* reached the shelves, the plan for a change of direction would get a strong confirmation that neither Harry nor Landis would expect or appreciate.

CHAPTER FOURTEEN

A NEW FORM OF COMBAT

> Belief has nothing to do with true or false. Never has. Never will.
> —Harry Crews, *Karate Is a Thing of the Spirit*

Harry and Sally headed up to Vermont in the late summer of 1969 to take part in another Bread Loaf Writers' Conference. About two hundred miles directly south, in Bethel, New York, another gathering was soon to be under way. The Woodstock Music & Art Fair would draw the Rolling Stones, the Grateful Dead, Jimi Hendrix, and four hundred thousand flower-powered hippies to a dairy farm. The resulting cornucopia of nudity, hallucination, and rock 'n' roll would come to symbolize the peak of the 1960s counterculture movement. At Bread Loaf, however, the vibe was slightly different. John Ciardi, the famed poet and esteemed contributor to the *Saturday Review*, ran the conference in those days. The writers would gather together for a meal, and when everybody had finished, Ciardi would gently tap his wine glass and say to the group: "Join together, everybody. The witch of fungi will lead a mushroom walk at three p.m." Those interested would then comb the woods in search of wild mushrooms, the nonhallucinogenic kind.

The conference was still a staid, traditional operation, and the energy and intensity Harry brought to it quickly made him a star in yet another venue. "He took over," remembered Landis. "He became a wild man up there. Pretty soon, everyone was leaving there with Harry Crews stories."

The novelist Dan Wakefield became one of Harry's first friends at Bread Loaf. They formed a pseudo drinking club called the Good Guys along with the poet Maxine Kumin, the writer Brock Bauer, and a few other faculty members. "He was the wildest, most entertaining guy at Bread Loaf, and that's saying a lot," recalled Wakefield. The group had formed associations the previous summer, so upon arrival they began drinking, always a top priority for the faculty, and getting reacquainted. As everybody was exchanging greetings, Wakefield stood nearby and listened as Harry spoke with Ciardi. "Harry was talking to him, and I was listening in. And Harry was sort of buttering him up. He was saying, 'Oh, Mr. Ciardi, this is just the greatest place. I really love your work.' And Ciardi's just beaming and thanking him. And Ciardi walks away, and Harry looks at me and says, 'Can't say I don't know how to kowtow!'"

The writers came from varied backgrounds, but not many came from the South. The majority came from the Northeast, and some of the older faculty members had been coming for years. Some of the veterans maintained a dignified air that Harry and the younger writers reveled in puncturing. On the first or second evening, he was part of a group conversation with Avis DeVoto, the widow of historian Bernard DeVoto and a writer of some repute herself. Harry decided to loosen the mood.

"What we ought to do here sometime is work out all our old frustrations and hostilities and all that," he said. "What we need to do is have a Mazola party."

DeVoto took the bait. "What's a Mazola party?" she asked.

"Well," Harry replied, with a wide grin, "you get a room that has tile floor, preferably, and you get about thirteen men and twelve women, or thirteen women and twelve men, and everybody takes their clothes off. And then everybody just pours Mazola oil all over themselves, just rubs it all around. And then you just rub and hug and slither around there with everybody's bodies, and I'm telling you, it just gets out all those old frustrations and fears. And you come out feeling great."

DeVoto looked at Harry, stunned, until laughter finally broke up the silence.

"In Middlebury, Vermont," Wakefield remembered, "that was not the kind of thing this bunch of straight-laced Bostonians heard very often."

The Good Guys often took it upon themselves to take the literary stiffness out of the occasion. One evening, the famed poet Anthony Hecht was giving a very formal reading. There was a raised stage behind the podium from which he was speaking. Near the end of the presentation, Harry, Kumin, and Wakefield appeared behind him. They had donned togas and put wreaths of flowers in their hair and began to pantomime regal dance moves. The crowd began howling with laughter, and Hecht could only smile as the formality drained out of the room.

Kumin remembered Harry as "wild and flamboyant." They became close friends, and Kumin would later come to speak several times at the University of Florida at Harry's invitation. "There were always drinks with dinner, and then there would be a lot of drinking after dinner. It was a very wet place," she said. After one night of drinking, Harry accidentally ended up in Kumin's room. "I opened the door, and he leapt out of bed and said, 'Jesus Christ, Max! I didn't expect to see you here.'"

Harry's entertainment value did not stop with the faculty. He was a favorite of the scholars, as the paying students were referred to, as well. Each faculty member would have one night where they would give a lecture to the entire conference. "That was your time to shine and be a hero and all that," said Wakefield. "And Harry gave his on Flannery O'Connor. And I've got to tell you, I've never heard a better literary lecture about a literary figure than I heard him give that night. I mean, he was incredibly passionate about it. He was like a preacher. He had worn some very amazing outfit, a sort of ruffled shirt and cuffs and all this stuff. He was all dressed up. And I remember him saying, over and over, 'You cannot dismiss Miss O'Connor! You cannot dismiss Miss O'Connor!' And people were just completely enrapt."

Bread Loaf in the late 1960s was still a very undemocratic place. The faculty and the fellows dined together and had their own separate living space; the scholars were, for the most part, kept separate. They would look longingly across the path to the building where the writers gathered and hope for an invitation. Occasionally, lucky students would get an invite to join the faculty, an initiation rite each hoped to receive at some point during the conference. Most of the scholars were college age, but Hilma Wolitzer was a stay-at-home mom who dabbled in fiction, writing about issues in her own life. She'd recently had a short story, titled "Today, A Woman Went Mad in the Supermarket," published in the *Saturday Evening Post* after a friend showed it to an agent, and now she had a scholarship to Bread Loaf. Each scholar would be assigned a faculty member as a mentor. Wolitzer's first mentor turned her off by singing the praises of Erich Segal, who was on the best-seller list that summer with *Love Story*. So, as a replacement mentor, she got Harry.

"Harry was just so accessible," Wolitzer remembered. "You know, you had such a feeling of hierarchy that I thought you couldn't really approach faculty members. But Harry just sat down on a step with me and talked about life in general." Despite their differences in background, Harry opened up about his own life, discussing the loss of his son, and Hilma told him about the pressures in the life of a suburban New York housewife. While many of the faculty members glossed over student writing, Harry offered Wolitzer in-depth critiques of her work in progress and, after the conference, read two entire novels of hers, offering blunt criticisms along with praise. "I never, ever lie or bullshit about fiction," Harry told her. "Even though I think of you as a dear friend, I would say what I think is true even if the truth was something awful. Fortunately, there's nothing awful about your work."

Harry liked to cross the line of demarcation to eat with the students. He would lay on his southern humor to lighten the mood. There were usually loose dogs roaming the grounds, and at one such lunch a female student became frightened when one mutt barked at her menacingly. The girl jumped up onto a picnic table in fear. Harry came over to rescue her but stopped in front of the table and began speaking to the dog. "Well, now you've treed her, boy," he said. "What are you gonna do with her?"

Harry would spend three more summers at Bread Loaf, the final one coming in 1973. Connections he made there would last for many years. He would invite several Bread Loaf writers to Florida to teach or read at conferences. He became extremely close with Ciardi, eventually dedicating a novel to him. After the trip north in 1969, he wrote to Lytle and told him of his exploits. Lytle was pleased. "It was pleasant to know that you made such a hit at Bread Loaf," Lytle wrote. "It's not wise to talk too much about what you are doing at a given moment, but it is good to talk around it and bring up what artists are interested in, certainly when you are young." Lytle's wish for Harry from just a few years before, that he remove himself from literary isolation, was now being fulfilled each August, as he not only interacted with his peers but sent home a generation of Bread Loaf scholars with stories that would be told for years to come.

Though he'd been a published author for just a little over a year, Harry now was part of the club, and he knew it. He was still riding high from the critical reaction to *Naked in Garden Hills*. He allowed himself to feel pride in what he'd accomplished, not just with that book, but with his life. Those who did not understand the blood he'd shed to reach this point could get on his bad side quickly. Amateurs who wanted Harry to write their novel for them fell into that category. In response to one such request, Harry laid out what would be his stock response to those who didn't understand the sacrifices a writer must put forth:

> I can tell by the things you say in your letter that you don't know the first iota about what makes fiction work. Try not to be discouraged by this letter. You wouldn't be discouraged if somebody told you you were not a brain surgeon, would you? Or a Stock Market Analyst? Well, writing fiction is just as complicated and hard to learn as juggling stocks or taking out somebody's brain.
>
> For the past fifteen years I have devoted all of my waking moments and all of my energies to becoming a writer. Why in the name of all that is holy would I take a year or two out of my life and write your novel? Novels are not made from ideas. They are made from a hundred thousand words put together in such a way that they make a reality that sucks the reader out of his skin.
>
> I know you are going to think I'm just being a bad guy sending you a letter like this. But believe me, I've got better things to do than to spend my time giving another human being a hard time. But unless you want to take a couple of decades and learn to write fiction (assuming you could, not everybody can), my advice is to throw your five hours of tapes in the sea and relax and enjoy whatever time God sees fit to allow you.

To those he respected, however, he was often extremely deferential. A reviewer for *Life* had been one of the many to compare Harry to Faulkner. Harry expressed his appreciation in a letter a few months after the review was published: "When I first saw your review, I wanted to write you a letter. As a matter of fact, I did . . . four of them. But I always ended by tearing them up. Whatever I wrote to you seemed gauche and strained. So I decided to wait and hope that something sensible would occur to me to say to you. I am indebted to you for the review."

Whether because of deference to his editor's gentle admonitions or due to his own self-determination, Harry had begun work on a novel that was quite different. Since his arrival in Gainesville, he and Sally had taken up the study of karate, the Japanese martial art. Harry had come across a karate demonstration in a supermarket and was immediately intrigued. The sport had begun to generate great interest in the United States in the 1960s. By 1961, it was being taught in more than fifty schools to over fifty thousand devotees. Harry and Sally took classes with a young teacher named Dirk Mosig, a graduate student in psychology who also happened to be a fourth-degree black belt in Okinawan karate and kobudo who competed internationally in the sport. Mosig viewed karate as a way of thinking more than an athletic endeavor and taught his classes that way. Harry threw himself into the pursuit and brought Sally along with him.

The classes could be intense. Mosig had unique training methods. One evening, he came to class with a cage filled with tarantulas. The students were broken into pairs and told that the winner of each fight would be given the privilege of eating a tarantula. Sally won her contest but, despite Harry's urging, turned down the "privilege" of ingesting the spider.

Sally turned out to have more talent for the sport than her husband. Both showed promise, however, and Mosig encouraged them to enter the Florida Open Karate Tournament, which was to be held at Gainesville High School. At the competition, Sally advanced all the way to the final round in her division. In the finals, she fought a girl ranked two belts above her and still managed to lose by only a single point. But the level of intensity was too much for her. "The competitors, they were just fierce," she recalled. "I remember the girl I fought was on another level. We were taught certain techniques where you would strike, but you weren't going to hurt anybody. But some of these people, they were out to hurt you. It was just a different atmosphere than in our class."

Harry won a few matches as well, but after the contest, it was Sally who had impressed their teacher. He urged Sally to travel with him to the national competition in Kansas City, which was scheduled for a few months later. But one karate competition was enough; Sally had decided she was through. She had joined to spend more time with Harry, not to be kicked and punched in front of a cheering crowd. "To see the kind of people who were there and how gung-ho they were, you knew they were gonna take it to the end. And I thought, 'I don't want to get hurt because I'm a mother and a wife,'" she said.

Done in by "awkward feet," Harry didn't have much chance at nationals. But something about the ethic of the sport, how the practitioners were expected to submit to the ways of karate utterly and completely, appealed to him. He began to see literary possibilities, and before long the outline of his next novel began to form in his head. The story would take place in Fort Lauderdale, where he had lived for six years but not yet used as a backdrop for one of his books. And the story would revolve around a character from *This Thing Don't Lead to Heaven*, Jefferson Davis Munroe, that book's resident midget (now Harry's record would move to four for four on midget usage). As with the phosphate mine or the nursing home in his two previous books, karate seemed a useful metaphor around which Harry could examine a larger theme. Karate was "self-justifying madness," and his characters, afloat in a godless world, would latch onto the practice as a way to attach meaning to the hollow existence that was modern life. Landis had expressed excitement about the possibility of a karate novel, so Harry set to work very shortly after he sent *This Thing Don't Lead to Heaven* to New York.

Landis and Harry prepared for their next book launch with confidence and anticipation. Advance reviews had been positive once again. With Sally's support, Harry had dedicated the novel to their fallen son, Patrick. Landis had called it a perfect book, and Harry felt it was his best work to date. Lytle and Kirkpatrick had not been given the manuscript in advance this go-round, so Harry moved toward publication, for the first time, with no negativity in the air whatsoever.

The negativity, this time, came after publication, and it was out there for everybody to see. The reviews, when all were added up, could be characterized as "mixed," but those who didn't like the book savaged it. No punches were pulled, and several haymakers were landed. In the *New York Times*, James Boatwright wrote, "It's a preposterous novel, but something's more seriously wrong. The offensive element is an all-too-common one: the irresponsible establishment of distance between the narrator and his subjects, a willed distance that allows the cheapest kind of god-playing, the setting up of these quaint, oddly named characters who frenziedly work out the destiny invented for them by their none-too-clever puppeteer." James Martin, writing for the *Los Angeles Times*, hated it even more: "Not only does this third novel fail to fulfill the promise of the earlier two; it ultimately betrays Crews' limitations as a storyteller and a perceptive critic of human nature." The general consensus seemed to be that Harry had gone back to the well once too often; now, to many of the professional critics, it was apparent that Harry had only one trick, and it had already become tiresome.

Both Landis and Harry were shocked by the reaction. Landis, though he had, upon reading the manuscript, felt it to be slightly derivative, still thought it a powerful, effective novel. He was somewhat dismissive of the criticism. "I'm sorry you have to be subjected to such stupidity, but there it is," he wrote to Harry.

Harry took it much worse, and his response was much less measured. He dashed a note to a friend about a particularly bad review in the *Atlanta Constitution:* "If you know or ever see the motherfucker who wrote the review of HEAVEN in the CONSTITUTION, tell him I said he was not only a motherfucker but a stupid motherfucker. That he wrote a bad review of the book couldn't mean less to me, but that he wrote badly about the book does."

Despite the defiance, he was shaken by the response to the book, and, for the first time since the acceptance of *The Gospel Singer,* he felt the nagging ache of insecurity. Because of the intensity of the reaction, he had difficulty not being convinced that he had indeed failed with the novel. He wrote to Henry Van Dyke, another friend made in Vermont, shortly after the reviews began appearing. "The HEAVEN book has had its problems. Maybe I blew it there. I don't, at this moment, think I did. But maybe so. A lot of people have said some very fine things about it. But a lot of people have thrown buckets of shit at it too."

For years after the critical reaction, Harry would think, and speak, of *Heaven* as a failure and deem it his worst book. The Boatwright review, in particular, stuck with him and became a signpost for Harry's overall strategy for how he dealt with book reviewing. "[Boatwright] was not just unhappy with the book," he said years later. "He was unhappy I was alive. About halfway through the review, it just switched from the book to me. I just believed the guy."

Once the initial shock had worn off, however, receiving such a lambasting from the editor of the *Shenandoah Review,* one of the most prestigious of publications, girded Harry to future reviewing shrapnel. He later changed his views on his own book and would eventually claim that he did not look at the critical response to his work. But for now, it was a shot to his confidence. He responded as he had when he faced all those rejections back in his Fort Lauderdale home office. "The only defense against all that sort of thing is work," he wrote to Van Dyke, and he plowed into his next project.

Prior to the release of *Heaven,* Harry had made another decision in relation to his career that would have long-term consequences. He had become disenchanted with his agent, Bert Cochran. The source of his disenchantment was his own editor. Over the course of the previous year, Landis had expressed his feelings about Harry's representation. Cochran was with a minor agency, and not very well known among the writers and agents on Landis's lunch list. One firm that did happen to be on the Morrow lunch circuit was the Paul Revere Reynolds agency. The agency had been founded in 1893 and was now under the control of the son of the original founder, Paul Reynolds. Over the years, the agency had represented Stephen Crane, George Bernard Shaw, Joseph Conrad, and, more recently, Alex Haley, Richard Wright, and Malcolm X.

Morrow did a lot of business with Reynolds's clients. John Willey, Landis's boss, approached him one day with an idea. It seemed that Paul Reynolds's daughter had married a man named John Hawkins, who was around the same age as Landis. Wouldn't it be a nice idea if Landis and his wife went out to dinner with Paul Reynolds's daughter and new son-in-law? Landis got the hint, and soon the two couples were social friends. Hawkins had degrees from Harvard and Penn and was a sharp intellect who proved to be good company. It wasn't long before it occurred to Landis that Harry, one of his top clients, was a great prospect to add to Hawkins's client list.

The decision was made, and Harry wrote a two-paragraph letter to Cochran. Harry, the letter said, was joining another agency. No reason was given. "I do appreciate all you have done for me," it concluded.

Cochran had been blindsided. He fired back with anger and threats. "In the light of all the work I have done from the first when you had a manuscript languishing at Universal, and the successes achieved, it seems to me that common decency demanded that you discuss with me any problem you thought existed, so that we could effect a solution."

The threat raised Harry's ire, and he ratcheted up the rhetoric. "I invite you to sue me anytime you like," he wrote. "I feel compelled to remind you that it has taken me twenty years of writing to get where I am. When we talk about these books, we are talking about my blood and guts."

The details remained to be hashed out, but the split was final. Landis consoled Harry through the breakup. "Please don't worry about Cochran," he wrote. "No doubt he's upset, but he's earned it with what has to be termed his incompetence, but more than that his inconsideration." No matter how nervous he was over the legal wrangling, the switch would be an enormous benefit to Harry's career, Landis told him. Harry was now a client of John Hawkins, and would be for the rest of his life. By the end of the month, Hawkins had reached an agreement with Morrow to publish Harry's next book, before the manuscript was even completed.

The smoke had cleared. Landis was pleased that his prized client was now in the capable hands of his new friend. The arrangement moved along swimmingly at first for Landis and all involved. A few years down the road, however, the agent-swap he had helped engineer would seem less like the brilliant move it initially appeared to be.

CHAPTER FIFTEEN BERKELEY OF THE SOUTH

> To believe what's here, you've got to disbelieve the rest
> of the world.
> —Gaye Nell Odell in *Karate Is a Thing of the Spirit*

College campuses in the early 1970s were the epicenter of conflict and culture in America. The Vietnam War and the military draft were still in full flourish, filling the average male college student with ample supplies of fear and rage. A large swath of the country had turned violently antiwar, which most believers took to also mean antigovernment, leading ultimately to anti-authority-of-any-kind. In May 1970 the Kent State shootings had sent a charge into the campus movement. A student-led antiwar demonstration, of the type that was occurring across the country daily, had ended with four young demonstrators dead at the hands of the Ohio National Guard. Now the tension was elevated for students and college administrators alike, as both sides waited impatiently for the next outburst.

It might not have been Berkeley, but the clash of generations was alive and well at the University of Florida. Demonstrations were commonplace; administrative threats to student activity were equally prevalent. In the fall of 1970, a UF doctoral student and instructor named Robert Canney made the mistake of using the word "goddamn" while rabbling the crowd at an antiwar event. He was arrested, charged with obscenity, and soon given his walking papers by the university. "They chose me as a scapegoat because

I spoke out against the war and tied it in with the whole Black Liberation Struggle," Canney protested.

A week earlier, the campus Reserve Officers' Training Corps building had been bombed by students, though it was done so ineptly that no actual damage was done to the structure. UF's administration walked the tight-rope, threatening to crack down on demonstrations that went beyond the bounds of the law while offering draft counseling services to its panicky student body. The tension would eventually boil over in 1972, with three days of violent clashes between students and police that led to 369 student arrests, a good portion of them sporting billy-club bruises.

Culturally, Gainesville, like most college towns during the crest of the Hell-No-We-Won't-Go era, was hippie from head to toe. Long hair, beads, and bell-bottoms were the uniform on campus, and a psychedelic mush-room potion was the drink of choice. Recreational drugs of all types were readily available; they were part of the anti-establishment package. In fact, in Gainesville, you didn't even have to go looking for drugs—they would find you. According to the *Florida Alligator*, the university's newspaper, on a walk down University Avenue, which ran along the north border of the campus, one might be offered Kentucky grass, acid, speed, or psilocybin. A graduate student told the newspaper on average he received unsolicited offers for illegal drugs at least once a day. And Gainesville itself developed a national reputation for marijuana production. Gainesville Green was a recognized brand name for a potent strain of pot grown in town. On the north side of University Avenue, in the student ghetto, was a small complex of houses known as Fort Ganga, where those interested in buying a bag of Gainesville Green knew it was available around the clock.

The creative writing program was a small, tight-knit group that was in some ways insulated from the university as a whole, and in other ways a microcosm of those larger trends. The classes still met in Building D on weekday nights. After the extended, intense sessions where the students would bare their souls for their peers to critique, many of the students would head over to the Winnjammer, a downtown restaurant that became the bar of choice for the writing program. The drinking and conversation would continue late into the night. Drugs were usually available for those who were interested, and, usually, everybody was.

As Harry would hold court during those late-night sessions, more often than not he was flanked by a younger but no less able storyteller named

Johnny Feiber. Feiber, who had become one of Harry's closest friends in short order, had a life story that read like a Bruce Springsteen song. Born into one of the founding families of Gainesville, he was a football star at Gainesville High School and went on to a standout career as a running back at the University of Florida, taking handoffs from Steve Spurrier for two seasons in the mid-1960s before an ankle injury ended his playing days. The U.S. Army thought his ankle was just fine, however, and he was sent to Vietnam, where he led troops on patrol for the Fourth Infantry Division from June 1968 to June 1969. He came back to the states physically uninjured but emotionally damaged, grew his hair long, and tried to keep his head down while the antiwar movement swirled around him.

Vietnam veterans with long hair and an attitude weren't very popular in the early 1970s with those doing the hiring in Gainesville. Feiber had a journalism degree from UF, but the *Gainesville Sun* politely turned him away, as did all the other employers he tried. By chance of luck, he ran into his old high school principal on the street one day and fell into a job teaching high school English. His mother had instilled in him a love of literature as a child. She was a voracious reader who would lie in bed with young Johnny and read him pages of the literary fiction she favored. She gave him Eudora Welty's *Powerhouse* when he was thirteen. Teaching high school reignited his passion for literature. He had studied with Kirk as an undergraduate at UF, and through Kirk he met Harry, began pursuing a master's degree, and ended up spending many of his nights at the Winnjammer.

Feiber often took on the role of Harry's sidekick and coconspirator. He was "gorgeous and southern and funny" and would go back and forth with Harry telling tales and entertaining the bar crowd, remembered Marie Speed, another of Harry's students at the time. "Harry ADORED him, and I think he wanted to be him."

The two inspired a level of hero worship among their followers, especially the men. Testosterone was in the air. Many wanted to prove their toughness to their leader. "It was this group of men, and some of them were woefully untalented," Speed said. "They just wanted to be writers, but they couldn't write their way out of a paper bag. They really believed that you had to suffer, and you had to drink and that whole thing—a real writer has been through hell and back. I'm not saying that some of that isn't true, but that was the mandate."

When Harry had arrived, Kirkpatrick was the unquestioned leader, and early on Harry had accepted secondary status. But that did not last long. Quickly, Harry's presence, and soon Harry himself, began to challenge Kirkpatrick's authority. The two had opposite personalities: Kirkpatrick was quiet and unassuming; students who bought into his message, that dedication to craft must be placed above all else, became deeply devoted to him. Harry was all charisma and show. Many young male wannabe writers didn't just want to learn from him, they wanted to be him. Harry had been declared the next Faulkner; Kirkpatrick still had yet to publish his first novel. Inevitably, Harry's following grew at the expense of Kirkpatrick's, and Harry began to overshadow his mentor.

With Harry proving to be a dynamic presence in the classroom, his superiors in the department decided early on to make use of his talents and his celebrity. He could play a big room, too. Marilyn Moriarity came to the University of Florida in the early 1970s and remembers her first encounter with Harry as part of the Humanities Series, a large lecture in which professors with different specialties would teach in a rotation to students from all disciplines. Harry was the professor chosen to discuss literature.

"I was this really shy undergraduate and I always sat at the back of the auditorium," Moriarity remembered. "And I always knew where the door was because I always tried to get out early. We'd had a few professors already, and this next guy appears, pacing back and forth. He had on jeans, he had on tennis shoes. I thought he was an assistant and I thought he was going to give us a message or cancel the class or something."

Harry paused at the center of the stage and said: "You don't have to make my job any easier, but I would appreciate it if you would come down here and sit and then I won't have to shout."

"It was shocking," Moriarity said. "Professors didn't speak like that in my experience. I'm the kind, I would have left, but he didn't even say y'all, he said you. So I knew I couldn't run away. So I went to the front."

"Then he started lecturing, still pacing back and forth, and he had this book. And he held this book up and he said, 'There are some people who when they see a word on a page, act like the word is the thing. So if they saw the word "shit" on the page, they would act like it was an actual piece of shit and they would say *ewwwww*.' He let that roll off his tongue for what seemed like forever. Then he said, 'But a word isn't a thing; a word is just a word and it can't hurt you." Harry was introducing a favorite story of his, O'Connor's "The Artificial Nigger." It was the kind of parry students rarely heard from English professors, and it was the type of thing that was quickly earning him a reputation across campus.

The advanced writing classes intermingled on campus and at the Winnjammer, students drifting from the orbit of Kirkpatrick to Crews and back again. William Mickelberry studied under both men in the late 1960s and early 1970s, becoming very close with both. Mickelberry grew up in Miami and was married with two kids by the time he entered the UF writing program. Nights at the Winnjammer, he recalled, were as integral to the learning experience at UF as time spent reading or writing. "It was the late sixties, early seventies, so there was a lot of turmoil all the way around and a lot of extracurricular activity," he said. "You know, there was the classroom, but the rest of it was probably more important. Well, I wouldn't say more important but more extensive."

Harry held court, and as the night went on and everybody became more and more inebriated, his minions would often feel the need to prove themselves to him, and to one another. "Harry was an incredible raconteur of the scurrilous kind. There was a lot of competition for that with some of the guys. There was sort of this macho kind of streak through it, certainly from Harry's side. Smith [Kirkpatrick] was not quite so enamored with that," Mickelberry said.

A rift between the two professors developed, gradually at first. Kirkpatrick began to show his disapproval of Harry's teaching style. He felt it was all flash and no substance, and that Harry was more interested in creating acolytes than he was in teaching the craft of writing. Soon, however, Harry's lifestyle became part of the issue. The Winnjammer gatherings on class nights were part of the story, but Harry was a regular at several other bars around town. His favorite was a downtown pub called Lillian's Music Store, but he could also be found regularly at Dub's Steer House, a club north of town that featured topless dancers, the Alibi Lounge, or any one of a number of other local haunts. He had also begun to avail himself of Gainesville's drug menu. Cocaine was now his drug of choice, but Harry was willing to partake in whatever was on hand. More and more, he began to show up late or not at all. Somebody might be dispatched to find him, or Mickelberry or another advanced student might be called on at the last minute to fill in.

Whatever the reason—his newfound fame, the no-rules climate of the times, the cocaine, or the whiskey—Harry's personality was changing. His behavior became increasingly erratic. One night, he was drinking at the bar at Lillian's with Scott. Harry was wearing a sixteen-inch gold necklace with a pendant dangling from it. In the middle of the conversation, he removed the necklace, balled it up, and swallowed it, and chased it with a long gulp from a mug of beer.

"What the fuck did you that for, Harry?" Scott asked incredulously.

"I'll shit in a box for a week and we'll see what happens," Harry said with a grin.

Harry prided himself on being the life of the party. Scott lived in a sixteen-room old house near campus with several roommates and often hosted get-togethers for the writing community. At one such affair, Harry was doing his best to make a dent in the whiskey supply. In the middle of the evening, he went to lean against what he thought was a wall but turned out to be a shower curtain. He fell over backward and, on his way down, grabbed the curtain and pulled it into the tub with him. The commotion riled up Scott's dog. The dog started barking and jumped into the tub on top of Harry, and soon the entire gathering had turned into an audience for Harry's shenanigans. "That was the kind of stuff he was always doing," Scott said. "We laughed our ass off about that. He was that kind of guy, he was funny as shit."

Harry was generous to a fault with his friends and students. He had given Scott the idea of a novel about high school football, and once he had read some of it, he told Scott to send it to Hawkins. Harry followed it up with a letter to Hawkins lauding both Scott and his novel. He made the same gesture to several of his students and friends.

But Scott soon found out that Harry's eccentricities weren't always a barrel of laughs. He was still reading Harry's works in progress and gave him some negative feedback on his karate book. Harry felt Scott was mimicking the criticisms of Kirkpatrick and Lytle, and some animosity developed. It boiled over at a party at Scott's house. Early in the evening, Harry brought up the subject and Scott again said that the novel "had not moved him." Later, Harry confronted Scott in the middle of the living room, surrounded by partygoers.

The situation escalated. Harry tried a karate kick, but Scott, who spent as much or more time in the weight room as Harry did, tried to gain control. "I said, 'Harry, what the fuck are you doing, man?' He said, 'C'mon, motherfucker!' He pushed me and challenged me! So I tackled him, knocked his ass across the fuckin' room. Then I said, 'I'm gonna let you up now, God dammit. Act like you got some sense.'"

After Scott let him up, Harry grabbed and broke a whiskey bottle and hurled it at Scott. He missed badly, so he grabbed a vase off a shelf and tried again. This time, Scott ducked out of the way, and the vase scored a direct hit on the head of another partygoer, one who happened to be a female biology professor. She began to bleed profusely. The wound would require several stitches.

"All hell broke loose," Scott remembered. "Smith was there, and I said, 'Smith, I'm going to get out of here, or one of us is going to kill him, or he's going to kill me, one of the two.'"

Harry remembered a slightly different version of events a few years later. "I threw a vase or something against a wall and it shattered," he told a reporter. "One of the pieces hit [a professor] on the head and cut her scalp and she bled all over the place. It was only a small cut but she really bled. I called them the next morning to apologize but they didn't take it too well. I thought they understood that when you went to *that* kind of party you expect things like that to happen."

Scott left the party, order was restored, and soon the two made amends. But Scott, like others who spent time around Harry, began to keep his distance. "I never turned my back on him again. I mean, I'm not going to hang out with a guy that halfway through the conversation, he's going to get too drunk and want to go outside and fight."

A similar situation around the same time exacerbated the conflict between Harry and Kirkpatrick. At yet another party, this one at Kirkpatrick's home, Harry got into a verbal altercation with Kirkpatrick's wife, and while dozens of partygoers looked on, screamed expletives at her as the two argued in the backyard. Harry was once again calmed, but the incident was another contributing factor in the cooling of their relationship.

A few years after arriving in Gainesville, Harry and Sally had purchased a house that had a backyard which ended at a creek. On the other side of the creek was Kirkpatrick's property. Soon, the two men who ran the University of Florida writing program were barely on speaking terms. The creek between their homes became both the literal and metaphorical line of demarcation between the two.

Though relations within the program were deteriorating, the outside world of Harry Crews was blossoming. Hollywood producers had been interested in Harry's work since *The Gospel Singer* was published. Some of the inquiries led to Harry's first brushes with fame. Elvis Presley, whose name during that era was drawing thousands upon thousands of fans into the casinos of Las Vegas on a nightly basis, had read the novel and envisioned himself in the title role. Colonel Tom Parker, Presley's longtime manager, didn't like the idea, and Presley reluctantly let it drop. But he still thought the book was Hollywood material and passed the idea on to a friend and disciple of his, Tom Jones.

Jones was another prominent Las Vegas act at the time. He was a Welsh-born sex symbol who was at the height of his fame in the late 1960s and early 1970s. He also saw the potential in Harry's book and decided it was his ticket into film production. A meeting was arranged, and Harry took Sally out to Los Angeles to meet the singer and his representatives. The group attended a cocktail party, and Jones was even more smitten with Sally than he had been with the book. Jones managed to get Sally alone and, with all the sex appeal he could muster, began to lay on the Welsh charm. Once Sally understood his intentions, she put a stop to it quickly.

"Are you crazy?" she asked Jones. "If Harry finds out about this, he'll kill you!" Jones did end up with the rights to *The Gospel Singer* for a time but lost interest in the project soon thereafter.

The Jones meeting did lead to a nice $5,000 check, but it was interest in his second book that turned Harry into a screenwriter. One evening shortly after the release of *Naked in Garden Hills*, he picked up the phone at his house and was surprised to learn that the voice on the other end of the line was Frank Perry.

Perry was an established Hollywood director with several big-budget dramas to his credit. He had recently directed *Diary of a Mad Housewife*, which had garnered numerous accolades, including an Oscar nomination for Carrie Snodgrass, who had played the lead role. Now Perry was interested in *Naked* and wanted Harry to write the script.

Though he had never even read a screenplay, Harry immediately took the job. Perry arranged to buy the option through Hawkins, and Harry was hired. Now he had a few weeks to figure out how to write a script. Perry sent him a script to use as a model, but Harry had no idea what the terms meant. What was a reverse angle? Why were some words underlined at random? What the fuck was a two shot or a three shot?

He called Pearce in desperation. Pearce had learned the hard way, as well, and now had an Oscar nomination for *Cool Hand Luke* under his belt. Once again, Pearce came through for his friend. He typed Harry a glossary of screenwriting terms—*interior/exterior, POV, moving shot*, etc. He offered simple, easy solutions. Get a cardboard tube out of a roll of toilet paper, and look through it at things in your living room. "This will train you to think in camera terms. It will also amuse your friends," Pearce wrote.

More importantly, he offered encouragement. "Don't worry. Shit, this is easy. I hadn't ever seen a script either when I got the job in Hollywood and I didn't have anybody to help me out and I got nominated for an Oscar on the first draft of the very first fucking try. Hell, it's just gotta be easy. Only the moron fakes out there keep insisting it's hard," he wrote to Harry.

With Pearce's glossary in his bag, he flew up to Manhattan to meet Perry and write a movie script. Perry put him up at the Plaza Hotel across the street from his office. The director sent a typewriter over to Harry's room in the Plaza, and Harry got to work. Each night, Perry would send a messenger over to the hotel, have that day's pages brought to his house, and in the morning the two would meet across the street in Perry's office and go over them. Perry would gently correct Harry's work, pointing out the differences between novels and screenplays. "No, you see, you can't do this. See, son, it's a *picture*." Harry realized he was getting a lesson that would be valuable to him down the road. "I was going to school with a master," he said later. "That's where I learned whatever I may know about writing screenplays." After three weeks, Harry had written his first script. Though it didn't get produced, and none of the subsequent scripts he wrote would either, he had learned a skill that would prove to be extremely lucrative, much more so than fiction, for the rest of his working life.

CHAPTER SIXTEEN

THE HAWK FLIES

> The pursuit of falconry enables nobles and rulers disturbed and
> worried by the cares of the state to find relief in the pleasures of
> the chase. The poor, as well as the less noble, by following this
> avocation may learn some of the necessities of life.
> —Emperor Frederick II, *The Art of Falconry*

*K*arate Is a Thing of the Spirit came out in February 1971. The book
was a departure from Harry's previous two novels. Those books
featured a cast of odd characters whose lives intersected in worlds
of Harry's creation—the condemned mine in *Naked in Garden Hills* and
the corrupt old folks' home in *This Thing Don't Lead to Heaven*. *Karate*
was rooted firmly in the real world. The backdrop for the book was Fort
Lauderdale; it would be the only one of Harry's novels that would make
use of his years in South Florida. The urban beach setting gave the novel a
more modern feel than his previous work. The book also included a distinct
protagonist, John Kaimon, a young drifter who is taken in and schooled
by a group of karate devotees and their grizzled leader, a karate master
named Belt. The group lives in an abandoned beach motel, eats, sleeps, and
trains together, and looks and acts more like a cult than a martial-arts class.
Karate also introduced a technique Harry would continue for the rest of
his career, the use of the same characters in multiple novels. The character
of Jefferson Davis, prominent in *This Thing Don't Lead to Heaven*, serves
as an unseen godlike figure to the members of Belt's beachfront karate cult.

The character of Kaimon was more of a standard protagonist who could serve as a stand-in for the author, a tactic that Harry would begin to incorporate in his fiction. The book would also mark the first in which Harry turned an obsession in his own life (karate) into a theme for his fiction, something that he would come to believe was part of the Crews fiction formula. He decided to include a disclaimer about karate, which, on Landis's urging, was eventually cut down to about 25 percent of its original length for publication:

> This is a work of the imagination. No particular system of karate is portrayed in this novel. What is portrayed here is karate as it is manifest in the lives of specific characters in a specific action. I respect the ancient and honorable way of life known as karate, and the uses I have made of karate here are just the uses a writer of fiction makes of any subject that enters his experience.

At the time he authored that note, Harry had already largely moved on from karate in his own life. His instructor graduated from the University of Florida and left town, and Harry, who had achieved the rank of seventh kyu in Kyokoshinkai, had graduated to other obsessions. To the reading public, Harry the person was still a mostly blank page; however, he already saw the risks of allowing his actual life to divert attention from his fiction. "This is as far as I'm willing to go into my experience with karate. At least as far as I'm willing to go in public," he wrote to Landis. "I think you begin to run a real danger when the life of the writer is mixed up with and confused with the thing he writes." His fear would prove prescient.

The karate that made it onto the page, however, was deemed a success by the nation's reviewers. The wave of negativity that had come with *This Thing* washed back out into the sea. To most reviewers, he was no longer a rookie trying to prove himself; he had assumed a place in the lineup. "Crews writes with a hand as sure, tough and trained as Belt's destructive paws," wrote John Deck in the *New York Times Book Review*. "He is on his own, absolutely sure of himself, and very good." The reaction was a relief to Harry. The shots he had taken still stung. He had not forgotten those who had penned the attacks. "KARATE hasn't had a bad review yet," he wrote to a friend. "But we can depend on Sydney and the *Atlanta Journal* right? Right. The next time I'm in Atlanta, I think I'll drop by and castrate him. But, come to think of it, I'm fairly sure somebody has already beat me to it."

Harry's graduation from rookie to veteran had been hastened by the astounding pace with which he was producing novels. Morrow had now released a new Crews book each spring for four straight years. He no longer wrestled with the longstanding advice from Lytle and others that he should slow down; instead, he had decided to drive full-speed in the opposite direction. Instead of writing and revising until a work had achieved perfection, he developed the habit of choosing a date upon which he would complete a novel, and then setting an unshakable course for completion. And the dates for completion that he would choose were moving closer to his start date. To friends, he confided that he had become his own arbiter of quality; what he sent up to New York would appear, as written, in print the following spring. "I could just put shit in a bag and they'd print it," he told Scott.

The topic of his next book, the next personal obsession he would choose to deal with in print, was the automobile. As a symbol of America's mad fascination with cars, Harry had decided to create a character that eats one.

Harry's descent into automotive addiction had occurred years before, after his stint in the Marines. Out of embarrassment, he had completed his entire tour of duty without learning to drive, but after his discharge he had gotten behind the wheel and stepped on the pedal with gusto. With the help of the maintenance knowledge he had acquired in the service, he quickly became a full-fledged greaser. He first owned a 1938 Ford Coupe, which he flipped on a rain-slicked road between Folkston and Waycross, Georgia. Next, he acquired a 1940 Buick, into which he installed a 1952 engine, along with numerous other improvements. The Buick met its end when Harry bet a friend who owned a pickup truck that his Buick could make it from Coffee County, Georgia, to Jacksonville faster than his friend's truck. The Buick got to Jacksonville first, but in the process four tires were ruined beyond repair, and, at the time, Harry lacked the funds to replace them, so the Buick went up for sale. The beginning of the end of his auto-obsession was his next car, a 1953 Mercury with three-inch lowering blocks, fender skirts, twin aerials, and custom upholstery. By this time, he had become completely hooked. "Nothing in the world was more satisfying than winching the front end up under the shade of a chinaberry tree and sliding under the chassis on a burlap sack with a few tools to see if the car would not yield to me and my expert ways," he wrote years later.

The Mercury proved to be both the high-water mark and the abrupt conclusion of his motor mania. A friend allowed him weekend use of a body shop, and Harry, then twenty-two, spent most of his free time massaging the engine, improving the sound system, and painting. He had finished his twenty-seventh paint job when he came to a realization: "I could keep on painting it for the rest of my life. If 27 coats of paint, why not 127? The moment was brief . . . but I did realize, if imperfectly, that something was dreadfully wrong, that the car owned me much more than I would ever own the car, no matter how long I kept it." He sold the Mercury the next day.

Sometime during the intervening fifteen years between the sale of the Mercury and the decision to write *Car*, Harry's love of the automobile had transformed into an intense hatred. As an adult, he drove nothing but junkers and came to see the automobile as a symbol of American excess. "I hate the stifling presence and abhor the sheer stupidity of the automobile industry," he wrote. "How much sense does it make for a 113-pound housewife to get into 4,000 pounds of machinery and drive 2 blocks for a 13-ounce loaf of bread?" To dramatize his disgust, he concocted his most absurd, and his most easily summarized, setup to date: a man eats a car.

The man in Harry's story was Herman Mack, a naïve son of a junkyard dealer, who signs up with a Jacksonville hotel owner to do his deed as a piece of public performance art. He has determined to, over the course of several years, swallow bite-sized pieces of a 1971 Ford Maverick in front of a live audience. He will also go behind a curtain and pass the pieces through his bowels and into a bowl, so that they can be cleaned and sold to fans as souvenirs. The rest of Herman's family is consumed by the auto industry as well: his father, Easy Mac, whose dreams are invaded nightly by Cadillacs; his sister, Junell, who drives a wrecker called Big Mama to salvage cars that have been destroyed in highway accidents; and his brother, Mister, who is desperate to monetize Herman's antics. While the novel is at its heart a metaphor for American auto obsession, it also was Harry's first attempt to deal with the death of his son Patrick in his work. He ultimately reveals the origin of Herman's pain to be the loss of a childhood playmate in a fatal junkyard accident.

The writing of *Car* was easier for Harry than any previous book, and it came quickly. In September, he reported to Hawkins that he had completed three chapters. By November, Hawkins was congratulating him on completing a first draft. The bulk of the writing, Harry said, was done over the course of six weeks, during most of which he stayed awake with the help of chemicals, moderated by whiskey. He sent a copy to Pearce, who called it a small masterstroke. In it, he saw similarities to his own masterpiece. "I am happy to say I can see certain influences of COOL HAND

LUKE. This sure beats eating fifty eggs. But washing a windshield with a pair of tits really is a bit better than just squishing her ass up against it," Pearce wrote. "You should have stolen a lot more, baby, because I sure as hell intend to steal a lot back—somehow."

The speed with which Harry was completing novels was now affecting his own publishing strategies. During the writing of *Car*, Hawkins had expressed his first feelings of displeasure with Morrow, and Harry had echoed some of his complaints. Now, Hawkins had a new manuscript to sell, with another novel, *Karate*, still yet to be published by Morrow. Together, the two wrestled with the question of whether or not to bring *Car* to Landis and Morrow. Both thought they had Harry's most commercial book to date in hand. The time had come, Hawkins said, to choose a path that would take Harry to the next level of success as a writer. The goal now, they both felt, was to get Harry's books into the hands of more readers.

The world outside Gainesville was beginning to take more of an interest in Harry Crews beyond his fiction. The character of Harry Crews himself was now coming into focus for those beyond his personal circle. In the spring of 1971, a writer for the *Miami Herald* came to Gainesville to write an extended magazine profile on Harry and found, to his delight, a much more interesting character than your average fiction writer. "He looks like a tormented Burt Reynolds and ends most of his sentences in exclamation points," the reporter wrote. "His face is strong, nearly handsome, yet when he emphasizes a point he contorts it into masks that resemble the things mothers threaten their errant children with."

The Harry Crews who had emerged from Fort Lauderdale to take the University of Florida by storm looked completely different just three years after his triumphant return to Gainesville. Gone was the necktie, the professorial jacket, the close-cropped Marine-style haircut. His hair was now cut short in front, accentuating his protruding forehead, but long in the back, flopping onto his upper back. He kept his sideburns long now, to just below the mouth, and left a few buttons open at the collar. His appearance stood out among the corduroy and tweed that populated the halls of the English Department. He was rail thin, thanks in part to a new obsession that had emerged in his life, jogging. Despite his ravaged leg, which gave him an outlandish limp that one observer said made it appear that he was riding an invisible unicycle, he ran five miles a day through the hills of his northwest Gainesville neighborhood. One regular running partner said he ran "as if he had some anonymous pursuer at his back," and he frequently outpaced students with much younger and healthier legs.

To go along with his running, he had taken up another hobby/obsession into which he could pour his seemingly unlimited reserve of intensity: the training of hawks. As a youngster on the farm he had developed a fascination with predatory birds. During the many hours and days he spent with his grandmother when he was too weak to leave the house, he would watch her feed and care for biddies, young chicks hatched in the pen next to the house. Grandma's biddies occasionally became lunch for the hawks that patrolled the skies of Bacon County. One of Harry's earliest memories was of Grandma's response to the deadly hawks. She put one biddy out in the yard to entice a hawk, but not before she put arsenic in the feathers on the biddy's head. As if on cue, the hawk descended on the farm, coming in low, right over the fence, its red tail fanned and its talons stretched. It grabbed the biddy without a sound, the last bird it would steal from Harry's vengeful grandmother.

As an adult, his fascination with hawks reemerged. "A bird that drinks blood and eats flesh seemed to me then, and seems to me now, an aberration of nature," he wrote. He began to study the history of falconry. He was delighted to learn that Attila the Hun went into battle with a hawk perched on his arm. He discovered *The Art of Falconry*, by Frederick II, emperor of the Holy Roman Empire, and it became his ornithological bible. He decided he would trap and train birds using the ancient techniques that Emperor Frederick had written about seven centuries earlier, using leather hoods and jesses for the birds, and feeding them off his wrist.

He trapped two hawks, a red-shoulder and a red-tail, at Paynes Prairie Preserve State Park, a twenty-thousand-acre savannah located ten miles south of Gainesville. Soon, he had converted his garage in their quiet residential neighborhood into a coop, nailing plywood across the garage opening from floor to eye level, and filling the top in with chicken wire. Not all the neighbors felt this was an acceptable use of the garage.

He also met with some resistance to his new hobby in the English Department. Word of Harry's hawk operation, like many of his colorful pursuits, had filtered through the faculty. A female professor heard that a hawk had died as a result of Harry and Frederick II's training techniques, which included starving the hawks into submission. At a cocktail party, Harry and the professor got into a heated discussion about "the noble bird," and the temperature of the discussion climbed higher and higher as Harry, several drinks coursing through his system, loudly defended his methods.

"You have no right! You have no right!" the professor screamed as yet another party was reduced to chaos. The scene would reappear a few years later, slightly fictionalized, when Harry's novel about hawk training was published.

Though he was dedicated to the ancient ways of Frederick, Harry would occasionally deviate from the text of *The Art of Falconry*. For instance, he liked to take a hawk with him when he went drinking. He would drive over to the big house where Ward Scott and Johnny Feiber lived, park his car, and emerge with a hawk on his arm, often with a tiny leather hood over its head, and bells on the leash that connected it to Harry's wrist. After a few hours of beer drinking, pot smoking, and conversation, he would get back into the car, one hand on the wheel, the other holding up the hawk. "We would look at each other, laugh, and say, 'This doesn't seem like a good idea,'" Feiber remembered.

On one such night, Feiber's friend George Grandy, a teammate from his football days, offered to take the hawk and its razor-sharp talons on his bare arm.

"I don't know if you should do that," Harry objected.

Grandy did it anyway, and lived to tell about it. Harry left later that evening with the hawk on his glove, a little chagrined.

Research for his latest book was always classroom fodder for Harry, and the hawks were no different. In one undergraduate class session, he was complaining about the insatiable hunger of the hawks. One student volunteered the idea of feeding them house cats. Harry approved of the idea, telling the rapt students that cats would make an ideal meal, since the hawks required fur and bones in their diet in order to survive in captivity.

Hawk training would eventually become another one of Harry's former hobbies. Once he had completed the manuscript that would later become his sixth novel, *The Hawk Is Dying*, he donated the birds to the zoo at Santa Fe Community College in Gainesville. Shortly after he had sent off the manuscript, he put all the leather accessories he had accumulated into a drawer in his desk and closed the hawk chapter in his life for good.

In the fall of 1971, Willie Mickelberry and his wife, Susan, offered to watch Byron so Sally could accompany Harry to New York on a business trip. Willie had been studying with and assisting Harry for three years, but it was Susan's first trip to the Crews's ranch-style house. To her, it seemed like the ideal home for the modern American family. It was Norman Rockwell, updated for the new, hip decade. The Mickelberrys arrived, ready for the weekend, and Harry and Sally said their goodbyes to Byron. James Taylor's *Tapestry* was spinning on the record player, the song "You've Got a Friend" echoing through the shag-carpeted living room and into the sparkling kitchen. Thanks to Sally, the home was immaculate from top to bottom. Coffee was brewing in the Mr. Coffee machine, another of the new items that symbolized suburban success in the early 1970s. "They had a charming young son in Byron, and a beautiful family," Susan said. "It just seemed to me like it was the perfect house." And Harry and Sally appeared, to Susan, to be doting parents. Halfway through the trip, Willie's mother and father visited with their little dog in tow. The dog nipped Byron, scaring him, but doing minimal damage. Willie called Harry and told him about the incident, and the trip was nearly cut short. "Harry was extremely protective of Byron," Willie recalled.

The scene of suburban bliss was a façade. Just as Harry had imagined about the pictures in the Sears Roebuck catalogs from his youth, the true story was far more sinister than the images that were portrayed to outside observers. The quiet neighborhood, the two-car garage, the picture-book family—to Harry, it had become a cage. Success and stability brought no peace; instead, he lived in a constant, growing state of barely suppressed rage. The source was nebulous. The demons from his childhood, the loss of his son, the relentless feelings of inferiority, which hadn't been checked by his success—none of it allowed for a comfortable existence in what he called "the normal life."

As his suburban angst grew, he spent less and less time with Sally and Byron. The bars and clubs of Gainesville were a convenient escape, and drinking was becoming less recreation and more part of the routine. And his writing always took precedence over family responsibility. When he was in the middle of a book, he had even less patience for domesticity. The dereliction of his duties as a husband and a father wracked him with guilt, but he could not fight it. Shortly after he had managed to live up to one of his self-imposed manuscript deadlines, he wrote to a friend who had invited him on yet another weekend away from the family: "I just finished a novel. That means that I have just come off a year of intense, isolated effort, a year during which time I neglected—along with a number of other things—my family. In another month or two or three I will be starting another novel.

In the meantime—like right now—I'm trying to give myself and my time (never an easy thing to do with me) to my family."

As the marriage deteriorated, Sally tried to hold the family together. Byron was eight and starved for attention from his father. While Harry chafed at domestic life, Sally saw it as her chief responsibility and Byron as her reason for living. She looked the other way at most of Harry's transgressions and concentrated on maintaining the home for Byron. "If I hadn't been a writer, I am convinced I'd still be married to Sally," Harry said years later. "She's a wonderful woman. But when I'm working I run on such a tight wire I'm impossible to live with. Friday comes, and she's been in the house all week, and she's accepted an invitation to a party that night. I get home from work and I say, 'No, darlin', you go, I ain't going.'"

As time went on and the deterioration continued, Harry's temper would occasionally flare. "There'd be other times when a book would be on you so bad you'd go to pieces, scream, say things you were instantly sorry for, break something, then leave. And while you were gone, you'd say 'You sorry bastard, you got it wrong. And what you gotta do is go home and make this right.' And more often than not you just went back and made it worse."

Monogamy was also another aspect of "the normal life" that Harry had little time for. As much as the neglect of his family hastened the deterioration of the relationship, his philandering had an even greater impact.He began renting a small apartment in Gainesville, ostensibly as a writing bunker, but it also doubled as a place to bring women he met on the side.

Most of these relationships were fleeting, but not all of them. In 1971 he went to Melbourne, Florida, with Pearce and another ex-convict author named Malcolm Braly to appear on a panel about violence at the behest of Lawrence Wyatt, a professor at Florida Technical Institute. At a reception held for the event, Wyatt's wife introduced him to her friend Charné Porter, a striking young photographer and sculptor with an eye for the eccentric. Harry and Charné had immediate chemistry. Her photographer's eye pegged Harry as the perfect subject, and the two left the party together so Porter could retrieve her camera and turn the lens on her new friend. Soon, they were seeing each other on a regular basis.

To the extent that Sally was aware of Harry's other life, it was another factor driving them apart. "Harry wanted more of everything, and Sally wasn't enough," Feiber said. "Sally is the sweetest person in the world. She let Harry do whatever the hell he wanted to do, I think. I never saw her ever say 'No' to him about anything, and I really never saw them fight, but of course I wasn't there all of the time. But I think she was devoted to him for the most part."

As Harry fought to break free from the entanglements of middle-class life, the same battle was being played out on the pages in his typewriter. The story he chose to tell in 1971 would mirror his personal life more directly than any he had written before or would in the future. The manuscript that would eventually become the novel *The Hawk Is Dying* told the story of George Gattling, a middle-aged, middle-class Gainesville suburbanite who, as his life is falling apart around him, devotes all his energy to the training of a red-tailed hawk.

Harry's protagonists had been growing in similarity to their creator— this time he invented a character that grew directly out of his current self. George Gattling wasn't a university professor; he owned a car upholstery business that catered to university professors and attended cocktail parties with university professors, who showered him with condescension. Harry's own struggles to fit in at the university were accentuated by Gattling's role as an unimportant outsider. Gattling came from Bacon County, where, like Harry, his father had died when he was not yet two. To drive home the point and leave no doubt whatsoever, Harry even used his own actual current address, at his house in northwest Gainesville, as Gattling's address in the book.

Gattling also becomes, in the course of the book, a man who loses a child to drowning. Harry chose to make his protagonist unmarried, instead living with his divorced sister and her mentally challenged teenage son, Fred. The character of Fred was modeled on Sally's younger brother Tony, who, according to Sally, was slipped hallucinogenic drugs when he was at a high school party and was left severely brain-damaged. He spent the rest of his life in and out of sanitariums. For a time, Tony lived with Harry and Sally in Gainesville. In the book, Fred is like a son to Gattling, and Fred's drowning pushes Gattling further into madness.

Like Harry, Gattling feels trapped by his empty suburban existence, and the symptoms are rage and despair, as if there were "something dangerously loose in himself." Gattling had been misled by the world, tricked into a life he never wanted:

> Looking through the window at the straining bird, beautiful and doomed
> in the slanting sunlight, he thought: I'm at the end of my road. I was

warned about everything except what I should have been warned about. I was warned about tobacco and I don't smoke. I was warned about whiskey and I don't drink except when I can't stand it. But I was never warned about work. Work hard, they say, and you'll be happy. Get a car, get a house, get a business, get money. Get get get get get get get. Well, I got. And now it's led me here where everything is a dead-end.

Gattling follows, to a T, the teachings of Emperor Frederick II and carries the hawk on his arm around Gainesville as he prepares for Fred's funeral and fights off the admonitions of his family and friends. As the hawk resists Gattling's attempts to man the bird, Gattling himself is finally and completely rebelling his own manning, at the hands of society.

A little sour ball of shame settled in George's stomach. The hawk was as docile as a kitten. He could touch her and she never moved, permitting any indignity. Wherever he put her down she sat until he came back and picked her up. To put a hood on the biggest, strongest and most magnificent raptor in the world was to reduce it to something any child could carry. George sighed. He was determined not to think about that, but he knew he would think about it anyway. It couldn't be helped. Hadn't his mother insisted all his life that nothing was free?

As Harry finished the final pages of the manuscript for *Hawk*, his second and last marriage to Sally was down to its last few chapters as well. Harry had concluded that, though he loved Sally and Byron, he could never find contentment in a domestic setting. If he stayed, they would both be the worse for it. It was a decision for which he would feel tremendous guilt for the rest of his life. He knew deep down that he was putting his own compulsions before the needs of his family. He was walking out on his son as he had been abandoned as a child.

By the summer of 1972, it was clear to both Harry and Sally that divorce was imminent. Though she had already hired an attorney, Sally was determined to resolve the situation in the best possible way for Byron. One morning, Sally came to campus to find Harry at his office. The two walked over to the Plaza of the Americas, a grassy square in the middle of campus filled with student activity. They sat on a bench and, away from the influence of lawyers, worked out between the two of them the terms of their impending divorce. There would be no set visitation times; instead, Harry could come see Byron whenever he wanted. And Harry would provide for Sally and Byron by whatever means necessary.

Sally felt strongly that she wanted Harry in Byron's life: "I went to the judge when the divorce was being finalized, and he said, 'Do you want visiting hours?' And I said, 'No, no.' I said, 'Harry's his father and I'm his mother, and Byron should have access to both of us whenever he wants.' And I thought that that was the best way to do that. So Byron could go see Harry any time he wanted."

It was an arrangement that both would adhere to for the rest of Byron's childhood. The amicability of the relationship that remained eased the transition. Still, though it was of his own making, his abandonment of his family was yet another piece of psychic baggage for Harry to carry around.

"Anybody who tells you they get a divorce and leave without scars or wounds never had any affection for their woman to start with," he said. "I felt like shit doing it. I always have since then."

CHAPTER SEVENTEEN

MELROSE

> If you're going to be anything or know anything or do anything,
> you've got to be abnormal. Whatever's normal is a loss. Normal
> is for shit.
> —Harry Crews, *The Hawk Is Dying*

elrose, Florida, is a quiet little village located halfway between Gainesville and the Atlantic Ocean. It lies between several lakes, the largest being Lake Santa Fe, and is home to several hundred vacation homes for boaters and fishermen from larger surrounding cities. The center of town is the intersection of State Road 26 and State Road 21, also the intersection of four Florida counties: Putnam, Alachua, Clay, and Bradford. Since the 1930s, the southwest corner of the intersection has been occupied by Chiappini's, a combination gas station, country store, and watering hole that has served for nearly a century as the social center for the town. It was the same bar where, after entertaining students at the local middle school, Marjorie Kinnan Rawlings would grab a stool and drink away an afternoon a few decades earlier. In the early 1970s, Mark Chiappini spent most of his days behind the counter at Chiappini's, as he does today, serving beer and sharing stories with the regulars. He still remembers the first time Harry Crews walked into the store.

"He came strolling up the street, looking like somebody from another planet," Chiappini said. "His head was shaved clean, and he had a Fu Manchu mustache and an earring in one ear. He had a can of beer in his hand, and he was wearing a white judo outfit. And I think he had on a pair of loafers. . . . He looked like a thug, somebody a mother would see and say, 'Let me hide my child.'"

The bar at Chiappini's was to become a place for Harry to find some human interaction when he needed an occasional break from self-imposed isolation. It was the isolation, however, that he craved when he removed himself from the suburbs, and he found it in Melrose. His close friend and student John Feiber had brought Harry to Feiber's brother Jim's house on Lake Melrose, and Harry immediately saw possibilities. Before long, he had identified a small, Cracker-style stucco cabin in the same vicinity and signed a rental agreement. The house would need some work before it was ready for a tenant. Since leaving Sally, Harry had slipped into a vagabond lifestyle. Without a permanent residence, he would take up with friends, or girlfriends, until he either wore out his welcome or stumbled on a better alternative.

While he was waiting for the Melrose cabin to be ready, Harry lived for a time with one of his students, Marie Speed, and her boyfriend. Speed had studied with Harry for several years and was in the tight circle of students who spent their Thursday evenings in Building D and at the Winnjammer.

"Back then, a lot of us sort of helped take care of Harry when he needed it," Speed remembered. "You know, we'd teach his classes if he was under the weather, so to speak. So we had a guest bedroom. Back then, you know, Harry sort of ran through people because he was a difficult person, and as you know, he had problems with his drinking. . . . But for us, he was actually a pretty wonderful house guest."

Speed and her boyfriend lived in a small house in the Duck Pond area of Gainesville, a tree-covered neighborhood with older homes just a few blocks from downtown. One morning, Speed came out of her bedroom and walked down the hall toward the bathroom. Harry was coming from the other direction, completely naked.

"It's okay, Missy Speed," Harry advised. "Just don't look."

Another time, Speed came into the kitchen ready to leave for campus around eight a.m. Harry came in, went directly to the fridge, retrieved a beer, and popped the top.

"Harry, you shouldn't be drinking that now," Speed told him.

"Darling, if I didn't have to, I wouldn't," Harry replied.

Harry was appreciative of the hospitality and made an effort to show his hosts his appreciation. Unannounced, he hired a massage therapist, who came to the house, set up his massage table on the porch, and was waiting for Speed and her boyfriend when they came home. On another occasion, Speed came home terribly upset after a confrontation with her boss had led to her quitting her job at a local health spa. Harry put her in his car, took her to Lillian's, bought her a drink, and took her dancing.

"It was really, really sweet," she said. "That's when he told me I was one of the only women that he was friends with."

Harry's generosity of spirit was evident to many of his students. Though his personal life was in shambles, he could still serve as a positive mentor, and often did. Feiber credits Harry with keeping him from dropping out of the graduate program.

"I got so disgusted so many times that I wanted to leave," Feiber said. Harry would sit patiently with him and lobby for him to stick it out. "One time he said to me, 'God dammit, you just have to understand that graduate school is like eating a big bowl of shit. You can put strawberries on it, vanilla ice cream, and chocolate sauce. But it is still going to taste like shit.' He said, 'So you just take one spoonful at a time, and pretty soon it is over with.' I thought, 'Well, shit, he's got it. That's exactly right.'"

When the cabin in Melrose was ready, Harry thanked Speed and her boyfriend, grabbed what few belongings he thought he needed from Sally's house, and pulled his car onto University Avenue, heading east. He drove a beat-up old Mustang, the backseat filled with assorted garbage—empty beer cans, crumpled manuscript pages, cigarette butts. The driver's seat had broken and wouldn't stay in the correct position, so Harry had jammed a piece of wood between the front seat and the back seat to keep it upright.

He applied the same minimalist standards to his new house by the lake. The house had been erected in the 1920s and showed its age. It sat on a dirt trail a few hundred feet from the highway, shaded by tall pine trees. It was one of the few livable houses in the vicinity, surrounded by several abandoned, rotting cabins of similar design. The interior of the house usually looked similar to the backseat of the Mustang. Harry did not install a phone and even took himself off the postman's route, picking up his mail at the post office instead. The cabin was furnished with a pair of beds, a fireplace, and a makeshift table upon which he placed his Underwood typewriter and a ream of typing paper.[4] All outward distractions had been eliminated.

With human interaction contained, he could now spend as much, or as little, time in front of the typewriter as he chose. He had several projects on his mind and in the Underwood. He had begun a novel called *The Enthusiast*, about a divorced Gainesville lawyer obsessed with weightlifting, handball, and concentration camps. Shortly after finishing *Car*, he had begun work on a play called *The Gymnasium*, about a deaf-mute midget who walked with his hands. And he had also started thinking about other ways to break out of the novel form. As his fiction became more biographical, the idea of a memoir had begun percolating in his mind.

Though he yearned for it, he could only stand so much isolation, so much time in front of the typewriter. He became a regular presence at the bar at Chiappini's as well as at the Blue Pines, another bar and pool hall down the road in Putnam County. He jogged nearly every day. Often, he would conclude his run at Chiappini's, settle down on his favorite stool for a series of Budweisers, and then bum a ride back out to the cabin on Lake Melrose. He also had purchased, for $175, a ten-speed Gitane French racing bicycle and could be seen regularly pedaling it along the highways.

The new freedom from restrictions allowed Harry to act on impulses even more than he had before. On a whim, he could drive east to Crescent Beach, his favorite spot to watch the sun rise over the Atlantic, or drive west, and watch it slip behind the Gulf of Mexico. With nobody counting on him, or at least nobody who couldn't wait, he was free to follow whatever path opened up. Mark Chiappini recalled one afternoon when Harry was at the store and an attractive young woman walked by the window. Somebody at the bar knew her, and Harry was introduced in the parking lot. Chiappini watched as they talked, Harry working his southern charms to the full extent of their capabilities. Soon they came inside to tell the assembled group that they were leaving—they had decided to go to Mexico together. Harry and his new friend hopped in his car, drove directly to the Orlando Airport, and were gone for a week.

The cabin wasn't completely limited to literary pursuits. It was a beautiful setting, and Harry invited friends, students, and women to his new home on a regular basis. He had become more reliant on cocaine and had added several other illegal substances to his repertoire. Chiappini remembered one occasion when Harry called him out to the house so he could borrow a tool. "I opened the wrong drawer, and there was every type of drug you could think of," Chiappini said.

Drugs were so readily available and so integrated into his life now that Harry could lose track of his own supply. One weekend, he called Feiber with a request: Harry was in Gainesville and his car was in Melrose.

Would Feiber mind picking up the Mustang at the lake house and driving it into town?

Feiber consented, got the car, and started driving. A few minutes into the drive, he went to light a cigarette. The hole on the dashboard where the lighter used to be was empty, because Harry had tossed it out the window a few weeks earlier when it wouldn't heat up fast enough for his liking. So Feiber reached one hand behind him and started rummaging around the refuse on the backseat, searching for a matchbook.

Instead, his hand settled on a plastic bag, which, on closer examination, was filled with cocaine.

Now, both the drive and Harry's request took on more sinister overtones, as Feiber found himself transporting illegal substances along Florida's highway system. He kept both eyes on the horizon for law enforcement but made it safely to Gainesville. He stopped at his house, took the bag of cocaine inside, and put it in freezer. Then he delivered the car to Harry, not mentioning the coke.

A week or so later, the two of them were at Feiber's house. Harry said that he had run out of cocaine and asked Feiber if he could help him get some more. Feiber casually walked over to the fridge, opened the freezer door, and pulled out the bag he'd found in the backseat of the Mustang.

"Look familiar?" he asked.

Harry looked at it, then up at his friend sheepishly.

"I was wondering what happened to that," he said.

On certain occasions, the drugs would be put back in the drawer, and Harry's cabin could be a place for entertaining friends and families. One weekend, Feiber was with a girlfriend at his brother's place on the lake. The two of them decided to take the boat over to Harry's place to say hello. As they approached, Feiber could see that Donn Pearce was visiting with his family. As the boat approached the shoreline and Feiber and his girlfriend could better view what was happening on the shore, Feiber realized that everybody there was completely naked. The Pearces had become nudists, and Harry was happily joining in. On the admonition of his girlfriend, Feiber waved and slowly turned the boat around.

Parties at the Lake Melrose estate were interesting, all-night affairs with a diverse crowd—writers, students, Harry's drinking buddies from the pool hall—with Harry always the center of attention. Pearce was a regular attendee. Partygoers who didn't know his connection to *Cool Hand Luke* would soon find out. He came equipped with a pair of leg irons, and would demonstrate his Houdini-like ability to remove his pants in seconds while the chains were locked around his ankles.

Charné Porter was a regular part of Harry's life now, and she lived with him on Lake Melrose a majority of the time. To her, the Harry who entertained the masses at all-night parties was not a true representation—it was just Harry putting on a show. The real Harry liked to be alone in the cabin with Charné, deep in his work. He would sip a vodka and tonic and bang away at the typewriter while, across the room, Charné worked on sculpture or a screenplay.

As time went on, more people knew where Harry was, and the party followed. The most memorable party at Lake Melrose, one that Harry would eventually immortalize in *Esquire*, was big enough to earn its own name: the Goat Day Olympics. The idea for the party was hatched at the bar at Lillian's, where Feiber worked as a bouncer. Harry casually remarked, late one night over whiskey, that the two of them should shoot a goat and roast it. Unlike many a plan drawn up in the wee hours of the morning at the bar at Lillian's, the two pursued this one, and a few weeks later Harry had come into possession of the goat. About thirty friends were invited out to the lake to take part in the ritual ceremony and consumption. Harry brought Byron along, and Byron decided he wanted to be the one to pull the trigger. The adults thought better of it, however, and Feiber, with his .30 caliber carbine, put a bullet in the condemned goat. The party was under way.

Goat Day became an annual tradition, an event marked on the Melrose calendar. A pig, which like the goat arrived at the festivities very much alive, was added to the menu, along with racks of ribs, oysters from Cedar Key (an island west of Gainesville on the Gulf of Mexico), and many other Florida delicacies. Feiber would spend a day cooking, grilling chicken three deep on the grill, feeding more than a hundred attendees, most of whom would wade into the lake once the sun reached the top of the sky. "Nobody is invited to the Goat Day Olympics," Harry wrote. "Everybody is invited." The party was usually called for ten a.m., and would still be going strong at three a.m. the following morning. To Harry, the ritual slaughter of the animals (in later years the deed was done with an axe) drew for him a connection to the ceremonial hog butchering of his youth on the farm. What was once done in the name of survival had become an all-day celebration of bacchanalian revelry.

For the summer of 1973, Harry planned his most extensive adventure since his cross-country motorcycle trip. He had signed on to attend Bread Loaf once again. This time, however, he planned to arrive on foot.

The idea of writing a memoir had risen up his priority list, and now he embarked on both a continental hiking trip and his first attempt at book-length nonfiction. With Charné coming along as his personal photographer, he planned to spend the entire summer walking the Appalachian Trail, starting at Springer Mountain in Georgia and traversing the eastern United States, all the way up to Vermont. He brought along a tape recorder, planning to interview the people he met along the way, with the goal of weaving a narrative out of the trip, his interviews with fellow hikers, and the story of his life. "I find myself wanting to write about myself naked, without the metaphor, or the comforting distance of the third-person pronoun," he wrote. He also found himself in need of escape from the guilt he still felt over his divorce, and from his increasing dependence on the bottle. "I haven't been to bed sober in a year. There's no liquor stores in the woods."

Before sunrise on June 15, Harry, Charné, and a farmhand named Ronnie Donnegar hopped in a rental car and headed from Atlanta to the trailhead. (Harry and Charné had met "Ronnie Dog" a few days earlier, and Harry, while he was "drunk and speeding my eyeballs out," had hired Ronnie to lug supplies for thirty dollars a week plus expenses.) Hoyett had reluctantly agreed to drive them and their two hundred pounds of backpacks to their starting point.

The trip turned out, at least in Harry's retelling, to be a comedy of drug-fueled errors that lasted seven weeks and, in the end, covered several hundred miles, though it stopped well short of the intended destination. In Georgia they took Darvon and Quaaludes, stole beer and a camping stove from a group of middle-aged, overweight suburbanites, then returned in shame to give back the stolen stove a short time later. In Tennessee they ran into a gang of fearsome Budweiser-drinking rednecks who didn't ap-preciate Harry's hippie-esque appearance. (He had let his hair grow down to his shoulders.) Ronnie Dog pulled a .38 on the rednecks, avoiding what Harry saw as a developing *Deliverance* situation. At Laurel Falls, right near the Tennessee–North Carolina border, Harry dropped acid with a suicidal Vietnam vet whom, later that evening, he saved from diving off the falls to his death by delivering an Okinawan reverse roundhouse kick, which he remembered from his karate training. In Virginia they met, and were utterly disgusted by, a vacationing family in a Winnebago that was stopping at each overlook in the Shenandoah National Park so the father and son could drive golf balls off the cliffs.

Mostly, though, they were alone in the woods, trudging for hour after hour with heavy packs weighing them down. The hiking was gruesome and difficult. Harry stayed off the bottle, but his weak leg made every step a struggle. The group would walk twelve hours and then collapse. Often they would come off the trail to a bus station, take a Greyhound to the nearest motel, rest up a few hours, and head back to the trailhead.

After each day, Harry spoke into his cassette recorder, creating a repository from which he would draw for years. Eventually, after they'd "been on the trail so long [they] were lean and mean enough to eat rocks," the adventure had run its course. Donnegar's pack was allegedly stolen by a bear, so he dropped out and hitchhiked back to Georgia. Harry and Porter made it as far north on foot as Harper's Ferry, Maryland, at which point they caught a ride with an air force sergeant to Union Station in Washington, D.C. They bought tickets on the Metroliner to New York, and, a few hours later, with their packs still on their backs and their bodies caked with remnants of the southeastern United States, they hiked their final few yards, through the grand marble lobby, past the staring tourists, toward the check-in desk at the Plaza Hotel.

CHAPTER EIGHTEEN

FREE AGENT

> Writing is a moral occupation, practiced by not necessarily
> moral men and women.
>   —Harry Crews, *Guilty as Charged*

If his personal life had become unloosed by the divorce, Harry's status as an emerging voice in modern literature seemed secure. New York was still ready and waiting to publish his novels just as fast as he could write them. And his reputation as a talent, among those who were in a position to decide such things, remained on an upward trajectory. Awards, and in some cases even money, were part of the benefits of such a position. In 1972 the American Academy of Arts and Letters and the National Institute of Arts and Letters chose to bestow on him a $3,000 prize for "contributions to literature." "It is a rare honor and one which I never had the vaguest notion of getting," he told the *Alma Times*, his hometown newspaper, when they called to salute him as a local hero.

To accept the award, Harry traveled to New York where he was to be presented his envelope and check along with the other recipients, which that year included Donald Barthelme, Eudora Welty, and Tom McGuane. He spent the three days prior to the luncheon drinking and contemplating his unworthiness for the honor that he was about to receive. When the time came for the luncheon, he waited nervously at his table to hear his name called. Jacques Barzun, the famed historian, was to present the award. Barzun announced his name, and Harry proceeded to the podium, took the envelope out of Barzun's hand, and looked him dead in the eye.

"I didn't learn to drive a car until I was twenty-one years old," Harry said.

"You're welcome," replied Barzun.

Though starstruck in his big moment, Harry was now comfortable among his peers in literary circles and had few inhibitions. He had developed relationships with many established writers through Bread Loaf and the University of Florida Writers' Conference he organized annually. After the luncheon, a reception was held in a tent nearby, where the winners and their guests sipped daiquiris and complained about the humidity. Harry invited Landis to join him, and Landis pointed out some of the honorees. The two made their way over to McGuane, who at the time was among the most celebrated of writers, the label of "the next Hemingway" having been bestowed on him by more than one critic. McGuane's wife, Becky, a gorgeous brunette who would later marry Peter Fonda, was standing nearby when they approached. Harry, always aware of a beautiful woman, took notice.

"You know, I'd love to fuck your wife," Harry told McGuane. The next Hemingway was suddenly at a loss for words.

"I'd never heard anything like that before," recalled Landis. "But it was said in good spirits, and McGuane took it that way. It was like to say, 'I want to pay you the ultimate compliment.'"

Shortly after he got back to Florida, Harry cashed the check from the American Academy, shaved his head for the occasion, grabbed a few friends, and went to St. Augustine "expressly to spend that money." A day of drinking turned into two, and then three, and the group found themselves running through their funds at a club called the Slipped Disc Discotheque. Harry had spent a few hours and what remained of his winnings buying drinks for and dancing with a girl in the club. He left her momentarily, then returned to find a sailor had taken over his position with the girl.

"He knew damn well I was with her," Harry said. "He was talking to her and he had his back to me."

The affront, at that time of the night, called for nothing less than a massive retaliation. He climbed up on the bar, unzipped his pants, and, as he unleashed a torrent of verbal insults, proceeded to urinate directly onto the head of the offending sailor.

The inevitable fight followed, the police arrived, and all involved ended up in the back of St. Augustine squad cars. Harry wound up in the backseat with the girl at the center of the dispute, who didn't seem to understand why she, an innocent victim, had been lumped in with the perpetrators. She voiced her displeasure to the officers.

"You can't do this to us!" she screamed. "You can't!"

Harry tried to calm her down. "Yes, they can, darling," he said. "Yes, they can."

A phone call to Harry's attorney earned them their freedom later that night. The attorney, after taking one look at his client's glistening head, advised Harry not to contest the misdemeanor, paid his bail, and the group quickly made their way out of St. Augustine.

If New York was showering Harry with free money, Hollywood was offering even larger pots, though there was a little more work involved. A producer named Larry Spangler, who had had some success with a series of blaxploitation films, most notably *The Soul of Nigger Charlie*, was the latest filmmaker to acquire the rights to *Gospel Singer*. He hired Harry to write another script, and on the second day of 1973, Harry received a check for $26,374. For the entire 1972–73 school year, he would receive, for his full-time job, a grand total of $12,000 from the University of Florida.[6] Other producers saw the big-screen potential in Crews novels. He was regularly cashing checks now from filmmakers who had purchased rights to the books and were sitting on them, waiting for financing, a script, or some other piece of the puzzle to fall into place.

For screenplay work, Harry's pace, which was astounding for novels, reached the speed of light. Shortly after *Car* was published, a producer bought the rights and asked Harry to write the script. Harry took the money and promptly forgot about the job. When he finally remembered it and looked at the contract, the deadline was looming. He called Mickelberry and explained the situation. Harry told his student that he planned to write the entire script in three days, but he would need a generous supply of cocaine to do it.

Mickelberry informed Harry that he wasn't a drug dealer. But Harry had a knack for convincing people to do what he needed done, and Mickelberry agreed to supply him with what he needed.

The fuel didn't quite get him to his goal, but he was close. He finished up the cocaine as he completed the script, and on the title page, he scrawled "This was written in 5 days with the aid of Grade A Cocaine. I'm not proud of it, but I'm not ashamed of it either. The luck of the draw."

Money and work were flowing, but the one area in which he still felt he was lacking was readership. And the blame for that failing, more and more in Harry's mind, was falling on the head of his publisher, William Morrow. Together with Hawkins, he had vacillated over the decision to publish *Car* with Morrow. Both were disappointed in the sales and marketing of his previous novels. Because of the nature of the book and the more modern themes, Hawkins had expected *Karate* to outsell Harry's previous efforts. Instead, it hadn't sold at all—just a few months after initial publication, weekly sales of the book were in the dozens. Hawkins was furious with the publishing house. "I am horribly frustrated and disappointed by the sales and what Morrow has done about the book," he wrote to Harry. "When HAWK is finished, I hope we can approach the sale with an open mind."

Landis and Harry had been working together for more than five years by this point. Landis had edited Harry's first four novels without ever meeting him in person, but since the publication of *Karate* they had spent time together at Bread Loaf, at Hawkins's home, and in Gainesville, when Landis came down for the Writers' Conference. Their friendship had deepened. "I feel as if we've made significant contact, established some tender feelings and also some necessary conflicts, without the latter of which we'd probably become dull to one another over the years to come," Landis wrote to Harry. "You're too big and full of being to encompass during a few days of scattered meetings. But I know I'm with you, as I've always been with your work."

"I tell you straight, I think you're a zonk inside guy," Harry wrote back. "The best thing I can say about any man. We've got it right now; we'll be all right."

Along with feelings of friendship, Landis and his colleagues at Morrow felt they had earned a share of the credit for establishing Harry as a talent. After all, Landis, and Morrow, had discovered him, and despite the fact that his books had lost money for the company, they had stuck by him and planned to continue to do so. "In those days . . . you didn't care all that much if it didn't sell that well because he was still writing well," Landis recalled. "This was not a commercial venture. It wasn't approached that way, he wasn't paid that way. If it became that, that was fine, but in those days, you just published. You were looking to live your life publishing books that interested you. You hoped that what your house sold would sustain you and your writers, all of them. So that's what you did."

Apparently, it was a business venture to Harry and his agent. As negotiations began for *The Hawk Is Dying*, Hawkins approached Landis and asked for a larger advance and a guarantee that Morrow would spend money to aggressively advertise and market the book. Landis went to his boss, Larry Hughes, president of Morrow, who agreed to meet both demands. Landis wrote to Hawkins to put the new offer on the table: a $5,000 advance and a $10,000 advertising and promotion budget. He also made his case to Hawkins as to why it was in everybody's interests that Harry remain at Morrow. Harry might be able to get a larger advance from a bigger publishing house, Landis told Hawkins, but if *Hawk* didn't earn that advance back, Harry might be out on the street shopping for another publisher. At Morrow, Harry had, and would always have, complete loyalty. "I want what's best for Harry and for Morrow and for me and for you," he wrote. "And I really believe that we all have the best, that the best will get even better (because that is made inevitable purely by virtue of Harry's continuing to write), and that for anyone involved to give it up would be to create a terrible sadness where before there was a lot of joy, struggled for, worked for, but a lot of joy."

As the negotiations were ongoing, Landis invited Harry to New York to meet with the staff at Morrow for the first time. At Morrow's expense, Harry flew up to New York, spent time with Landis, and toured the Morrow facilities on Fifth Avenue in Manhattan. Harry poured on the charm and was an enormous hit in the halls of the publishing house and later over drinks (which would eventually appear on Harry's expense report). Landis had told everybody beforehand that Harry might break out into song, and, as if on cue, Harry let loose with some of his favorite gospel tunes. Soon, everybody had joined in, and a memorable moment in Morrow history had been created.

Unbeknownst to the singing Morrow employees, Harry spent part of the trip going from one New York publishing house to another with Hawkins, shopping his services. One company they visited was Knopf, a larger house with a more literary reputation, though it also produced its share of best-sellers. (Despite the presence of Harry and a few other writers with literary reputations, Morrow was known mostly at the time as a commercial publisher.) Knopf doubled the Morrow offer: a $10,000 advance and a two-book contract, plus the added prestige that came with having the Knopf name on your book. And, as a cherry on top, were Harry to accept the Knopf offer, he would now have as his editor Robert Gottlieb, the man behind *Catch-22* and someone known throughout the publishing industry as the boy wonder with the golden touch.

It was too good to turn down. Shortly after he returned to Gainesville,

Harry told Hawkins that he wanted to accept the Knopf offer. Hawkins was fully in support of the move. He called Landis and delivered the news. The relationship, which had held a different meaning for each participant, had been severed once and for all.

Landis expressed, through Hawkins, a sense of betrayal at how the entire incident had been handled. He understood Harry's leaving and even saw the logic in the move for Harry's career. "I remember telling people, 'After you've done five books in five years at the same house, it's time to look around for yourself to find something else,'" he remembered. "But we had paid his way to New York, and for his hotel. I really got pissed off that we had paid for him to come up and screw someone else."

Harry saw things differently. "I neither understand your animosity toward me, nor do I sympathize with it," he wrote. "You did not publish me for reasons of friendship, although I came to think of you as a dear friend; rather you published me because I wrote books which for one reason or another you liked or wanted."

Harry also denied having talked to Knopf or any other publisher in New York and took offense at the suggestion. All he had done, Harry wrote, was follow the advice of his agent, whom Landis, if he would recall, had recommended to Harry himself. "Now dig this! My honor cannot be questioned with impunity. What is said about my work is one thing; what is said about me is another. All I'm saying is that any man who speaks against my name—and speaks lies—will get an opportunity to see if he can whip my ass. If that is childish, or sophomoric, or whatever, make the most of it." Harry was clearly conflicted, however, and followed his threat with a declaration of love: "You read and took my first book. You have been my editor—and the best one I ever hope to have—through the publication of five novels. Nothing can change that."

Landis took a few days to reflect, then responded with a more conciliatory letter. He did not question Harry's honor, he wrote. He had felt betrayed, was saddened, and his self-esteem had been wounded, as had that of some other Morrow employees. (Morrow had formally asked to be paid back for the New York trip Harry had taken on their dime.) "I have told myself to be angry with you, but when I feel around I find I'm not; and if I were, I'd be fucking sure to tell you."

Harry had sent a copy of his letter to Hughes. The president of Morrow, like his subordinates, couldn't understand what had gone wrong. But he worked to smooth relations and even invited Harry to return to Morrow should the circumstance arise. And he told Harry that the support he received from Landis was considerable. "Hardcover book publishing is a tough business from which to make any money," Hughes wrote. "Jim fought like a tiger to see that all your books here were well promoted and sold. I think it's fair to say that he did this in many cases with some opposition from the guys who wear those steel-rimmed glasses in the accounting department."

The contentiousness drained away quickly. Landis wished Harry success on *Hawk*. It would be a strange sensation, he said, reading it for the first time in its printed edition. Harry let the affront to his honor pass. After a few years, he would unfailingly rank Landis as his best editor and express regret at leaving him and Morrow. At the time, however, Harry's was an economic decision. The writer, he had come to feel, is left with so little power in the publishing game that when the opportunity came to wield some, it must be done, regardless of the collateral damage. "When my work is in with me and the legal pad and the pencil in the room where I write, it's—I hope—art. Or at least I have pretensions to art," he said. "When it gets outside that room, it's a business."

CHAPTER NINETEEN

NO MAN'S LAND

> But a goddam American, who can eat TV dinners and drink
> Cokes and lie split-level in his house waiting for retirement,
> doesn't need discipline or difficulty because the President and his
> B-52's have all the discipline the country or anybody in it needs
> and he and they will take care of whatever is difficult.
> —Marvin Molar in *The Gypsy's Curse*

Robert Gottlieb had something that was rare in the world of publishing: a name and a profile, recognized not for writing, but for editing. Everybody in the business, and many outside it, knew of him. He had played a starring role in what had become lore in the halls of New York publishing houses. The glorious tale of the discovery, creation, and success of Joseph Heller's *Catch-22* was the kind of yarn everybody in that line of work dreamed about.

The manuscript that would eventually change Gottlieb's life first came across his desk in 1957, when he was a twenty-six-year-old editorial assistant at Simon & Schuster. He had grown up on the West Side of Manhattan, graduated from Columbia, spent some time at Cambridge, and then talked his way into his first publishing job, one he'd been destined for since spending his childhood devouring book after book from the neighborhood lending library.

He had precisely one book under his control at Simon & Schuster when he first read seventy-five rough pages of Heller's dark comedy about a group of World War II bombardiers serving in Italy. That was the plot, but the real story was about the absurdities of war, the lives of soldiers in war, and military authority. Heller was unpublished and unknown at the time, and Gottlieb not only championed the book, he worked on it, page by page, revision after revision, for years before it finally saw the light of day in 1961. The editing was an intense experience for both writer and editor in which pages and chapters would be laid out on the floor of Gottlieb's office, reordered, rewritten, or cut, until, after years of work, the complicated structure came together for both men. *Catch-22* caught a wave on the anti-authoritarian vibe that was taking off during that era, and within a year it had sold more than a million copies. Gottlieb's reputation was cemented.

The success propelled him up the ladder at Simon & Schuster, where he would soon become editor in chief. In 1968 he was lured away by Knopf, and he took over the position of president of the company in 1973. By then, his modus operandi had been established. He wore dark-rimmed glasses, rumpled polo shirts, unkempt brown hair, and looked a bit like a taller Woody Allen. After years of lunching with agents and writers, he had reached a level where industry people would come to him, which was how he preferred it. Writers would ride the elevator up to his office for his guidance, where he often liked to get down on the carpet to examine the manuscript in question. It was common for him to ask for major rewriting and restructuring of manuscripts he had accepted.

The suggestions of editors were not something that Harry, by this time, relished. He had a tendency to view editing as criticism, and he did not like criticism. His patience with Lytle and Lytle's persistent calls to "go deeper" had run out years earlier, leading to the end of their mentoring relationship. Landis had offered little in the way of rewrite demands at first, and when he began to request changes, Harry rejected most of them. During the editing of *Karate*, Landis had felt there was a problem with the conception of the book. He had written Harry a nearly thirty-page letter detailing his problems with the manuscript. Harry was impressed and later remarked that Landis "hadn't read the book, he'd eaten it."

But no matter how it tasted, Harry thought the book was fine just how he'd written it. "My memory is that Harry said, 'My God, this is incredible. Thank you very much. But I think I'm going to leave it the way it is.'"

Still, when Harry went to New York to meet with Gottlieb for the first time, he knew of, and was impressed with, Gottlieb's reputation. Both he and Hawkins believed the move to Knopf offered the chance to raise Harry's stature significantly. Harry arrived on schedule and was sent to Gottlieb's office, which he said "was big enough to stable a team of draft horses." Gottlieb entered the office and, according to Harry, "sat in the middle of the floor, even though there were couches all over the place and a perfectly good chair behind a desk that a grown man could have slept on."

Writer and editor have different memories of their one and only face-to-face meeting. To Gottlieb, it was a pleasant meeting in which the two didn't quite find a way to communicate. Over a career in which he had worked with hundreds of authors, Harry would go down as one of the few writers with whom he could not connect in any way. To Harry, it was the case of an empty reputation with nothing concrete to offer, but more importantly, it was another piece of evidence that writing was a solitary game. His work would and should be his vision, and his alone. He would use a description of his meeting with Gottlieb as proof of this truism and, three years later, include it, without mentioning Gottlieb by name, in an article in *Esquire:*

> "I leaned forward. He leaned forward. This was what I'd come to get: the word, the brilliance of genuine literary direction.
>
> "Here, Harry, is what you've got to do." I waited as he concentrated to get it just right. "Harry, you've got to open up the end of your novel and . . . let it breathe."
>
> "Let it breathe?"
>
> "Right," he said. "That would be my advice: open up the end and let it breathe."
>
> "I stayed in his office for two hours trying to discover what that could mean and then left without ever knowing."

Later, Harry's retelling would include the fact that he responded with his own metaphor. "I leaned back and I said, 'You know, I've got hotel reservations for two days. But your comments have been so pointed, so precise . . . it has let the book blossom for me.' If he's gone do a metaphor, I might as well do one too."

After many years had passed, Gottlieb discussed the meeting with an interviewer from *The Paris Review*. In his portrayal of the meeting, he was far gentler to Harry than Harry had been to him: "I knew exactly what I meant, and another writer would have known exactly what I meant, but the comment was useless to him. It wasn't a bad thing for me to say, nor was he being stupid or resistant—it was just that my ways of communicating were never going to work with him. It was not a proper marriage, and luckily we got a quick divorce."

In fact, the relationship continued for two more years. Harry worked with Gottlieb on two books, *Hawk* and *The Gypsy's Curse*, and on another manuscript, before the two parted ways. After the failed New York meeting, Harry took the *Hawk* manuscript back to Florida, revised it on his own as he had with his previous books, and submitted it to Knopf. Gottlieb was happy with the revision, and *Hawk* was published in the spring of 1973 to generally positive reviews. Knopf sold the paperback rights to Pocket Books, and Gottlieb soon put Harry's next novel on the schedule to be published the following spring. However, his advance would, due to the sales of *Hawk*, drop from $10,000 to $7,500.

Despite their communication issues, Gottlieb liked Harry's work and saw him as a talent for Knopf to cultivate. *Hawk* wasn't a best-seller, but Gottlieb had not expected it to be. "His books as I remember them, the texture of them was quite wonderful, charming, and interesting," Gottlieb said. "There wasn't a subject or a story that would grab people and propel them into immediate readership success. With a writer whose main quality is tone, that takes time for people to discover it, adapt to it, and pursue it. . . . There is really no formula."

The Gymnasium, Harry's first attempt at writing for the stage, which he had started three years earlier, had not come together. He tabled the idea of playwriting and decided to adopt the story as his seventh novel. During his late teen years, he had trained with Hoyett in a place called the Fireman's Gym, and he had met a deaf-mute who could balance on his hands. The gym and the hand balancer were the germination of *The Gypsy's Curse*, Harry's first and only attempt at first-person narrative. The story was told from the point of view of Marvin Molar, a deaf-mute with useless legs and a square head who had been left at the gym at age three with a note that read: "We are your normal people and we cain't stand it. Whoever you are, we would be ablidged if you would take care of this for us because we cain't stand it anymore. Thanks you, His people. P.S. It cain't talk."

Marvin lives in the gym with its owner, Al Molarski, a gruff septuagenarian who had performed feats of strength in his youth, and two punch-drunk fighters (one a teenager from Bacon County, a character loosely based on Hoyett). Marvin uses his hand-balancing act to entertain children and enthrall gym customers. The plot follows Marvin's infatuation with Hester, a beautiful "normal" girl who is the living embodiment of the curse in the novel's title and who will be Marvin's undoing. The novel was a significant departure for Harry, heavier on dialogue than his previous work, perhaps due to its earlier incarnation as a play, and with a matter-of-fact, deadpan voice he created and sustained for his protagonist.

The book employed another technique Harry hadn't tried before: Marvin's narration was revealed, in the last pages, to be a murder confession given to the police. (*The Gypsy's Curse* ends with a technique decidedly *not* new to Harry's work—a concluding bloodbath.) When he sent the manuscript to Knopf in the summer of 1973, Gottlieb was complimentary. "You've got the boy and the life . . . beautifully," he wrote to Harry. "It's funny without being yocky, and it's moving without being sentimental. Most important: I believed absolutely in Marvin."

Gottlieb's one major reservation was the confessional element, which he saw as a failed gimmick. He also echoed a criticism Harry had heard on much of his work—brutal violence was not the best way to deliver a satisfactory conclusion. Still, Gottlieb felt, in this case, it worked with the rest of the novel and should remain.

The Gypsy's Curse was published in March with the original structure intact, minus the police-confession element. Harry reworked the ending slightly to appease Gottlieb, while maintaining the violent conclusion. Critical response was once again positive. Gottlieb even wrote to report that he had shown it to Heller, who had offered his praise. However, Heller saw the same flaw that Gottlieb had pointed out (a comment that Gottlieb was happy to relay to Harry): "He felt the ending was just a little too easy, but was very impressed nevertheless. And Joe is no one easy to impress. So be pleased."

His next effort would be another departure, one that Harry had planned prior to his hike up the East Coast. Upon his return from that adventure, he had begun the memoir that had been in his mind, and by early 1974, a draft of *Take 38* arrived in Gottlieb's office.

The exact nature of the work, however, was difficult to define. Originally, it was to be a straight narrative of the hike, based on Harry's own experiences and the characters he would meet and interview on the trail. After the trip was over, however, his vision became more autobiographical. He wanted to write about himself and his experiences, to explain where his work came from. "I mean to propose a theory of literary creation by

Harry graduated from Andrew Jackson High School
in Jacksonville in 1953. He was the first member of
his family to finish high school. Harry Crews Papers,
Hargrett Rare Book and Manuscript Library,
University of Georgia Libraries.

Harry's unit in the U.S. Marines. He served three years, stationed in Florida, mostly in airplane maintenance. Harry is fourth from left in the back row (see also detail at left). Harry Crews Papers, Hargrett Rare Book and Manuscript Library, University of Georgia Libraries.

After his discharge from the Marines, Harry enrolled at the University of Florida on the GI Bill. University of Florida Archives.

Andrew Lytle ran the creative writing program at the University of Florida. Mr. Lytle, as he was known to his students, became a mentor and father figure to Harry. Vanderbilt University Special Collections and University Archives.

Smith Kirkpatrick looks over a story in the creative writing classroom in Building D at the University of Florida. Harry would later dedicate his first book to Kirkpatrick. University of Florida Archives.

Sally Ellis, pictured here in her high school yearbook, came to the University of Florida in 1959 and met Harry soon thereafter. They would be married twice and have two children together. Wright Memorial Public Library, Oakwood, Ohio.

After graduating from the University of Florida with a master's degree, Harry taught English at Broward Junior College in Fort Lauderdale from 1962 to 1968. He wrote constantly but struggled to find a publisher. Harry Crews Papers, Hargrett Rare Book and Manuscript Library, University of Georgia Libraries; Broward College Archives & Special Collections.

THE GOSPEL SINGER

Chapter One

Enigma, Georgia was a dead end. The courthouse
had been built square in the middle of State Road
229 where it stopped abruptly on the edge of Big
Harrikin Swamp like a cut ribbon. From the window
of the cell on the north side of the courthouse,
Willalee Bookatee Hull could see the whole town.
He swayed gently, shifting his weight from first one
foot to the other. Behind him on a wooden table a
plate of peas was congealing in a gauze of pork fat.
Two biscuits lay at the side of the plate. There
was a slop bucket in one corner of the cell and

The Gospel Singer (1968) was Harry's first published novel. He found the setting
when he took a wrong turn and ended up in Enigma, Georgia. Harry Crews Papers,
Hargrett Rare Book and Manuscript Library, University of Georgia Libraries.

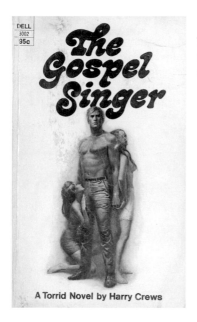

The paperback version of *The Gospel Singer*, a violent psychodrama, was marketed as a romance novel by Dell.

This flyer announced a talk given by Harry a few weeks after his triumphant return to the University of Florida in 1968. He was hired by UF shortly after publication of *The Gospel Singer*. University of Florida Archives.

Campus Speaker Series

Has written "The Gospel Singer" & "Naked in Garden Hills"

HARRY CREWS

(Nationally acclaimed novelist,
U of F graduate, and NOW an instructor)

Lounge 123
J. Wayne Reitz
Union

Free

Monday, Nov. 17,
4:30 P.M.

Sponsored by
J. Wayne Reitz Union

Harry teaches class in the creative writing classroom in Building D. Harry and Smith Kirkpatrick ran the University of Florida creative writing program in the late 1960s and 1970s. Harry Crews Papers, Hargrett Rare Book and Manuscript Library, University of Georgia Libraries.

An advertisement for Harry's second novel, *Naked in Garden Hills*, compares him to Faulkner, O'Connor, and other literary luminaries. *New York Times*.

From left, Ward Scott, Sally Crews, Charlie Wilson, and Harry Crews attend a party at Scott's home. Courtesy of Anna Kirkpatrick.

Johnny Feiber, a former University of Florida star running back and Vietnam veteran, became Harry's student and close friend after Harry returned to Gainesville. Courtesy of Charné Porter.

Harry began attending the Bread Loaf Writers' Conference in Vermont in 1969 and continued through 1973. Sally accompanied him in 1970. Courtesy of Middlebury College Special Collections and Archives, Middlebury, Vermont.

The 1972 Bread Loaf faculty: (*rear*) Joy Anderson, John Ciardi, Miller Williams, John Frederick Nims, James Whitehead, Isaac Asimov, Seymour Epstein, Diane Wakowski; (*center*) Robert Hayden, Harry Crews, Judith Ciardi, Robert Pack, Jonathan Aldrich; (*front*) William Lederer, John Williams. Courtesy of Middlebury College Special Collections and Archives, Middlebury, Vermont.

1973 was Harry's final year at Bread Loaf. He hiked the Appalachians from Georgia to Virginia on the way to Vermont that summer. Courtesy of Middlebury College Special Collections and Archives, Middlebury, Vermont.

Harry profiled actor Charles Bronson for *Playboy* in 1975. He spent a week in Idaho on the set of the movie *Breakheart Pass*. Courtesy of Ken Bell.

Harry watches the action on the set of *Breakheart Pass*. Courtesy of Ken Bell.

In an article titled "Carny," Harry wrote about the carnival circuit for *Playboy*. He had worked as a carnival barker in his youth. Courtesy of Charné Porter.

Myrtice Crews, Harry's mother, raised Harry and his brother, Hoyett, by herself for most of Harry's childhood. She was remarried to Alfred Turner and settled in Ashburn, Georgia. Courtesy of Don Haselden.

Throughout his teaching career, Harry was known as an energetic performer in the classroom. There were often long lines to sign up for his classes. Harry Crews Papers, Hargrett Rare Book and Manuscript Library, University of Georgia Libraries.

Maggie Powell was Harry's companion through much of the 1970s and 1980s. The couple lived together off and on. Courtesy of Maggie Powell.

Maggie was a competitive bodybuilder in the late 1970s, with Harry serving as her pseudotrainer. The experience was the genesis of Harry's novel *Body*. Harry Crews Papers, Hargrett Rare Book and Manuscript Library, University of Georgia Libraries.

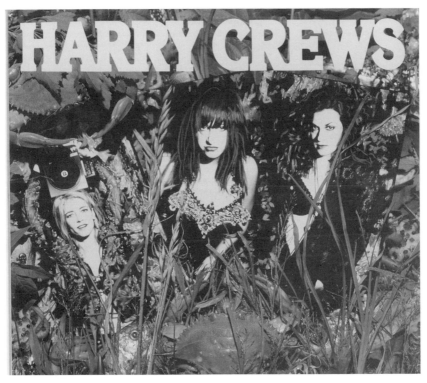

Punk musicians Lydia Lunch, Kim Gordon, and Sadie Mae formed a band and named it Harry Crews in 1988. Most of their songs were titles of Harry's novels. *Naked in Garden Hills* was released in the United States by Widowspeak and in the UK by Big Cat.

Madonna and Sean Penn
invited Harry to be their
guest at the Tyson-Spinks
heavyweight title fight
in Atlantic City in 1988.
Courtesy of Ron Galella.

Harry's friendship with Penn led to Harry's appearance in the Penn-directed film *The Indian Runner*. Harry played a grieving father who is thrown out of a court hearing. Columbia Pictures.

In the early 1990s, Harry got several tattoos and began wearing his hair in a Mohawk. He said these were efforts to remain an outsider. University of Florida Archives.

From left, Huntley Johnson, Harry, Huntley's son Huntley Jr., and Byron Crews. Huntley became a close friend and confidant of Harry's. Courtesy of Huntley Johnson.

Harry returned to Bacon County to interview his aunt Eva Haselden about family history in 1996. Pictured with Harry and Eva is Eva's son Don Haselden. Courtesy Don Haselden.

Maggie's dog Heidi became one of Harry's closest companions.
Courtesy Maggie Powell.

In 2004 Harry's novel *The Hawk Is Dying* was made into a movie. Paul Giamatti played the lead role, which had similarities to Harry's life in the early 1970s, when he trained hawks in Gainesville. Copyright © County Line Films LLC.

Ed Nagel poses in his home in Gainesville, 2015. Nagel and Harry were roommates at the University of Florida. Nagel became a close confidant of Harry's when the two reconnected in 2005. Ted Geltner.

Jay Atkinson, who took Harry's class for eight straight semesters in the early 1980s, visited Harry in 2010. In later years, Harry spent much of his time sitting in his recliner is his sunken living room. Courtesy of Jay Atkinson.

One of the houses Harry lived in as a young child still stands today in Bacon County.
Ted Geltner.

Harry was still writing whenever he was physically able until the day he died.
Courtesy of John Zueli.

examining my own life—where I lived, the books I read, the culture out of which I came, the influences both good and bad of formal education and certain teachers, the consequences of a tradition in which nightly around the fireplace our lives were remade in the narrative exchanged by uncles, fathers, and grandfathers."

Take 38 contained elements of all the above, all built around a drug-infused backwoods adventure that seemed to straddle the border of fiction and memoir. The long walk north provides the structure of the book. Several of the encounters Harry and crew had along the way are used as set pieces, each on its own a seeming representation of reality, but the entirety, by the end, has the distinct scent of fiction. Harry even hinted as much in his introduction: "I don't care much for facts. What concerns me is memory and belief. So what you read in these pages is what I remember and what I believe." Interspersed throughout, however, are crystal-clear reminiscences of Harry's childhood—the death of his father, the reimagining of the Sears Roebuck catalog, riding mules with Hoyett—that have a recognizably different tone and feel than the rest of the manuscript.

To Gottlieb, *Take 38* was not a single book, but parts of half a dozen books in various stages of completion. Each of these efforts showed promise; none, he felt, were anywhere near ready to be published. The weakest element, to his mind, was the Appalachian Trail sections, which read to him like straightforward journal writing and had not been shaped into literature. By far, the strongest element was the flashbacks to Harry's childhood, which Gottlieb felt were fully realized: "It's as if you were ready to write an autobiography of your first eight years—or even your first 22 years, but not those last 16." This was a criticism that Harry clearly took to heart.

However, Gottlieb recognized that he was delivering a rejection to an established writer, and a judgment he had to know might end their relationship. He sought to soften the blow and hold firm to his convictions at the same time:

> It *isn't* an autobiography. It isn't a book about the Walk. It's a patchwork of where your mind is now (the working part of your mind), and so a fascination—but for me, not the public. Which will no doubt plunge you into gloom—but I should tell you that I'm elated by the book, because it *does* promise so much that's rich and good. Cold comfort for you and easy for me, since my work isn't at stake. But they pay me to say what I feel, so I must.

Knopf did not publish *Take 38*, nor did any other publisher. Harry would not publish another book with Knopf, nor would he submit *Take 38*, in its original form; instead, it went into the drawer. But Harry remembered where it was; nearly every word of it would eventually be published in one form or another. And Gottlieb's offhand idea, an autobiography of Harry's childhood, would resonate with Harry and eventually help remove the fog from the autobiographical vision that had been forming in his mind.

The isolation of Melrose had accelerated his output, and Harry was now producing what would be some of the best writing of his life. The recognition continued to flow, too. The *New York Times* and *Los Angeles Times* were now hiring to review books on a regular basis. The National Endowment for the Arts awarded him a creative writing fellowship grant—$5,000 of what Harry called "genuine spendable United States dollar bills." When he was away from the typewriter, however, life was much less in control.

Willie Mickelberry was finally approaching the finish line on his master's degree from the writing program in the spring of 1974. He had a teaching job secured; the degree was the final stepping stone to legitimate employment. The final obstacle that had to be overcome was getting Harry's signature on the proper form. The problem, as was often the case in that era, was that Harry was nowhere to be found and hadn't been seen in days.

Mickelberry searched campus and Harry's favorite haunts with no luck. Finally, word came that Harry had surfaced at his house in northwest Gainesville. Mickelberry drove to the house late in the evening and knocked on the door, determined to get the signature. The door opened, and a girl from his writing class was standing in front of him, completely naked.

"Where is Harry?" Mickelberry asked, keeping his gaze at eye level.

"Well, he's in the bedroom," the girl said, "but he is heavily armed. You might not want to mess with him right now."

Mickelberry's anger had been building during the days that he was searching for his teacher, so he decided to dismiss the girl's warning. He went to the bedroom.

With the girl one step behind, he opened the bedroom door and saw Harry, also naked, pacing around the room, holding a shotgun and muttering to himself. The noise of the door opening broke his trance, and he looked directly at Mickelberry.

"I need you to sign my master's thesis," Mickelberry said.

From the door, the girl begged Harry, "Put the gun down, please put the gun down."

Harry, eyes bloodshot and unfocused, was silent for a moment, then seemed to grasp the meaning of the question.

"Well, I haven't even read the damn thing yet," he said.

Mickelberry's thesis was a short novel that required the approval of Harry and two other committee members for him to earn his degree. The idea of Harry actually reading it, at that point, hadn't crossed his mind.

"I need you to sign it and have it in the English Department by ten o'clock tomorrow morning," he told Harry. Then he threw the pages down on the bed, turned, and left.

The next morning Mickelberry went to the English Department office at ten a.m., expecting to be back where he started, lacking the necessary signatures. To his surprise, Harry, dressed and presentable, walked into the room.

"Did you read it?" Mickelberry asked him.

"She read it to me," he replied.

Harry sat down at the desk, picked up a pen, and signed the paper.

"It was a lot better than it deserved to be," Harry said. Then he stood up, handed Mickelberry the form, and limped out the door.

Bizarre behavior was not reserved for Harry's graduate students. Harry started his own end-of-semester tradition, one that he kept up for a few years. On the last day of class, Harry showed up completely drunk, dressed head to toe in a gorilla suit, toting a basket filled with bananas.

He jumped up on his desk, thumped his chest, and scratched his backside. Then, one by one, he began pulling bananas off the bunch and throwing them at the students, as they stared up at him in disbelief.

"Life is just a bunch of bananas!" Harry bellowed. "Get 'em while you can, my friends, for tomorrow they're gonna drop the big one!"

CHAPTER TWENTY **PLAYBOY JOURNALIST**

> When I took a job, I always knew from the start I wasn't going
> to write about what they told me to write about. I was going to
> meet some people, get into some shit, and see where it took me.
> — Harry Crews, interview with author

In the summer of 1974, while most Americans were preoccupied by
Washington, D.C., and Richard Nixon's final, futile attempts to wiggle
out of Watergate, Harry was five thousand miles away.

He had spent most of two days in airplanes, each craft progressively
smaller as he approached his final destination. His journey began in Atlanta, with stops in Chicago, Seattle, Ketchikan, Juneau, Yakutat, and
Cordova. His final destination was the tiny seaport town of Valdez on
the edge of a narrow fjord that spilled into Prince William Sound. What
felt like hurricane-force winds buffeted the aircraft. Out the window, he
could barely make out the snowcapped peaks of the Chugach Mountains,
rising five thousand feet above, blanketed in clouds and mist. The pilot,
a twenty-something Texan who'd been in Alaska just over three months,
brought the plane down through the squall with one hand, lighting his
cigarette with the other.

"It's a little choppy today," he said calmly, taking the first drag off his
Lucky Strike, "but I think it'll be all right."

Harry's adventure into the far north was the first of many excursions
he would take into the world of journalism. The genesis of this particular

trip had come less than two months before, when he received a short note from a junior editor at *Playboy*.

"I just read *The Gypsy's Curse*. This is a fan letter because it was so goddamn good." The fan was Laurence Gonzales, a young Northwestern graduate who would become a close confidant of Harry's over the next few years. Gonzales had joined the staff of *Playboy* in July 1972, less than a year removed from college, becoming the youngest editor the magazine had ever hired. He had been freelancing for a small Chicago magazine called *Earth*, founded by an ex-*Playboy* editor. When *Earth* went out of business, the editor arranged an interview, and Gonzales, despite having essentially no experience and no real job description, found himself working for one of the most widely read magazines in the United States of America.

"I had absolutely no qualifications," Gonzales recalled. "But *Playboy* had so much money, it didn't make any difference. We were so overstaffed. If they liked you, they'd hire you, and see how it worked out. They kind of liked me, and I said, 'Give me six months, and if you don't like me, fire me.'"

Hugh Hefner had started *Playboy* with a $3,600 loan and an idea: twentieth-century American men could be interested in fine wines, luxury vehicles, and intellectual concepts and still want to take an extended peek at a girl lying suggestively on a rug wearing nothing but a pair of bunny ears. He had distinguished his vision from the nude pin-up rags that came before him by refusing advertising altogether until he could attract highly respected Madison Avenue clients that gave *Playboy* a unique stature in the marketplace. By 1974, the strategy had paid off in spades and showed no signs of abating. *Playboy* had a monthly circulation of 6.5 million, and Hefner's umbrella company, Playboy Enterprises, was pulling in nearly $200 million in annual revenue. To Hefner's delight, Americans were proving over and over they would buy anything with a bunny-ear insignia on it.

The endless spigot of money meant the editorial division had a nice fat wallet and a lot of time to plan spending it. "We had so much money, we didn't know what to do with it, literally," said Gonzales. The editors tried valiantly, however. It was a close-knit group—many, including Gonzales, had literary ambitions and were friends in and out of the office.

Playboy had built a strong reputation for publishing literary fiction. Recent issues included stories by John Updike, Vladimir Nabokov, Saul

Bellow, and Sean O'Faolain. And the so-called New Journalism was still coursing through the veins of the American magazine industry. Coined by Tom Wolfe, New Journalism was the application of techniques more commonly associated with fiction to works of nonfiction. In the late 1960s, Wolfe had gained ample acclaim by using this technique at *New York* magazine. Gay Talese and Hunter S. Thompson had earned similar reputations. Renowned novelists like Norman Mailer had jumped on the train as well. The *Playboy* gang wanted in and had the money to do it. The editors would gather at the Bow and Arrow, an art deco–themed bar near *Playboy*'s Chicago headquarters, start a tab, dream up story ideas, and match them with famous writers.

Gonzales had been instrumental in bringing Thompson into the magazine the previous year with "The Great Shark Hunt." He was trying to lure Ken Kesey, vanguard of the Beat Generation and author of *One Flew Over the Cuckoo's Nest*, into doing something. They had yet to convince a fiction writer of Harry's stature to try journalism.

Gonzales wasn't the first to broach the idea of magazine writing with Harry. Pat Ryan of *Sports Illustrated* began courting Harry in April 1973, offering to publish either fiction or fact. *Sports Illustrated* also had a long history of luring name fiction writers. Hemingway had chronicled his big-game hunting trips to Africa, and the magazine had sent Faulkner to cover the Kentucky Derby. Jim Harrison and Tom McGuane, successful fiction writers of the era, had appeared regularly in *Sports Illustrated* recently. Both were acquaintances of Harry's and had recommended Harry to Ryan. Harry had been interested, but the time and topic had not yet appeared. The previous December, Harry had turned down Ryan's latest salvo, using a screenwriting assignment as his excuse.

Now, though, everything fell into place. Harry was between novels, summer was approaching so class wouldn't be in session, and the heat was just beginning to descend on Florida.

The *Playboy* team had concocted a fully funded trip into the cool environs of southern Alaska. It sounded like an intriguing summer getaway to Harry.

"They wanted me to come to Chicago and meet them before I went to Alaska," Harry remembered a few years later. "I didn't know anybody at *Playboy* and nobody there had ever met me. They were very nice, intelligent people. I think I asked a silly question. I said, 'What do you want me to write about? What do you want me to do?' And they said, 'Just go and have a look and do the town of Valdez, that's a boomtown, and the pipeline. We don't know what we want you to do. We want 12,000 words."

Harry had long been intrigued by *Playboy*. In his decade as an unpublished novelist churning out page after unread page of fiction, he had submitted stories to the magazine and still kept the form rejections. Pearce was now writing regularly for *Playboy*. Pearce's advice still rung in Harry's ears: If you're offered money to write, take it. You can figure out how to do it, whatever it is, later.

Indeed, the meeting in Chicago had more to do with the bar at the Bow and Arrow than it did with the development of the Valdez piece. "Harry came up and we became buddies and had a lot of fun together," Gonzales said. "I was a natural choice to be his editor because Harry and I were basically drinking ourselves blind."

Playboy was not the only publication with Valdez, Alaska, on its mind. In the summer of 1974, it was a natural place for a journalist to parachute into and take the cultural temperature. Writers from the *New York Times*, the *Los Angeles Times*, and several other news organizations had either been there already or would be shortly. Valdez, which had been a forgotten little port in a barely accessible part of the world, was undergoing a massive transformation, and it was happening at the speed of light. Oil had been discovered on the North Slope of Alaska in 1968, and shortly thereafter the oil oligarchy began plotting how to physically, and politically, get it out of the ground and into the Chevys and Fords that filled the highways and byways of America. The political end of the equation had just recently fallen into place, thanks to OPEC (the Organization of Petroleum Exporting Countries). The Saudis, Kuwaitis, and the other Middle Eastern countries that sold America much of its oil had collectively decided to stop doing so because they weren't too fond of the U.S. support of Israel in the 1973 Yom Kippur War. OPEC imposed an oil embargo, American motorists began waiting in long lines at gas stations to buy rationed gasoline, and, magically, all the environmental and legal concerns about the pipeline melted away. In January 1974 Congress passed the Trans-Alaska Pipeline Authorization Act by an overwhelming margin, and the oil companies finally had their green light.

Valdez residents drove 660 miles round-trip to Anchorage for groceries, there were no shoes for sale in the entire town, and the medical community consisted of two doctors, one of whom was eighty years old. It was also the only year-round ice-free port where the oil could transfer from pipeline to tanker. The pipeline, the largest single private capital investment project in history, was scheduled to be active in three years. It would drive the population to eight thousand within a year and much higher once the oil started pouring through the pipes.

By the time Harry climbed off the Piper Aztec and stepped onto the dirt runway in late June, four hundred miles of steel pipe, in thirty-foot sections, were on the ground in Valdez. The influx of workers had begun, and with it prostitution, narcotics, and organized crime. "The mob is dividing up Alaska right now," an unnamed source told the *Anchorage Daily News.*

Harry got a ride from the airport to the Pipeline Club, and as he pulled his luggage from the taxi, his eyes locked with those of a legless man, perched atop a dolly. He immediately felt right at home. Valdez, it seemed, was just the kind of place that could pop up in one of his novels.

The Pipeline Club was one of the three bars in town. Harry ordered a double vodka and tonic. He offered to buy the bottle of vodka from the bartender. No dice. Liquor, like everything else, save ice and now oil, was hard to come by in Valdez. He headed back out into the rain and found his way to the Club Valdez, a sprawling one-room bar with two pool tables, a dance floor, and country music always on the jukebox. He ordered another vodka and tonic and followed the smell of marijuana to the men's room, where he encountered one of the first wave of Alaskan drug dealers.

"What you selling a lid for?" he asked.

"A weighed ounce is worth ninety dollars," replied the dealer, a kid in a beaded headband and fringed leather jacket.

"Not to me it isn't."

"All right, then, sixty dollars."

"You're hurt," said Crews. "Something's burned in your fuse box."

The dealer shrugged. "People expect to be robbed up here. Anythin' is worth anythin' you can git for it. But sixty's all right. Sixty wouldn't cheat me."

"I bet it wouldn't," Harry said, walking out the door.

After a few more drinks and conversations at the Club Valdez, he managed to find a room for the night at a work camp, but not before learning his first lesson of journalism: don't tell people you're a journalist. His constant scribbling in his notebook had attracted stares and comments from the bar clientele, who were developing an eye for interloping writers. At the work camp, the manager had a similar reaction when Harry told him he was on assignment from *Playboy.*

"No way," he said. "Take you a year to write this and you wouldn't have it right. You'd have it wrong. The only way to measure what's happening here . . . is with a six-inch ruler made out of rubber that stretches to seventeen feet." Crews, though confused, diligently took it down in his notebook.

He started day two in Alaska by following the footsteps of the mainstream reporters to the authority figures of Valdez—the mayor, the city manager, the police chief. He was unable to connect with the mayor, who doubled as a mail carrier and was out delivering letters, but he interviewed the city manager and the police chief and got the requisite quotes. Too many people coming to town, not enough sewers, said the city manager. There might be an increase in crime, but nothing so far, said the chief.

One morning of straight reporting was more than enough, and Harry settled into what became his preferred method of working a journalistic assignment. He went back to the Club Valdez and found people to drink with. He spent the next few days going from the work camp to the bar, meeting Alaska natives, construction workers, Eskimos, and assorted characters, some angry, some affable, who told him stories and offered him insight into the local attitude toward the coming population explosion. Everybody who wasn't from Alaska, he learned, was considered from "The Outside," and those who had spent at least a few winters in Alaska had contempt for the outsiders. "Goddamn Texans took over this state and never fired a shot," one of the more angry drinking buddies told him.

A few nights later, he hooked up with a pair of construction managers, one of their wives, and a few others. The group drank through the afternoon and into the evening, then one of the managers invited everybody to his trailer for a fish fry. Harry still had his notebook, but he was becoming one of the gang. The art of interviewing was not in his repertoire. He was garrulous by nature. He was an innate performer, and his conversational style tended more toward talking about himself than inquiring about others. What grew from this disposition was an interview technique in which he barely questioned his subjects at all. "I would be the world's worst interviewer," he would later say, "if I ever actually interviewed anybody." Somehow the style worked for him. His affability allowed him to get beyond the reporter-source relationship quickly. His willingness to bare himself to others often allowed him to get the same, and more, in return. His journalism reflected this, often revealing as much about Harry Crews as it did about the actual subject of the article.

At the fish fry, the drinking and eating continued late into the night, stories were swapped, and when everybody was tapped out, Harry started out toward his room at the work camp. He ended up instead at a Volkswagen van owned by a pair of Los Angeles–transplant tattoo artists he had encountered earlier in the day.

"I'm from LA. I worked for Lyle Tuttle, tattooist to the stars," one of the artists had said. "Do you know him?"

Harry had waved him off, but the morning after the fish fry he awoke, head pounding, in the backseat of his rental car, parked directly next to the Volkswagen van. He felt a sharp stinging sensation in his arm. He slowly adjusted his gaze down to the source of the pain only to find a freshly tattooed hinge on his right elbow. Further investigation determined his wallet was sixty-five dollars lighter. He ran across the lot, found the tattooist, and screamed he had been both robbed and defiled. The tattooist calmly told Harry he'd been charged the regular rate for an elbow hinge.

Harry had no tattoos at the time and felt they were the mark of assholes, but it led him to another of the many colorful characters of Valdez. A prostitute named Micki wanted a tattoo of a butterfly on her backside. (She'd seen the movie *Papillon* a few weeks earlier and was captivated by Steve McQueen and the butterfly tattoo on his chest.) Sitting in her double-wide trailer, Harry learned that until a few weeks ago, she'd been turning tricks at the behest of her husband, Buddy, in Los Angeles. The happy couple had heard about a girl who had gone to Alaska to sell subscriptions to *Argosy* magazine. She'd been arrested two months later with five subscriptions to *Argosy* and $19,000 in her pocket. (The same story was reported in the *Los Angeles Times* a few weeks later.)

Micki had been doing a similarly brisk business in Valdez and was happy to share the details with Harry and *Playboy* magazine.

"They mostly want head. Hell, I don't mind giving head. I'm in the business. It comes with the package," Micki said matter-of-factly.

"Well," said Harry, unable to form a sensible response, "it's so cold and wet here in Valdez."

Micki ignored him and went on. "I think they think I might have the clap or something. Shit we got a doctor who looks after me. See, most of 'em have their old ladies Outside in Seattle or up in Anchorage and they fly out to see 'em every couple of weeks and I don't think they want to risk carrying home the clap."

Micki went on, and on, and within a few minutes had dumped the contents of a small bag of cocaine on the table and began snorting freshly cut lines with a rolled-up hundred dollar bill.

"I figured one day I took nine yards of cock," she said casually, in between snorts. Harry instinctively did rough calculations in his head. "Later on, I won't have to work so hard. Once all the men are here and the camps are full, Buddy plans to expand and take the load off me."

Harry was now firmly into sourcing that had eluded the *New York Times*. A client arrived—a fisherman who brought with him a strong scent of salmon—and Micki went into the bedroom and took care of him in less than five minutes. When she was done, Harry did his best to frame the conversation as an examination of the logistics of her profession. Business seems to be good, he offered.

"Oh, this is slow," Micki said. "The middle of the week is never any good. But weekends? You ought to see weekends. It's a madhouse around here. They all seem to be hornier on the weekends."

He talked to Micki for a while longer, learning the intricate, anatomical details of her business, waiting for the return of Buddy and the tattooists. Buddy was more cuckolded husband than pimp, though he did like to dress the part when he was lounging in the couple's trailer: ruffles-and-lace, earrings and gold chains, amber-colored goggle-style sunglasses.

Buddy was strongly against the butterfly tattoo for purely financial reasons. "You won't be able to fuck for a week," he exclaimed to Micki. If she couldn't have a tattoo, she had turned her last trick, Micki retorted. The couple went back and forth on the issue in front of Harry, getting more and more heated.

"It was all very embarrassing," Harry wrote later. "I hate to witness family disputes."

Eventually, Buddy tacitly acknowledged his status in the relationship and acceded to his wife's wishes. He headed out into the snow but only after donning a pair of muddy Levi's and a tattered flannel shirt, the requisite Valdez uniform, to track down the tattooists. Harry was still there when his new friends from the Volkswagen van showed up, met their new client, and began to apply the *Papillon*-style butterfly to her snow-white posterior. Blood dribbled down her thigh, but Micki, gilded by the coke, didn't seem to notice. The following morning, Harry was on a plane to the Lower 48.

Back in Florida, he researched the history of Alaska and the logistics of the pipeline and followed what the mainstream journalists filed on their parallel trips to the north. By the end of the summer, the 12,000-word manuscript was on the desk of Gonzales in Chicago. Upon reading, it was clear to him that *Playboy* had found a novelist who could make the leap to nonfiction. Harry's submission was thoroughly researched, expertly constructed, and an extension of the voice that lived in his fiction. Gonzales asked for a few minor changes and a rewrite of the ending. "Thanx for the new ending, you old writin sumbitch. Goddamned metaphors and everything. Well, I want you to know I expected nothing less from a good old Georgia boy like yourself," he wrote to Harry. "I gotta run cause there's a young lady undressing in the hotel across the street and I gotta set up my telescope."

In early January 1975, *Playboy* put out a news release heralding its new discovery. "The brutal transformation of Valdez, Alaska, from a sleepy little village to a roaring boomtown is poignantly explored in the February issue of *Playboy*. Harry Crews watches an army of carpenters swarm over this community of 1,000, changing it into a company town of 17,000 workers who will handle the flood of oil soon to come from the North Slope fields."

A few days later, the issue was on newsstands across the continent. It included eight pages of nude photos of Linda Lovelace, the star of the wildly popular X-rated film *Deep Throat;* an interview with Mel Brooks; fiction by Nabokov; and playmate of the month Laura Misch. "Going Down in Valdeez," took up the largest portion of the 206-page edition, covering 12 full pages. Gonzales also added a contributor's note that ran several paragraphs. "Crews has gathered a loyal, almost cultish following," he wrote. "Most of his characters you would generously call freaks. What Crews does with these grotesques is make them human, believable and painfully sympathetic. You might gather that we are fans of Harry Crews. Yes. We think him among the very best of our novelists."

"Going Down in Valdeez" opens with one of those freaks, the legless man sitting on the dolly. The character echoes the legless hand-dancer who was the narrator and protagonist of *The Gypsy's Curse*, which was still sitting on tables at the front of bookstores nationwide. Harry first believes the beatific look on his face to be a sign he was "a religious mystic famous in Valdez for seeing through to the heart of things." Alas, he learns the look signified something else. "The legless man put his padded fists down and gave himself a shove, shooting his little dolly past me. There on the cement where the legless man had been sitting were two symmetrical, perfectly formed human turds. . . . I knew I'd been given a sign."

Harry had followed the example of Hunter Thompson. In the article, he himself was the main character, his co-star was Valdez, and the inhabitants of the town were the supporting players. The piece chronicles his attempts to find a room, his many hours in the Club Valdez, his accidental tattoo, and builds to a final set piece with Micki and the butterfly. Finally, he delivers the powerful metaphorical ending Gonzales had asked for:

> It was no doubt gratuitous, even sentimental, but looking at the butterfly on the young whore's ass, I thought of the long snaking pipeline falling from Prudhoe Bay across the interior of Alaska to the Bay of Valdez. I thought: If Alaska is not our young whore, what is she? She is rich, but who can live with her? She is full of all that will pleasure us, but she is hard and cold to the bone. And if we scar her, leave her with pestilence and corrupted with infection, irrefutably marked with our own private design, who can blame us? Didn't we buy her for a trifling sum to start with?

The article was well-received and gave Harry a taste of the reach beyond novels. Novels required far more time and toil; he was usually ecstatic if he was able to sell 10,000 copies. *Playboy* sold 6.5 million copies. And while it was Linda Lovelace and her ilk who drove the sales, many, many more people read Harry's writing as a result. He liked the feeling.

Shortly after publication, Gonzales received Harry's expense report, in the form of a small spiral notebook in which Harry hand-wrote notations for each expenditure. It was a very colorful little book report, Gonzales remembered. Along with the numerous bar bills and the sixty-five-dollar charge for the hinge tattoo, one particular entry near the end of the report made him laugh out loud: "Micki, for services provided."

GRIT JOURNALISM

> There was an incredible din, the noise of violence, viciousness,
> and the lust for blood and money. The naked American. Nothing
> fake here. Life insurance and retirement plans were forgotten,
> children were forgotten, there was no future, only the moment,
> and the moment was savage.
> —From "A Day at the Dogfights," 1979

Everything about the Valdez article—the wining and dining of Harry, the wild tales from the road, the finished product, and the final affirmation—added up to ensure Harry's continued relationship with *Playboy* and its editors. Arthur Kretchmer, *Playboy*'s editorial director, was a converted Crews fan, and he relayed the newly created Crews legend to Hefner, who ate it up. Soon, Harry was known throughout the Chicago headquarters as the magazine's "resident weirdo."

Harry's *Playboy* coronation took place in the winter of 1975 at the company's end-of-the-year awards gala. "Goin' Down in Valdeez" had been chosen by the editors as *Playboy*'s top nonfiction piece of the year. The event was held at Hefner's Chicago mansion and attended by much of the Playboy establishment. Harry had arrived early in Chicago and spent several days leading up to the event drinking steadily and ignoring basic personal hygiene and health issues. On the night of the gala, Harry got lost and did not find his way to the mansion until the event had been under way for more than an hour. He had not shaved in weeks, and the scent of alcohol preceded him by several yards. The security guards manning the gates got a whiff and told him that, despite his intentions, he would not be attending the gala that night.

Harry became enraged. He bellowed: "There's an award in there and a thousand dollars, and it's mine, and I've come to claim it!"

Luckily, an editor happened by and heard his protestations, and Harry was escorted in to the event in time to accept his prize.

He had started, with his very first article, at the pinnacle of the magazine industry. Opportunities abounded. Harry viewed journalism as yet another revenue stream, and he was always in need of income. He had found that he enjoyed the adventurous aspect of it, though he felt it a less worthy pursuit than fiction. Gonzales, who had literary ambitions himself, held the same view and shared it with Harry when recruiting his new star writer to continue to perform under the *Playboy* banner: "How about some real cheesy, hack journalism to line your pockets and rot away your backbones?"

For the next two years, Harry could be considered nothing less than a full-time journalist. The bulk of the magazine writing he would do in his lifetime took place during this period. He still had no phone in his cabin on the bank of Lake Melrose, so his "office" was the pay phone in the parking lot outside Chiappini's. He would take calls from editors in Chicago or New York, then come into the store and announce that he'd just gotten off the phone with Hugh Hefner. He traded in his car for a silver Dodge van that became his road vehicle for assignments, since he preferred driving to air travel if possible. "I do not get on airplanes unless I'm profoundly drunk," he wrote to Gonzales after submitting an unusually large airport bar bill on an expense report.

Gonzales and his fellow editors devised Harry's next *Playboy* assignment before the Valdez piece was published. The idea was to put him in the position to produce what articles editor Geoffrey Norman, Gonzales's boss, called "highly literary magazine journalism." Well down on the list was the idea of offering Harry the most commonplace magazine story on the menu, the celebrity profile. But the editors had been kicking around the idea of profiling Charles Bronson, at the time the reigning box-office king of Hollywood, thanks mostly to the returns on *Death Wish*, a violent revenge fantasy that had been one of the top grossing films of the previous year. *Death Wish* had made Bronson a hot property. He was rumored to be the highest-paid actor in Hollywood and had made five movies in the past year and a half. The sixth would be a western called *Breakheart Pass*, to be filmed in the mountains of Idaho in early 1975.

Bronson was known as a tough guy, onscreen and off. He had a rags-to-riches backstory that was a northern version of Harry's own personal narrative. He was the son of a Russian-Lithuanian immigrant who had supported fifteen children as a coal miner in western Pennsylvania. As a youth, Bronson, then Buchinsky, had spent time in jail for robbing the company store. He'd been a tail gunner on bombers during World War II, and then had spent twenty years handling horses on movie sets before somebody put him in front of the camera. Now, at age fifty-four, he was a newly minted movie star. His screen roles, combined with his quiet, intense personality, had made him a somewhat mysterious and slightly dangerous figure on the American celebrity landscape. "Somebody said Charlie Bronson and Harry Crews; everyone in the room said 'perfect,'" Gonzales remembered. Harry felt the same way. Soon, he was planning his first trip to Idaho.

The production was based in Lewiston. Harry checked in for a seven-day stay at the Lewis and Clark Hotel. Each day, he would join the cast and crew and climb onto a train, ride deep into the mountains, climbing more than four thousand feet, and film all day and into the night. Bronson and his wife, actress Jill Ireland, who was also in the film, spent most of the time shut off in a luxury boxcar that served as their trailer, while the rest of the crew milled around the set waiting to be called. Bronson was notoriously taciturn, and Harry spent the first few days trying in vain to get him to say anything remotely quotable, instead receiving only a few monosyllabic greetings and nods. "After I'd been there three days, I had half a page of notes—nothing on tape," he said. "I got a little frantic."

He continued to hover near Bronson, waiting for just the right opportunity to approach. In his notebook, he had written out several pages of questions in case he was granted an extended sit-down: Who are your favorite actors? Do you participate in sports? If you had a day in a big city and could do anything, what would you do? The right opportunity, however, never seemed to appear.

After a few aborted attempts, he spotted his target alone, several paces away from the production, tossing rocks off the side of a mountain. Harry made his move. He walked over and took a shot with one of the questions in his notebook.

"I've read where you said, 'I don't have any friends and I don't want any friends. My children are my friends.' Did you say that?" Harry asked.

Bronson remained silent for several uncomfortable seconds. "Yeah, I said that," he replied.

"Doesn't that strike you as a strange thing to say?"

"No."

"Jesus, come on," Harry pleaded. "Everybody has friends. What reason is there not to have friends?"

Finally engaged, Bronson for the first time offered Harry a few syllables strung together. "There's no reason not to have friends. Just the opposite is true," he said. "There's every reason to have friends. But I don't think you ought to have friends unless you're willing to give them time. I give time to nobody."

It wasn't much, but that last line, it would turn out, would work nicely to structure an article around.

Bronson's reticence forced Harry to teach himself the trick that all journalists use when confronted with the silent subject: the Write Around. The technique was in fact a staple of New Journalism, the type of literary nonfiction that Harry's editors were counting on him to turn in. One of the seminal works of the genre, a 1966 *Esquire* profile titled "Frank Sinatra Has a Cold," by Gay Talese, had been written without a single interview with the subject. Talese created memorable scenes by getting as close to Sinatra as he could and observing. Harry did some of that but eventually moved on to another tactic. After he got what he could out of the actors and assorted set denizens, he retreated back to Lewiston and hit the bars. He spent Saturday night and into Sunday morning going from one beer joint to another, tape recorder in hand, interviewing the townsfolk about their interactions with the Hollywood interlopers.

Later in the week, Harry got back on the train and this time changed his strategy. If Bronson wasn't going to talk, then Harry would be happy to. It was one of the things he did best. During one break from shooting, Harry was regaling Bronson's publicist, Ernie Anderson, with his escapades of the previous night, when his South Georgia drawl caused Bronson to take notice.

"Where do you come from with that accent?" he asked.

"A farm near the Okefenokee Swamp," Harry replied. It was the opening he needed, and he took full advantage. He told Bronson about farm life, about how he hadn't driven a car until age twenty-one, and then began to go into a story about driving mules when Bronson broke in. He too, it seemed, had grown up around mules, on the farm in Pennsylvania.

It was the bonding moment Harry needed. Bronson became, for him, positively garrulous. The two farm boys traded their mule stories and then moved on to tales from their years in the service. Harry had been beaten by a cruel sergeant; Bronson had picked one up and tossed him onto a dance floor. Later they moved on to discuss their shared hatred of critics. Harry complained about his old nemesis, James Boatwright of the *New York Times*. Bronson promised vengeance on Jay Cocks of *Time*. Critics, they both felt, were a scourge.

"I realized that when [Bronson] has something he wants to talk about, he is articulate and talks with great animation," Harry wrote. "He just doesn't seem to want to talk much with very many people."

Bronson had likely opened up more to Harry than the previous dozen reporters who had made the attempt. Still, it wasn't much to go on, and when Harry turned in his twelve thousand words to Gonzales, there were barely three hundred from Bronson. The line "I give time to nobody" made it in five times. Once again, though, Harry's editors were ecstatic with what they received. The piece he turned in was not strictly a Gay Talese–style Write Around but Harry's own twist on the celebrity profile, recalled Norman. "I couldn't stand to read movie-star stories, even as an editor, but I can still remember how much I laughed when we got that Bronson story in," he said.

A manuscript of more than fifty pages arrived at the *Playboy* offices soon after Harry returned to Florida, and the bulk of it appeared in the October 1975 issue. Upon publication, Harry experienced another of the pleasures of journalism: taking the heat for a ridiculous headline. The title the editors had bestowed on his piece was "Charlie Bronson Ain't No Pussycat." Adjacent to the first page was a photo of Bronson's face superimposed over the body of a pit bull. Harry was more than displeased. He quickly dashed off a letter of apology to Bronson, laying the blame on the editors. "If it had been me, I'd be in jail somewhere in Illinois, because I'd be going up there and kicking somebody's ass," he told his new celebrity friend.

The silver Dodge van rolled up thousands of miles over the next several months. *Playboy* sent Harry to Raleigh, North Carolina, to cover the trial of Joan Little. Little was a twenty-one-year-old black robbery suspect who stabbed a white jailer to death after he forced her to perform oral sex. It had all the elements of a Crews story, but it never materialized into anything more than a long expense report.

The next idea to gain momentum was another celebrity profile. The success with Bronson led the *Playboy* team to try another big-screen tough guy, Robert Mitchum. After a few rounds with his publicist, however, that idea went down the drain, too.

The next successful *Playboy* assignment originated with Harry. He had met a carnival operator named Duffy who was on the carny circuit in Pennsylvania. Harry himself had worked in carnivals after the Marines and told Gonzo "he had some incredible experiences to relate." Gonzales pitched it to Norman, and pretty soon Harry was rolling up I-95.

"Carny," published in September 1976, was another Thompson-esque romp, in which Harry pops Biphetamine twenties and unveils the inner workings of the sideshow, introducing the readers to the "ride boys" and "lot ladies," the "sticks" and the "marks." This carnival, and the ones of Harry's memory, were not the G-rated, state-fair type event; Duffy's festival was heavy on freak shows and featured a performer named Rose who specialized in firing eggs out of her vagina. Harry used the article as an opportunity to shed light on the freaks who populated his fiction. In an extended aside in the article, he related a revelation made years earlier, on his first trip to the carnival circuit:

> I woke up one day in an Airstream trailer in Atlanta, Georgia. The trailer was owned by a man and his wife. They were freaks. I was a caller for the show. My call was not particularly good, but it was good enough to get me the job and to keep it. And that was all it was to me, a job, something to do. The second week I had the job, I was able to rent a place to sleep in the Airstream from the freak man and his freak wife. I woke up that morning in Atlanta looking at both of them where they stood at the other end of the trailer in the kitchen. They stood perfectly still in the dim, yellow light, their backs to each other. I could not see their faces, but I was close enough to hear them clearly when they spoke.
>
> "What's for supper, darling?" he said.
>
> "Franks and beans, with a nice salad," she said.
>
> "I'll try to be in early," he said.
>
> And then they turned to each other under the yellow light. The lady had a beard not quite as thick as my own but three inches long and very black. The man's face had a harelip. His face, not his mouth. His face was divided

so that the top of his nose forked. His eyes were positioned almost on the side of his head and in the middle was a third eye that was not really an eye at all but a kind of false lid over a round indentation that saw nothing. It was enough, though, to make you taste bile in your throat and cause a cold fear to start in your heart.

They kissed. Their lips brushed briefly and I heard them murmur to each other and he was gone through the door. And I, lying at the back of the trailer, was never the same again. I have never stopped remembering that, as wondrous and special as those two people were, they were only talking about and looking forward to and needing precisely what all of the rest of us talk about and look forward to and need. He might have been any husband going to any job anywhere. He just happened to have a divided face.

Soon after he had begun writing for *Playboy* on a regular basis, a story that seemed to be perfect on its face fell into Harry's lap. In October 1974 he began receiving letters with a return address of Florida State Prison, Starke, Florida. His former creative writing student from Broward Community College, Gerard John Schaefer, now made his home in the solitary-confinement hall of that particular institution.

After BCC, Schaefer had enrolled in Florida Atlantic University, where he had both earned a degree in geography and been deemed so completely disturbed and frightening that he was recommended for psychological testing. It was determined that he suffered from "impairment in reality." Armed with that knowledge, he embarked on a career in law enforcement. He flunked the psychological examination for the Broward County sheriff's department but managed to find work as a police officer, first in the town of Wilton Manor (where he was fired for "lack of common sense") and later in Martin County, up the coast from Fort Lauderdale. Soon after taking a patrol in Martin County, he picked up two young female hitchhikers, tied them to a tree, and threatened to hang them. When they escaped and reported the crime at the same police station where Schaefer worked, Schaefer told his supervisor he wanted to teach them a lesson about the dangers of hitchhiking. He was in jail for that crime when he was arrested for the gruesome deaths of two teenagers. Evidence found during the investigation tied him to as many as twenty more murders, dating back to before his association with Harry. He was convicted of the two murders in late 1973, sentenced to life, and sent to Starke.

Schaefer's rambling narcissistic letters began arriving in Harry's box in the English Department just as *Playboy* was hounding him for stories. His disturbed former student appeared to have one. "I will give you enough facts that are heretofore unknown to blow the mind of the entire country," Schaefer wrote. Harry had been chosen for his sensitivity and talent, Schaefer told him. He had considered Tom McGuane and even spoken to Mario Puzo, but had decided that only Harry was up to the task.

Harry pitched it to *Playboy*, and the editors were interested. On a Saturday morning in December, he made the drive out to Starke. Schaefer had been nineteen when Harry had known him previously, a quiet, clean-cut kid. Now his psychological damage was right on the surface. He asked Harry if he would testify that Schaefer's writing was born in Harry's creative writing class. "Man, I can't do that," Harry said. "If you'd have written any of that shit, you'd have been tossed out of the class."

Schaefer talked and talked, and as he spoke, Harry became less and less interested. That his former student was almost definitely a serial murderer wasn't the problem to Harry. Worse, he was a bullshitter, and he was boring. He talked and talked about his celebrity status, his lawyer, the international rights to his sensational story. Before Harry had even left the prison, he'd decided to kill the story.

In the end, Schaefer became one of Harry's more successful students, if judged solely on publishing. Two collections of his "killer fiction" would eventually be published. In other categories, he didn't fare as well. He would spend the next twenty-one years in the prison in Starke, before being murdered by a fellow inmate in 1995 in an argument over a hot-water dispenser. As the inmate inflicted the first of forty-two stab wounds on his victim's body, he gave Schaefer a fitting send-off: "You ain't gonna need no hot water in hell, Motherfucker!"

If *Playboy* was the magazine industry's leading money machine, *Esquire* was the gold standard for literary merit. It was founded in 1933, when a young editor named Arnold Gingrich decided to start a new magazine that would be to American men what *Vogue* was for American women. The magazine was to "have ample hair on its chest and adequate cojones," its founder bragged. Gingrich wrote to a new acquaintance of his who seemed to have those attributes, Ernest Hemingway. Gingrich sent him some stylish new shirts he had received, complimentary, from advertisers, and begged for a submission for his first issue. Hemingway obliged, though he thought the name *Esquire* far too snobbish for readers during the depths of the Depression.

Luckily for Gingrich, Hemingway was wrong, and *Esquire* flourished. In subsequent decades, the magazine published a high percentage of the top names in American fiction. In the 1960s, it was at the forefront of the New Journalism movement, publishing Talese, Wolfe, Mailer, and others who were experimenting with the emerging form. The legendary editor Harold Hayes was credited with bringing in and molding those and other talented writers during that era.

In 1976 Geoff Norman left *Playboy*, moved to New York, and took a position as editor at *Esquire*. One of the top names on the masthead at *Esquire* at the time, Lee Eisenberg, told Norman he wanted to bring Harry along as well. The magazine already had a number of high-profile columnists: Roy Blount Jr. wrote regularly on sports, Pulitzer Prize winner Taylor Branch had a column on Washington politics, and humorist Nora Ephron was a regular as well. The plan was for Harry to join the ranks of the columnists; the magazine would add a southern literary eccentric to its all-star lineup. It took very little convincing by Norman to bring Harry on board.

For a writer with only a few journalistic assignments under his belt, he was given enviable independence. Under the arrangement he worked out with his editor, Norman was to offer some occasional guidance, but Harry would be on his own to choose and develop topics. "We want the most interesting thing that happens to you every month," Norman told him. "The voice of this magazine, which is carried by columns as much as anything else, has been getting more and more urban and rarified and we think it's time to put a little sweat back in it. So what we would like from you every month is an experience, idea or person you came across that seemed to you baroque enough to interest readers of *Esquire* and to inspire you to write. Like I said, 1,500 words in my hands around the fifth of the month."

The column was christened "Grits" and made its debut in the July 1976 issue of *Esquire*. Norman included an editor's note, introducing readers to the magazine's newest contributor: "There isn't much Harry Crews hasn't done in the twenty-odd years since he left Georgia. In the last seven years he has written many books dealing variously with religion, snakes, karate, weight lifting and hawks. Nobody, not even Crews himself, is sure what will engage his attention next, but he has promised to tell the world about it in this space."

It was now entirely up to Harry to fill that space. The fifth of the month, he soon learned, came around very quickly. He was essentially his own editor, and the independence that he had been granted came with a downside. "At the time, I thought it was a great deal," he said later. "But it turned out not to be a great deal, because you've got to come up with something; then you've got to get some kind of slant on the son-of-a-bitch so you can write about it. It was hard. It was only a twenty-five-hundred to three-thousand word column. That's not much for one month. But I was writing other things at the same time."

Luckily, he had a secret weapon to fight the continuous deadline. He dusted off *Take 38*, the manuscript Gottlieb and Knopf had rejected a few years earlier, and commenced cannibalization. He went through it looking for passages that could be converted into a magazine piece and found several. A scene from the Appalachian Trail in which he and Charné had watched a suburban family hit golf balls off the Shenandoah Parkway became a "Grits" column. Ditto an extended anecdote from his experiences as a Marine recruit at Parris Island. A reminiscence of his Bacon County youth, in which he recalled listening to his elders spin yarns by the fire, served perfectly to meet another *Esquire* deadline. Norman and his colleagues accepted what Harry submitted with satisfaction, and very little revision.

In addition to the *Take 38* material, Harry began to find column fodder in his own everyday existence. He wrote about decidedly nonurban experiences, as Norman had requested. Drinking buddies from in and around Melrose became characters in *Esquire*. Cody and Jimbo, a pair of good ol' boys who liked to tie a chain between their pickup trucks and see which one could pull the other, became the stars of the column one month. Another month it was Buck, a melancholy grit, driven to violence because a girl in the saloon would not allow him to "feed in her lilies."

"Grits" was written in the first person and, more than anything he'd produced previously, allowed Harry to introduce himself to readers unfiltered. The Harry Crews of "Grits" was a man of his characters, a wild card living on the edge with a drink in his hand, but self-aware enough to observe the proceedings with a raised eyebrow to his readers. His notoriety increased as each issue of *Esquire* hit newsstands across the country. And now there was an image forming in the culture that would register with his name.

In Gainesville, some of his friends saw the public Harry as a calculated maneuver. Pearce, who had preceded Harry into the magazine world, had created his own character in hopes of propelling his career, that of the ex-con who viewed life on the outside with a jaded prison mentality. It was, Harry observed, an effective way of distinguishing oneself from the vast sea of magazine writers. "Harry realized he didn't have a persona," said Ward Scott. "He had to invent one. And the one he invented was a crazy motherfucking freak from Georgia."

Harry's quick success as a magazine journalist cooled his relationship with Pearce. Once again in Harry's life, his star was on the rise while one of his mentors seemed to be headed in the opposite direction. Pearce's follow-up to *Cool Hand Luke*, a novel called *Pier Head Jump* about his experiences in the Merchant Marine, had come out a few years before and been virtually ignored. His magazine work was well respected but wasn't nearly enough income to support his family. And, unlike Harry, he didn't have the safety net of a university job.

"After he got the assignment up in Alaska, he was getting two or three times as much money as I did," Pearce recalled. "And, I was really pissed off about it. I guess I still am, I don't know. He had an agent who apparently was a real agent, and I did not have either one."

Somehow, each month a column arrived at the *Esquire* offices in New York. Norman found working with Harry to be a breeze. "It was one of the remarkable things about the man. We all know what a wild, sort of off-the-rails life he led, but professionally he was flawless. He never missed a deadline, the copy came in, at least when I was working with him, the copy came in, and it was hard to find anything to do to his copy. It was clean, polished, syntax was great, there were no grammatical errors, there were no punctuation errors. I mean he was just a joy to work with."

The editors at *Esquire* had found a workhorse, and they kept adding to his load. It was extremely rare for writers to have multiple bylines in the magazine, but Harry accomplished the feat several times, contributing his column and writing features for the same issue. If a personality appeared on the radar who seemed to fall within Harry's strike zone, a call was made to Melrose, and soon Harry was on a plane. He wrote about Garner Ted Armstrong, a popular radio evangelist who had been hit with allegations of gambling and adultery. He pitched the idea of a profile on an independent trucker, Mike Parkhurst, who had embarked on a quest to unionize the trucking industry. And in the most prescient example of editorial match-making since the Bronson story, Harry was sent to Los Angeles to profile Robert Blake, ex-military, rugged individualist, star of the hit TV police drama *Baretta*.

Blake had starred in *The Little Rascals* as a child and spent his life in Hollywood, but by the mid-1970s he was a self-styled renegade at the peak of his acting fame. (Later in life, he would achieve a greater notoriety when he was put on trial for murder in the shooting death of his then-wife.) Blake's story was similar to that of Bronson, but unlike Bronson, Blake was happy to chat, and the more he did, the more Harry felt himself to be looking in the mirror. Like Harry, Blake had a desperate childhood featuring a violent, angry father figure. Blake liked to ride motorcycles. Blake, like Harry, was filled with a "seething, source-less rage" that could lead to either creativity or danger. The similarities were almost too much for Harry to handle. "Something beautiful and dreadful and mysterious had been happening all day," he wrote. "I felt it every time Blake spoke directly to me, but I had no name for what it was, did not then, do not now. I kept thinking that what Blake was saying, I'd said before. That what he had done, I'd done, too. And it all went as deep and intimate and mortal as blood and bone."

Identification, it was now clear, was Harry's journalistic style, and each subject was another opportunity to look inward. "Television's Junkyard Dog," published in the October 1976 issue of *Esquire*, was a look at the life of Robert Blake as it related to Harry Crews. Harry dug into his own past and told the story of his cross-country motorcycle trip, of his final meeting with his stepfather Paschal, and several others seminal moments in the life of Harry Crews, including the epiphany, ten years before, that led to his finding his voice as a writer:

> For many and complicated reasons, circumstances had collaborated to make me ashamed that I was a tenant farmer's son. As weak and warped as it is, and as difficult as it is even now to admit it, I was so humiliated by the fact that I was from the edge of the Okefenokee Swamp in the worst hookworm and rickets part of Georgia I could not bear to think of it, and worse to believe it. Everything I had written had been out of a fear and loathing for what I was and who I was. It was all out an effort to pretend

otherwise. I believe to this day, and will always believe, that in that moment I literally saved my life, because the next thought—and it was more than a thought, it was dead-solid conviction—was that all I had going for me in the world or would ever have was the swamp, all those goddamn mules, all those screwworms that I'd dug out of pigs and all the other beautiful and dreadful and sorry circumstances that had made me the Grit I am and always will be. Once I realized that the way I saw the world and man's condition in it would always be exactly and inevitably shaped by everything which up to that moment had only shamed me, once I realized that, I was home free. Since that time I have found myself perpetually fascinating. It wasn't many weeks before I loved myself endlessly and profoundly. I have found no other such love anywhere in the world, nor do I expect to.

When he signed on as an *Esquire* columnist, Harry committed to at least a year, and after he'd been around the calendar once he was ready to be released from the deadline merry-go-round. The constant pressure had weighed on him, even landing him in the hospital for a stretch to deal with what his doctor pronounced "nervous exhaustion brought on by overwork."

During the year that he'd been a regular contributor, the magazine had undergone a major transformation. The sun was setting on the heyday of New Journalism, and magazines in the mold of *Esquire* were feeling the pinch. In 1976 alone, revenues dropped 17 percent. What worked in the experimental 1960s no longer held water in the cynical 1970s. The magazine installed a twenty-nine-year-old editor, Lee Eisenberg, to revamp and redesign. "Those were the beginning of the bad days for those kinds of magazines," Norman said. "*Esquire* was still very long on content but very short on advertising. We were beginning to see the new kind of product; *People* magazine and that sort of thing was coming in."

Arnold Gingrich, the magazine's founder and arbiter of taste since 1933, had died in July 1976, and *Esquire* was soon up for sale. A little over a year later, in August 1977, it was purchased, ironically, by a group led by Clay Felker, the editor extraordinaire of *New York* magazine, the man most often credited with ushering in the wave of experimental journalism in the previous decade.

That Harry closed the curtain on his column as *Esquire* was adapting to the new industry reality was sheer happenstance. Independently, he had begun to feel that the column had run its course. For his final piece, he took his penchant for identification to the extreme. He had been invited to the University of Texas to give a reading and take questions in a seminar on southern literature. The professor who had invited him offered an unsolicited, impromptu tour of the site of the university's infamous mass murders, where Charles Whitman had gunned down dozens of people in the middle of campus eleven years before. Harry took it all in, gave his lecture, and then, after several rounds with a bottle of vodka, returned to the base of the tower to meditate, all night long, on the incomprehensible act.

Whitman, Harry wrote in the final installment of "Grits," had succumbed to a weakness that exists in all of us. Everybody spends their lifetime resisting that climb up the metaphorical tower, the climb that Whitman had been unable to resist. Once you give in and climb it, there's no way down except death. "If I believe anything, I believe that the tower is waiting out there. I have no answers to why it is out there, or even speculations about it, but out there somewhere, around some corner, or in some green meadow, or on some busy street, it is. Waiting."

It was a dark and disturbing way to close the book on "Grits." When he was finished with the column, he put the pages in an envelope, along with a letter to Norman informing him that he would be reading Harry's last column. He drove the silver Dodge down to the Melrose post office, bought a stamp, and mailed the package off to New York.

Though he would continue to write for magazines intermittently for the remainder of his career, the most significant journalism of his life was now behind him, completed in less than three years. It had accomplished the goal of raising his profile, but his attention was now elsewhere. "I wrote as well as I could," he said later. "I wrote things that I thought were real and of some consequence. But I also thought it might get my name around and might help my books to sell. I want my books to sell. I ain't ashamed of that."

Norman, who was also to be swept out with the change in ownership at *Esquire*, understood Harry's departure. He took great pride in his discovery of a true talent for literary journalism. "Crews had this wonderful baroque, gothic sense of humor and the absurd that he always found in his stories," he remembered. "You knew what you were going to get from a Harry Crews story. It was a ride, it was to be carried along by that sensibility and that imagination. . . . In the case of Crews, it was always about the writer. The subject matter was interesting, but in the end you were there for the writer."

END OF THE FEAST

Harry Crews looks a little like a primitive who has tried
civilization and was unimpressed.
—*Miami Herald*, June 30, 1974

The first time Maggie Powell laid eyes on Harry Crews, he was buck
naked and unconscious, the comatose host of a party that was just
kicking into gear. She had just walked into Harry's Melrose hide-
away with Johnny Feiber, searching for a place to keep the night alive after
the lights were turned off at Lillian's. In short order, Harry was roused,
donned a "loincloth," and another night by the lake careened toward dawn.

Maggie was the granddaughter of a president of the University of Georgia
who was raised in Gainesville and had recently returned to town. Her father
did soil conservation work for the federal government, and her mother
worked in the University of Florida Athletic Department. After getting her
undergraduate psychology degree at Florida State in Tallahassee, she was
back, accepted into a prestigious program to pursue a graduate degree at
UF in clinical psychology. She was tall, lithe, and athletic, a former high
school and college gymnast who was now a devoted runner. She was also
emotionally raw, having lost her father the year before, after he succumbed
following a year-long struggle with heart disease. Within weeks of coming
back home to begin her studies, she was in a devastating car wreck after
a UF football game. The crash left her with brain injuries that would not
be fully revealed for decades.

But that first night in Melrose, Harry took notice of Maggie and soon was asking Feiber about her. Feiber gave Harry the green light, and what would become a lifelong relationship for Harry began.

Maggie and Harry had their first date in early December 1976, and by the end of the year they were a couple. On New Year's Eve, with Sally out of town, Maggie came over to the Crews house in northwest Gainesville, and they ushered in 1977, drinking first at home, then at Lillian's, then wherever else they could find a drink. "We got good and drunk," Maggie remembered. "From then on, Harry and I started hanging out together all the time."

Harry would eventually pack up his things and move into Maggie's small Gainesville apartment near the university. Her life was consumed with her graduate studies, but she assumed the role of Harry's personal assistant as well. Harry was still using the old Underwood typewriter he'd acquired back in Fort Lauderdale, but he'd recently thrown it against the wall in a fit of rage and had started writing in longhand on legal pads. Maggie became his typist. Another of the duties she assumed was teaching assistant. On days when Harry had started drinking too early, or too heavily, students would get to class for the Thursday-night seminar to find Maggie instead of their instructor. She'd pass out assignments, assure the class that Harry was alive and well, and that he would be back the following week. Or, when he was up to teaching, she would accompany him to class and sit silently by his side as he delivered his performance.

The performances for which he was now famous occurred less and less often, and his absences were much more common. On one occasion, Harry had missed several classes, and word had gotten back to him that his superiors were aware of the situation. Harry became convinced that he was about to be fired. After several hours of drinking at home, he made his way to the office, ready for a confrontation. Somewhere along the way, he'd lost track of time. When he finally arrived, the building was nearly empty; all his colleagues had long since left for the day. Harry sat down at his desk and drunkenly scribbled out a resignation letter, which slid onto the floor when he drifted off into unconsciousness, head down on the desk. Somehow, the letter was discovered and brought to the department chairman, who called Harry in and told him to forget it. We don't want to fire you, he assured Harry, and we won't let you quit.

A nationally renowned author was a valuable commodity to a university. Still, a segment of the department would have been happy to part with that commodity, and Harry felt the same way toward them. To him, that golden academic designation, PhD, denoted a parasite, an arrogant "footnoter" who couldn't write anything, yet still had the audacity to turn his or her nose up at real, honest writers. "Writers scare the hell out of PhD professor types," Harry wrote. "They distrust us and dislike us. If a writer is to be in a university, it is simply a burden he has to put up with."

"Harry was not an academic in a typical sense," said Melvyn New, an English professor who went on to chair the department in the late 1970s and 1980s. "I can remember faculty meetings where he let it be known that he thought that all academics were stiff, formal, pompous, and he made it very clear. He never really protected himself."

Faculty meetings often put the division between Harry and the department on full display. "They brought out his rebelliousness," New remembered. He would often take pains to show his boredom and contempt. One of his favorite ways to pass the time was to take his wallet out of his back pocket, open it up, and begin rearranging the bills, over and over. When sufficiently angered, he was prone to blurting out rebuttals while another professor was still talking. "For any assistant professor, which is what he was, for any other assistant professor, he would have had to have been very, very drunk to do what Harry did at meetings," said New.

At one such meeting that lives on in department lore, Harry's sights were trained on an English professor named Gordon Bigelow. The trigger to Harry's anger has been long forgotten, but something set him off and he stood up and began to lash out at his colleague. At the end of each sentence, he spat out "Gordon Bigelow, PhD!" with as much contempt and vitriol as he could muster. The diatribe went on and on, with Bigelow sitting, head bowed, just a few feet from Harry, waiting desperately for the attack to subside.

At another memorable faculty meeting, the subject on the floor was how "creative" works should be measured against scholarly work when the department made tenure decisions. A remark was made that, in Harry's mind, disparaged the writing of actual fiction. He leapt to his feet, and announced to the room that he was ready and willing to "put his books on a goddamn scale" and match them, pound for pound, against the production of any goddamn "scholar" in the room. Nobody took the challenge.

After yet another meeting, one in which Harry had walked in long after it had started, New chastised him for his lateness.

"Sorry," he told his boss. "I was out making literature."

Faculty meetings weren't the only venue in which Harry would show his disdain for his colleagues. Departmental social gatherings could serve the purpose as well. Once, Harry was hosting such an event, becoming increasingly unstable as the night wore on. Several hours in, he told some of the attendees to gather round in the living room so he could show them a little Bacon County trick. He called over his dog, a hundred-pound German shepherd, rolled him over, and began to massage the dog's genitals, offering a play-by-play as the dog's enjoyment increased. By the time Harry's massage achieved the intended outcome, a good percentage of his audience had left the room, gotten their keys, and headed to their cars.

The department, and even the university, profited from his name, however. UF's annual writing festival annually brought in national literary figures, thanks in large part to Harry's increasing circle of friends. In October 1976 the Pulitzer Prize–winning playwright Tennessee Williams was persuaded to travel up from Key West to speak on campus. Williams agreed to the appearance on the condition that Harry would introduce him.

Due to previous incidents, Harry had been barred from such introductions, but the department made an exception in this case. On the night of the appearance, Harry took Williams to Lillian's, and the two "drank their dinner." When it was time for the event, they made their way back to the university auditorium and climbed up to the stage. Harry was introduced and limped to the front of the platform, stumbled, and nearly drove the podium into the audience. He regained his balance and stared into the front row, where the top officials of the University of Florida administration were seated.

"Ladies and gentlemen, it is customary on these occasions to say where a writer went to school and where he was born and the honors he has won," Harry intoned. "But who gives a shit?"

He allowed the wave of shock to reverberate through the audience of 750, said a few more words, and waited for Williams to walk forward.

"That's rather the nicest introduction I've ever had," Williams purred.

Trips back into his home state seemed to generate ideas for Harry, and one such trip across the border had been the spark for the novel he worked on in between magazine assignments. He'd attended the Claxton Rattlesnake Roundup, an annual small-town festival where men, women, and children gathered to kill, skin, and eat rattlesnakes and engage in other state fair–type activities, like beauty pageants and taffy pulls. The former Georgia governor and strident segregationist Lester Maddox was in attendance the day Harry spent at the roundup. Maddox shook hands and warmed up the crowd with a hymn played on his mouth harp to officially open the snake massacre. The event had that surreal quality which immediately felt to Harry like the setting for a novel. "I want to find out what this means," Harry told an interviewer as he was starting the book. "I watched those ladies. They want to eat some of that rattlesnake and they just been hanging on the pen looking at 'em where they're all writhing in there. And they get over there and the husband says, 'Aw, come on Delores. Just put it in your mouth honey. It's just like fried chicken.' I don't know what that is, but I want to know."

His association with Gottlieb and Knopf had run its course, so he was once again a literary free agent. Charles Corn, an editor for Atheneum Publishers, had begun pursuing Harry after the release of *Gypsy's Curse*. Corn was a Georgia native and a Marine, and he worked those angles to develop a friendship with Harry. Corn was also a respected editor who already had, or would soon, edit such authors as Paul Theroux, John Irving, Joyce Carol Oates, and Jorge Luis Borges. Corn made it clear he was a viable alternative to Knopf. "I hope you won't feel pressured or get tired of hearing me say that I'd love to be your editor," he wrote to Harry.

A little more than a year later, Corn got his chance. The manuscript he received from Hawkins was Harry's darkest, angriest, most violent work to date. The protagonist, Joe Lon Mackey, was a rage-filled, illiterate ex–high school football star with no prospects. Each episode in the 170-page book was more grisly than the next: a sheriff gets his genitals sliced off by a delirious young black woman while raping her; Joe Lon's mother suffocates herself with a plastic bag, cinching it with his father's only tie; his father tortures dogs in the guise of training for dogfights, then kicks one to death after it loses a match; his insane sister rubs feces in her hair while watching the evening news. The few pages that weren't devoted to characters murdering, raping, or defiling each other were used for creating many snake-as-penis, penis-as-snake metaphors. And, with what had become the Crews trademark ending, it closed with a storm of violence, this time of the human-on-human, human-on-snake, and snake-on-human variety.

Though Corn had repeatedly begged for a chance to work on a Crews manuscript, this one was not quite what he had in mind, at least initially. This new novel, as Corn saw it, contained brilliant passages that equaled Harry's earlier work. But it also had too many underdeveloped and overdeveloped characters. It had too many seemingly unrelated scenes and structural flaws. It was "scattered and diffuse," with an "uneasy arbitrariness as it develops." Still, Corn had a strong desire to work with Harry and was salivating over Harry's next project, the Bacon County memoir, so he did not want to reject the snake manuscript outright. Instead, he sat on it.

As weeks went by, Hawkins increased the pressure for Atheneum to make a decision. Corn continued to vacillate. "Short of marching to Atheneum and physically relieving him of the manuscript, I am not sure what else to do," Hawkins wrote. In the interim, Harry, as was now his modus operandi, lashed out against the criticism. He and an unnamed coconspirator dissected Corn's letter, offering their own critiques of Corn's comments, in the form of letters back to the editor scribbled in the margins. "Dear Mr. Corn: Please be advised that we'd be pleased if you would run it up your asshole sideways and swivel continuously until further notice."

Eventually, a truce was reached. Atheneum would publish *A Feast of Snakes*. Corn would furnish Harry with editorial suggestions, which Harry would agree to consider. Corn line-edited the manuscript page by page and sent it back to Gainesville along with four more pages of commentary. With time to digest Corn's criticism, Harry reevaluated. "I'm going to rewrite it, but only because I want to," he wrote to Gonzales. "It will be just as it is now, but ten times as tight."

He spent six weeks at Charné's home in Winter Park, Florida, working on the revisions, and by early 1976 a new version of the manuscript had been accepted by Atheneum and was making its way through copyediting. Harry sent Gonzales an early copy of the manuscript, and soon *Playboy* had agreed to pay $3,500 for the rights to publish an excerpt a few weeks prior to the release of the book in July.

Feast of Snakes was Harry's most disturbing novel, and a certain segment of readers, publishers, and reviewers were sufficiently scandalized. In South Africa, the Directorate of Publications decreed that anyone found distributing or importing the book was in violation of the law and subject to heavy penalties. Harry's London publisher expressed reservations, calling it "the kind of novel which is likely to shock British booksellers and librarians, who are a strange, insular and puritanical lot." Harry took tremendous pride in these reactions.

American newspapers and magazine reviewers recognized the increased shock value and either found it to be more, better Crews or too much Crews. Lloyd Zimpel in the *Los Angeles Times* was among the former, calling it "a spare and artful tale, often macabre and coldly humorous." The *New York Times'* Christopher Lehman-Haupt was staunchly in the latter camp: "What comes as a surprise is the gratuitousness of it all . . . the sense you get that Mr. Crews is piling it on for the sake of shocking us."

A letter that arrived in Harry's mail slot in Melrose, however, likely made a greater impression on him than anything that appeared in print. Corn had sent an advance copy to Joseph Heller. Heller shared Harry's penchant for instigation and instantly recognized the strain in the pages of *Feast*. His letter described to Harry a discussion he had recently had with Kurt Vonnegut. "I . . . started telling him about the book, and it warmed my heart to hear him laugh uproariously at the part that, literally, isn't funny at all, but in your book is as funny and impertinent as all hell—the slicing off of that dick, and the way the news is received and passed around," Heller wrote. "It's indeed a fine novel you've written . . . and I think it's going to cause some commotion. I hope it does. It deserves to."

The overall reaction to *Feast of Snakes* conveyed the sense that Harry had taken his novelistic vision to the limit and beyond, and perhaps reached some type of crossroads in doing so. Read on its own, it is a powerful and unique descent into the depths of human misery and angst. Read against his other books, it can appear derivative and gratuitous. During the writing of the novel he had been heavily involved in his foray into journalism; his continued interest in memoir was growing out of that undertaking. *Feast* was a culmination. Though he would always continue to say that writing novels was his true purpose and the rest of it was just for the money, he was in the process of stepping away from fiction. After producing eight novels in eight years, another eleven years would pass before he published his ninth.

A SENSE OF PLACE

> Nothing is allowed to die in a society of storytelling people. It is
> all—the good and the bad—carted up and brought along from
> one generation to the next. And everything that is brought along
> is colored and shaped by those who bring it.
> —Harry Crews, *A Childhood*

One Saturday morning, when Harry was still living by the lake in Melrose, Johnny Feiber made the drive out from Gainesville. It was a cool winter day, and Harry had a fire going in the fireplace. He asked Feiber to go get a case of beer and then come back and have a seat by the flames. He had been thinking about something, he told his friend, something that might turn into a book, and he wanted to say it out loud to somebody for the first time. "Then he just started talking," remembers Feiber. Over the course of the morning, "he told me, pretty much, the story of *Childhood*, from beginning to end . . . the entire bones of it, and all of the events."

It was in the tradition of oral storytelling, in which history remains in the collective memory of a people, passed from the lips of the older generation to the ears of the younger, around a fire, that Harry conceived of his most personal work. Listening to these stories had made him a storyteller himself. "When I was a boy, stories were conversation. And conversation was stories. For me, it was a time of magic," he wrote.

He had been working, in his life and his writing, toward this project, the story of his Bacon County youth, for several years. By 1976, he had

213

accumulated a drawer full of material to include, both from his aborted Appalachian Trail project and his "Grits" column in *Esquire*. This time, however, he had come around to the idea of an exploration of his youth and an examination of the world in which it took place. And now, he had finally determined, it was to be a straight memoir. "Something in my head resists that," he told an interviewer. "But it can be nice, if done right."

With the help of some more free grant money, this time $5,000 from the National Endowment for the Arts, and an indefinite leave of absence from the University of Florida, he traveled up to South Georgia and committed to research. He spent the entire summer of 1977 talking to as many people as he could find who still had memories reaching back into the unrecorded past of the Crews family. Byron joined him for much of the time, and the two would climb into Harry's van and drive the dirt roads of the county, going from farmer to farmer, tape recorder in hand.

It was the first significant time Harry had spent in and around Bacon County in more than twenty years, and it was a rude awakening. He found that the alienation he often felt at the university also existed, albeit in a different form, among those he thought of as "his people."

A deep rift had developed between Harry and his brother Hoyett. Wounds from childhood were always just below the surface between the two brothers. Hoyett had married and become a born-again Christian. Never one to understand Harry's literary ambitions, he was aghast when Harry began writing for *Playboy*, and especially when he found out Myrtice had seen it. How, Hoyett asked in disbelief, could Harry show that pornography to their mother? Myrtice felt no such negativity toward Harry's work and gave her full consent to her son's autobiographical project. She was even inspired to begin her own handwritten account of the family history, which Harry would eventually incorporate into the manuscript.

Harry felt an even deeper sense of alienation, however, among his more distant relatives, his uncles and aunts and cousins with whom he hoped to reconnect through his research. "They act like I'm a goddamn leper," he said. On the surface, they were pleasant to Harry. They would invite him into their homes and were willing to share their stories and discuss the past in depth. But he could feel that he was no longer one of them. "If I go into their house and it's cold or there's something there they think's not quite right, they apologize to me in a way they would not apologize to their other blood kin. It doesn't make you feel good. It makes you feel bad."

The disconnect went both ways. Harry's cousin Don Haselden remembered noting a change in the Harry he'd known during his childhood. Don and some of the others were proud of how one of their own had educated himself. But, on occasion, Don felt Harry used his intellect condescendingly. Once, Don asked a question that seemed to annoy Harry. "His answer went on and on, and I said, 'Now Harry, will you interpret that so I can understand what you're saying?'" Don recalled. "I was just thinking to myself, 'Hey, that boy's got an education now. He wants to say all these words that we just don't understand out here," Harry himself would write in *A Childhood* about his own peculiar ability to change his speech patterns and behaviors, depending on the education level of those he interacted with. With some people, Bacon County Harry would appear; with others, the erudite professor was on display. It was not an ability he was proud of.

As he got further and further into the research, Harry began to see the entire enterprise as a search for his father. He had not consciously set out to do so, but the psychological void left by his father's death seemed to color every episode he turned up in his investigation of his desperate youth. For as long as he could remember, he said, his dreams had been haunted by his dead father. He had gone into the project with the idea that staring directly into the past, and learning as much as possible as he could about his father and the events that surrounded his father's life and early death, would be a soul-cleansing experience. Instead, dredging up the past seemed to magnify his psychic pain.

The difficulty was reflected in the writing process as well. Words, he found for the first time in his life, would not come. He had rarely experienced writer's block while writing fiction, but now, when he sat down to put ink to paper, he failed. Again he returned, figuratively, to the place in front of the fire, the telling of the story, to get past the block. If he couldn't write, he would talk. He got his tape recorder, turned off all the lights, and, sitting by himself in the dark, told the tales into a microphone. Once a tape was full, he would give it to Maggie, who would transcribe it for him. It was unusable, of course, but it was a start, and it was enough to get him past the blank page and at least a few steps down the road.

The manuscript began to come together and, by late 1977, he could see the finish line. The progress was now regularly interrupted with extended bouts of drinking. Charné had begun to escape to Orlando when it escalated past the point she felt she could control. Around this time, the owners of Harry's Melrose cabin decided it needed renovation, and the work could only be done in the absence of Harry. He and Charné were unable to find a suitable replacement in Melrose, so Harry rented an apartment in downtown Gainesville and Charné spent more and more time in Orlando.

A businessman named Harvey Heller had offered Charné the use of a beautiful home on a lake in a central Florida orange grove. When Charné would allow it, Harry would come down and spend time on the estate, working out the final puzzle of his memoir while Charné worked on her sculpture.

A reporter named Steve Oney who had become friendly with Harry after earlier assignments came down to interview Harry at the orange grove. He remembered it as a "surreal scene." Charné was "sexy and beautiful," clad in short shorts and a tight T-shirt, her partially completed sculptures, which appeared to be cement phalluses, displayed all around the grounds. Harry grilled steaks, and the three of them sat among the orange trees, drinking bottle after bottle of wine, smoking pot, and eating the steaks with their bare hands.

The *Childhood* project had taken on immense importance in Harry's mind. He began to carry the manuscript around with him everywhere he went. He found that he was making the most progress at Heller's house in Orlando. Yet another auto accident had left him without his own transportation, so he began to take the Greyhound down from Gainesville. On one of his final trips down, a few of Charné's male friends, one a lawyer and the other a Vietnam vet, came over to the estate for a visit. Everybody was getting along at first, but an innocent comment by the vet sent Harry into a jealous rage. Charné took her friends out to a bar to calm the situation, leaving Harry at the house to stew.

A few months earlier, Harry had presented Charné with a Revolutionary War–era antique musket as a gift. When Charné and her friends returned from the bar late in the night, Harry was waiting for them, wielding the musket. He cocked it and pointed it at the vet. The vet, understandably scared that he was about to be punctured by a two-hundred-year-old musket ball, turned and ran. Harry pursued. The vet came to a fence that enclosed a dog run and attempted, unsuccessfully, to scale the fence, instead ending up injured in a heap in the dirt inside the dog run. While Charné screamed at Harry and tended to her friend's wounds, Harry grabbed his manuscript and ran off into the orange trees.

Hours later, Charné got into the car to track him down. As the sun was just beginning to trickle over the horizon, she came upon Harry, more than a mile away, the musket hanging from one hand and the manuscript under his other arm, limping, slowly and dejectedly, down the long dirt road that led to the exit of the estate.

Once again, Harry was changing publishers. Harper & Row had signed on to publish the Bacon County memoir, along with an anthology of Harry's nonfiction articles to be called *Blood & Grits*. "I hope that we will be able to give you the feeling that you have finally found a properly appreciative home," wrote Harvey Ginsberg, next up in line as Harry's editor. Harry titled the book *A Childhood: The Biography of a Place* and sent the two manuscripts to Ginsberg in early 1978.

Prior to mailing it off, Harry called his mother. He was writing about real people, people in his own life, for the first time. Going over the manuscript for a final time, he realized it opened with a scene in which his father had a testicle removed after contracting gonorrhea from an Indian prostitute. It was one of dozens of anecdotes that could cause potential embarrassment. He asked Myrtice if she'd like to read it before it went out to the world.

"No, son," she told him. "If it's the truth, write it."

Of that one thing, he was sure. And by then, he was also confident that he had a masterpiece on his hands.

Ginsberg concurred. It was, he wrote to Harry, "quite simply, a beautiful book." He sent Harry a page and a half of minor suggestions, some of which Harry accepted, and the book was set for publication in the summer of 1978.

Harry said often that he had labored for hours over the first sentence of *A Childhood*. It had become his philosophy to craft an opening to set the tone for each book. "I try to write the strongest beginning I can write and try to live up to it," he said.

> My first memory is of a time ten years before I was born, and the memory takes place where I have never been and involves my daddy whom I never knew.

"I can quote that sentence," he said years later. "Sentences like that don't just pop out of your head. It's not antithetical, but it is classically balanced. I'm proud of that sentence. I was proud of that sentence when I finally got it."

He had initially conceived *A Childhood* as an autobiography of his life in Bacon County, ending when he left the region for good and joined the

Marines at age seventeen. In the process of writing, though, the focus narrowed. The final version concluded around age seven. It was written in a voice that had not been present in his previous fiction or in his journalism. Much of the Crews attitude, the reliance on the bizarre, had been leached out of the writing, and in its place was a detached yet crystal-clear voice, devoid of self-pity but tinged with vulnerability. It was an effort to both discover, and to communicate as directly as possible, his own voice. "I have always slipped into and out of identities as easily as other people slipped into and out of their clothes," he admitted early in the text. "It was for just this reason that I started this book, because I have never been certain of who I am."

A Childhood moved from episode to episode, with moments of tragedy—his father's death, his own brushes with death, the breakup of his family—and humorous scenes that can evoke the flavor of a Depression-era Huck Finn. Harry interspersed the dialect of the region and the time and put to paper many of the legends he'd heard the adults spin around the fire or the sewing circle, often through the voices of his elders, brought back to life from his own memory. Willalee Bookatee's grandmother, known as Auntie, was one of many such vivid characters who were used to tell the story:

> Auntie was not just right in the head, and I knew it. She was, as they said in Bacon County, *that way*. You couldn't go crazy in Bacon County; you were just *that way*. She was a little, frail thing who had an amazing strength in her spidery hands. Under the voluminous skirts she always wore, her bones seemed as brittle as a bird's. She was born, she was quick to tell you, a slave. But she did not know how old she was. If you asked her, she would say "Round about a hundret." More than once mama had told me Auntie was *that way* because of her age.
>
> In a deliberate, whining voice I knew she could accept, I said, "I wish you'd tol me about the birds, Auntie."
>
> Her head cocked again, listening. "You know a bird can go ahead and spit like a snake," she said. "Spit jest like a snake. I know you know that."
>
> I didn't know a bird could spit like a snake, but once she said it, it sounded marvelously, horribly right to me. After the words came out of her old shrunken mouth that had known everything and said everything, it was hard for me to imagine a bird not spitting like a snake. And never mind that I had no idea how a snake might spit.

"Birds spit like a snake and never hit you but in one place," she said, pausing, holding the silence like a measure while she looked at me expectantly. Then, when it was obvious I didn't know: "Right in the mouf."

Upon its release, *A Childhood* was universally praised. The reception would produce the best critical reviews Harry received of anything he wrote in his career. An excerpt published in *Shenandoah* a few years earlier had already been cited as the "best nonfiction work in America" by the Coordinating Council on Literature in America. Reviewers in major publications across the country followed suit. *Time* chose it as one of the ten best books of the year, and other publications gave similar designations. In *The Nation*, Michael Mewshaw wrote that *A Childhood* "maintains a precarious balance between sentiment and sensation, memory and madness, and manages to convince the reader of two mutually exclusive imperatives which have shaped [Harry Crews's] life—the desire to escape Bacon County and the constant ineluctable need to go back." "What Harry Crews has done," wrote Betty Lukas in the *Los Angeles Times*, "is retrieve in written language the powerful, touching, grisly, funny, tragic episodes of his early childhood with an unforgettable reality." To John Leonard, writing in the *New York Times*, the book was "a splendid memoir" in which "the truth is in the terrible beauty of his stories."

Once again, however, critical success did not translate into material success. Sales lagged, at least behind where Harry and his agent felt they should be. Hawkins wrote to Ginsberg, urging more effort on the part of the publisher to drive sales. "How far is Harper willing to go to back a distinguished book that isn't making any money?" he asked. "I'm pleased that Harper is going to make millions on Linda Goodman, as I was pleased to be the agent for ROOTS. If anything, the big money means we have a greater responsibility to be creative about some of the books that don't generate millions."

A Childhood would be the pinnacle of literary recognition for Harry. The response would, over time, lead to a reexamination of his entire body of work, which, correlated with *A Childhood*, began to take on the shape of a cohesive literary vision of the South, one that began to merit academic attention. His memoir would go on to be anthologized over and over and taught in high school and college classrooms for years when the topic of the Depression-era Tobacco Road was next on the syllabus.

In his imagining of *A Childhood*, Harry had hoped to achieve something other than literary success, however. And on that level, the project proved to be a dismal failure. He had said he wanted to find himself, to answer certain questions so completely that he would no longer be forced to deal with them in his dreams. "I thought if I could relive it and set it all down in detailed, specific language, I would be purged of it," he wrote. "It almost killed me, but it purged nothing. Those years are still as red and raw and alive in memory as they ever were." If he couldn't kill the demons with words, then, what was there left to do? It proved to be a question for which Harry did not have an answer.

"After I'd written it," he said, "I just woke up one morning and realized I didn't give a shit anymore."

Now I was on the roster. Every few weeks, I'd get a call, sometimes before dawn (I soon got into the habit of turning off my cell phone to preserve my night's sleep and that of my family), when Harry needed a driver. There were a few of us—Ed (when he and Harry were getting along), Harry's barber, a couple others—among whom he divided the responsibilities.

I'd park in the gravel driveway, enter through the unlocked front door, and find Harry, in the same old recliner, but usually ready for action. "You're looking well today," he'd offer, and then he'd give me the day's itinerary, usually the bank, or the doctor, or the drugstore, all within the two-mile radius that had become the horizon of his life in his current state. Most of the time, he was in a talkative mood, happy to field my questions and delve back into the endless story archive.

If it was near the end of the month, however, he could be in a sour mood. The purpose of the call on those days was inevitably to refill his Oxy supply, so he'd be in pain, reeking of desperation. Often, he'd run out of pills early and the mission would be to convince the doctor or pharmacist, or both, that it was a good idea to fork over the meds now. Once he had them, he'd open the bottle, down one, and count the rest of the capsules, one by one, in the palm of his hand, a habit from the thousands of such transactions he'd completed in younger days. When the medicine reached his bloodstream, he'd begin to feel better and tell me about the street value of the drugs we were now holding. Sometimes he'd drift off to sleep before we made it back to the house.

After a few visits, I thought I had a grip on Harry's daily life. Most of his time was spent in the recliner, I imagined, interrupted by the occasional excursion or visitor. The life he was known for, it seemed, was way in the rearview mirror. Sometimes, however, that life seemed to reach out of the past and grab him.

One morning when I came to pick him up, he looked up from the recliner with a black eye that extended across a third of his face. He smiled through the deep purple bruise, obviously proud of the injury. He offered no details, other than claiming that far worse damage was done to the perpetrator who had caused his wound.

We went to the doctor that morning, and Harry waited in the car as I went in to pick up some medicine. A nurse must have seen him through the window and noticed the condition of his eye, because the doctor ran out to the parking lot waving his arms before we could pull away.

"Harry, what are you doing?" he asked, with a mixture of confusion and disgust. "Come in and let me take a look at you."

Harry dismissively waved him away, cursed him under his breath, and we drove off. Once we were out of range, he softened, remembering that his doctor wasn't an enemy.

"He's an army doctor, served two tours in Korea," he said appreciatively.

The past was never really the past, it seemed. Once, he called with a proposition. He was working on a big story for *Playboy*, he said. It was about the drug trade in Gainesville. He'd let me in on it if I would drive him over to east Gainesville, the other side of the tracks, for some "research."

Luckily, I had to go out of town when the research was supposed to take place.

On another occasion he called, more desperate than usual. An old girlfriend had come over. She'd brought a friend, and after Harry had gone to sleep, they'd stolen his Oxycodone.

Two of his old concerns, drugs and money, were usually on the agenda. Once, he had a box full of cash that had to be deposited in the bank. Again, no details were offered.

When he was handling a lot of money, as was often the case if a check arrived from California, where his agent was still selling options on his novels, he'd offer me a cut in exchange for the ride. He seemed disappointed when I declined the money. To Harry, payment for services was of the utmost importance.

Once, I called with a request. I needed a signed letter from him to get copies of his papers from the UGA library. I left a message explaining the situation and waited for him to call me back. No return call came.

A few days later, I got him on the phone. Why hadn't he called?

"Well, you said, if you're willing to do bap, bap, bap, then I should give you a call. I don't want to do bap, bap, bap," he said derisively. Soon, he got to the point.

"We live in a quid pro quo world, chief," he said.

We negotiated, settling on the signed letter in exchange for a ride to the dentist later that afternoon, one he clearly knew he could have had just by asking.

On better days, he'd dispense the kind of advice he used to offer his favorite students, advice about writing, or love, or whatever was on his mind.

One day, he was sitting on the bed, struggling to pull his boots off.

"That's when you know it's over with a woman," he said. "When you're stripping down buck naked on one side of the bed and she's doing it on the other side. If it's love, there's supposed to be some licking and sucking going on."

Sex, he continued, was the one thing in life that you could never have enough of. You could reach your limit on cakes, or ice cream, or heroin. But it was a definitive law of nature: it was impossible to have too much sex.

He asked few questions, but when he discovered I had a wife and two children, he expressed what felt like sincere admiration. He wanted to meet the kids, take the family out to dinner. He'd tried and failed at it, he said, and had passed up later opportunities to have a family and raise children, unwilling to take the plunge again, a decision he now regretted. He'd made a choice to devote his time on Earth to words and stories, he said.

Harry had spent a lifetime giving writing advice, and it rolled off his tongue without a second's thought. Since I was a reporter, talk often turned to journalism.

"I never wrote what the editors in New York told me to write," he said. "I said I would, but I didn't. I just got into some shit, and then put it on paper."

One day I was complaining about the fleeting nature of journalism, how you poured your heart into a story, and by the middle of the next day it was gone, never to be read or discussed again. He concurred. A novel was forever, he said. And you don't have to worry about an editor telling you what to write. Then he went into a soliloquy that perfectly distilled the plight of the journalist.

"And when you're a reporter, you get to write, but you have to get past editors," he told me. "You always do, before you get to do what you want to do, or what you'd rather do. You say: 'Why don't you let me go cover this or that?' Maybe you want to go cover the rodeo, so you can get deep into it, and write about the stink of shit. But they say, 'Uh, we don't think so, we'd rather you go cover the lemon pie bake-off, at the junior high school, or something or other.'"

He took a long drag of the cigarette.

"And there you find yourself, up to your ass in lemon pies."

HARD WORK

> I am one of the all-time sloppy, disgusting drunks, the kind
> mothers can point out to their children as an example of the
> final evil of alcohol.
> —Harry Crews, *Take 38*

T he audience was steadily dwindling, as groups of twos and threes quietly made their way up the aisles toward the exits at the back of the auditorium in the Arts & Letters Building on the campus of the University of South Florida in Tampa. Sitting on the edge of the stage, boots hanging over the side, the keynote speaker on the second night of the Celebration of Literature was stumbling, barely audibly, through a reading of the essay "Climbing the Tower," dying a slow death. A deep purple bruise began at his nose and expanded outward across his face. Speckles of gray had begun to creep into his unkempt hair and his thick mustache, and his eyes were several shades of pink. His face was beefy and reddish now, and his once solid body was puffy, with a substantial gut hanging over his belt. He had downed, in a single suck, an entire fifth of Gallo wine in the car ride to the event. As the exodus grew, he tried to reassure those who remained.

"This won't take along," he said repeatedly, pleadingly. "Only a few more pages."

The USF professor of literature who had introduced him a few minutes before decided to throw his fallen star a lifeline and get him off the stage.

He approached Harry and whispered something into his ear. In a split second, the shame on Harry's face transformed into anger.

"I've only got one more paragraph," he shouted, tears glistening in his eyes.

The professor enlisted another of the evening's speakers, the author William Price Fox, to help get Harry off the stage. Harry rose, reenergized, and began to stagger around the stage, leaning on Fox. He took off his reading glasses and slammed them to the floor, and dropped the book from which he had been reading. Then, from memory and with a newfound dramatic presence, he bellowed the final paragraph of the essay, his words echoing through the now half-empty room. The remaining audience members rose in applause.

When the room quieted, one of those members shouted a question to Harry: What did it take to become a real novelist?

Harry moved to the front of the stage and replied, as powerfully and deliberately as he could manage, with a prolonged pause between each word, "Blood! . . . Bone! . . . Marrow!"

For the next several minutes, he wandered about the stage, responding to real and imagined questions, and periodically shouting "Marrow!" at Fox in a show of pretend rage. It was, one attendee said, "a sensational performance, antagonistic and existential, something Norman Mailer might have delivered . . . if Mailer had been, oh, say, Davey Crockett."

Eventually, Harry was carried out of the building to a waiting car, shouting incoherently through the parking lot. Fox and a few others managed to get him into the vehicle and a few minutes later deposited him, unconscious, in his room at the Travel Lodge.

It was how each night now concluded for Harry, more or less. He had begun a phase during which, he said, he would not go to bed sober for nine full years. And most mornings would begin with a long tug on a bottle of vodka, just enough, he would say, to steady his hands so he could shave. His life was now ruled by alcohol. During an average day, he would consume a quart of vodka, a case and a half of beer, and several bottles of wine.

His battles with the bottle were often on public display. He was now a sought-after speaker on the university circuit, and such appearances were ripe for heavy drinking and outlandish behavior. His reputation preceded him, so he was usually handed a drink as he was stepping off the airplane, expected to lubricate and perform the role of tortured drunken artist. He obliged.

In April 1979 he was invited for a two-day speaking engagement at Agnes Scott College near Atlanta. With an all-female student body and strong religious ties, it was an unlikely place to import the Crews Show. It was a paying gig, however, so he signed on. "I'll be honest," he told a reporter. "I've spoken at five different colleges in the last few months, Jack, and it's all for the bread."

He arrived drunk and was ushered into a frilly upstairs bedroom in the Anna Young Alumnae House. He lay on the bed and began to hold court, pontificating for the assembled students and members of the English faculty. He offered a "rambling discourse on the virtues of women's breasts and the complementarity of male and female genitals," sending most of his hosts toward the door. Those remaining eventually escorted him to the Letitia Pate Evans Dining Hall, where he looked around at his fellow diners and pronounced to whoever would listen, "Oh, Lord, they sure are some fine-lookin' thangs. I tell you, Jack, if I taught here, I'd be guilty of everything I've been accused of."

That evening, a group of professors and students took Harry to Manuel's Tavern after his first speaking engagement, where he proceeded to work his way through several vodka and tonics. A reporter from the *Atlanta Journal-Constitution* who was following him for the day was at the table. She had a butterfly bandage on her head, and, in a show of some kind of ill-conceived chivalry, Harry leaned across the table, licked the bandage off her head, and swallowed it. After challenging another patron to a fight in the parking lot and "confessing to an embarrassing array of carnal sins," he was brought back to the Anna Young Alumnae House, where he passed out among the frills. In the morning he emerged from the upstairs bedroom, completely naked, putting an exclamation point on a story that would be told through the halls of Agnes Scott College for years to come.

Sometimes, Harry made it to the university that had invited him but never actually reached the stage. On a trip to Anderson University in South Carolina, he made an unfortunate pit stop at the university library to check his name in the card catalog (a detour he made ritually upon arriving on campuses) prior to his planned appearance. The Anderson University library, he discovered to his horror, did not own a single Crews title.

The only proper response, Harry felt, was to drink himself out of commission, which he proceeded to do. When the time arrived for the reading, he sent his assistant, David Johansson, to the now-filled auditorium. The organizer inquired about Harry's whereabouts.

"He's not coming," Johansson told him.

"Why not?" the professor asked incredulously.

"Because you don't have any of his books in your library."

The assembled academia of Anderson U. went home, but some diehards found Harry's room at the hotel later that evening. Harry was convinced to invite them in, and an impromptu reading took place, with Harry and his fans sitting on the floor, joints and whiskey bottles moving from hand to hand around the room. Harry signed books, took reading requests, and the party lasted into the early morning.

After such an aborted appearance, word would often get back to Gainesville. A department chairman who had brought Harry to campus would call the English Department to complain about an inebriated appearance or a no-show. Most of these complaints barely registered; Harry's own colleagues, of course, got to see the same type of show firsthand, on a regular basis. Brandy Kershner was a James Joyce specialist who had taught English in the department nearly as long as Harry. One evening while Kershner was serving as interim chairman of the department, he went out to dinner at a fashionable downtown Gainesville restaurant with his wife. While the two were being led to their table, Harry was being escorted out of the establishment in the other direction, his arms draped around the shoulders of two friends. Harry was barely conscious, but he gained focus enough to recognize Kershner as the two colleagues crossed paths.

"Oh, my god," Harry shouted in horror for the entire restaurant to hear. "It's my boss!"

Gainesville restaurants were often the site for one of Harry's drunken performances. A friend of Feiber's graduated from the University of Florida School of Law, and Harry offered to take her, Feiber, and several others out to a celebratory dinner. The group settled on Twelve East, a swanky downtown dinner spot. Harry was drinking martinis that evening, ordering one after another. When dinner was served, he pushed aside his silverware and proceeded to eat his entire steak with his hands, as the rest of the dining room looked on in shock. It was his own twist on Mr. Lytle's soup-slurping statement, more than two decades before. When dinner was over, Harry fell out of his chair and needed help out of the restaurant.

He did not sip a drink, he "bubbled the bottle." He was drinking not to be social but to get drunk. Social drinking, he said, was not drinking.

"When Harry drank, you would give him a glass of something, and he would drink it in one go, and then he would order another one," Feiber remembered.

Feiber saw him less and less as Harry's drinking increased. Once, after he had not seen Harry in many months, Feiber paid him a visit. "He said, 'Well, let's have a drink.' I said, 'Fine.' He poured himself a full, twelve-ounce glass of vodka, and then he poured me one. I said, 'Harry, wait a minute, I gotta have ice.' So, he said, 'OK,' and he poured some out, and he put one ice cube in it. I said, 'Let me do this.' I poured most of it out and put some ice in it. Then, I nursed that thing. The bottle was maybe two-thirds full when I got there, and by the time I left it was [empty]."

Part of the problem was proximity. In Melrose, he had been far enough removed from bad influences to keep his situation in check when necessary. Now he was in town, accessible to all his drinking buddies, and minutes from a dozen bars. Cronies arrived nightly with bottles and plans, and Harry offered little resistance.

Feiber recognized the conundrum and offered Harry a solution. Feiber himself had gotten his own place on Lake Melrose and moved out of town full-time. After a particularly rough stretch for Harry, Feiber invited his friend to stay at the lake house, so Harry could dry up and get his life back on course. Harry accepted, and for a few days he curtailed his drinking and seemed to be straightening up. Feiber taught English at Santa Fe Community College in Gainesville at the time, and he would say goodbye to Harry in the morning and make the drive into town.

On the fourth or fifth day of the arrangement, Feiber arrived home from work and sensed a different vibe. "I could smell a woman had been in the house," he said. Feiber kept an extensive wine collection in the cabin. Now, he looked around and saw more than thirty open bottles of wine scattered around the room. Harry had opened bottle after bottle, drinking the ones that pleased him, and leaving the remainder half-full on the floor. Feiber proceeded out the back door to the bank of the lake. From the water's edge, he saw Harry and a female companion, both completely nude, in Feiber's boat, in full view of all of his neighbors. Very soon after that, Harry's return to Melrose was quietly aborted.

Drinking all the wine that was available and ending up naked had been on Harry's playlist for years. Now, however, his binges often derailed him for weeks. He would start drinking and not emerge for days at a time. At his lowest points, he would drink himself into a state of unconsciousness, sleep for six or eight hours, then awake just long enough to grab the nearest bottle, gulp continuously for a few minutes, and pass out again for several more hours. "I've never seen any other human drink alcohol as quickly. He could drain a fifth of vodka, half of it, in thirty seconds," Johansson said. When he would run out of whiskey, he'd call a friend, or an acquaintance, to replenish his supply. The chosen delivery person would often find Harry in the corner of his apartment, surrounded by empty bottles, covered in his own excrement.

Huntley Johnson, who began acting as Harry's lawyer in the early 1980s, often found him in this "wretched, filthy" state. "He would stay on the ground in one place, and hold court there—eat, shit, piss, sleep. Harry did not have good bowel control when he was drinking," Johnson said.

The problem, Harry said, was that once he reached this state, he physically did not have the power to stop himself from drinking. These types of binges could reach a conclusion only with a trip to the hospital, a rehabilitation clinic, or jail. Many benders ended with Harry taken to the emergency room and then, on doctor's recommendation, checked into the Vista Pavilion mental health facility in Gainesville, where doctors would use all means necessary to dry him out. He told friends about an incident when, upon admission to the facility, he was out of control and had to be restrained by employees. Once he had been calmed, he was shown a metal bathtub and told that if his behavior regressed, the tub would be filled with ice water, and he would be placed in it with a canvas cover that had a single opening for his head. Harry took the advice that time and stayed calm. But the time between rehab appearances was shrinking. One year during this period, he made sixteen separate trips to the clinic.

He was still, however, a functioning alcoholic. He took and completed writing assignments; he appeared often enough in class to stay employed. Doctors prescribed him Anabuse, a drug that induces vomiting and other effects when alcohol enters the system. It would work for a while, but then Harry would occasionally drink despite having the drug in his system and end up paying a severe price for it. During writing projects, he would often take Anabuse, and then, when he was nearing the conclusion of the project, he would gradually reduce the dosage down to nothing, in effect scheduling his next drinking binge to coincide with completion of the manuscript.

He did his best to keep signs of his drunkenness away from the workplace, canceling class when he deemed himself unpresentable. But occasionally Turlington Hall was the nearest crash point when he could not make it home, and he would be found unconscious in the office suite by his colleagues arriving for work the next day. One morning, he landed a few yards short of the office. Larry Hetrick smelled the stench as he arrived ready for class. Outside the office suite, the janitorial staff was cleaning up piles of vomit, from which, moments earlier, Harry had been removed. Such incidents cemented resentment among some of his colleagues, even those, such as Hetrick, who considered Harry a friend.

Such behavior was not limited to Gainesville. On one trip to meet with editors in New York, a group took Harry to lunch at Tavern on the Green. Bob Mecoy was an editor with Dell at the time. In the midafternoon, he received a call from a friend begging for assistance extricating Harry from the restaurant. "We did the next best thing to carrying him out head and foot," Mecoy recalled. "I mean he was 98.6 percent unconscious. Somehow, we got him back to his hotel and put him to bed."

A call from Harry often would mean one was in for a difficult few hours. Steve Oney received one such call from a pay phone at the Atlanta airport. Harry told Oney he had been beaten and robbed in New York and had been awaiting his connection to Gainesville when he was attacked by airport security. Oney and a friend drove to the airport and found Harry covered in scrapes and bruises, sitting on the curb. They offered him a bottle of whiskey, which he readily accepted. Later, after Oney got Harry back to his apartment, Harry began making advances on Oney's girlfriend, before he mercifully passed out for the evening.

Usually, his writing projects were bookended by benders. Michael Cimino, a well-respected Hollywood director who had enormous success with *The Deer Hunter* and equally enormous failure with *Heaven's Gate*, hired Harry in 1983 to write a screenplay about Emmett Kelly, the famed circus clown. Harry signed the contract. Soon, the deadline neared. He had been drinking heavily for two months and could not seem to clean up long enough to write the script. He appealed to Rodney Elrod, a student of Harry's who had become a close friend. Elrod's wife, Debbie, was a nurse, and the two took Harry in. Their home in Cross Creek served as an amateur rehab clinic. For a week, they attended to him, helping him through the DTs, until he was finally sober enough to write.

With his discipline returned, Harry focused solely on the project for the next two weeks. He woke early, sat at the kitchen table and typed until midmorning, took fifteen minutes to eat a sandwich and drink a glass of orange juice, and then sat back down at the table. The afternoon and the evening was the same, day after day, until the script, titled *Clown*, was ready to be sent to Cimino. Harry had a drink in his hand shortly after the manuscript left Gainesville. When the check from Cimino arrived from Hawkins, Harry paid the taxes on it and then signed half of it over to Elrod.

Those who encountered Harry at his worst, after he'd been drunk for an extended period, often would come away from the encounter thinking death was imminent. Predictions of Harry's demise became rampant. Harry made such an impression on fellow Andrew Lytle disciple James Dickey, with whom he had begun a friendship through joint appearances at writers' conferences. Harry and Dickey spent time together in the dead of winter at the University of North Dakota Writer's Conference in Grand Forks, North Dakota, where Harry "gave himself a hell of a bad time with alcohol." Dickey, a notorious drinker himself, tried to get in touch with Harry afterward to check on him. "I still can't locate him," he wrote to a friend. "I have some doubts, knowing him from those ice-bound days, as to whether he's still alive . . ."

Those who had known him years before could not believe the depths to which he had sunk. After a visit to Gainesville, a former student, Lawrence Jordan, wrote to Kirkpatrick, in despair over Harry's state. "Smith," Jordan wrote, "you all simply cannot sit there and allow him to do that to himself. . . . Tormented as he himself is, his vision is even more tormented and dealing with him personally is sometimes as bad as being crucified. But he is worth an attempt. No one can save a drowning man who does not himself want to be saved, but those of us safely ashore can be lighthouses."

Editors, who before had seen his behavior as a selling point, saw that now it was out of hand. When they called him now, they were never sure what to expect. "I spoke with Harry today and he is not too well," one editor wrote to a colleague of Gonzales. "He sounded positively awful, could not make complete sentences and did not seem to know where he was or what was going on. He did tell me he was beaten up badly, said he had what sounded like a large hematoma or even hemorrhage on his stomach. He spoke about 'getting' the guy who did it."

Many of those people with whom he had been close for years before began to pull away as his alcoholism worsened. "Harry was a drowning man. Being his friend was hard work," Feiber said. "It got to the point that I told him I just couldn't be there for him anymore."

The predictions piled up, and Harry made attempt after attempt to turn things around. "Alas, can't drink anymore," he wrote to Gonzales during one such effort to clean up. "I have brutalized and terrorized my body and—after a long lapse—I am physically and mentally tough again. I say it, as you can tell, with some pride. Why not? All my friends were predicting my death."

Publicly, however, he was defiant. One New York writer made the mistake of observing that the final chapter of Harry's life was winding down, and his death was imminent. Elrod asked Harry about the article in question. "That just goes back to those wimps who say I'm burned out, that I had a mind and talent and destroyed it with alcohol. . . . Most people can't deal with chaos. They can't deal with blood and bone and pain. They think that once you're hurt, you're hurt forever. And of course, you are if you're a wimp. Immodest as it is of me to say so, I ain't a wimp. I get down sometimes, but I always get up again."

Anybody who believed they were going to outlive Harry Crews was mistaken. He would be back, he declared, no matter what was being written about him.

"To answer your question," he told Elrod, "I'll piss on his grave."

MUSCLE MEMORY

> When writers don't write, they tend to do immoral things.
> —William Faulkner

Building D had finally been demolished in the mid-1970s, and the University of Florida English Department was now located in Turlington Hall, a sprawling red-brick building that housed much of the College of Arts & Sciences. Harry's office was now in the Creative Writing suite in Turlington. When he worked on campus, part of his daily routine was to walk from his office to Krystal, a hamburger joint, for coffee. Susan Mickelberry had an office in a neighboring building. From her window, she could see Harry on his daily sojourns, limping toward traffic, and noted his sporadic transformations. When he was deep into the bottle, Susan Mickelberry said, he looked like "walking death." But, just months later, his appearance would be completely different. She could tell he was back at the gym and that his latest comeback was under way.

"He was a testament to the recovery powers of the human body," she recalled.

Harry's binging was debilitative, but it was also intermittent. After a stint at the clinic, or when he was deep into a writing assignment, he could be productive. He would regain his discipline, mentally and physically, often subsisting on a diet of fish and vegetables to get his weight down. His alcohol consumption would be somewhat under control, and he would settle back into his preferred routine. The early, early morning had become his chosen time to write. He'd awake at four a.m., brew a pot of coffee, and plant himself at the table. The Underwood had been largely rendered inoperable due to multiple collisions with the wall, brought on by fits of rage, so he wrote in longhand most of the time, smoking cigarettes and drinking cup after cup of black coffee. (He'd read many years earlier that Graham Greene thought five hundred words a day was sufficient output and would often stop in the middle of a sentence when he hit the magic number, and Harry had long ago adopted the same daily finish line for himself.) Once his writing was completed for the day, it was time to don his gray sweatshirt and sweatpants and hit the gym, where he would move from machine to bench to machine for three hours, shower, and finally make his way to campus.

Harry had been living off and on with Maggie in her small apartment near the university for two years when Maggie's sister moved to St. Petersburg. Maggie inherited her sister's small rental house in downtown Gainesville, and Harry followed. Less than a block away stood the Gainesville Gym, a new establishment that catered to "iron freaks" and had recently begun to host an annual bodybuilding competition.

Maggie had dropped out of graduate school at UF and taken a job as a drug abuse counselor at Lowell Correctional Institution. Running was her preferred method of staying in shape, but a foot injury had sidelined her, and soon she was accompanying Harry to the Gainesville Gym on a daily basis. The determination she had been channeling into her studies was soon redirected to the weight bench. The gym added a female division to the bodybuilding event, and Maggie, after some convincing from John Babb, owner of the gym, and Harry, agreed to start training.

The sport of female bodybuilding was just starting to emerge on the American cultural landscape in the late 1970s. Male bodybuilding had come of age in the 1950s and rocketed into the national consciousness in 1977 with the popularity of *Pumping Iron*, a documentary about the sport that marked Arnold Schwarzenegger's introduction to American audiences. The film, combined with the country's growing obsession with physical fitness and the expanding influence of the women's-lib movement, had produced the perfect climate for a new, media-friendly fad.

The first female bodybuilders were closer to beauty-pageant contestants than their bulked-up, disproportionate counterparts on the male side of the sport. In competition, they wore bikinis and posed like models as often as they flexed for the judges. Rachel McLish, a "5-foot, 6-inch, 120-pound beauty with auburn hair and a golden smile," won the first Ms. Olympia competition in 1980. Lisa Lyon, a dancer at UCLA who became another pioneer of the sport, measured in at 5' 3", 105, with the "lean, athletic appearance of a swimmer or a runner." She parlayed her sudden notoriety into television appearances and photo spreads in *Esquire* and *Playboy*. The rules of the game, early on, had been established: be beautiful, be strong, be thin.

Maggie latched on to those ideals. She bought a book about Lyon and began to use her own training in physiology to transform her body. She won the local competition easily and assumed the title of the first Ms. Gainesville. She was hooked.

By now, Harry had twenty-five years inside gyms. He'd lived it, and he'd already written a novel, *Gypsy's Curse*, about gym life. Now he took on the role of bodybuilding trainer. He would be Mick to Powell's Rocky. At numerous times during his life, he'd exhibited incredible physical discipline, willing himself into becoming a runner and cyclist, despite his weakened legs. He taught discipline in the classroom as well. In Harry's world, physical pursuits, though, were the great equalizer. "In athletics, I can find truth," he said. "You say you can lift 440 pounds on the bench—well, I just happen to have 440 pounds and a bench. No more talk. Let's see what you got."

After she won the Gainesville Gym event, Maggie jumped into the sport with both feet. She lifted weights and trained aerobically every day, moving, day by day, from one muscle group to the next. She saw immediate results and soon moved up to statewide competitions. When an event was approaching, she would often train eight hours a day.

Since she was after the Lisa Lyon look, a large part of preparation involved dieting. At times she would consume just five hundred calories a day, subsisting on tuna, carrots, and air-popped popcorn. "I was just skin and muscle . . . and bones. There was no fat on me at all," she said. "That's the way that I could win. The judges needed to see that I looked like an anatomy chart."

Harry's most important role as trainer was to coexist with an extremely hungry, constantly angry trainee. "I wasn't a very nice person, I don't think. When you're starving to death, it's hard to be," she said. Harry monitored her workouts and occasionally tried to ration her food intake. In an incident that would, years later, become a literary set piece, he once followed her through a workout, barking at her all the way, insisting that if she performed a particular set as he had asked, he would relent and allow his starving trainee to eat a single cube of ice.

But it was largely a singular pursuit, in Maggie's eyes. "Harry liked to tell people he was my trainer, and at times he was," she remembered. "I didn't take him too seriously most of the time. But he did help me."

Maggie's pursuit went on for several years, and she accumulated a wall full of trophies. It consumed much of her free time and, when in heavy training, most of her life. In 1984 she entered a regional event in Georgia, the highest level of competition she had yet attempted. She dove back into training and dieting and, with Harry along for the ride, traveled north to compete in the event.

In the few years in which she had participated, the sport, and the competitors, had evolved to become more in line with the men's divisions. Petite and toned was slowly being replaced by bulging and swollen. The new champion was Bev Francis, an Australian athlete who had started out as a power lifter. She tipped the scales at 168 pounds, with 16-inch biceps and a 39-inch chest that was all pecs. She could bench-press 330 pounds comfortably. When she first appeared in competition, one reporter wrote, it "seemed like a very special bull had appeared in a shop full of Barbie dolls."

Another addition to the sport was steroid use, already rampant on the men's side. The combination of the changes had begun to sour Maggie on the entire endeavor. "I was a bodybuilder, I wasn't a power lifter. I was doing exercises. I learned enough about it in school to sculpt my body, not to grow huge," she said. "When people like Bev Francis—it was hard to tell if she was a guy or a girl—when she started winning, it was not for me. I don't know that they did steroids, but I believe they did. I worked out pretty hard, but I knew I could never get to be like that."

Maggie placed second in her weight division in the southeastern competition and promptly retired for good. She and her trainer stepped off the women's bodybuilding circuit and moved into the next stage of their lives. But Harry had been watching closely, and now he had a full notebook stored away. The entire bodybuilding scene—the Barbie dolls, the Amazons, the beauty vs. bulk debate, the needles, the starvation, all of it—had begun, somewhere along the way, to edge into focus as the canvas for one more work of fiction.

For Maggie, however, life with Harry was not all training and travel. Alcohol was a constant part of their lives. Maggie at first had sought to control it, removing alcohol from the house or urging Harry to attend Alcoholics Anonymous meetings. "Most of the time when he and I were together, he was drunk. He did get sober from time to time, but it was infrequent," she recalled. "I couldn't control him, or his drinking. He wouldn't be drunk all the time necessarily, but you never knew when he was going to be and when he wasn't going to be."

The relationship bottomed out often. At times when Harry was drinking and a certain mood came over him, he could be frightening and dangerous. He had a hair-trigger temper that emerged suddenly. With Maggie, his anger came to the edge of violence but never crossed the line, she said. He called her every name in the book, but his attacks remained verbal. On many occasions, the situation would become untenable, and Maggie would tell Harry he needed to find another place to live. "I'd get to a point where it would be just too exhausting," she said.

It was the natural state of affairs for Harry. He was now used to moving along to the next stop, if it were to be a dumpy apartment in the student ghetto, another girlfriend's place, or somebody's couch. He had few belongings; as a point of pride he wanted to, at all times, be able to put all his possessions in the back of his truck and leave town. "I'm the easiest person in the world to get rid of," he said. "All someone has to say, as long as they don't say it belligerently, is that they don't want me around, and I'll leave. Walk. Fuck, I'll go. I don't like to argue or fight with women. I'd rather put my feet in the street, and have, more times that I can remember."

On several occasions, he moved back in with Sally and Byron at the house on Eighth Street. That arrangement also had a short shelf life, and he was usually back on the street soon after moving in. (In later years, he increased the number of times that he would tell people he had been divorced from Sally, depending on how recently he'd moved out.)

As often as he was thrown out by women, there was usually another woman waiting. Monogamy was another part of the married-children-house lifestyle he had no use for. And, working at a university with thousands of young women, there was always opportunity. "Nobody could be around Harry without becoming aware of his sexual proclivities or his absolute preoccupation with sex," said his friend John Morefield.

Harry had little concern for professor-student boundaries, and the mores of the day were far less restrictive in that area than they would eventually become. "That's the great thing about being at a university; you can fuck yourself to death if you want to," he told an interviewer. "But I don't want to."

Age was no barrier. Teresa Burns arrived in Gainesville at age seventeen in the early 1980s and enrolled in Harry's creative writing course. She hadn't heard of him or his books, but it didn't take long to realize he was somebody important. Famous names were dropped in the classroom—Rip Torn, Kris Kristofferson—and the class members were made aware of Harry's bibliography and fame. Young and impressionable, with dreams of being a writer, Burns was, like many of the students that fell into Harry's orbit, absorbed by the atmosphere of art and rebellion he fomented among his closest students. She joined the current group of cronies that followed Harry to the Winnjammer or other bars after class, drinking round after round and talking for hours about writing and art, among other things. It all played into her sense of the romantic, and soon, like many before and after her, she was in a sexual relationship with her English professor.

"It was easy to get caught up in the hero worship," Burns recalled. "I was seventeen and a freshman, and at the time, I characterized it as, 'Oh, a famous person is paying attention to me.'" And, as someone with ambitions as a writer and artist, she viewed it as an invitation into a hidden world, one she dreamed about being a part of. She wasn't the only one, she said: those of us in his circle felt "that we were more talented and creative and have a greater capacity for the threshold for experience. We can do these things that would screw up the average person, but we're not the average person, we're better than they are."

It was no deep dark secret that Harry slept around with students. "Harry had many, many girlfriends," said his former student Marie Speed.

And Harry, on occasion, would brag about his conquests. "You got to be holding a rap—to be able to talk. But it helps if you got some credentials," he said years later. "But I'm not sure if those two things are necessary. Talk, the rap, and the credentials. . . . And young girls, for some curious reason—and young girls, what I mean by that: Let's get them old enough so we ain't going to Raiford [a prison in north central Florida]. I don't know. Nineteen. Twenty. Eighteen. Nineteen. Twenty. Twenty-one. Twenty-two. Twenty-four becomes very old for what we're talking about here. Now, and they just . . . love old, wrinkled, ruined guys. It's incredible."

Burns said Harry was interested in women like her—students whom he felt he could seduce, and whom he didn't believe to be the type to broadcast the realities of his existence. "He would never have targeted the type of female teenage student who would be conscious enough to say, 'Hey, wait a minute, I don't want to sleep with those three guys.' Intuitively, he wouldn't want someone like that. In fact, someone like that would steer clear of him because maybe they would have good intuitive sense that maybe there's something the matter with a fiction-writing class where the professor is drunk and doesn't teach half the time."

As Harry's girlfriend, Burns was pulled into a world she had never imagined. Parties at Harry's apartment were the epitome of bacchanals. Harry would often goad his young lovers to have sex with his friends. While people drank and got high in the living room, orgies would take place in Harry's bedroom. Once, he attempted to send a friend over to Burns's apartment for sexual favors. And, Burns said, there were others who received the same treatment; each one Harry pushed to see how far they would go. She knew several female students who ended up in therapy shortly after leaving the program. "He destroyed the lives, psychologically, of a lot of people," she said.

What had seemed like a window into a thrilling new adult realm eventually, with the romantic gauze removed, began to feel like a seedy, demeaning existence in which she was one of many pawns. When she was supposed to be learning and growing as a writer, too much of her time was spent caring for and servicing a drunken, horny, middle-aged man. To avoid driving-under-the-influence arrests (of which he'd already had his share), Harry would ask Burns to drive him around from bar to bar. She reached the breaking point one night when Harry, in a completely inebriated state, stumbled out of her car to urinate on a tree, lost his sense of direction, and instead peed all over her car. For the first time, she began to scream at him in anger. Harry was too far gone to hear it, though, and when he was done, he stumbled a few more steps and crumpled into the grass by the side of the road.

Even in the anything-goes, doped-up early 1980s, such behavior by a professor would be actionable if it came across the desk of the right administrator. Harry was a tenured professor now, however, and, of course, he was Harry Crews. But Burns felt many in the English Department administration knew at least some of the story and preferred to look the other way. Her relationship with Harry ended early in her undergraduate career. Afterward, she stayed on at UF and earned a master's in fiction writing and would go on to become an English professor herself. "I find it rather unconscionable that the university allowed him to do the things that he did," she said. "I would get fired if I got anywhere close to any of the behaviors he did and anyone knew about it. But people just seemed to say, 'Oh, that's Harry.'"

The fiction-writing program still fostered a tight-knit, closed environment, where little light shone from the outside. William Logan served as the director of creative writing in the mid-1980s. Relationships between students and professors were more common during that era, with less of the stigma attached than in the academic environment that emerged a few years later. He remembers rumors about Harry, but little more. "What I learned in this profession [concerning the behavior of professors] is that unless students complain, there is no complaint," Logan said. "And students never complain."

Burns recalls speaking with Logan near the end of her time in Gainesville. Logan was sympathetic and seemed to acknowledge what she had gone through. "He was the only one there who ever said, you know, 'I'm really sorry.' It was not on behalf of the department, but I knew what he was talking about. And he knew. And I said, 'Thanks, I was an adult. I made my choices. If I hadn't run into a Harry, I would have run into someone else.' And he said something to the effect of, sarcastically, or ironically anyway, 'Yeah, that's why we have Harry here—to help young women through their issues.'"

Sometimes, the young women he helped were not students but avid readers. At the height of his celebrity, Harry's phone number was always listed in the white pages, and it didn't take much for an interested woman to get an invitation. One afternoon, Johansson was sitting in the apartment when Harry was opening mail.

"I got a letter from this girl in Ohio who says she wants to come down and fuck me," he said.

"Really?" Johansson replied. "She send a picture?"

Yes, she had, and soon she arrived at the apartment in the flesh. Harry and his guest got along swimmingly at first, and soon they were planning a trip to Daytona Beach. Predictably, the whirlwind romance between author and fan descended quickly into chaos and dysfunction.

Johansson stayed at Harry's apartment while they were gone. Just a few days into the planned trip, Harry called him from the beach.

"You gotta come get this girl," he pleaded.

There had been an incident in a restaurant. There was screaming and disruption. Tables were overturned. The honeymoon was clearly over.

Johansson picked up a case of beer, made the drive to Daytona, and took the elevator up to Harry's room. The scene when he arrived was desperately sad. The girl from Ohio had been crying and was standing next to the bed, methodically placing her clothes into her luggage. Harry was staring blankly out the window toward the horizon. Down below, children played in the surf, families clustered in the sand. Johansson joined him at the window. Harry was melancholy.

"It's a beautiful day out there," he said. "The ocean, the birds, the sky. And I can get no pleasure from any of it."

Johansson handed Harry a beer. Harry took it and looked at it silently for a minute.

"Son," he said, "skip this movie if you can."

CHAPTER TWENTY-SIX VIOLENCE FINDS US

> Nothing gets you back in touch with yourself like a little of
> your own blood. A broken nose or a broken rib centers a man
> emotionally like nothing else can.
> —Harry Crews, "The Violence That Finds Us"

By the early 1980s, there was an oft-repeated line around Turling-ton Hall concerning Harry's prowess with his fists. "When he first arrived in Gainesville, Harry Crews had to go a long, long way to find somebody who could kick his ass, but he always managed to find someone willing to do the job," new arrivals were told. "Now, he doesn't even have to leave the city limits."

The truth, in fact, was that, regardless of time or place or circumstance, the most common result when Harry came to blows was indeed an ass-kicking, with Harry himself on the receiving end. It happened often enough that friends knew it was a possible outcome of any evening spent with Harry. He could be quick to anger, was always prepared to escalate a verbal confrontation, and, with his reputation as a brawler long ago established, attracted violence even when he wasn't looking for it. Even his countenance could lead to violence; he had a face that when viewed by bank security guards, he said, caused them to immediately unholster their weapons. When he was looking for a fight, he wasn't particularly interested in proving himself to be the toughest guy on the block. Rather, at least when writing about his violent incidents in hindsight, he professed to be striving for the satisfaction of receiving the beating, and the soul-cleansing powers that existed in the act of feeling pain and tasting his own blood.

"I don't remember him ever winning a fight," said Willie Mickelberry. Mickelberry was an early representative of what would later be referred to in Gainesville as "Crews's Crew," students who would take it upon themselves to follow Harry to the bars and keep him out of harm's way. For Mickelberry, the job sometimes entailed rushing down to a bar where he would find Harry, inebriated and in immediate jeopardy after antagonizing one, or all, of the patrons. (The mission was often even more perilous for Mickelberry, who wore his hair long, making him a target at some of the honky-tonk bars Harry frequented.) More commonly, Mickelberry would be called after the fact and asked to bring Harry something to ease his pain or expedite the healing process. "He had a little masochistic taste for suffering," Mickelberry recalled.

The results of combat were usually visible, and if they weren't, Harry was happy to show off his battle wounds. He would regale journalists with an ever-expanding list of the injuries he had sustained through the years: concussions, razor cuts, broken knees, shattered ribs on both sides, a broken neck, a broken sternum, his nose broken multiple times, and bruises on all areas of his body where bruising was possible. He bruised easily, and extensively. His friend John Morefield came out of Lillian's one evening just as Harry was parking his car across the street. Harry stepped out of the car and Morefield saw that his face "was just one big purple bruise." It was enough to send Morefield scurrying in the other direction, an offense that Harry held onto for weeks.

Many of the incidents, in Harry's portrayal, were of the wrong-place, wrong-time variety. On a trip for *Esquire* to profile radio evangelist Garner Ted Armstrong in Oklahoma, his itinerary landed him in the Dallas–Fort Worth airport with a long layover. He jumped in a taxi and asked to be taken to the nearest pool hall. He found a playing partner who happened to be of Mexican descent, and a few games later, a group of Texans in cowboy attire sauntered up to the table. The Texans began to harass Harry's new friend, showing off their vast vocabulary of Latino slurs. Harry eased away from the table. After a few more comments, the Mexican, who turned out to be an American Vietnam vet, took a pool cue to the face of one of his harassers.

The Texans quickly gained the upper hand, got the vet down on the floor, and worked him over with their boots. Harry still avoided the fray. This wasn't his fight, he thought, and his flight took off in a few hours. But the Texans took one too many shots, and Harry could hold back no longer. He jumped in, and the pool-cue-wielding Texans immediately turned their attack on him. Instead of a flight to Oklahoma, he ended up with several facial wounds and a ride in a police cruiser. He and the vet were handcuffed and taken to jail, while the Texans resumed their evening at the bar.

Trips to Texas were always dangerous for Harry, and a number ended similarly, prompting him to begin telling journalists that he never had set foot in Texas without ending up in a cell. But it was not just in Texas where he encountered dangerous episodes; trips of any kind could result in bodily harm. On a trip to Los Angeles for *Esquire*, he spent an evening drinking with the actor Vic Morrow. On the way home, Harry asked Morrow to let him out of the car so he could walk back to his hotel; instead, he stumbled into an alley where he was mugged and beaten. When the mugging was concluded, he thought to himself how nice it was of his assailants to take only his money and leave his wallet on the ground beside him.

On another *Esquire* assignment, he traveled to Naples, Florida, to write about an underground dogfighting event. At the fights, he asked the wrong fan to move out of his view of the pit and ended up with more lacerations and lost blood than any of the pit bulls that had been the evening's entertainment.[7] On yet another ill-fated journalism assignment, he flew to New York, ostensibly to research an article on homeless people who lived in the subway system. Before any actual research took place, he was robbed and beaten. On the flight home, he got into an altercation with airport security during a layover in the Atlanta airport and had to be rescued by friends. He returned to Gainesville with lacerations all over his face; he was unsure when he had received them. It was a pattern that students and colleagues began to notice—if Harry had visible wounds, he must have recently returned from an assignment.

Injuries were par for the course for Harry. When William Logan first arrived on campus to begin teaching for the English Department, a colleague pointed Harry out to him. Harry was once again on crutches, the result of a "bike accident," he was told. Logan assumed Harry had been on a motorcycle, but when he met Harry later, he learned the truth. Harry had been drinking, climbed on his Schwinn, and rode it into a brick wall.

If Harry's wounds weren't the result of drinking or antagonizing, they were often the result of unpaid drug debts. Mark Chiappini recalled one afternoon when Harry limped into the store and took a seat, seemingly in far more distress than usual. Upon questioning, Harry lifted his shirt to reveal a deep black bruise from his sternum to his waist. His entire torso was discolored. Las Vegas drug dealers were the culprit, Harry told him. They had administered the beating and then told Harry if he set foot in Nevada again, they'd kill him.

Larry Hetrick, his friend and English Department colleague, said Harry often suffered beatings because he just didn't feel he should have to pay for drugs. Once, Hetrick saw Harry limping to his office, moving slower than usual. Finally, Harry's progress stopped completely and he fell into the wall. Hetrick approached to help.

"What happened this time, Harry?" he asked.

"They chain-whipped me, Larry," Harry answered. "They got me real good. They tied me up on the bed and chain-whipped me."

At the time, Hetrick's apartment was just a few blocks away from Harry's in downtown Gainesville. Hetrick walked over for a visit one afternoon and found Harry sitting on a metal cot with no mattress, reading a book of Emily Dickinson's poetry. Save for Harry, the book, and the cot, the room was completely empty. Harry again blamed his greedy drug dealers.

"Can you believe this? They took everything I had," he complained. "What really pisses me off, though, is they made off with my typewriter. They can have the rest of it, but you don't take a man's typewriter."

His combatants weren't always anonymous attackers; friends, students, colleagues could be drawn into confrontations, too. Michael Garcia spent a good deal of time with Harry in the early 1980s. Garcia was a writer, musician, and small-business owner who ran a restaurant and other establishments at various times. The two lived together in a small house near an area referred to as "the hobo park" in downtown Gainesville for most of 1981. One night, they were drinking with a group of friends at Twelve East, a restaurant near Lillian's, and Harry began to provoke Garcia, riding him about a debt that Garcia said had long ago been paid off. Garcia reached his breaking point and stood up to face off with Harry. The rest of the group eased away from the table as the rhetoric grew hotter. Finally, Garcia struck first and punched Harry in the eye. Harry managed to stay on his feet, but it was a one-punch TKO, and Garcia left the bar.

Garcia went to see Harry the next day. Whatever the source of Harry's rage the previous night, it had evaporated, and the two laughed about it. Harry posed for photos to display the black eye Garcia had given him.

"He could get angry in a heartbeat if somebody said something to him," Feiber recalled. "I mean, Harry could turn on you. You could be his best friend right now, and an hour later, he would tell you, 'I don't ever want to talk to you again.' Of course, the next day, he would call you and be ready to go anywhere with you."

Feiber occasionally found himself on the wrong end of Harry's explosions. One morning, after a long night bouncing at Lillian's, Feiber was driving with his girlfriend to St. Augustine, on the Atlantic coast. The two pulled up at Chiappini's in Melrose to get some beer. Harry was already at the bar. Feiber had hurt his leg the night before and was still in pain, so he sent his girlfriend in and waited in the car. Suddenly, Harry appeared in the doorway, screaming and gesturing violently at Feiber. "You motherfucker, you think you're too good to come in and say hello to me!" he yelled. Feiber put his head down, waited for his girlfriend to climb back into the car, and continued on to St. Augustine. A few days later, he went to see Harry to patch things up, and Harry barely remembered the incident.

The wrong move in the classroom could also often lead to potential fisticuffs. On his first day at the University of Florida in the fall of 1980, Jay Atkinson strolled into Harry's classroom. Atkinson was a graduate student who had just recently arrived in Gainesville. Before class, he had asked for directions from a man wearing jeans and a tattered golf shirt, whom he had assumed to be a janitor, recruited from a "moldy old boxing gym or a soup kitchen."

The janitor was, of course, his new professor, and when class started, Harry sat down at the table and began to speak in his deep Georgia drawl. Atkinson had grown up in Massachusetts, had just arrived in the South, and had never heard of Harry Crews. Harry concluded his introduction.

"Excuse me, Professor, but I couldn't understand what you said because of your accent," Atkinson asked innocently. "Could you please repeat it?"

Harry stared blankly at Atkinson for what seemed like a minute, and then, in his most menacing voice: "I don't much like your accent, either. We can go outside and settle it, if you want."

Atkinson had been in his share of fights as well and knew nothing of Harry's reputation, so a stare-down commenced. The tension reached a crescendo in the classroom before another student, a veteran of Harry's classes, leaned over and spoke under his breath to Harry. Harry nodded and responded out loud to the student.

"Why, what do you think of his fucking accent?"

"Jay's accent is memorable, Harry," the student responded in a calm voice. "Just like yours." This time, the crisis was averted, and the first day of class went on without incident.

Atkinson would go on to become one of Harry's most dedicated students, signing up for his fiction workshop for eight straight semesters, and also receiving much of his education outside Turlington Hall. One evening, on Harry's invitation, Atkinson and a friend showed up at Harry's latest apartment. Harry was on one of his forced vacations from Maggie's house and was living in a rented second-story room on University Avenue. The room was decorated with empty beer cans, and Harry was sitting on the lone chair with another beer in his hand when Atkinson and his friend arrived. Harry had requested they bring several quarts of Miller High Life, and the three spent some time disposing of it and reading Shakespeare before heading to Lillian's.

The Miller beer Atkinson had supplied, combined with what Harry had been drinking prior, had given them a hefty buzz. After several more rounds at the bar, Harry began to challenge Atkinson and his friend to bouts of arm wrestling and knuckle wrestling, another of his favorite manly contests, in which competitors would hook middle fingers and twist until one either loses a digit or screams for mercy. The matches became increasingly louder, drawing more and more attention from patrons and bar staff, until Atkinson twisted Harry's finger several degrees past Harry's pain threshold, sending him out of his chair and onto the floor of Lillian's, yelping in agony.

Despite Harry's status with the staff, the display, and what had preceded it, was disruptive enough to get the three ejected from Lillian's. Harry was far beyond the walking stage now, so Atkinson put Harry's arm around his shoulder and dragged his professor out onto the street. A light drizzle was falling and Atkinson continued to hold Harry up, when a pickup truck drove up beside them. The angry driver leaned out the driver-side window and began to jeer them.

"Harry Crews is nothin' but a lousy drunk," he sneered. "Big shot writer! You're a fuckin' loser and a bum."

Atkinson attempted to balance Harry in a standing position so he could approach the driver, a thirtysomething tough guy sporting a cowboy hat.

"What's your fucking problem, buddy?"

As Atkinson moved toward the truck, Harry's balance gave way, and he collapsed to the sidewalk, then rolled off the curb and into the gutter, rainwater streaming onto his clothing. He looked up, emitted an audible groan, and then kept one eye open to watch as the situation escalated between Atkinson and the driver. Harry remained prostrate in the gutter, not moving a muscle, as a confrontation played out a few feet in front of him. The cowboy-antagonist pulled a gun, tussled with Atkinson, and finally drove away, after his girlfriend, sitting in the passenger seat, locked the gun in the glove box. When the battle of wills was concluded, Atkinson and his friend retrieved Harry, now thoroughly drenched and barely conscious, carried him to the car, drove him home, and watched him stumble back through the door to the house on University Avenue, another potential crisis averted.

Harry returned home that night unscathed, but that was often not the case when he encountered strangers with bad intentions. On another night in another Gainesville establishment, he walked through the doors and noticed a couple sitting at a table near the bar. The girl greeted him, and Harry vaguely recognized her.

"Hey, how are you?" he asked casually. "You're lookin' good."

Thinking the interaction was over, he walked over to the bar, sat down, and ordered a drink. He was raising the glass to his mouth when the fist of the girl's boyfriend arrived first, at a high rate of speed. It knocked Harry off his stool and took out a row of teeth as well.

It didn't always happen that quickly, but Harry's fights often ended with him in a prone position. Despite all his experience, his karate training, his time in the gym, and his intimidating presence, he usually managed to come out on the losing end.

"As menacing as Harry was, he was one of the most un-athletic people that I have ever known," Feiber said. "He was menacing looking, but I don't think there was that killer instinct in him at all. . . . And usually, when he did get into a scrap, he was so drunk that you could have [tapped him on the shoulder] and he would have gone right over."

Alcohol didn't always have to be involved for a confrontation to develop, and Harry was more than happy to go looking for one. On one early-morning bike ride, Harry and a friend were on the road when a young man ran them into a ditch and drove off. Harry clambered to his feet in time to see the license plate of the offending vehicle. Later that day, he traced the tag number, got the address of the man, and biked over to his house. When he knocked on the door, a much older man appeared in the doorway. Harry pointed at the vehicle, now sitting in the driveway.

"Whoever was in that car, I want him out here on the grass," Harry demanded.

The man told Harry that his son was driving the car, and the son wasn't coming out. Harry began shouting over the father's shoulder into the house.

"What we ought to do is get down right here in the door, but because your daddy's here and your mama's inside and I don't want them to get all upset, we'll just forget it."

Harry started walking toward the street but then stopped and turned back around.

"Let me say one more thing: If you get to thinking about this, and change your mind, here's my name and where I live. And if you ever do this again, like we say in Bacon County, we'll get to find out whose ass is the blackest."

Those were the types of episodes that built Harry's reputation, and, once built, it was hard to stop the momentum. As time passed and he moved beyond reasonable fighting age, he began to complain of being approached in bars, or elsewhere, and being told stories of his own exploits, which were far different than reality or completely fictional. Often, those relating the story wanted to see Harry back it up. A piece of Harry could do wonders for one's own reputation, it seemed.

One afternoon, Harry was taking a short break from writing and sat down to eat his lunch on a bench in downtown Gainesville. A neatly dressed young man of college age approached. Harry had never seen him before.

"You're Harry Crews," the young man said. "I've read all your books. I really like what you do. All right if I sit down?"

Harry agreed, and the two had a short chat about Harry's novels. Abruptly, the man asked, "How does it feel to be famous?"

"You'd have to ask somebody else about that," Harry responded, perplexed. Something about his new friend didn't seem right.

"Oh, you're famous," the man said. "I know you."

The man saw that Harry was drinking whiskey and asked for a drink. Harry obliged.

"I've had a drink with Harry Crews," he said triumphantly.

By now, Harry had caught onto the vibe that he was dealing with somebody more than slightly unhinged. He tried to extricate himself from the situation, telling the man that he needed to get back to work.

It was too late. The young man jumped to his feet, pulled out a blade, and sliced a six-inch gash in Harry's arm. Blood poured down his T-shirt.

The man turned and ran, and this time Harry chose not to pursue his attacker. "Anybody who chases madness deserves what he gets," he wrote about the incident later.

As the years went by, Harry began to back away from confrontations, particularly those brought on by people who'd heard some part of the legend of Harry Crews. He'd deny the story, attempt to calm the situation, and head for the door as quickly as possible.

More damaging to him than a cut or a few bruises was the effect the reputation eventually began to have on the reception to his work. And by this point in his life, there was less work appearing and more bar stories about Harry the wild man. The legend had begun to detract from, or at the very least compete for attention with, his writing. He met more and more people who had not read a single sentence he'd written but could recite numerous anecdotes, factual or not, about what he'd done after the clock struck midnight. Of course, it was a blessing and a curse. He himself had done much of the job of creating and augmenting his image as a drunken brawler and had profited from it as well. Editors wanted to hire the wild man, and universities wanted to invite him to campus, pour him a drink, and watch what happened. But when it overshadowed his books, it became something of a detriment in Harry's eyes.

"More people are more interested, it seems, in talking about what I'm supposed to have done and what I still do than they are interested in my books," he told an interviewer. "It's a mistake I started making early, and I never knew it was a mistake until it was too late."

THE RACIST GENE

> I rushed off to the desk in the office and got the necessary
> little card that allowed me to rush to the bar, where I had to
> sign in on the necessary little register so I could swallow the
> necessary amount of vodka that would dull my growing
> certainty that Duke knew something about the human heart
> and its predisposition to violence that I did not know, could
> only dimly sense.
>
> —Harry Crews, *The Buttondown Terror of David Duke*

In *A Childhood*, Harry recounted the morning he found out his best friend, Willalee Bookatee, should be called a nigger. Harry was five years old, and he and Willalee spent most of their free time together. The two friends were inseparable. After one particular day of exploring, young Harry was telling a story to some relatives about one of the family's black neighbors, Robert Jones:

> "So me and Hoyett was passing the cotton gin and Mr. Jones was stand-ing there with his wife and—"
>
> My aunt leaned down and put her arm around my shoulders. Her great soft breast pressed warmly at my ear. She said: "No, son. Robert Jones is a nigger. You don't say 'mister' when you speak of a nigger. You don't say 'Mr. Jones,' you say 'nigger Jones.'"

I never missed a stroke in my story. ". . . So me and him was passing the cotton gin and nigger Jones was standing there with his wife . . ."

We were all dutiful children in Bacon County, Georgia.

In his youth, racial attitudes hadn't advanced much since slavery in Bacon County. According to Harry, every member of his family was racist, and blacks were known exclusively as niggers and lived in a neighborhood known to all as Niggertown. Yet among the poor, the lives of blacks and whites were intertwined. The adults worked together, the children played together. It was from this dichotomy that Harry formed his own racial attitudes, distinct from that of his kin, and observant enough to allow his work to serve as a window into the complicated racial relationships of the people of his childhood.

In his writing, this clear-eyed examination of race relations among the lower class brought an element of realism to his work. *The Gospel Singer* had opened with the character Willalee Bookatee lamenting that his name had been replaced with "the nigger" once he'd been accused of his crimes. Throughout Harry's novels, the word "nigger" is commonplace and unremarked upon. A class system between the races is apparent and adhered to, and rarely a thematic element in the plot. Instead, it usually becomes part of the landscape navigated by characters, who are preoccupied with far greater concerns.

Race took center stage, however, in one of his more celebrated journalistic assignments for *Playboy*. By 1979, the fortunes of a young Ku Klux Klan leader named David Duke were just coming onto the radar of the national media. The charting of the rise and fall of the Klan had been going on since the organization was formed by ex-Confederate officers to intimidate newly freed blacks in the wake of the Civil War. Its ranks had swelled into the millions in the 1920s, shrank to nearly nothing by midcentury, and then crept back up during the Civil Rights movement of the 1960s. In 1979 the Anti-Defamation League estimated that Klan membership was on the rise again, with ten thousand members and one hundred thousand sympathizers. And Duke, a handsome, tan, well-spoken Louisiana racist not yet thirty years old, was riding on the bow of the reemergence.

The trend caught the attention of *Playboy* editor James Morgan. The KKK itself didn't excite Morgan; it was an ancient story that had been plowed again and again by newspaper journalists. But to Morgan, something about Duke signaled a change in the direction of the organization. Duke was young and fresh and ambitious, and his modern methods led to clashes with the old guard of the Klan. A phone call with Duke only confirmed Morgan's beliefs; Duke was more interested in talking about the KKK's new PR magazine than he was in discussing the evils of the blacks and Jews. Duke, Morgan felt, represented "a new style, one tailored to the Age of Hype."

Soon, Harry was on a plane to Louisiana to meet and profile a different type of societal outsider. Duke, twenty-eight, had run a wing of the Klan since 1974. But he looked nothing like the stereotype the organization had perpetuated for a hundred years. He preferred slacks and sport coats to white robes and hoods; the *New York Times* had dubbed him the "ultimate gray flannel racist." Unlike the shadowy, publicity-adverse KKK of the past, which made its public statements with burning crosses, Duke bought advertising on radio, debated civil-rights heroes at universities, even ran for state senate. He organized a KKK "border patrol," in which a dozen Klan members stood guard against Mexican infiltrators while fifty reporters, notified by Duke, watched the proceedings.

Harry took the assignment and spent a week tagging along as Duke went from Klan rally to meet-and-greet to television studio to interview session, in New Orleans, New York, Boston, and Tulsa, Oklahoma, with numerous stops in between, all the while Duke "singing the same three or four songs" about the diminishing plight of the white race in America. Early on, Harry, due to his accent and appearance, was branded by most onlookers as Duke's bodyguard, a label that he could not shake, despite Duke regularly championing Harry's literary qualifications to all who would listen. (Duke even worked Harry's overcoming of his Georgia sharecropper roots into conversations as proof of the genetic superiority of southern whites.)

In Tulsa, Duke and his new pseudobodyguard were picked up at the airport by a pair of Klan-affiliated college professors, who drove them three hours through rural Arkansas, at increasingly high rates of speed, spewing bigotry as Harry and Duke squeezed tightly on the upholstery in the backseat, bonding in fear. Over the course of the week, Harry had challenged Duke on his views to a point, but had mostly let him ramble on, compiling Duke's rhetoric in his notebook, rhetoric he called "the same old sad bullshit I'd grown up on in Bacon County." Now they were headed to a rally in Rogers, Arkansas, scheduled for later that evening. The professors let them out at their hotel, and they walked across the parking lot to check in.

"How long have you had an organization here in Rogers?" Harry asked.

"Two months," Duke replied. "Two months ago, there wasn't a Klansman in this town. I don't know what to expect tonight. There may only be five people there. If that happens, I'll still give it everything. Every man who is willing to stand up with us is important."

Harry had taken the assignment with the belief that Duke was a con man, but the regularity of this type of statement, and the constant unsmiling, slightly crazed look in Duke's eyes, had now convinced Harry that he was dealing with something much more frightening: "that scariest of beings: the True Believer. There is never a doubt in his head or heart that the job he is doing has to be done, done at any cost, and he is the best qualified one to do it, the only one to do it."

A driver picked them up that evening and drove them through Rogers to the rally, where they were greeted by robed, hooded Klansmen as well as dozens of police, representing the city of Rogers, Benton County, the State of Arkansas, and the Federal Bureau of Investigation. Apparently, *Playboy* wasn't the only organization that had caught wind of Duke's charisma. Despite himself, Harry played the role of bodyguard, sticking by Duke's shoulder and scanning the windows and roofs of adjacent buildings for snipers. There were indeed men with guns in those locations, but all were representatives of law-enforcement agencies. The police hurried Harry and Duke into a room and checked them for weapons.

The rally, it turned out, had a lot more than five people in attendance. The armory where it was held was standing-room only. Hooded men, giving the Nazi salute, chanted "White Power! White Power!" in unison. The streets outside were filled with people straining their ears to hear Duke proselytize. Throughout Duke's ninety-minute speech, attendees stomped, applauded, and rose in standing ovations. The reception to Duke's performance was a final dénouement in the judgment Harry had formed over his week as a traveling Klansman: Duke was both charismatic and dangerous, and had tapped into a source of growing rage and resentment in society. "All of this in a little town where two months before there had been no Klan organization and where there had not been a Klan rally in 50 years. I figured I was sick enough to go home," he wrote.

The following morning, Harry checked out of his Holiday Inn and waited with Duke for a car to arrive and take them to the airport. Despite being sickened over and over by Duke's whitewashed rhetoric of hate, he admitted to developing a fondness for Duke personally. The car was late, so the two walked over to the motel pool, which was dry. There, Harry found the perfect closing to his profile:

> Duke took off his shirt, hung his feet over the lip of the pool and dropped onto the dusty bottom and started doing one-armed push-ups. Thirty with each hand. While he pumped up and down, he grunted, "Not one in a hundred men can do this."
>
> I thought he was probably right. I also thought that while it was a ludicrous sight, silly in the extreme, he was getting stronger by doing it. He *was* getting stronger. A sign. A real sign.

Harry sent the manuscript to Morgan a few weeks later. "I'm having a hard time being humble about having the brains to put Harry Crews on this story," Morgan wrote shortly after receiving the pages. "Obviously, the combination was absolutely right."

In his response to Morgan, Harry was far shriller in his denunciation of the Klan than he allowed himself to be in the body of the article. "There was a time when Hitler had no more than two thousand followers and he was laughed at and called a Boy Scout and scorned for his strange ways," he wrote. "Ten years later, he owned Germany. A melodramatic observation, perhaps. But we ought to remind ourselves from time to time that it is only the truth. It did happen."

"The Buttondown Terror of David Duke" appeared in the February 1980 issue of *Playboy*. In it, Harry emphasized Duke's personal charm and ability to disguise his radically racist views as mainstream philosophies. The movement around Duke was a cult of personality, and it was Duke himself, more than the KKK, where the danger lay. "Not one single instance—not one—did anybody take final issue with him, tell him that he was full of it or refuse to continue with conversations whose subject was race hatred," Harry wrote. "I would not have believed it had I not been there."

The piece proved prescient. Less than a year after publication, Duke had resigned his position with the Klan and formed his own organization, which he christened the National Association for the Advancement of White People. He softened his rhetoric, stopped appearing in Nazi garb, even reportedly underwent surgical procedures to change his appearance. He began to call his prior association with the KKK "youthful excess." His political positions began to fall in line with the far right wing of the Republican Party—against affirmative action, in support of Americans of "European descent."

By the early 1990s, Duke was a player on the national political stage, albeit one who was treated like nuclear waste by the mainstream of both parties. He managed to be elected to the Louisiana State Senate in 1989, then lost a bid for the U.S. Senate. The high point of his political career came in 1991, when he made it into a runoff in the election for governor of Louisiana against Edwin Edwards, a former governor whose most recent term had included standing trial for mail fraud and bribery. Duke was on the national news night in and night out. It was billed as the race between the crook and the wizard, Louisiana politics at its finest. Duke's past became the story, national money poured in to stop the former Klansman, and he was easily defeated. When Duke ran for the Republican presidential nomination the following year, he played to empty houses and garnered little support. The national media, and the public, had had enough, and Duke was ushered off the stage.

Still, as Harry had foreseen, Duke had been able to tap into a segment of southern society by preying on racial fears and attitudes that existed very close to the surface. (Against Edwards, he had received a majority of the white vote.) It was a belief system Harry understood equally as well as Duke did, because it was the system under which he had been reared. "All the dos and don'ts of segregation were in the air you breathed," he wrote. "All the business about Jews and Catholics and blacks and people from other countries was the Truth because the people I was raised among believed it was the Truth." The week with Duke offered him the chance, for the first time, to put his own racial beliefs on paper. Years later, Harry was still confused as to the origin of these beliefs. "How did I manage to miss the racist virus, as I am convinced I did, and as I am convinced my life demonstrates?" he wrote. "I know what I know, and the virus simply did not take, which seems something like a miracle to me."

The Duke piece was a success, but such successes were becoming far less frequent. His byline would not appear again in *Playboy* until 1984, and his last article for *Esquire* came out in September 1980. He began an association with *Playgirl* magazine, writing several pieces in the early 1980s. He traveled to Liberty Baptist College in Lynchburg, Virginia, to profile the Reverend Jerry Falwell, whom he found to be even more dangerous than David Duke. He was on set for the filming of *Cross Creek*, the Marjorie Kinnan Rawlings memoir of Cracker Florida, and contributed a glowing portrait of the lead actress, Mary Steenburgen, to *Playgirl*. (This assignment led to a friendship with Rip Torn, who had a role in *Cross Creek*, and whom Harry took on a whiskey-fueled alligator hunting expedition.) Intermittent assignments came in from other publications, but his interest in such work had clearly waned. "I'm like an old whore these days," he wrote to Morgan, "still getting plenty of work, but not enjoying it as much as I once did."

Maggie returned to graduate school to pursue a master's degree in exercise physiology and, as time went on, was less willing to put up with Harry's lifestyle. And Harry often required more assistance to get through the day. One day Atkinson asked Harry to sit down for a taped interview, and Harry obliged. When the interview was concluded in the early afternoon, Harry asked Atkinson to go with him to the Orange & Brew, an on-campus pub, for a few beers. Atkinson had rugby practice later that afternoon but agreed to come along and watch Harry drink.

At the pub, Harry quickly went through a pitcher and a half and soon reached the word-slurring stage. He had recently been paid, and in the front pocket of his Penguin golf shirt was a roll of twenty-dollar bills that added up to his biweekly salary. (Harry didn't trust banks and liked to keep his money in cash when possible.) Harry excused himself to go to the bathroom, and when Atkinson glanced in his direction, there was the roll of bills, sitting in the middle of the floor. He picked up the money and gave it back when Harry returned to the table. When it was time for Atkinson to leave for rugby practice, Harry went to the pay phone and called Maggie for a ride. He was stumbling now and having difficulty forming words. He stood up once more and lurched toward the bathroom. "I watched him walk around the corner and I'm thinking, he's gonna drop that fuckin' money again," Atkinson said.

He did, and Atkinson picked it up again, this time putting it in his pocket until Maggie arrived. She drove up, and as he helped Harry into the passenger seat, she locked eyes with Atkinson, shaking her head in disgust. Atkinson pulled the money out of his pocket, walked around to the driver-side window, and handed the roll of bills to Maggie. "Here you go, here's Harry's money." Maggie snatched the roll, threw it down, and, without a word, put the car into gear and drove away.

Harry's money came and went quickly. When he had some, he could be extremely generous, a trait that was accelerated by alcohol. In the right mood, he would come out of a bar and hand a hundred-dollar bill to a homeless person. Or he would call a taxi to go out and get him some whiskey, paying the driver hundreds for the job. Or grab the check for a full night of food and drinks for two tables full of students at the Winnjammer. As a result, his financial situation was usually a mess, and the alimony he paid annually to Sally made matters worse. His full annual salary from the University of Florida would go to pay alimony, and he would still start each year $4,000 in debt, he said. The financial pressure forced him to take screenwriting jobs and magazine work to make up the difference, another force pulling him away from fiction. "I've been carrying enough alimony for twelve years to kill two other men," he told an interviewer. "I mean, to feed a damn horse for twelve years you ain't been riding—that's hard. I'm sick of it."

His constant state of pennilessness, for Harry, dripped with irony, because his ex-wife was the daughter of a millionaire. He liked to relate a story about one day when Sally brought her mother by his apartment to drop off their dog after a trip to the vet. Mother and daughter arrived in the student ghetto in his mother-in-law's shiny new Corvette. They entered through the squeaky screen door, looking furtively at the scattered remains of Harry's latest party. Sally's mother, bedecked in jewelry and designer clothing, glanced around the tiny room, taking in the squalid conditions. She walked over and examined the peeling wallpaper and then complimented Harry on his decorating prowess. "Excellent choice, Harry," she told him, running her fingers over the curling plastic. "It's so very quaint."

Sally remained a presence in Harry's life. Periodically, they were drawn back together. One day in 1983, Atkinson told Harry he would be going with some friends to a new restaurant in Gainesville, the 13th Street Fishery. Harry said he would be there too; he was going on a date with Sally. When Atkinson and his friends arrived, Harry and Sally were sitting across from each other, staring into each other's eyes "like they were in high school." Harry waved Atkinson and his friends over to the table. "I want to introduce you to the woman with the finest facial bone structure of any woman I've ever met," he declared.

Despite his resentment over the alimony, Harry rarely said a negative word about Sally. "None of it was her fault," he said. "She is the most decent human being you want to meet in your life."

He also never missed an opportunity to publicly profess his love for Byron. Harry's relationship with his son was complex. Sally and Harry had split up when Byron was an adolescent, and Harry had remained involved as a father at varying levels. In the years immediately after the split, visits with Byron would often be sources of extreme stress for Harry. When Harry was living with Charné in Melrose, Byron, then nine or ten years old, would be dropped off for the weekend. Harry would sometimes go immediately to the bottle, leaving Charné to figure out something to do with his son. "Sometimes, it was like they didn't have a relationship at all," she said. "It was weird. Crews was very weird about him."

By that time, Byron was well acquainted with his father's drinking habits. Less than a year before he separated from Sally, she went to Ohio for a week, leaving Harry in charge of Byron, then seven years old. One night, Byron went to play with a friend down the block, promising to be back at dinnertime. He showed up an hour late and blamed his failure to return on time on the rain that had begun falling late in the afternoon. Harry didn't buy the excuse. He wasn't drunk but had been drinking steadily through the evening. As punishment for Byron's tardiness, Harry told his son that he could stand out in the rain for a few more minutes. Harry went inside, collapsed into his recliner, and promptly dozed off for two hours. He woke shortly before nine, opened the door, and found Byron in exactly the same spot, his "blond hair plastered and every thread of him soaked."

It was one of many incidents in his childhood that hardened Byron to Harry's actions. When he was a few years older, Byron brought up the incident in a conversation with his father. He politely asked Harry to replay the events for him. Harry obliged and then asked his son what he had been thinking as he stood out in the rain for those hours. "I thought, 'That drunk fucker thinks I'm going to call and ask him to come in out of the rain, but I'm not.'"

Byron spent the majority of his time with Sally; Harry's presence was unpredictable. When his disposition was good, he would make an effort to increase his presence. One summer, the two made their own expedition to the Appalachian Trail. Harry made occasional appearances at whatever activity Byron was pursuing at the time, from horseback riding or team sports to, in his teen years, rock music. When he was around, Harry would take Byron jogging or to the gym to lift weights. Once, Harry made an appearance at Byron's school, waxing poetic about the glories of writing for the entire student body. After the talk, Byron came onstage and kissed his father in front of an auditorium full of adolescents, an anecdote Harry would continue to share to emphasize how close he was with his son.

There was no alternate reality on display for his son, however, so Byron often got to see up close his father's self-destructive nature. Once, when

Byron was older, he went to visit Harry at the room Harry was currently renting. There was no answer when Byron knocked on the front door, but he noticed a cord coming from a window and snaking across the lawn. He followed the cord, which led him to a bush on the side of the building. The cord ended under the bush, where it was attached to an electric blanket. Byron pulled the blanket down and discovered Harry, unconscious. To one side of him was an apple with a single bite taken out of it. Byron moved the blanket a little bit further to reveal a Vidalia onion. Harry had apparently taken a bite of the onion also before calling it a night.

"I've never hidden myself from him—never," Harry said. "I told him, 'If I go down tomorrow, I don't want you to find out about me from somebody else.'" The strategy often left Harry explaining to his son why he lived how he did. After one extended binge, Byron came to Harry's office on campus for one such talk. Father and son were both in tears. "Daddy," Byron asked, "I know you got to do what you do, but does it have to be this bad all the time?"

Music became the focal point of Byron's life as he entered his late teens, and he often devoted hours each day to practicing his guitar. He became more comfortable in Harry's circle and occasionally would move in with his father. Harry's friend Michael Garcia operated a Cuban restaurant downtown and would sometimes invite Byron to perform with him.

After high school, Byron enrolled at the University of Florida and soon took a seat in his father's writing seminar. One night, Harry showed up drunk and in the mood to sing the blues. He alternated between belting out tunes and ranting about the blues and fiction in completely incomprehensible fashion. Byron was noticeably embarrassed and stopped coming to the class shortly thereafter.

When Byron decided to leave the university to pursue a musical career a little while later, Harry initially objected but was eventually encouraging. A few years later, Byron was interviewed about his father for a documentary and spoke reverentially of Harry's intellectual capabilities, his skills as a storyteller, and his father's ability to survive despite the abuse he heaped on himself. Byron became emotional, however, when discussing Harry's difficulties in fulfilling the role of father: "In terms of seeing Harry Crews, the writer, crash and burn, it was very painful. But seeing your daddy crash and burn, it was a fucking nightmare. I'm still working my way through that today."

A MESSY BUSINESS

> I see teachers killing students every day. Students' papers come
> back to them with so many red marks on them that they cannot
> even see what they originally put down on the paper. The student
> has been left with nothing. Everything has been taken from
> him. He has been left with nowhere to begin again. That's not
> teaching, that's slaughter.
>
> —Harry Crews, "Teaching and Writing in the University"

The world might have thought Harry had one foot in the grave, but on the University of Florida campus he was still in high demand. Students interested in taking his classes had to rise early on sign-up day, wait in long lines, and hope a seat was still available. The hardest of the hard core were not turned away easily. Rod Elrod was studying writing at the University of Montana when he picked up *A Childhood* for the first time. A Louisiana native, Elrod had been to several universities in the South, finally earning a general studies degree from the University of Louisiana–Monroe. He was unfamiliar with the work of Harry Crews. A few pages in, however, he felt a kinship he had not previously experienced in all his years of reading literature. He called Harry on the telephone and said he wanted to study with him in Gainesville.

"Don't come," Harry told him. Elrod had a teaching assistantship at Montana, and Harry urged him to stay put. "You've got a good thing going up there."

Elrod applied to the University of Florida anyway and was accepted into the writing program. Once again, he called Harry.

"Don't come," he was told, again.

Elrod and his wife, Debbie, decided Florida was as good a place to learn to write as Montana, so they packed up their belongings and moved to Gainesville. Rod enrolled in Harry's class and contacted him to let Harry know he was in town. Harry did not return his calls. Once class started, Harry ignored him for the first six weeks.

"I know exactly, now that I'm older, what he was doing," Elrod said. "Writing is a messy business. . . . Nobody should be a writer unless they can't be anything else. That's what Harry was telling me."

After six weeks, Harry relented, and Rod soon knew what it meant to be a member of Harry's inner circle. They began to spend time together outside the classroom, at each other's homes, and at Harry's favorite haunts. "I think I took three or four classes. I don't really remember how many. I had such unfettered access to him that the workshops didn't mean anything. I signed up and got A's, but I saw him every day."

Rod and Debbie bought a little house in Cross Creek, and Rod got a job cooking at the Yearling, a short-order joint near the Marjorie Kinnan Rawlings Home, which had by then become an official historic site. With his unfettered access, Rod received much more than just writing lessons. He got to see Harry go on a binge and "load the hammer" on many occasions. But when Harry was sober, Rod marveled at his power of concentration and the energy he poured into evaluating student work. "When he concentrated on reading a manuscript, it was *read*," Rod said.

Once they became close friends, Harry would even agree to read the manuscripts of Rod's friends from Montana, who sometimes made the trip to Florida to meet Harry. "He would give the manuscripts back and start talking, warm up to it, and he'd say, 'Well, on page 19, where you say this, that phrase really clanked on my ear, you know? And then on page 180 . . .' He would make references to the manuscript, and scenes in the manuscript, without ever looking back at it."

You didn't have to be a member of Crews's Crew or spend your free time at Lillian's to be the beneficiary of Harry's evaluation, either. Marilyn Moriarity enrolled in several of Harry's workshops in the early 1980s. At the end of one semester, a story she had submitted was discussed briefly in class but didn't receive much attention. Moriarity thought little of it and left town once the semester had concluded. Many months later, after she had changed the focus of her degree and was no longer studying creative writing, Harry noticed her and stopped her in the hall one evening.

"Ms. Moriarty, I've been thinking about that story, and it finally came to me," he told her, unprompted. "You need a better balance of summary and scene. You had too much summary and not enough scene."

He was a demanding taskmaster. It quickly became apparent to everybody in the room that Harry was far more educated and well read than any of his pupils. He would mention a certain writer, and experienced students knew that meant they ought to read that writer's work and be prepared to discuss it in depth the following week.

Membership in the inner circle did not exempt students from Harry's harshest criticism. At one workshop, Rod read a story to the class and was lavished with praise. Harry did not share their view and tore into Rod's story with a ferocity that shocked everybody in the room. When he was done, he asked Rod to respond.

"Well, I don't know what you're mad at, but this story is not measurably different from others that you've liked," Rod told him. "So it must be something personal." The class moved to another student's story, and later that evening Rod and Harry continued the discussion, this time at a lower temperature, over oysters and beer. Harry had decided, for whatever reason, that Rod needed to be challenged publicly.

Harry's classroom could be a tension- and testosterone-filled environment, and he liked it that way. Critics in the department would say that his workshops were dominated by young men trying to impress their mentor with their toughness, both in their writing and in their attitude. Physical boundaries didn't exist with members of the boys' club; Harry would exchange punches to the stomach, arm-wrestle, or throw down a weight-lifting challenge. Moriarity was aware of the male camaraderie among Harry's students. When she would see him outside class, she would receive a polite "Hello, Ms. Moriarty" from Harry. After one class, she brought up the issue with Jay Atkinson, who was also enrolled that particular semester. "I said, 'You know, Jay, he calls me Ms. Moriarty, and I just feel like you guys seem to have more fun, and I feel excluded. All I am is Ms. Moriarty.'"

The following week, she was walking down the hall when she saw Harry coming around the corner. Harry noticed her and began to smile. He approached her.

"How you doin', Marilyn?" he asked. Then he moved in closer, bent down, and threw a soft rabbit punch into her gut. "You been workin' out?"

Male or female, Harry was apt to challenge his students. He was looking, he would say, for writers "who are ready to eat nails to get where they're going." Critiques of writing came in the form of verbal exchanges; Harry eschewed written comments on papers, preferring one-on-one conferences, in which he would "in a gradual and terribly time-consuming fashion, try to get [the writer] to see what he has done."

Each student needed to be pushed at his or her own level. "Some students are tougher than others. Some take criticism better than others," he said. Though he, like Lytle, could be highly critical and would occasionally bring students to tears, he did not lack compassion for his pupils and condemned his peers who did. He recognized the raw nature of teaching creative writing: "My students bring me manuscripts that deal with some of the most intimate and sensitive aspects of their lives. The manuscripts purport to be fiction, but, as is usually the case with apprentice fiction writers, what the story actually deals with is thinly disguised biography. They are bringing me their blood and bone. And they understandably don't want to hear me say that their writings, their visions of who they are, are crippled, mutilated and mangled."

Those who bought into the vision, as Harry had under the tutelage of Lytle and Kirkpatrick, accepted the role of apprentice in the craft of writing. He would liken the path of his students to opera singers or violinists, who were expected to practice for years under the eye of a master. An anecdote he told regularly concerned a karate master who had achieved the level of tenth-degree black belt. When asked if his incredible level of skill and decades of training made him a true master of karate, he replied only, "I am a student of karate." In Harry's view, passed down to him from the Fugitives half a century before him, one must submit to a lifelong journey in which each will always and forever be a student of writing. To become a writer, "to climb to the mountaintop," he told his students, they must realize "that no man ever held in his hands an instrument more delicate, more complex and full of mystery than the instrument of language."

Conveying his own passion for his craft, ultimately, was his greatest skill as a teacher and his gift to students. "After a class with Harry Crews, you wanted to just go home, get the typewriter, and get going," said his student Marie Speed.

Rod Elrod studied on and off with Harry for four years without receiving a degree. He eventually went back to the University of Montana to complete his MA. He needed only a few credits to graduate, but he had burned some bridges on the way out and was not granted an assistantship from the English Department at Montana. Short on funds and forced to pay crippling out-of-state tuition, he was trying, and failing, to support himself and Debbie by earning handfuls of dollar bills playing poker and pool in Missoula beer joints. One dark, cold day in the middle of winter, the phone rang, and Harry was on the other end, calling from sunny Gainesville. Harry asked his friend how he was doing.

"Well, I'm doin' fine," Rod lied.

"Look," Harry said, sensing the situation. "This is not your mama you're talkin' to. How about you tell me how you're really doin'?"

"Well," Rod said, "now that you mention it, it's twenty below outside, everything's covered with black ice, I haven't got a job, I can't get a job, and I won't see the sun for another three months."

"Well," Harry asked, "how would a thousand dollars make you feel?"

"A thousand dollars makes me feel pretty good."

The following day, Harry air-mailed a certified check for a thousand dollars to Missoula. Elrod used it to get out of the pool halls and to survive the long winter. In the spring, when the town thawed, so did the English Department. Elrod got the assistantship he needed to finally earn his degree. Harry never mentioned the thousand dollars again.

Not all of Harry's students left his tutelage with positive feelings. Sterling Watson was a member of the first wave of students who fell into Harry's orbit at the University of Florida. Watson had graduated from Florida Presbyterian College (now Eckerd College) in St. Petersburg, Florida, in 1969 and come to UF for the master's program. Once in Gainesville, he became a close friend and confidant of Harry's, partaking in all that position entailed. Unlike many in the group, Watson was a uniquely talented writer in whom Harry saw great potential.

Watson graduated from the program and went on to teach English at Raiford Prison about thirty miles outside Gainesville. He used that experience to write and publish his first novel, *Weep No More, My Brother*, for which Harry provided a cover blurb. Harry had also helped set up his protégé with an agent.

For his next novel, there would be no blurb from Harry on the book jacket. Inside, however, Harry was on every page. *The Calling*, published in 1986, told the story of an aspiring young writer drawn into the web of a pill-popping, heroin-shooting, gang-raping, lecherous, burned-out writing professor who uses and abuses his students and anybody else who happens to share his airspace. Most people who knew anything about Watson read it as a transparent portrait of Harry. Reviewers mentioned Harry by name. The supporting characters seemed derived from an inside view of Harry's life—Sally, Lytle, Charné, classmates of Watson, all received thinly veiled portrayals throughout the text.

Watson braced for the expected reaction from his mentor. He disingenuously told anybody who asked that the Harry character, called Eldon Odom in the book, was entirely invented. "The book is a work of fiction," he told the *Orlando Sentinel*. "Any belief that the character is based on a living person is fanciful. Harry Crews and I were at Florida at the same time, but that's all. The major teacher in Florida's writing program for twenty years has been Smith Kirkpatrick. He's a great teacher, and he's still teaching."

Watson sent a copy to Harry with a note that said the book was meant as a tribute, and he hoped Harry would view it that way. Harry did not. Instead, he saw it as a knife to the back, an act of "gratuitous malevolence," and Watson as Judas. "It was a cheap shot which I am at a loss to explain or understand," he told a reporter. "He didn't need my wife, my son, my dog to write his novel. . . . I never did anything to the guy. All I did was teach him what I could about writing fiction, and on occasion buy his whiskey."

Privately, Harry stewed over the book and plotted his revenge. He told friends that he was considering using his underworld connections to hire a hit man to resolve the situation. He called Watson and threatened him. "I told him it was a blood offense he'd committed, one that only blood can satisfy."

The book was positively reviewed in Florida newspapers and did extremely well for a novel from a small publisher based in Atlanta, selling five thousand copies on first printing. Even Harry acknowledged the novel's quality. "He has shown and continues to show great promise," he said of his former student. Watson, by then, was teaching creative writing at his alma mater in St. Petersburg. He made no attempt to satisfy Harry's request for a blood donation, choosing instead to avoid the confrontation. Harry attended a literary fair in St. Petersburg expecting to see Watson, but no meeting occurred.

Beyond the anger, Harry was genuinely hurt by the portrayal. He had considered Watson a friend, even a surrogate son. His vision of his relationship with Watson, and others like him, was far different than the depiction of him in *The Calling*. Harry always exempted students when he disparaged all the other inhabitants of academia. For the most part, he enjoyed their company and thought it reciprocal. In his mind, teaching and mentoring were as elemental and essential as writing, and were functions he believed he performed admirably. It was an honorable role he felt he could serve even when he was unable to write sentences and paragraphs that met his own standards. *The Calling* was a glance in a mirror that offered a canted reflection, a similar image viewed in vastly different light. "It didn't bother me that much of what he wrote was true," Harry said years later. "What bothered me was the tone of it, the stance that was taken in it. How this was a guy that hurts people, that fucks over people, that doesn't care about people."

Relationships in the English Department had changed as well. The department, which in the 1960s and 1970s had contained a large faction that wanted to euthanize the creative writing program, now changed directions and sought to build up its academic credibility. Melvyn New took over the chairmanship of the department in 1979 and went about recruiting credentialed writers and poets. "When I took over the chairmanship, we had really no creative writing program," he said. "We had Smith Kirkpatrick and Harry Crews. Smith was a fairly unproductive writer, and a fairly unproductive member of the faculty, and I think he kind of hid behind Harry, although Harry felt dependent on him. But it was the other way around: Harry *was* the creative writing program."

New began to expand the ranks of the creative writing program. Richard Eberhart, a poet with a Pulitzer Prize and a National Book Award on his résumé, began teaching one semester each year. Donald Justice moved from the prestigious Iowa Writers' Workshop to Gainesville in 1982, two years after he, too, won a Pulitzer. In 1983 Logan, a student of Justice's and a renowned poet in his own right, came aboard and was named director of the creative writing program.

Harry may have felt threatened by the new blood, but his reaction paled in comparison to that of Kirkpatrick. The feud between the two had thawed over the years, and they now had more than a decade of copiloting the program with little interference. Now, however, the program was being dragged out of the wilderness and into the publish-or-perish arena inhabited by the rest of their colleagues. Kirkpatrick hadn't published anything in years. The new administration gave lighter course loads to younger, productive professors, leaving Kirkpatrick to cover more classes than he had in the past. His resentment grew. He barely spoke to Logan and came into the office less and less. Eventually, he stopped coming to campus altogether. To make the point even more perfectly clear, he locked the door to his office and left his windows wide open. Soon, the office was discovered by pigeons, which made themselves at home and turned it into a pigeon bathroom and bird apartment complex for an entire flock. A while later, the pigeon headquarters was discovered by University of Florida maintenance staff, members of which opened the door to find a cesspool of feathers and bird excrement, enveloped in a vomit-inducing stench. The office had to be professionally fumigated before humans were again able to enter.

With Kirkpatrick's role diminishing and multiple award-winning poets now in the lineup, the department was in need of an injection of youth and energy in the area of prose. The injection that was chosen was a young writer named Padgett Powell. A graduate of the College of Charleston with a degree in chemistry, Powell had undergone a drastic change in career path, moving to Houston to work as a roofer and study under the experimental writer Donald Barthelme. His first novel, *Edisto*, a semiautobiographical coming-of-age story set in South Carolina, had given him immediate literary cachet. The book came out in early 1984 and was heaped with praise. It was excerpted in the *New Yorker*, a finalist for the National Book Award, and compared to *Catcher in the Rye* by Walker Percy. The *New York Times* called it "a sparkling read, so full of energetic inventiveness, intelligence, love of language and love of people."

In the midst of its effusive praise, the *Times* also saw fit to compare Powell's writing to another "voice of the New South," none other than Harry Crews. The comparison in the newspaper concerned writing, but in Gainesville it went further. A young, southern writer with a long, strange trip to literary stardom, his first novel getting rave reviews, comes to the University of Florida to revive the writing program. It was part of Harry's bio from fifteen years earlier, but now it was being repeated, only this time Harry was playing a different role: the less-than-productive, stagnating faculty member with a brilliant upstart now on the scene to illuminate his deficiencies.

Powell joined the UF faculty in 1984. Word had gotten back to Harry that Powell had said he was not a fan of Harry's fiction but thought his new colleague a first-rate journalist. Harry, of course, took this as a backhanded compliment, and his resentment grew. Soon thereafter, Powell invited Harry to dinner at his home. The two eminent writers were going to break bread together, pour some whiskey, and toast to the future of literature at the University of Florida. Harry brought Maggie along, and the two did some drinking to prepare for the occasion.

Midway through the dinner, the conversation turned to Harry's magazine writing. Powell praised a recent piece Harry had written for *Esquire* a few years before called "A Day at the Dogfights." The story, which chronicled Harry's adventures observing an underground dogfighting ring in central Florida, was tremendous, Powell said. But, he asked Harry, it obviously couldn't have all happened in a single day, right? Hadn't Harry rearranged the facts, just a little, for dramatic purposes?

Harry felt his integrity had been questioned. He rose violently to his feet.

"Are you accusing me of paddin' a story?" he demanded.

Immediately, the two new colleagues were nose to nose, and the get-to-know-each-other dinner never made it to dessert. Maggie shuffled Harry out of the house before blows were struck. "That's what Harry did in those days," Maggie remembered. "He got drunk and got into people's faces."

Powell and Harry worked together for nearly a decade after that fateful meal with little or no interaction. Harry's relationships with most of the members of the department, though, were cordial. He got along well with New, the chairman. Without that relationship, some in the department believed, Harry's antics would have had much more damaging consequences. And whether or not the arrival of Powell had anything to do with it, he began to make progress toward ending his novel drought. He'd begun work on a story called *The Enthusiast* in 1972 and taken it up several times in the intervening years, only to drop it again. The book had taken many incarnations over the years, but it had evolved into the story of a Gainesville lawyer and handball player named Duffy Deeter who lives in a Winnebago with a built-in gym, spies on his ex-wife (who happens to be sleeping with his law partner), both loves and is repulsed by his pudgy, candy-inhaling son, and generally rails against the inadequacies of living on planet Earth. By early 1986, the manuscript was complete, contracts were signed with a publisher, this time Harper & Row, and, finally, another Crews novel was on its way to the printer.

Productivity in the area of fiction did not carry over to his lifestyle, though. His drinking continued to affect him at home and at work. Visits to the rehab center were becoming more frequent, as were absences in class. In 1986 he was unable to finish out a semester; after six weeks, he cashed out, and Logan took over his seminar for the remainder of its run. The revolving wheel of his existence kept returning him to the same self-destructive outcomes. A change was needed. He began planning for a radical move. What was called for, Harry felt, was new surroundings, a place to rid himself of the old habits and develop new ones. He had moved away from Gainesville twice before, once east, once south. This time, he packed up his things and pointed his truck to the west.

CHAPTER TWENTY-NINE THE WORM FARM

> That was the great, grand secret of writing, the secret certain
> students lusted after, the secret some people wrote him letters
> about, the secret he was sometimes paid money to lecture on, the
> great, grand secret of writing: Put your ass on the chair. Repeat:
> Put your ass on the chair.
> —Harry Crews, *Where Does One Go When There's No
> Place Left to Go?*

If you're looking for a place to turn over a new leaf, a place where you could avoid distractions, stay sober, and get some writing done, New Orleans probably wouldn't be your first choice. A city where the bars have no mandatory closing laws, where drinking in public is legal and encouraged, and bartenders will pour your leftover hurricane into a plastic go-cup, where your waiter at even the most cultured of restaurants is liable to offer you a wine list at breakfast—a city like this would not be the place to go if you wanted to clean yourself up and jump onto the wagon. "New Orleans," said his friend Rod Elrod, "was not the place Harry needed to be."

But that, indeed, was Harry's plan. He wanted to get away from Gainesville, from classes, students, and faculty meetings, from Lillian's and the Orange & Brew and the Rathskeller. It was to be an escape from the familiar haunts of Gainesville, the ones that had become a force of stagnation. It was time to pack up and ship out, change the scenery, reshuffle the cards and see what came up.

Maggie, Harry's longtime, on-and-off-and-on-again girlfriend, had found some direction in her life, direction that had escaped Harry ever since he had completed *A Childhood*. On a tip from a friend of Harry's film agent, Maggie had, a few years back, set herself on the path to becoming an exercise physiologist. It wasn't quite psychology, her chosen field, but it was a subject she knew a little about, and once she cracked the books, she found she had an aptitude for the subject. She had spent years refining her own body through exercise; it wasn't much of a jump to do the same thing for patients. So she had chipped away at it, class by class, and in December 1985 she earned her master's, with a thesis titled "Physiological Profiles of Female Competitive Body Builders," based on hard-earned knowledge from her years pumping iron on the amateur bodybuilding circuit. Degree in hand, she was now ready to embark on a new career. She had secured a job as the assistant director of a wellness center at a brand-new hospital in New Orleans and made plans to leave Gainesville and start her new life as the calendar turned to 1986. Her sister bought her a golden retriever, which she named Heidi, and the two of them made the trip west on I-10 and moved into an apartment on Audubon Park, right near Tulane University.

A few months later, Harry was headed down the same stretch of I-10. For the first time in twenty-six years, a fall semester would start without him. His supervisors in the English Department at the University of Florida had happily approved a sabbatical for the 1986–87 school year. He had clearly earned it. With nearly two decades of service, he was now one of the senior members in the department. And a little separation might do a world of good, for both Harry and the denizens of the department.

So it was set. Harry would move into Maggie's apartment, put the bottle aside, and dedicate himself to a new novel, starting from scratch. He hadn't published a novel in nearly a decade. (*All We Need of Hell* was at the publisher and on track for release, but he had written much of that book in the early 1970s.) Now, cleansed of all the burdens of home, he was ready to start on an entirely new work of fiction.

The plan went bad quickly.

Harry arrived ready to tackle his New Orleans novel, and at first he seemed to be mentally and emotionally prepared to do just that. He tried to develop a strict writing routine, as he often did when he was in a productive period. He woke early, walked Heidi three miles around Audubon Park, had a light breakfast, and set up in front of the typewriter. For a short while, progress was on schedule.

But the lure of Bourbon Street proved too strong. While Maggie was working long hours at the hospital, Harry began spending long hours in the bars of New Orleans.

Gainesville had offered familiar barstools and friendly bartenders, but New Orleans was a major-league drinking city. Harry spent time in the French Quarter, ostensibly to do research for his book, but his research was always participant research, and he spiraled into a binge that he couldn't pull out of. He spent less and less time at the typewriter. The cycle that had happened time and again in Gainesville reemerged. Maggie began to feel she was losing control as Harry went deeper and deeper into his binge. He was powerless to stop drinking, and Maggie was unable to help. But now she had a fledgling career to protect, and she needed to do something before things spiraled completely out of control.

When she reached the point at which she felt there was no other option, Maggie sat Harry down and, quietly and dispassionately, told him he would have to leave. "There was not enough from our years together for her even to be pissed," Harry said.

After another night of excess, Harry somehow found his way back to the apartment and crashed on Maggie's bed, vodka bottle in hand.

"This shit has got to stop," he told her.

"I keep telling you that."

"I think I've redlined again. I don't think I can get back without some help. You've got to take me to a hospital."

Maggie knew the drill from a dozen times prior. "I don't know where to take you. Where do you want to go?"

"A hospital, any hospital," Harry demanded. "If I go down for the count before we get there, just tell them I have to detox from alcohol. It ain't a fucking big deal. Any hospital will do."

But this time, the choice of hospital proved extremely important. Harry woke up the following morning in pajamas he'd never seen before. He began to detect that the level of sanity among his fellow patients was very low. And then he noticed that all the doors on the hall were locked from the inside. The hospital Maggie had chosen was DePaul Tulane Behavioral Health Center, and Harry, unbeknownst to him, had signed a consent form that called for him to be locked down for seventy-two hours.

When he was lucid enough to understand where he was, he quickly realized he didn't want to be there. He asked for a phone call, then a lawyer, only to be told again and again that he had signed away his rights.

Eventually, he convinced a nurse to let him talk to the doctor. The doctor silently puffed on a cigarette while Harry pleaded his case. Harry told the doctor that he was a writer and a professor and a respectable member of society. "And," he said, "I'm committed to give two lectures later this month."

The doctor looked at Harry, bleary eyed, unshaven, and wearing institutional pajamas, and scoffed.

"Do you think you can lecture? You can't lecture."

"Give me a podium and I'll show you," Harry protested.

The doctor was unconvinced, and Harry was becoming more desperate. "I can go down to the French Quarter and find you five guys in five minutes drunker than I was last night," he said.

"You're not going anywhere," the doctor retorted. "Try to relax and be comfortable."

Another day of desperation and internment followed before Harry struck upon the bit of information that won him his release. DePaul was a private hospital, and this time, Harry's lack of funds worked in his favor. He told another doctor that he didn't have the insurance to pay for a stint in such a prestigious facility, and, once his story checked out, he was quickly transferred, via ambulance, to East Jefferson General Hospital, where the rules were far less stringent and the patients less frightening.

Still in his DePaul pajamas, Harry performed a reconnaissance mission in his new surroundings and learned that a simple request, to the right nurse, could grant him his immediate release. He spent another twenty-four hours playing pool, watching football, and wandering the corridors before he deemed it safe to request parole, and after a three-day hospitalization, he was once again free on the streets of New Orleans.

Once on the outside, Harry called Rod, his former student, who had moved back to Franklin Parish, a backwater in the northeast part of the state. Rod drove down to New Orleans to pick up Harry, the two of them went to Maggie's apartment, packed up, and, with Heidi in tow, drove back up to tiny Winnsboro, Louisiana, population four thousand, which Harry would call home for the next year.

Elrod had grown up in Franklin Parish, and after leaving the University of Florida, he had earned his MA at the University of Montana. He and his wife, Debbie, had moved back home to Winnsboro to raise a family. Debbie had given birth to their first child six months prior. Now Rod was teaching English at University of Louisiana–Monroe and considering a run for state representative. The couple lived on the farm where Elrod had been raised. His family was in the worm business, raising worms for fish bait, and now he and Debbie had taken up residence in a small house on the farm, about twelve miles from Winnsboro, about thirty from Monroe, the nearest city. And about a mile away from the house, across the farm, sat an empty worm barn. Rod understood how Harry worked best, and he knew instantly that with a little work, it could be an oasis.

"It was just a little barn, and it didn't have a toilet," said Elrod. "That was the main thing. So we built an outhouse. Dug a deep hole, built a little outhouse, put a little curtain on it, and he moved right in."

To visitors, it appeared to be nothing more than a shack sitting in a giant field of mud. Harry and Elrod outfitted it with a woodstove, some bookshelves, a few chairs, and a plywood desk. The bookshelves quickly filled up. On one wall, Harry posted Muhammad Ali's famous phrase of defiance, "No Viet Cong Ever Called Me Nigger," and on the opposite wall, "Only the Dead Have No Fear." And on the desk, he placed a placard with his Number One rule of writing: "Get Your Ass on the Chair." There was no electricity, and Harry had to get his water out of a jerry can.

The Elrods had experience sobering Harry up from their days in Cross Creek. They cleaned him up once again, and Harry pledged not to touch another drop until he had a completed manuscript.

Harry had stumbled into the exact situation he needed to recapture his gift. All his life, his best writing had come in isolation—in a makeshift study attached to the back of a trailer, in his house on Lake Swan with no TV, radio, or mail, in his hidden rented room in Gainesville—and now here he was, in a barn on a swamp, often without a soul in sight, just him, his dog, his typewriter, and the worms.

Once sober, he quickly settled into a routine. Rod got him a fishing pole, and Harry would catch two or three fish in the pond behind the barn, bake them on his wood stove, and eat them with some lemon for his meals. He had his old truck with him, and he found a little gym in Winnsboro, really just a metal structure where the owner had thrown some weights and benches. But it had a locker room, and Harry was there six days a week for a workout, a hot shower, and a shave. And every day, at four a.m., he was at his Underwood, ass in chair, a fresh page in the roller.

The subject was boxing. He'd devoted a fair amount of time and energy to the sport over his lifetime but, until now, hadn't devoted an entire novel to it. His introduction to the sweet science had come early on in life. When

Harry was ten, his older brother Hoyett had somehow come across a biography of Jack Dempsey, heavyweight champion and larger-than-life legend of the Roaring Twenties. Hoyett devoured the book, and then decided he was going to be a boxer. The family was on another tenant farm in Bacon County at the time, living hand-to-mouth, but Hoyett managed to save up enough money to buy himself some gloves and headgear, and he soon launched his ring career.

On Sundays, they would hitch the mule to the wagon, and Harry would drive Hoyett across the county looking for fights. Age and weight were unimportant. Anybody willing to scrap with Hoyett was acceptable. Harry served as his big brother's trainer, cut man, and second. The fights were often just glorified wrestling matches, but they served the purpose of allowing Hoyett to experience the sensation of taking a glove to the face and coming back for more. Eventually, Hoyett boxed professionally, compiling a 22–2 record before breaking his hand, and Harry spent many hours in the gym with him. Later, in the Marines, Harry took up the sport himself and fought as a light heavyweight, winning a base championship belt. Now boxing, and New Orleans, would make up the backbone of his next novel.

Needless to say, it wasn't to be a straight boxing story, where the bloodied underdog gets up off the canvas to gamely defeat the arrogant champion at the climax. In fact, there would be precious little actual boxing, as the general public understands the sport, in the book at all. There would be, however, a generous helping of perversity, debauchery, and one of Harry's most memorable freaks. Harry declared it a "novel with an absurdity at its center." The protagonist of the story was Eugene Biggs, a young fighter from Bacon County, Georgia, who finds himself in New Orleans after a quick trip from promising contender to washed-up pug before his twenty-third birthday. With his boxing career over prematurely, he learns accidentally that he has a special skill: the ability to knock himself cold with his own right hand, a trick he discovers spontaneously after his trainer and surrogate father abandons him in the dressing room following his final defeat. The trick was Harry's "absurdity at the center of the novel." Eugene performs it for cash, entertaining the New Orleans underworld of sexual deviants and bizarre misfits. Eugene's girlfriend is a Tulane graduate student who views Eugene as source material for her dissertation, and his best friend is another ex-boxer who now shows snuff films to tourists in the French Quarter. Eugene eventually rejects his profitable trick and goes to work for the undisputed king of the pervert underworld, J. Alfred Blasingame, a powerful businessman by day and a human oyster by night:

> But even before Eugene finished speaking, an enormously fat young man wearing an Adidas warm-up suit came into the room. He had chin after chin rolling down his chest toward a ballooning stomach that ended in a flap of fat even the warm-up suit could not hide. It hung across his thighs like an apron. His eyes were no more than slits in his swollen face. He had a leash in his right hand, the end of which was attached to a leather collar decorated with steel studs and fastened about the neck of an extremely thin man whose head was entirely bald, showing not a single wispy strand or a trace of stubble. He was dressed as a boxer and was as tall as Eugene but could not have weighed more than ninety-five pounds. Every bone in his body was insistent under his skin, skin that was diaphanous and desiccated. Eugene couldn't take his eyes off him. He was the most unhealthy-looking human being he had ever seen. As he watched, the man reached up and scratched his chest. A little shower of skin fell to the thick red carpet.
>
> "Knockout," said Georgie, "may I have the honor of introducing you to Oyster Boy."
>
> Eugene acknowledged him by simply repeating his name: "Oyster Boy." He did not offer his hand.

Harry's short stay at Maggie's apartment in New Orleans and his research provided much of the backdrop for the story, as did the time he spent in northeast Louisiana. "We'd take drives and tour the countryside around the area," Rod said. "Went down and showed him some of South Louisiana, some of the antebellum homes, things like that. Then it all turned up in the book."

Rod would later spend many years as a writer and editor at the *Franklin Sun,* the local newspaper in Winnsboro, but at the time he was still writing fiction and would regularly join Harry in the barn. The two would chat about the weather or how the fish were biting in the pond and then commence typing, Harry at the Underwood and Rod at a word processor across the room. The two had developed a rapport back in Gainesville, and they fell back into the same rhythms now.

"I've got a lot of the same stuff Harry has," Rod told a reporter who had come to record the story of Harry on the farm.

"Compulsion," Harry said.

Rod laughed. "Compulsion, I think, is the word. When I'm with Harry everybody thinks I'm the sane one. But when Harry's not around, everybody looks at me the way they look at him."

But most of the time nobody was looking at Harry. He kept to himself to a large degree, stayed on what he called "his program," spending days at a time by himself. Winnsboro was the anti–New Orleans, a town that Rod called the most conservative place in the world. He knew that one night of the wild Harry on the quiet streets of Winnsboro, the kind of performance that was a regularly scheduled event in Gainesville, would mean the immediate end of the Worm Barn experiment. Harry made a well-received appearance when Rod brought him to the university to read for his students, but for the most part, Harry remained on the farm.

"He wasn't trying to attract any attention, and I wasn't trying to give him any. He was here for a reason," Rod said. "He'd concentrate for several hours, and spend the rest of the day in a daze. I don't mean like in a trance or anything, but just letting things stew and getting ready to do it again. Might listen to NPR or something, you know? Talk about the news a little bit, but it was mainly just waiting to do it again the next day."

About halfway through Harry's stay in Winnsboro, in January 1987, *All We Need of Hell* was released to generally positive reviews. And, more surprisingly, people were buying it. The first printing of 7,500 copies sold out in twenty-three days, and the publisher cranked up the press for another batch. And, because it was his first novel in eleven years, reporters smelled a story. *"Crews is alive! And he's back!"* When they learned that he had become some kind of literary Mr. Kurtz living on a bayou outpost with only a typewriter and a bottle of Jack Daniels, the smell got too strong to ignore. *People* sent a reporter down to Winnsboro for a profile, and other media outlets made inquiries, all wanting a piece of Harry. Rod acted as the dutiful secretary, scheduling appointments, and Harry would trek up to the main house to tell the tale of the outlaw novelist typing away in the swamp.

Harry told *People* and the rest of the reporters that he had exorcised his demons for the time being and was bone dry, but the exorcism was not fully successful. More than once during his stay, Rod made the trip to the barn to find Harry in the grips of one of his binges. Harry would be on the floor hours, or days, deep into the bottle. The bare-bones literary command center would have transformed into the miserable pigsty of an alcoholic, the stench of urine in the air, waste of all kinds strewn around. While under the spell, Harry would stop eating or bathing; the longer the binge, the more time and effort would be required to clean him up. Rod would clean the barn and then drag Harry to his truck and drive him into Winnsboro, where a country doctor, a friend of the Elrods and a hard-core Christian, would help sober him up and send him back to the barn with a Bible and an admonition to follow the Lord.

Harry's final binge, near the end of his stay, nearly pushed Rod over the edge. Rod wasn't the carefree student he'd been back in Gainesville any-more; now he was a family man trying to build a career and a reputation in his hometown. Watching over Harry, a task that had been exciting and new in Florida, was now becoming more and more of an aggravation. "Of all the years I've known Rod, that was the angriest I'd ever seen him," recalled Debbie.

Harry took his Bible back to the barn after the last binge and, clear-headed once again, wrote the final chapters of *The Knockout Artist*. It was spring now, which meant the sweltering Louisiana heat was beginning to emerge, making life on the worm farm a little less pleasant. And in more ways than one, his sabbatical felt like it was reaching its conclusion. He composed a coda to *Knockout* in which his Bacon County antihero gets in his truck and heads east, all the while planning to do the same himself. On Easter Sunday 1987, Harry typed the final sentence of the novel and shortly thereafter packed up, bid the Elrods farewell, and pointed his pickup toward Gainesville.

The Knockout Artist would be dedicated to Harry's Louisiana hosts: "For Rod and Debbie Elrod, who made every effort to keep me sane—and very nearly succeeded—during the struggle to write this book," he wrote. Late in his year on the farm, Harry had asked Rod to take on the respon-sibility to carry out a task he'd been thinking about most of his adult life: the scattering of his ashes when he died. He asked Rod to take his ashes to Bacon County and pour them into Big Hurricane Creek, where he had played as a child.

It would be a year before *The Knockout Artist* showed up in bookstores. When it did, it was taken as a confirmation that *All We Need of Hell* was not some aberration; Harry Crews was indeed back on his feet. Reviewers uniformly noted that his skills as a storyteller and satirist had not dimin-ished. "Harry Crews writes like an angel, but one, of course, who is trapped in hell," wrote Chauncey Mabe in the *South Florida Sun-Sentinel*. The majority of the reviews had reservations, however, and they were all over the map. The book was either too much of a comic book, or not enough of one. The female characters were either too stereotypical, or too evil. And the vision was too dark, the story too outlandish, or the passages too cute. Charles Nicol, writing for the *New York Times*, discerned a change in Harry's work as he moved into late middle age: "Perhaps Mr. Crews has got too close to the sophisticates or, like his hero, has begun to find himself the subject of a dissertation or two. Has he quit knocking himself out, or is he just beginning?" And Christopher Lehmann-Haupt, also for the *Times*, wrote that when reading a Crews novel, "One doesn't pick up on its shortcomings; one allows oneself to be seduced. But one never forgets that one is being seduced. Or that Mr. Crews is a carnival barker of a slick and profitable freak show."

Perhaps the most important development in Harry's life to come from the publication of *The Knockout Artist* wasn't the critical reaction or the sales figures, or even the acknowledgment in literary circles that he was once again a productive and formidable writer of fiction. What would have even greater ramifications for Harry's life was the fact that *The Knockout Artist* somehow wound up in the hands of a pop-music superstar who counted herself among the exclusive club of celebrities so famous they didn't require a last name. And to Madonna, the book was a genuine, once-in-a-lifetime masterpiece.

CHAPTER THIRTY

AN ACQUIRED TASTE

> Could you love someone who constantly revolted you? The
> answer was easy: certainly. Revulsion seemed to be a necessary
> part of love.
> —Harry Crews, *All We Need of Hell*

It took very little time for Harry to resume his Gainesville lifestyle where he had left it a year before. He moved into a tiny two-room, $195-a-month apartment, replete from ceiling to floor with stained, deteriorating Formica, a couple of blocks from campus. On May 20, when he'd only been back a few weeks, he smashed his truck into a Cadillac while on the way to a morning workout at the gym. Both vehicles were totaled. Thanks to the accident, Harry reunited with colleagues and friends in Gainesville sporting a cracked cheekbone, among other assorted bruises.

Mary Voboril, a reporter from the *Miami Herald*, drove up to spend the day with the newly productive literary genius, now back in the state from exile. Harry met her with a sixteen-ounce can of Budweiser in his hand, at 10:15 in the morning. At his request, the reporter drove him down to the Yearling restaurant in Cross Creek. Harry ordered a shrimp salad, of which he would eat three forkfuls during a lunch in which he downed six glasses of white wine, gulping half a glass at a time. After being helped out of the restaurant, Harry directed Voboril to a convenience store, where he bought another six-pack of Bud. She drove him to the Rawlings House, now a state historic site open to interested visitors. Voboril had hoped to observe Harry in the historic home of another literary icon, but Harry refused to get out of the car in his condition. "Not when I'm like this," he told her. "I'm not always like this. I wish you could see me when I'm not like this."

On the way back to town, Harry downed the rest of the six-pack. Voboril helped Harry out of the car and back into his apartment. Harry, who had been alternately combative and reflective during their day together, now slipped into the role of kind uncle. "If you ever, ever get in trouble and need help, call me. Collect," he told her in slurred sentences. "And will you get me another beer before you go?"

Voboril ended her *Herald* profile with the scene as she left him at his shabby, dark apartment: "The refrigerator light is burned out. The wire shelves are empty, except for a cellophane bag of hard candy and five sixteen-ounce cans of Budweiser. He reaches for the fresh can and holds it protectively, as if he fears someone might wrest it away. He takes a long, flooding swallow. He cannot stand without falling. It's 3:15 in the afternoon."

Harry called Voboril to apologize and explain himself after their encounter but before Voboril's piece had run in the *Herald*. When it was published, Voboril tacked on an unconvincing addendum: "Since this story was written, Crews says he has gone on the wagon."

David Johansson spent a lot of time in Harry's squalid apartment during this phase of his life. Johansson had taken a number of Harry's classes as an undergraduate, and after he earned his degree he went to work as Harry's "all-around gopher," doing a wide variety of errands, from typing manuscripts to chauffeuring to buying beer. He also occasionally acted as Harry's call screener. He was playing this role one afternoon, sitting in the front room as Harry slept off the previous night's escapades in the bedroom. The phone rang. Johansson picked it up to hear a reporter from *Time* magazine. She also had heard of Harry's reemergence and wanted to do an interview. Johansson woke Harry to tell him the supposed good news.

"Tell 'em I'm sleeping," Harry growled.

Johansson dutifully returned to the phone and relayed the news to the shocked *Time* writer.

"Does he understand that it's *Time* magazine calling?" the reporter asked.

Johansson cupped his hand over the receiver and called out to Harry in the bedroom: "Harry, she wants to know if you know that it's *Time* magazine."

After a moment, Harry bellowed his response. "Tell her I don't care."

Though much of the attention mattered little to Harry, his level of national relevance seemed to be on the uptick. One late morning, he was waking up with a few beers in the living room with Johansson, perusing the books he'd been sent by publishers for one reason or another. He picked up Norman Mailer's latest, *Tough Guys Don't Dance.* Mailer was often associated with Harry by reviewers who placed the two in the "modern Hemingway" camp, but the two had never met. Harry cracked it open for the first time and began to leaf through and read passages. Mailer's protagonist was a writer named Spider, and Harry read a section where Spider discussed his literary influences:

"One night we would look for the faults in McGuane, next came DeLillo. Robert Stone and Harry Crews were saved for special occasions."

Harry stopped reading, placed the book down on the table, and looked at Johansson.

"Have I gone crazy, or did I just read my own name in this novel by Norman Mailer?"

It was one of those "incredibly surreal" moments, Johansson remembers, moments that were now occurring regularly in Harry's world.

If he was back in the crosshairs of *Time*, the *Miami Herald,* and other segments of the publishing media, Harry had also crept onto the radar of much less likely areas of the American entertainment scene. Some of the members of Sonic Youth, a hard-core New York punk band, began passing around a copy of *Gospel Singer*, and soon Harry Crews, more the concept than the actual person, was being discussed in the upper levels of the alternative music community in and around the clubs of lower Manhattan.

Lydia Lunch latched on to Harry's canon as much or more than any of the New York rockers. Lunch was at the time punk-music royalty. She had come to Manhattan as a teen and gained fame by performing vicious spoken-word rants about her childhood sexual abuse, eventually becoming lead singer of a band called Teen-age Jesus and the Jerks. She aimed to shock, writing songs about killing cats with shovels, and lyrics such as "Little orphans running through the bloody snow." Lunch had a literary sensibility, however, and spoke not of musical influences but of writers such as Hubert Selby and Henry Miller.

Lunch and Kim Gordon, Sonic Youth's lead singer, decided the work of
Harry Crews was worthy of its own punk band. "We wanted to do something musically, and I think, maybe, the name came first, because it was
so outlandish for a three-piece female group to be called Harry Crews,"
recalled Lunch. "Just the sound of it alone is pretty raunchy."

The two recruited a third member, drummer Sadie Mae, and got together
in New York in the summer of 1988 to write songs for the new entity.
They composed a list of songs made up of the names of Harry's novels,
even penning a song titled "About the Author," with lyrics directly lifted
from the jacket copy on one of Harry's books.

During the short existence of the band Harry Crews, Lunch put together
a packet of press materials and recordings of her and the other members
and sent it to the real Harry Crews. When it arrived at his apartment in
Gainesville, Johansson opened the package, examined the contents, and
began reading parts of it aloud. "Harry wasn't really interested," he said.
"But I knew this would tickle his fancy. I said, 'Harry, her boyfriend's name
is Fetus.' He said, 'I like that, Fetus! Sounds like a Crews character name,
doesn't it?'"

Once Gordon and Lunch had written a full playlist of novel-inspired
songs, Harry Crews the band flew across the Atlantic and went on tour,
barnstorming through Europe. In September 1988 the band played in Am-
sterdam, Hamburg, London, Rotterdam, and several other cities, receiving
positive, if confused, reactions from European punk fans.

"People really liked the idea," said Lunch. "They really liked the name,
Harry Crews, even if they didn't know how it was spelled or what it meant.
And I think people just thought it was a pretty outlandish idea. I don't
think it had ever been done before, an homage, a musical homage that's
not a musical, to an author."

The tour would eventually result in a live album, the only one in the
short existence of the band, titled *Naked in Garden Hills*, which featured
a head shot of a scowling, menacing Harry on the back cover. Lunch never
met Harry in person, and the band dissolved shortly after the members
returned to the United States. Sometime later, however, Harry received
an invitation. Sonic Youth would be performing in Jacksonville in an
MTV-sponsored concert event. Gordon and the other members of Sonic
Youth wanted to meet the inspiration for the now defunct all-girl band.
Though he was unimpressed by the band's sound (in a comment that got
back to Lunch, he said their music was "everything you don't want to

hear"), Harry was genuinely excited about the chance to go to the concert. He showed his enthusiasm sartorially, personally designing a pair of pants for the occasion. The concert pants had leather bell-bottom flares on the sides, a series of studs down the leg, and, in an inspired touch that Harry was exceedingly proud of: a patent-leather crotch.

Johansson, who served as driver and bodyguard for Harry's trip to the concert, remembers Harry gleefully showing off the outfit. "He said, 'We can trick ourselves out however we want to, whatever persona we want. We're gonna meet some of these *rock* people.'"

Gordon invited Harry backstage, and the two were filmed for an MTV segment. Harry enjoyed the attention and yucked it up with the band and its hangers-on. As time passed, though, he began to take a more critical view of the entire enterprise. "Anybody who thinks this album in anyway illuminated my work . . . has misread me," he told *Spin* magazine in 1990, when *Naked in Garden Hills* was released in the U.S. The music was terrible, Harry said (he preferred Lightning Hopkins); in fact, it was barely even music. "I wish the band well," he concluded, while seeming to do just the opposite. "My feeling is, if you want to do something with your life, that's great. But don't jack around with mine."

The sixth song on the A-side of *Naked in Garden Hills* was called "The Knockout Artist," the Crews novel that was still in the front of bookstores in the spring of 1988. And boxing would be the impetus for Harry's relationship with another popular musician who had developed an interest in the fiction of Harry Crews. A phone call came into the English Department one day, with a proposition for Harry: how would he like to attend a boxing match at the behest of America's reigning pop queen, Madonna?

The sport was on everybody's radar, it seemed. It was an opportune time to be the author of a popular book about boxing, as the sweet science was about to receive more attention that it had since the reign of Muhammad Ali had ended a decade earlier. The heightened level of interest was due to the emergence of Mike Tyson, a twenty-one-year-old former Brooklyn hood who had been discovered by a benevolent boxing trainer and turned into what *Sports Illustrated* called "a true warrior" with "the best of bad intentions." Following a ho-hum decade in heavyweight boxing, Tyson had emerged and won thirty-four straight fights, thirty by increasingly vicious knockouts. He was now scheduled to face Michael Spinks, a former Olympic champion known more for finesse than power, for the undisputed heavyweight crown in June. Tyson had also recently married television actress Robin Givens, garnering further publicity as rumors about turmoil and violence in their relationship swirled. The fight was to be Tyson's crowning, and with the hype propelled by his growing status as a media-created villain, the event had crossed over from sports circles into the wider entertainment culture.

If Tyson was about to claim the iconic title of Heavyweight Champion of the World, the belt that signified the World's Most Famous Couple was currently around the figurative waists of Madonna and Sean Penn. Madonna was the pop singer who had come to New York from Bay City, Michigan, in the late 1970s as a teenager with dreams of stardom. She had achieved those dreams in 1983, unleashing a string of dance/pop hits and fashion trends to go with them. Teenage girls from coast to coast began wearing black-lace tops, fishnet stockings, and dozens of bracelets to ape the new face of 1980s feminine cool.

Sean Penn was Hollywood's reigning bad boy. His name reached household status when he played the iconic stoner Jeff Spicoli in the teen comedy *Fast Times at Ridgemont High* in 1982, and since then he'd played a series of James Dean–type characters and established himself as both a bankable movie star and an extremely talented actor.

The two met on the set of Madonna's "Material Girl" video in early 1985 and were married later that year in a wedding that attracted most of Hollywood's A-list, along with twenty helicopters full of paparazzi, which had quickly become a part of the couple's daily existence. Penn, by then famous for his regular attacks on photographers, wrote "Fuck You" in six-foot letters as a message to the media air force that hovered above the Malibu ceremony. Once married, they made a movie together—*Shanghai Surprise*—which was summarily panned, separated, and reunited, all the while maintaining or increasing their fame and paparazzi desirability. And now they were on Donald Trump's guest list for the Tyson-Spinks fight, scheduled to take place June 27, 1988, at Trump Plaza Hotel in Atlantic City, New Jersey.

A few weeks prior to the fight, Harry received a message from the English Department in Turlington: a representative of Madonna had called and would like to speak with him as soon as possible. Harry was about as impressed with the music of Madonna as he was with that of Teen-age Jesus and the Jerks. But when he returned the call to Madonna's office, he learned that Madonna had read *The Knockout Artist* and been "blown away." She had passed the book along to Penn, who had a similar reaction.

Now they were inviting Harry to attend the Tyson-Spinks fight as their guest. They would cover all expenses: airfare, hotel, limousine, and fight tickets. Harry was ecstatic. He accepted immediately and began making plans to write about the experience.

Later, Harry told Byron about his conversation and plans with the Madonna people, and Byron relayed the story to Sally. Soon, she dropped by the apartment to see if it was true.

"I hear you got a call from Madonna," she asked him excitedly.

"Yeah, I guess she's a fan of mine," Harry responded nonchalantly. "I ain't a fan of hers."

Arrangements were made, and on the day of the fight, Harry met his famous admirers at their tony Central Park residence. The three spent some time getting to know one another before the planned three-hour limousine ride to Atlantic City. Penn was still sporting a close-cropped Marine buzz from his role in the Vietnam film *Casualties of War*, giving Harry the opportunity to discuss his own Marine experiences. Madonna sat down on the couch next to him, and Harry's nervousness was palpable. "My first thought was this: If you lived next door, sweetheart, I'd never ask you out," he wrote later of the introduction. "But my second thought was: Jesus Christ, the sweet musk of sex, the look of it, the vaguely salty smell of it, the move of it, comes off you like heat off a stove."

The fight was to be a Trump-manufactured spectacle. The publicity-seeking real-estate mogul used his personal helicopter fleet to fly in celebrities from both coasts. Elizabeth Taylor came with Frank Sinatra. Jesse Jackson, in the midst of a presidential run, was on hand. In the ballroom where the rich and famous were shepherded, University of Miami head football coach Jimmy Johnson was casually leaning against the wall when Warren Beatty barreled into him, knocking Johnson's drink to the floor as the actor scurried away from trailing photographers. Jack Nicholson and Paul Simon sipped Dom Pérignon and chatted while sports artist Leroy Neiman sketched them on his drawing pad. At a nearby table, Billy Crystal swapped stories with Rob Reiner.

The limousine shuttling Penn, Madonna, and Harry pulled up to the ballroom of the Atlantic City Convention Center amid a crush of fans and cameras. When the door to the limo was opened, a roar went up in the crowd—a sound, Harry said, "one would expect to hear at a football game or a lynching." Trump security guards, two deep, shielded them as dozens of flashes popped with each step. Penn shouted invective and threatened photographers who managed to get within spitting distance of him and his wife. As Harry inched forward, he took blow after blow to his torso and was hit repeatedly about the shoulders and head by flailing cameras. Penn kicked a television cameraman on the way into the building. The cameraman hit Penn with a forearm, and Penn responded by pinning him up against the wall before being pulled away. The incident would be reported in newspapers the following day.

Inexplicably, the mob of photographers had been allowed into the ballroom, causing Madonna's temper to flare. "Why were those fucking people allowed in where the guests are?" she demanded of a Trump representative. She continued to hurl expletives at the Trump employee as the little group was steered toward a waiting elevator. As they were waiting for instructions, Jack Nicholson, sporting dark glasses and holding a beer in his hand, stepped past the bodyguard and stood next to Harry. Beatty climbed aboard and nonchalantly leaned against the wall. The scene was surreal. Harry stood silently as Nicholson and Penn assessed the situation and Madonna "said unkind things about Donald Trump, including speculations about his ancestry."

After killing time in a hidden conference room, the three were finally led into the arena and taken to their seats, seven rows from the ring. Celebrities dotted the chairs around them, most chatting quietly, unbothered. Madonna, however, was still being swarmed by fans and photographers and reacting with vitriol, as her bodyguard fended them off. Shortly, Donald Trump himself made his way through the chairs, leaned down, and presented Madonna with an offer. Would she and Sean like ringside seats?

"We can't," she said firmly. "We have a guest."

Trump looked blandly at Harry.

"Go ahead," Harry told Madonna. "I'll be fine."

Madonna reiterated her position to Trump, who touched Harry on the shoulder and ushered the three of them down the steps, to a spot directly in front of the ring. He waved over a tuxedo-wearing underling, who brought over two chairs. Trump pointed to a spot two rows back for Harry, but again, Madonna refused. Instead, she sat on Penn's lap and offered Harry the remaining chair.

The tension grew thick in the arena as the crowd awaited the appearance of the combatants. The ring announcer introduced celebrity after celebrity to the crowd. Madonna drew cheers. The fans showed their disdain for

Penn, but he was quickly overshadowed by the tremendous cascade of boos saved for New York Yankees owner George Steinbrenner.

Tyson entered the ring at 11:25 p.m., wearing black trunks and black shoes, "with no socks, no towel, no robe and no pity." By 11:31 p.m., the fight was over. Tyson knocked Spinks down with a left hook sixty seconds into the fight and finished him with a vicious right to the chin at 1:31. So much for the evening's featured entertainment.

The Madonna entourage was quickly whisked away, once again fighting off the swarm. They hid in the kitchen for fifteen minutes before their driver brought the limo around. Madonna remained in a barely concealed rage after a night of harassment. As they sat in traffic, waiting to make their escape from Atlantic City, Penn announced that he needed to use the bathroom. No way, Madonna told him, we're not stopping. Penn objected, and Madonna handed him an empty champagne bottle and told him to piss in it. Penn hung his head like a dog being disciplined. I don't want to take a piss in front of Harry, he said. It was an awkward moment in a night filled with strangeness, and Harry saw it as a peek behind the curtain into the inner lives of his new celebrity friends. When traffic subsided, so did emotions in the limousine. Madonna put her head on her husband's lap and slept as the limousine made its way back to Manhattan.

Madonna didn't particularly enjoy the events of their first evening together, but she had enjoyed Harry's company immensely. She had a driver pick him up the following evening and bring him to a showing of *Speed-the-Plow*, the Broadway production in which she was currently starring (and getting viciously panned by critics). The two spent time together after the show, discussing Madonna's theater career and Harry's books. Harry had recently begun work on a novel about his experiences with Maggie in the world of bodybuilding. He explained the story to Madonna, and the two made plans for her to play the role of Maggie (to be called Shereel Dupont in the fictional version) onscreen. Harry clicked with Penn, too. Penn would buy the screen rights to *The Knockout Artist*, they decided, and write the script for an eventual movie adaptation.

Two days after the Tyson fight, while Harry was en route south, Madonna phoned the English Department herself. The stunned department secretary dutifully wrote down a phone message. Tell Harry, Madonna told her, that she loved the first eighteen pages of Harry's bodybuilding book. She would be writing him a letter shortly to expand. And, Madonna told the secretary, tell Harry that she is madly in love with him.

To show his appreciation to his gracious new friends, Harry decided he had to send a thank-you gift. He settled on the idea of mailing a set of signed first editions of each of his novels. The problem with the plan was that he did not currently have any first editions, having given all of them away over the years. His friend and attorney Huntley Johnson, an avid book collector, agreed to supply the books and sent them to the couple's Central Park address under Harry's name.

Soon after the gift was sent north, a return gift arrived. During their conversations in New York, Harry had told Madonna that he didn't watch television and, in fact, didn't even own one. Madonna was flabbergasted. How could he stay current with American culture or, more importantly, her latest videos? The retaliatory gift was Madonna's attempt to rectify the situation.

On a rainy morning, a truck from a Gainesville department store arrived outside Harry's tiny apartment. Employees carried an enormous box containing the largest wide-screen television set on the market up to Harry's front porch. Despite their valiant efforts, the box would not fit through the door. Johansson explained the situation to Harry, who was still in bed.

"Tell them to leave it on the lawn," Harry said dismissively.

The employees, who felt it was a bad idea for a high-end television to be left outside in a downpour, protested.

"Tell them," Harry said, "that if they don't do it, Madonna will buy their store and fire them."

The television survived the rain, and after expressing his gratitude to Madonna, Harry sold it without ever plugging it in.

Madonna's interest in Harry remained high. A postcard soon arrived. "You are definitely the coolest guy in the universe—next to my husband, of course—but it's a close race," she wrote. "Hope you had as much fun as me in New York, despite the bullshit."

She told Harry that Penn was still interested in *The Knockout Artist*, as she was in the bodybuilding book. "I hope you keep writing it cause I wanna be Shereel Dupont in a movie," she wrote. "As long as she doesn't die in the end." The book, when published two years later, would end with Shereel fatally slitting her wrist in a bathtub.

Circumstances would cut short Harry's association with Madonna. He paid her a visit in New York later in July, conducting a lengthy interview, the substance of which he would use in a profile of her for *Fame* magazine. By the time that profile was published in December, however, the World's

Most Famous Couple was about to be no more. On December 28, six months to the day after Tyson had cut down Spinks, an argument escalated, and Penn threatened to cut Madonna's hair off. Madonna took the threat literally, and soon a SWAT team arrived at the couple's Southern California estate. Madonna filed for divorce a week later. In the subsequent divorce negotiations, one of the items the couple squabbled over most intensely was the set of signed Harry Crews first editions.

It soon became clear that Penn had also acquired Harry himself in the divorce. True to his word, Penn bought the rights to *The Knockout Artist* and, between other projects, began writing a script for the movie himself. Harry's trip to Atlantic City had coincided with the beginning of his work on the bodybuilding book, eventually to be called *Body*, which monopolized his time for most of 1989. It wasn't until the beginning of the following year that their stars aligned again.

A lot had changed in a year for Penn. Around the time that he split up with Madonna, he had decided that he hated acting. He pledged to finish the jobs he'd signed up for, then move behind the camera to direct his first feature. On one of the last of his previously scheduled acting jobs, he'd met his future second wife, the actress Robin Wright, and had also begun to affect a softer public persona, which included less verbal and physical abuse aimed at photographers and extras.

On January 2, 1990, Penn called Harry and invited him to spend a few days at his home in Malibu, California. Penn had the germ of an idea for a movie, and he had some people he thought Harry might like to meet. Harry agreed, and days later Penn picked him up at the airport and drove him to Malibu. Over the next four days, Harry saw only a few hours of daylight; instead, he slept away most of the California sun. At night, however, he got a true taste of Hollywood.

"I'd had a movie idea for Levon Helm and Harry Dean Stanton, a brother story for these guys to play musicians," Penn said later. "And I wanted Harry Crews to get involved. . . . We had a fairly drunken night to see what Levon and Harry were like together."

More of Penn's Hollywood friends came over: Ed Harris, his costar from his latest movie, *State of Grace*, along with the actress Mare Winningham and several others. The party continued and tequila was introduced, and soon it became a musical celebration. Helm played guitar, Stanton joined in on the harmonica, and Winningham sang. Harry just tapped his feet and watched for a while, but after hours of drinking, he could keep silent for only so long. He waited for his moment and then launched into his favorite song to perform, "The Ballad of John Henry." It was a performance straight out of the Okefenokee Swamp, one he'd given on dozens of drunken nights in bars across Georgia and Florida. It was unlike anything that had preceded it and left the professional performers in the room in silent awe.

"When Harry started singing 'John Henry,' I thought I'd lost him," Penn said.

Harry's rendition was the highlight of the party. It also turned out to be his audition for his first and only acting appearance in a major motion picture. At the time, Penn was writing the script for *The Indian Runner*, which was to be his directorial debut. The script, inspired by a Bruce Springsteen song called "Highway Patrolman," was a working-class family drama set on the Great Plains. As the Malibu party went on through the night, Penn became convinced that the "John Henry" performance needed to appear somewhere in his first film. He had Harry sing it several more times as he contemplated its cinematic virtues.

Harry left Malibu after four days with both a pending acting gig and a screenwriting assignment. The trip, and the nights of partying, had also sent him into another one of his binges. This one was particularly debilitating because of his increased efforts at maintaining sobriety. The California trip derailed the latest attempt, and less than a week after his return to Gainesville, he checked back into the Buena Vista Pavilion for an enforced detox session.

If the trip had tossed him off the wagon, it had also been professionally fruitful. Penn had decided Harry and Helm did indeed mesh, and Harry was perfect to write the musical brother movie, which would be called *Picking and the Payback*. In his room at the rehab center on January 13, 1990, Harry began work on what he termed a "short-story play outline with scenes," featuring characters for Stanton, Helm, and Winningham. He worked on the screenplay off and on through the spring, and by September, 120 pages were in Penn's possession, and Harry had been "well paid."

Penn, however, had more difficulty turning *The Knockout Artist* into a script. He wrote 800 pages and still could not get the 120 needed for a two-hour movie. As filmmakers had been discovering for two decades now, Crews novels seem cinematic but are immensely difficult to translate to film. Penn said: "Harry Crews is a tall-tale-teller, and what is on his page has the sleight of hand to avoid archness in, say, a villain—every moment I wrote was like a sting on the score. And I just couldn't beat it."

Penn and Harry met again in the fall of 1990 in Omaha, Nebraska. *The Indian Runner* was now in production, and, as promised, Penn had written his literary buddy into the story. Penn met Harry at the airport in a beat-up pickup truck and drove him to the Midwestern mansion he'd rented for the duration of the filming. Harry was introduced to Robin Wright and later driven out to the small town of Plattsmouth, where the filming would take place. The cast included Viggo Mortensen, David Morse, Valerie Golino, and Harry's old silent acquaintance from his *Esquire* years, Charles Bronson.

The Indian Runner centered on the relationship between the Morse and Mortensen characters. The two played brothers; Morse's character is a tortured cop, Mortensen's a tortured Vietnam vet–turned-criminal. Of the many sources of angst hanging around the neck of the cop brother, one is the fact that he has recently shot a man in self-defense. Penn cast Harry as the dead man's father and Penn's own mother, Eileen Penn, an accomplished actor in her own right, as the dead man's mother.

Harry spent the next few days doing what he now knew constituted the majority of one's time spent on a movie set—standing around and waiting. When he could, he spent some time with Penn, gathering interview material for a profile he would write for *Fame* magazine. Finally, his scene came up on the shot chart. Harry and his screen wife were to confront Morse in a courtroom proceeding concerning their dead son. On cue, with Eileen Penn weeping beside him, he locked a baleful but deadly gaze on the movie cop who had killed his movie son and began a sorrowful, defiant version of "John Henry." His voice echoed through the movie-set courtroom for a single verse before the actors playing the courthouse officers dragged him through the revolving doors, still singing. The vision that Penn had when he first heard Harry sing translated nicely to the screen, and Harry was praised up and down by director, cast, and crew.

The Indian Runner was released the following year to mixed reviews and minor box-office receipts. Reviewers focused on Penn's directorial debut and his new image. No longer was he the rage-fueled brat-pack bad boy; now he was the reformed directorial artist. He had vision. The appearance of a cult southern gothic novelist in a supporting role did not go unnoticed. "What with casting Charles Bronson and Dennis Hopper in supporting roles and using novelist Harry Crews (very effectively), in a cameo, Penn has turned his film into a veritable Bad Boys Convention," Kenneth Turan wrote in the *Los Angeles Times*.

Months before the movie reached American audiences, a small group of Gainesville residents had received a sneak preview of one particular performance. Upon his return to campus after the trip to Nebraska, Harry showed up late to his evening fiction workshop. His on-again, off-again attempts to kick the alcohol habit were back in the off-again phase. His students quickly realized there would be no actual class that night and instead begged their teacher for some stories from his foray into cinema. Instead, Harry did them one better. Making every effort to remain steady on his feet, he re-created his onscreen moment. Soon, the sounds of West Virginia folk echoed through the halls of Turlington, as Harry belted out his favorite tune one more time:

> Captain said to John Henry
> Gonna bring that steam drill round
> Bring that steam drill out on the job
> Gonna whip that steel on down, Lord, Lord . . .

He'd made her somebody, made her hear the thundering applause
and shouts of approval, even love. He'd given her a cause in the
world, a cause such as she had not known existed for anybody.
And for that, she had done everything he had asked of her.
—Harry Crews, *Body*

The long drought was safely behind him now. *The Knockout Artist* had followed *All We Need of Hell* with respectable sales. Hawkins had negotiated a $55,000 advance for his bodybuilding novel. Harry now had a little extra money for the first time in years and had grown tired of moving from one ratty apartment to the next. He asked Huntley Johnson to help him find a more permanent living arrangement. Harry maintained a distrust of financial authorities dating back to the Depression, however, and did not like the idea of living in a home owned by the bank.

Johnson and his wife, Melissa, who was also a lawyer, picked up Harry for what was planned as an afternoon of house hunting. Melissa had made a list of several properties within Harry's price range and set aside several hours for shopping. The extended list did not prove to be necessary. The second house they came to was a wood-cabin-type ranch-style home in a secluded area, with tree-canopied property backing up to a meandering little brook known as Rock Creek. Though it had a rustic feel to it, it was still a suburban three-bedroom residential home, the kind that declares "I'm a proud member of the American middle class"—exactly the type of living arrangement Harry had been rejecting for years. It had a carpeted sunken living room, large plate windows with a panoramic view of the property, and a raised deck in the back. "He said, 'This is it. Boom. We're done. I don't want to do any of this anymore,'" Johnson recalled. "He moved straight from this awful apartment he lived in, into this nice house in a really beautiful area." The deal closed quickly, with cash, and Harry was once again a homeowner.

An opportunity that had presented itself shortly after his return to Gainesville allowed Harry to fulfill an ambition he'd harbored for decades. Jon Jory, the producing director of the Actors Theatre of Louisville, contacted Harry and Hawkins to see if Harry would like to write an original play. The Actors Theatre had started an annual festival in 1976, and in the years since had premiered more than two hundred plays. Several had gone on to win Pulitzers, including *The Gin Game* and *Crimes of the Heart*. To increase interest in the festival, Jory had begun to solicit works from well-known writers who hadn't previously written for the stage. Jimmy Breslin, E. L. Doctorow, and William F. Buckley were among the nonplaywrights to accept the offer. The price, for Harry, was set at $12,500. He accepted, and by the fall of 1988 his script, titled *Blood Issue*, was being workshopped for an early 1989 premiere.

Though he would unconvincingly deny the work was autobiographical, Harry essentially used *Blood Issue* to put his family on stage. And at the heart of the play was the central mystery of his life: the identity of his father.

The action takes place at a family reunion. The matriarch of the family, Mabel Boatwright, tries to hold her tongue while her two sons spit venom at each other. George Boatwright is a Bible-thumping racist; Joe Boatwright is a drunk, alienated writer. Bits from Harry's fractured relationship with Hoyett appear in the dialogue. Hoyett had been outraged when Harry sent Myrtice copies of *Playboy* to read his articles. The dispute resurfaces in the play:

> GEORGE: Damn you and Alaska both. I read what you wrote. Somethin anybody decent would've been ashamed to have in his hand. Bunch a naked women touchin theyselves, touchin theyselves while they tongues hung out dripping spit like a wind-busted dog.
> JOE: You sure do have a way with words, George. Must run in the family.
> GEORGE: At least I ain't never had nothin to do with a tits and ass magazine.

JOE: You don't like tits and ass, George? There are people, you know, who would say that wasn't normal.

GEORGE: Don't you talk to me about normal. The only reason I read that damn magazine anyhow is because I found it right here in this house. Our mother somehow got aholt of it. Damnedest thing I ever heard of. Our mother readin a tits and asses magazine!

JOE: I don't think you give Ma enough credit, George. I suspect she knows there's tits and asses in the world. Besides, I didn't give her the magazine and I didn't tell her to read it. If you've got a quarrel, it's not with me. It's with her.

The outline of the story closely follows the family relationships in *A Childhood*. As the less-than-cordial reunion proceeds, Joe, the writer, begins to ask questions about a third brother, one who died shortly after birth. Other family members curse him for picking the scab of an old wound, but Joe persists. He continues to pry into the past, trying to determine the relationship between his mother, Mabel, his father, Frank, and Frank's brother, Lonny. Whose blood truly runs through his veins? He must know, he tells them, so he won't have to spend his nights lying awake, "eating his liver."

In the climax of *Blood Issue*, Mabel, the matriarch, drops the fifty-year-old bomb: Joe's real father is Lonny. Mabel's husband, Frank, was impotent (his blood tainted by an Indian prostitute) but desperately wanted a family. After much verbal warfare and a few shotgun blasts, Mabel unlocks the secret: Frank asked his brother Lonny to father his children, and Mabel agreed. Everybody onstage is horrified to learn the truth behind a scandal that has been whispered about through the county, but Joe is relieved to finally know who his real father was. "I've got blood and now I know whose it was and where it came from," he says.

In the play, Harry brought ultimate finality to an issue for which, in life, there would be no closure. He had asked many of the same questions about his family history when researching *A Childhood* and would continue to wrestle with them. Finding truth where there might be none was a writer's job, he maintained, consequences be damned. "People [will] say I have no compassion to drag my family onstage so nakedly," he told the *Atlanta Journal-Constitution*. "But these people don't have the foggiest notion of the creative act, how the facts of one's life are transformed into a different truth on the page. I was a drunk writer, but not *that* drunk writer. My daddy lost a farm, but *that* daddy is not mine."

Jory edited the play and helped prepare it for production, and *Blood Issue* was workshopped through the fall of 1988. In April 1989 Harry made the trip up to Louisville to see, for the first time, his words in the mouths of real, live actors. Johansson accompanied Harry and remembered his bizarre preparations for spending a week away from home. Along with his clothes, Harry placed twelve cans of tuna fish in his suitcase and then, as an afterthought, unplugged his rotary phone from the wall, wrapped the cord around it, and put that in the suitcase as well.

In Louisville, the theater crowd was treated to Harry's interpretation of a southern playwright. He had acquired a Resistol cowboy hat, which remained on his head throughout his stay. With it, he wore a safari jacket with no shirt underneath and unzipped the jacket halfway to reveal his bare chest, creating an image that, one reporter said, "on any other novelist . . . would look like a macho gag, a Hemingway Halloween costume."

Harry attended rehearsals and at first did not like the feeling of seeing his work onstage. As certain lines fell flat, he would lower his cowboy hat over his eyes and avoid the gaze of the actors. With Jory's help, he rewrote large chunks of dialogue prior to the debut. "The cynicism is comin' off the walls in this place," he complained. "You can put that in the bank."

But despite the heavy undertones, Harry had loaded *Blood Issue* with humorous side plots and one-liners. Blatant racism is played for laughs; characters spend pages debating the virtues of a "Jap coffee pot." The ignorance and isolation of South Georgia is also a source of humor; Florida is called, by one character, a place "where there ain't a tree that don't have a light in it or ain't held up by a stick." The southern dialect throughout, along with Harry's coaching, had the actors laughing as the production grew sharper and opening night approached.

Jory's strategy of attracting big names had produced mixed results. Even with the help of theater script doctors, some of the writers proved unable to make the transition to stage writing. Breslin's effort, *The Queen of the Leaky Roof Circuit*, was called woeful; Buckley was revealed to be "a total tyro," according to one reviewer.

Blood Issue, however, proved to be a genuine crowd pleaser. The crowd at the festival, made up of experienced theatergoers, laughed out loud throughout. The performance was punctuated by gasps at the revelations, and when the performance was concluded, the audience rose for an extended standing ovation. Harry tipped his cowboy hat to each of the actors as they took their bows and reveled in the applause.

With his first and last play, he had written the festival favorite. He did not hide his satisfaction. It was, he said, "the biggest thing that has happened to me in a quarter century of writing." The success did not lead to a new career path, however. Harry revised *Blood Issue*, and it was produced and performed the following year by the Spirit of the Horse Theatre, in Minneapolis, Minnesota, and again a few years later in North Carolina. But the theater itch had apparently been scratched, and Harry's attention soon was directed to the next novel, one that was now bubbling to the surface.

If *The Knockout Artist* had confirmed that he was once again a productive novelist, it was *Body* which showed that he was back to writing at top form. Upon returning from his extended vacation in Louisiana, Harry had decided it was now time to use his experiences with Maggie on the bodybuilding circuit as the landscape for his next novel. Progress was steady through the first half of 1989. As was now his habit, most of his writing was accomplished in the early morning hours. He rose in the middle of the night, brewed a pot of Luzianne coffee, which he'd developed a taste for while in New Orleans, drank cup after cup, black, while chain-smoking cigarettes and constructing sentences in longhand on yellow legal pads. When the sun came up, he'd break for the day and head to the gym for a morning workout.

Because Maggie was still in Louisiana, Harry was without a typist. He arranged to have one of the secretaries in the English Department transfer his handwritten pages to typescript. She dutifully completed the job and turned it in, and when Harry began to read through the freshly typed pages, he realized that the secretary had taken it upon herself to correct all the southern dialect to proper grammatical English.

Johansson took over the role of typist shortly thereafter. He soon became aware that what he was typing was going directly into an envelope and being mailed to Hawkins in New York.

"Harry," Johansson asked, "is this a first draft?"

"Well, yeah," Harry responded sheepishly. "I suppose it is."

First draft or not, he had used the bodybuilding community to create a milieu that was vastly different and as satisfyingly complete as any he had previously created. His protagonist, Shereel Dupont, the character that Madonna coveted and which had been generously appropriated from the life of Maggie Powell, was a South Georgia grit trying to transform herself inwardly as she went about re-creating her outward appearance, turning herself into "a single shining muscle of a girl." Even her name was a creation—she had been christened Dorothy at birth and was a member of the Waycross, Georgia, Turnipseed clan. Now her family, literally and figuratively caked with Georgia clay, had followed her to the Ms. Cosmos championship in Miami Beach, where tanned, greased muscle reigned supreme. Her family threatened, by their presence, to reveal her true identity. For her trainer, Harry brought back the character of Russell Muscle, first introduced years before in *Gypsy's Curse*. (Recurring characters from novel to novel had become a Crews trademark.) Muscle lorded over Shereel, dispensing pain and withholding pleasure, callously rejecting to her pleas of thirst: "In two hours, you can have four ounces of water or four ice cubes to suck on, whichever you prefer. I'm a reasonable man."

The manuscript included an author's note in which Harry attempted to draw a line between where his experiences on the circuit ended and his fiction began. Within, he delivered a razor-sharp satire of the bodybuilding subculture, where vanity and narcissism reach steroidal proportions (the incursion of *actual* steroids, as Maggie had witnessed, was also present). The introduction of the Turnipseeds, hairy, violent, and distinctly unsculpted, was used to comic effect; indeed, the novel would eventually run with the subtitle "A Tragicomedy." Shereel's sociopathic ex-fiancé, Nail Head, a Vietnam vet with an ever-present switchblade, set on dragging Shereel back to her roots, would supply much of the drama and tragedy.

Body was to be published by Poseidon Press, an imprint of Simon & Schuster run by a young editor named Ann Patty. Patty received the manuscript in the fall of 1989 and was delighted with what Harry had produced. Still, the positive response she sent back to Florida included five pages of requested revisions. Harry's penchant for rejecting criticism was kept in check to a degree. He took two months to address her concerns, one by one, writing in the margins as he either completed, or rejected, Patty's requests. Most were rejected. Through their limited dealings he had developed a respect for Patty, and it shone through in his partial compliance. "I have done the very best I could to accommodate you and at the same time remain true to myself," he wrote to Patty. "I love the novel and hope you can trust me enough to allow me to go with my best instincts."

Patty accepted Harry's second draft and sent the manuscript along to printing. It hit the shelves in the early fall of 1990 and received a critical welcome that both accompanied its release and bolstered Harry's reputation in the fiction ranks. The September 9, 1990, cover of the *New York Times Book Review* ran with the headline "Three Crazy Novels" and teased to *Body*, Kurt Vonnegut's *Hocus Pocus*, and T. Coraghessan Boyle's *East Is East*. Within, English novelist Faye Weldon gave *Body* one of the most ebullient raves of Harry's career. Weldon noted Harry's deft handling of a female protagonist (a standard reviewer knock on Harry was his clumsiness with female characters): "Not for a moment, such is this male writer's skill, the throttled-back energy of his writing, do I doubt Mr. Crews's right to be as intimate as he is with his female characters," she wrote. "'Body' is a hard, fast, brilliant book. I hope the world it describes is less terrible in the flesh, or lack of it, than on the page."

The second-phase career success in book sales continued with *Body* as well. The response was enough for Hawkins to extract another $55,000 advance from Simon & Schuster for Harry's next effort. A more meaningful reaction to the book came from Maggie. She had recently moved back to Gainesville to care for her mother, who had been diagnosed with Parkinson's disease. Though she recognized Harry's fictional flourishes, she was touched by some glimpses of their relationship that peeked through in the text. Late in *Body*, Russell Muscle finally softens as he prepares Shereel for the decisive competition:

> "You have made yourself special in a way very few people are ever privileged to know. Hold on to that, keep it in your heart and in your blood."
>
> While he talked he had drawn her ever more tightly against him. And his hand had kept stroking her hair. She felt something coming off him she had never felt before, off his voice, his hands, the heat of his body. And it was a shock to her when she realized it was the purest kind of caring, and concern, and love. And all of it entirely untainted by anything sexual. It made her want to kiss him. And she knew she could have without doing violence to the moment. She could not help thinking it would be the kind of kiss she might give her father.

Maggie was proud of the book and honored that Harry would use her as a model for a protagonist. "I am not Shereel, although he based her on me in a lot of ways," she said. "I'm not from Georgia. There are a lot of things about Shereel that are not me, but a lot of the stuff that happened to her, happened to me."

The paternal aspects that appear in the pages struck a nerve with her.

She had examined and reexamined the choices she had made since meeting Harry. "I try and psychoanalyze, if you will, what was going on in our lives, and I think that Harry filled something of a fatherly figure role. My father died right at the time I met [Harry]. . . . He took care of me at times when I wasn't working. He was seventeen years older than I was. And what I've come up with in my psychologizing is that he took care of me. I won't say he was like my father, because my father was totally different from Harry. But I think in a lot of ways, I took him in because he filled that need for me at that time."

OUT OF THE BOTTLE

> I did not become a drunkard and stay drunk for X amount of
> years because I'm a writer. I became a drunkard like every other
> drunk does. I drank too much.
> —Harry Crews, *Gainesville Sun*, October 10, 1995

Gary Hawkins was a young filmmaker in Chapel Hill, North Carolina, looking to make a film about literature and the South, when one of his film subjects mentioned the name Harry Crews. Here was a subject who could really light up a camera, Hawkins was told. It was 1990, and Harry, according to Hawkins's friend, had recently been sober more often than not and, when he was, would make a lively film subject. Hawkins packed up his equipment and made the nine-hour drive from Chapel Hill to Gainesville. He knocked on the front door, and as soon as Harry ripped it open, with a searing intensity, he immediately began directing Hawkins's movie for him.

"You Hawkins?" he asked.

"Yes."

Harry began waving his arms, directing Hawkins and his cameraman around the property.

"We've got a pisser at each end of the house," he told them, leading them around his property. "You can set up in the back. Let's go."

For the next hour and change, Harry hypothesized, preached, and moralized on his favorite subjects for Hawkins's cameras: writing, sports, violence. He was, as Hawkins recalled, lucid and completely on point, and he delivered Grade A footage, every minute of it interesting and sharp. Hawkins would pose a question; Harry would briefly acknowledge it and then answer his own question instead.

After a little less than two hours had passed, Harry brought down the curtain.

"Well, I don't know when I've had a more pleasant afternoon," he said.

"The interview's over?" Hawkins asked.

"It sure is, bud."

Eight months later, Hawkins loaded up the equipment and made the drive a second time, to shoot some voice-overs. The man who answered the door on the second visit seemed to have aged years instead of months. Harry was sixty pounds heavier, and his mind seemed to be operating about thirty miles per hour slower. Hawkins set up his cameras in the back again, but the results were completely different.

"The laser focus and rapid-fire delivery were gone," Hawkins remembered. "I'd raise a topic and he'd address it, then he'd digress, then he'd digress from that digression, moving further afield until he grew bored and rolled to a stop. If the first interview was a lean, mean final draft, the second was a meandering first draft."

Health issues, alcohol, traumas of all varieties, physical and mental—all were beginning to bleed through to Harry's outward appearance and demeanor. He was in the second half of his sixth decade now. Injuries and age kept him away from the gym regularly, leading to weight gain. He was thicker now, gray woven through his hair and mustache. His limp was more pronounced, and when his legs were particularly bad, he walked with a cane. The passion and intensity for which he was known could still come out in force, but not nearly as often and now interspersed with forgetfulness and wandering attention.

He was invited to the Southern Festival of Books in Nashville in October 1990, where he delivered, without a single note, an hour-long recitation on the power of literature. He quoted Shakespeare from memory throughout, finally walking into an enraptured audience, shaking hands and patting backs as he orated. Hours later, however, his old friend John Morefield, with whom he had been close through the 1960s and 1970s, came to greet him at a book signing, and Harry seemed to be unable to remember him. At another book festival in the early 1990s, this one in Miami, Maxine Kumin, with whom he'd been extremely close during his summers in Vermont, came to see him. Harry seemed "completely out of it" and did not recognize Kumin.

Changes in his appearance were not all due to the passage of time. To perpetuate his outsider image, perhaps as much for his own internal benefit as for the public, he devised ways to make himself appear more bizarre. His hairstyles became increasingly peculiar. He began to wear a thick Mohawk, leaving the sideburns intact. It was a look he said he designed "with malice and forethought." (During a television appearance on *The Dennis Miller Show* in early 1992, Miller called his look "a cross between G. Gordon Liddy and Vanilla Ice.")

He also decided to add another tattoo; this time it was a conscious decision, with much deliberation. The ink was administered, and he now sported a smiling skull on his right arm, above the hinge, along with a quote from a famous E. E. Cummings poem: "How do you like your blue-eyed boy, Mr. Death?" It took little effort for admirers to get him to display his new adornment, and he went sleeveless as often as possible to bare his new motto to the world.

The effect, Harry said, was his attempt to counteract a perceived acceptance. With age, he felt he'd become something of a de facto Gainesville mascot—that slightly crazy, kindly old writer wandering around campus. Acceptance was not a reaction he could stomach. A tattoo or a haircut might just make him appear outwardly like the freak he was on the inside. "When folks see me now," he told Hawkins, "I can feel the hate coming off 'em like heat off a stove."

Despite his best efforts, though, he was finding acceptance in areas he would not have imagined years before. Academics had begun to accept, even study, his work, though not most of the academics who shared his office space.

The first academic articles on Harry's writing had begun to appear in the early 1980s. David Jeffrey had been introduced to the Crews canon in the early 1970s while he was coeditor of the *Southern Literary Review*. He was drinking coffee late one night with Harry's college friend Pat Waters. "You need to read this guy," Waters told him. "He's funny."

Jeffrey began to use Harry's books for his own personal respite from the eighteenth-century literature he was tasked with reviewing. A few years later, he proposed the idea of a Crews interview and got some interest from *The Paris Review*. He and his friend Don Noble, a professor at the University of Alabama, traveled to Gainesville, chased Harry from bar to bar for two days, found him after "he'd just dropped two bootleg Quaa-ludes," and eventually got six hours' worth of tape, much of which would eventually be published in *The Southern Quarterly*.

After the interview, Jeffrey became something of a champion of Harry's work. A few years later, he began soliciting academic pieces from friends and acquaintances at universities. A scholar named Frank W. Shelton, a professor at the University of South Carolina Salkehatchie, had discovered Harry concurrently and published some journal articles. Eventually, Jeffrey had enough content for a book. He took it to the University Press of Florida first but was rejected. "Frankly, I think they thought he wasn't worth it," Jeffrey said. After several more rejections, he found a willing publisher, Associated Faculty Press. *A Grit's Triumph: Essays on the Works of Harry Crews* was released in 1983, made little impact around academia, and disappeared from print soon after, along with the publisher, which, Jeffrey was told later, was actually a publishing house acting as a cover for the Mafia.

Academic evaluation of Harry's work cropped up more and more as the years passed, however. More pleasing to Harry was the fact that he had also become an icon to a good many up-and-coming writers, particularly those who shared his regional and economic background.

The lineup of southern literature now all seemed to pay homage to Harry. Barry Hannah, a Mississippi writer who earned the "modern-day Faulkner" tag for a time in the 1980s, had been a disciple since Harry reviewed his first book years earlier. Hannah had asked Harry about the possibilities of coming to work with him at the University of Florida. "Tell the chairman there that I'm a genius and at some later date when you might need me to say this about you, somewhere, I'll be there to plug you, if you can imagine that," he wrote to Harry.

Hannah was somewhat of a contemporary of Harry's, but in the early 1990s Harry's oeuvre began to seep into the younger generation. The new breed of southern writer sopped up not only Harry's subject matter but his outcast persona. Tim McLaurin was an aspiring writer who had grown up poor in rural North Carolina and joined the Marines as a teen. He spent years living the life his characters would eventually occupy in his fiction: finding odd jobs, from carpentry to delivery man to snake handler. He harbored literary ambitions and felt an immediate kinship when he read *Feast of Snakes* and began to investigate its author. He read the rest of Harry's work and modeled his own after what he read.

Like Harry, McLaurin wrote in anonymity for years. He was thirty-five when he found a willing publisher, and, with his first novel in galleys, he decided to pay a visit to his hero while on a trip through Florida. He stopped in Gainesville, checked into a motel, and was astonished to find Harry's name in the phone book. He drank a few beers and dialed.

Harry picked up the phone and offered his customary answer, bellowing his own name into the receiver. After McLaurin showered him with praise, the two agreed to meet. At nine a.m. the following morning, McLaurin was waiting excitedly outside Harry's office. "He turned the corner in the hallway, a large man, limping, craggy-faced with intense, piercing eyes," McLaurin remembered. "He looked about as much like the public imagined 'John Updike' image of a writer as Peter Pan did to Godzilla."

The meeting led to a friendship after Harry read and admired McLaurin's work. He offered a cherished cover blurb for McLaurin's debut novel and several subsequent books. In some of McLaurin's books, grits made an appearance, both as a breakfast item and a metaphor. It was, of course, one of Harry's favorite self-descriptors. The line from Harry to McLaurin, and his generation of "poor South" genre writers, would begin to fall under the umbrella of Grit Lit.

Larry Brown was another young southern writer who admired and then sought out Harry. Brown sported the requisite dirty South résumé: his father was a sharecropper, he served in the Marines, he wrote in obscurity for years, tapping out five manuscripts that went unpublished. Early on, he had discovered Harry and then read every word he'd published, combing the stacks at the University of Mississippi to find Harry's early novels, by then long out of print.

Brown published his first novel in 1989, and his work soon made its way to Harry's desk. Harry published a rave review about Brown's story collection, *Big Bad Love*, for the *Los Angeles Times* in 1990. "I read the book in a single sitting, then I read it again," Harry wrote. "In 25 years of writing, it was the first time I picked up the phone and tried to call the author."

The phone call never went through, but a month later, Brown struck up a correspondence through the mail. He began to compose long, boozy letters to Harry, describing his own childhood, his battles with alcohol, and his devotion to Harry's work through his years of literary solitude. Before he saw Harry's review, he had attempted to approach Harry at a book signing but had been too shy to go through with it. Now, he made his introduction through the mail. "Harry, you're one of the high priests of Southern literature is what you are," he wrote.

Harry showered his new protégé with holy water with his reply. "You are the goods, Larry Brown," he wrote. "The one-of-a-kind goods that cannot be planned for, or studied for, or prepared for or even prayed for—not with any effect anyhow. People like you just happen."

The correspondence continued, in letter form and on the telephone. The two exchanged stories, and Brown continued to compose multipage, intimate letters to his newfound mentor. "I'm just writing to shoot the shit and I don't expect you to answer every letter, cause I can talk much better in a letter than I can on the phone," Brown wrote. "I ain't much of a conversationalist on the phone nor in person, neither. I just kind of like to write to you so you can get a letter from me."

In Brown, Harry found a kinship he rarely found in his own students. Brown had begun to receive some recognition, but after giving up his career as a firefighter to concentrate on writing, he was going broke. In 1991 he was under consideration for a fellowship from the MacArthur Foundation. In his recommendation letter, Harry related one of the bonds shared by the two writers: "[Brown's] vision and sensibilities are rare enough and important enough that he will find very few readers. Or at least for a very long time. Perhaps for the rest of his life. Sounds contradictory, doesn't it? But it is not. Art is aristocratic, not democratic. The more folks who love your work, the less merit it probably has. Perhaps you wouldn't want to bet on that proposition. I would. I have. I have bet my life on it." Brown did not receive the fellowship.

Harry arranged a reading for Brown at the University of Florida in 1992 and invited Brown to stay with him. When Brown's plane touched down at Gainesville Airport, Harry was leaning against the wall, wearing an Oakland Raiders sweatshirt with the sleeves cut off, Mohawk, and a silver skull earring in one ear. At Harry's house, Brown discovered Harry had stocked the fridge with his favorite beer and whiskey. They quickly found that they enjoyed each other's company. "They were completely simpatico," said Huntley Johnson.

Harry brought Brown to Johnson's house, one of the stops as he ferried his new friend around Gainesville, to campus, to his favorite restaurants. Brown was quiet but comfortable in Harry's presence. "I probably did most of the talking when the three of us were together," Johnson said.

For the next decade, Brown would find a level of success similar to what

Harry had enjoyed. His novels and collections were published and highly regarded. *Big Bad Love* even became a Hollywood movie in 2001. In 2004 Johnson was driving through a rainstorm when he heard on the radio that Brown had died of a heart attack. He drove to Harry's house to deliver the news in person. "Harry was devastated," Johnson recalled.

A few years before his death, Brown wrote a tribute to Harry for *The Southern Quarterly*. He wrote of burning failed manuscripts, as Harry had done during his apprenticeship. "The incredible amount of things that have to be written and then thrown away is probably what discourages a lot of young writers. I don't think Harry ever thought of quitting," Brown wrote. "I know I certainly did, but something kept me going. To a large degree it was Harry Crews and his work."

For most of his writing life, Harry had been able to conquer alcohol long enough to do what was required to complete the job in front of him. His reemergence after his decade of silence was due, not to a commitment to sobriety, but more to a personal rediscovery of fiction as the reason for his existence. Even in his later novels, he had mostly employed the same rules for life: stay dry and write, then pop the cork when you finish. What he had been unable to do was remove alcohol from his life entirely.

Of course, there had been numerous attempts. Goals were established after each visit to the Vista Pavilion, after reprimands from his boss, after drunken episodes landed him in the hospital or jail. In 1985 he told the *Atlanta Journal-Constitution* he was done drinking. "Alcohol whipped me," he said. "We laughed, we talked, we danced at the party together; then one day I woke up and the band had gone home and I was lying in the broken glass with a shirt full of puke and I said, 'Hey, man, the ball game's up.'"

It was an empty declaration he'd made a thousand times before. The ball game would continue for several more innings and many more proclamations of success. The fall of 1988 included another prolonged stretch of sobriety. Harry was a groomsman in Johnson's wedding. For the wedding party gift, he signed copies of *All We Need of Hell* for each member. "We sat by the pool, I would tell Harry about each guy, and he would write some shit and sign a book for them," Johnson recalled. At the reception, however, Harry was noticeably absent. He stayed away, he told Johnson, because he did not want to be in the presence of alcohol.

Johnson and his bride went to Barbados for a honeymoon after the wedding and offered Harry the use of their condominium while they were gone. Barbados did not agree with them, and they returned early to find Harry very much off the wagon, living in their condo with a pretty young Crews fan who had taken a bus down from Minnesota.

The attempts continued. Desperation deepened. He availed himself of each and every method he could find for achieving lasting sobriety but found himself unable to fully commit to a single one.

For a time he tried acupuncture, which proved effective for a stretch, but eventually failed. He went back, again and again, to talk therapy, which also succeeded at times, but did not prove to be a cure.

He attended Alcoholics Anonymous meetings, finding strength in the support of the other members of the organization for a time. Soon, the strength he found was outweighed by boredom and annoyance. Ultimately, his disgust with both the exercise and its participants forced him out of the program. "They all tell these sad stories—the time they took a shit in somebody's ice box—well, we've all got a million of these stories and I found it tremendously depressing," he said. "I'd leave wanting a drink."

The very heart of the program, following the same steps as everybody else, acknowledging the same weakness as the rest of the everyday drunks, proved to be anathema to him. And the flavor of organized religion, which he had long ago sworn off, also helped drive him away. Being a member of a support group, no matter how personally beneficial, seemed to be something Harry was unable or unwilling to endure.

The trip to California to see Sean Penn and his Hollywood friends ended another long run of sobriety and landed him back in Vista Pavilion. It would be his last visit, and he marked the date of his entry as the official date of his last drink. The language of the reformed alcoholic began to creep into his public statements more and more. He found a therapist whom he could tolerate, one who used a combination of hypnosis and one-on-one psychoanalysis sessions. By the beginning of 1992, he was touting a two-year anniversary of being totally and completely alcohol free.

Another documentarian, Tom Thurman, came to interview Harry in the throes of his extended wagon ride. Harry spoke like a man who had finally bought in. "The truth of the matter is, you've got to do whatever's necessary," he said to Thurman's camera. "The problem is, you're a layperson. You're not a doctor or a psychiatrist. You don't know what's necessary. Whatever any of those told me to do, I did it. Maybe it wasn't the right thing to do, but I did it anyway."

Close friends—Johnson, Feiber, even Maggie, now back from New Orleans—got in front of the camera to offer affirmation to the new Harry. "Everybody in the world knew he had to do something about it before he did," Maggie said, with just a trace of exasperation in her voice, "but it finally reached him."

Though everybody stuck to the script onscreen and in public, there would be relapses. And though the specifics would change, substance abuse would remain part of Harry's life. Alcohol was mostly phased out; a myriad of pain medications, prescribed or not, would soon take its place.

It may have been a Pyrrhic victory, but the resultant lifestyle change was real. Less time drinking and recovering meant more time to devote to his writing projects and his teaching. It also meant a shrinking social circle. Life had been lived on a barstool for so long. Many of his relationships began and ended there. The lure of the bottle was far too much for him to risk reentering that world. So friendships that had been sustained by whiskey now withered and died. "I can count [my friends] on one hand," he said, "and still have enough fingers left for a grocery list."

Women were also something that had come with nightlife. He'd been living without a female presence in his house since his return from Louisiana (except, of course, for Heidi, Maggie's golden retriever, which he'd annexed in their split). When he took a woman out for dinner now, they'd decline to drink out of sympathy for his plight. "It doesn't bother me a bit," Harry would tell them. "Please, get drunk as a dog."

The solitary existence of a writer, he'd found, was creeping into all aspects of his life. He enjoyed solitude and quiet, but only to a point. Increasingly, loneliness would become the enemy. In *Blood Issue*, Joe, the autobiographical writer character, is asked why he spends so much time alone if he doesn't like it. "I didn't plan it for myself," he responds. "I just looked around one day, and that's the way it was."

CHAPTER THIRTY-THREE **SCARRED OVER**

> A lot of horseshit had been written about Heaven and Hell and
> coming back after death as a dog or something. But all of it was
> horseshit guessing. You could line up all the holy men of history,
> including Jesus, and the lot of them would not do as much for
> you as a good cup of coffee.
> —Harry Crews, *Scar Lover*

In the spring of 1992, Harry informed his superiors in the English Department that he would be resigning his position as professor on the first of June. He would enter a "phased retirement," teaching only one class a year, his spring creative writing seminar, for the next five years, before taking his leave of the university once and for all. He had twenty-five years in and, despite the friction over the years, was now a venerated elder statesman in the department and university. Still, his retirement announcement came and went with little fanfare. For his final year as a full-time professor, he earned $47,926, a lot less than many of his colleagues—it was just one slice of the grudge he harbored against his employer, one that would calcify and continue to grow over time.

Gone were the days of close friendships with students; now he mostly kept his distance, as he did with his colleagues. He was still revered by a certain type of student, and seats in a Crews seminar were limited, so prospective students had to show up early on sign-up days to gain entrance. His appearances on campus were less frequent, but he could still make a flourish. One morning during an enrollment period, he announced his presence by strapping on a pair of inline skates, the latest campus fad, and skating through the halls, acknowledging students with a wave as he rolled by.

His class was still like no other at the University of Florida. Maud Newton was a young aspiring writer from Miami when she took her place in Harry's classroom for the first time in the early 1990s. She was already somewhat a devotee of southern literature but knew little of Harry's work. Sitting in class with Harry at the head of the table was "an energizing, exciting, terrifying experience."

Newton jumped right in and volunteered to be the first to turn in a story. She had only a page written at the time but managed to complete it and submit it in time for the second class meeting. Harry handed it back to her with a big red C–. "My only consolation lay in a mystifying note he had scrawled beneath the grade: 'I think you'll do well in this class.' I was sort of weirdly encouraged by it." Harry hated the story but had liked a particular detail, a grandmother who lifted up her deflated breast to reveal a heat rash. His appreciation of that particular passage gave Newton insight into both her new professor and her own writing style.

"He could be incredibly withering," Newton remembered. "Sometimes he would just be really brutal about someone's story, so you were never entirely sure how he was going to react." A friend of Newton's in the class also turned in a story early in the semester. The story included a protagonist who "may or may not have had sex with a dog because she thought it was the reincarnation of her old heroin-smoking lover." The following week, Harry sat down at the table, pulled out the story, and told the assembled students, "I just want to read you all something, because this might be the stupidest thing I've ever read."

As it had always been, some students bought in, others tuned out. Harry entertained with stories he'd told a thousand times before; by the end of the semester, the class had heard some of them on multiple occasions. "He would sometimes start shouting about things, sometimes enthusiastically and sometimes angrily," Newton said. "I'm sure I and my friends laughed about things he said and the way that he behaved in class, but I was just really impressed, at the same time, by this real, truth-seeking need in him. . . . I feel really fortunate to have encountered it when I did."

His diminishing role at the university, and in the bars of North Florida, afforded Harry much more time to spend in front of the typewriter. His

output now was greater that it had ever been. A year into his semiretire-
ment, he already had nearly complete drafts of all the novels he would
publish during the 1990s, along with others that would never see print. He
was working toward a lifetime goal he'd made for himself, one in which
he constantly moved the bar. In the 1970s, he regularly told interviewers
he wanted to write twenty titles during his lifetime. A few years later, the
figure was twenty-five; by the 1990s, the number was up to thirty. The true
goal, he said, was an unattainable one: to write a perfect book. "If you
ain't got no lines in the water, you ain't gonna catch no fish," was another
oft-repeated Crews mantra.

With his newfound time, he was juggling several lines at once. *Scar Lover*
was completed in late 1991 and published the following year. By 1993, he
had completed two more novels, *The Horse Hog Gator Connection*, about
a South Florida alligator hunter, and *Circus Act*, set in a Florida retirement
village. He'd shelved both of those to tinker with the endings and begun
work on *Soap*, about a door-to-door soap salesman. He kept to his early
morning schedule and resisted, more than ever, incursions on his time. He
resented the imposition each January of the single annual writing seminar
he still taught at UF.

Under the direction of Ann Patty, Poseidon Press and Simon & Schuster
had paid another $55,000 advance for *Scar Lover*. It arrived, according
to Patty, "much more of a mess than *Body*," but she was pleased with the
manuscript nonetheless.

Scar Lover told the story of Pete Butcher, a drifter running from an
emotional wound left over from a childhood accident in which he hit his
brother with a hammer, leaving the brother brain damaged for life. The
event destroyed Pete's family, and the story, set in the paper mills and slums
of Jacksonville, follows Pete's attempts to heal, with the help of an ensemble
of variously scarred characters. Though dark and twisted throughout, it
was an uncharacteristically positive tale for Harry, a novel in which love
is a healing force that scars over open wounds.

The shift wasn't lost on Harry. "I just got this premonition I'm gonna
get killed in the *New York Times* over *Scar Lover*," he said for one of the
profile articles in support of the release. On the promotional tour, he emphasized his recent conversion to the church of love. He was flown out to
Los Angeles for *The Dennis Miller Show*, a short-lived talk show hosted
by the former *Saturday Night Live* cast member. Miller brought up the

issue, describing the sentiments found within *Scar Lover*. "Are you an old softy at heart, Har?" Miller asked kiddingly.

"Yup," Harry replied. "This is a departure from what I've previously done. But I just happen to believe that love, uncommitted love, without reservation, will heal anything. Somebody meets you and they love you that way, Jack, you got a harelip, or a crossed eye, or whatever. Don't matter. They love it all."

His premonition regarding the critics did not come true. The *New York Times* saw *Scar Lover* as another solid Crews effort, good enough to be a notable book for 1992. Other reviewers saw the same thing: one more clever, comic novel from an established writer, noteworthy for its slightly sunnier attitude but not diminished by it.

Ann Patty, at Simon & Schuster, was encouraged by both the response to *Scar Lover* and the sales. She and Harry worked well together, and he was becoming one of her favorite clients. Many of his books from the first phase of his career were now long out of print, so Patty came up with the idea of reprinting some of them. It was a mutually beneficial service she performed for her authors—reviving the backlist and making them, and hopefully Simon & Schuster, a little extra money.

Classic Crews: A Harry Crews Reader appeared the following year. It included *A Childhood*, *The Gypsy's Curse*, and *Car* in their entirety, plus several nonfiction pieces. Harry hated the title and made sure to let everybody who interviewed him know it. He claimed to be receiving letters from writers across the country deriding him for his narcissism. Embarrassing title or not, he happily deposited the $15,000 advance he earned. His only fresh contribution to the collection was a seven-page autobiographical introduction, an afternoon's work.

Another work completed in an afternoon earned him an honor he did not expect nor particularly want. Through a mutual friend, he was contacted by Ellen Datlow, an editor who had published several anthologies of fantasy and horror stories. Her titles included *Snow White, Blood Red* and *Alien Sex*. Now she was putting together another horror anthology, and this one would mix horror and sex. Would Harry like to contribute a story to such a project?

His reflexive answer was an immediate and resolute "no." For decades, he had included a line in his course syllabus forbidding his students from handing him genre writing of any type. "We will concern ourselves with literary fiction, that is, no sci-fi, fantasy, children's or other genre stories, no talking cats," he admonished his new students. He had nothing against it, he said, or those who wrote it, but he himself was just not interested.

Soon after he turned Datlow down, another writer and friend of Harry's called with a challenge. Harry had turned down the offer because he knew he couldn't do it, his friend intimated. The offer had now metamorphosed into a dare. "Bullshit," Harry told him. "Of course I can do it."

The result of the following afternoon was a story called "Becky Lives," which would be included in Datlow's anthology *Little Deaths: Twenty-four Tales of Sex and Horror*. Harry's submission had no mystical elements, no vampires, no talking cats. It was a simple tale of revenge. A spurned husband pays a prostitute to pretend to be his long-dead daughter in order to fool his ex-wife, who left him for a richer man years before. The devious plan is outlined, the tension rises, and a bloody twist is unveiled in the final paragraph.

Harry sent it to Datlow and forgot about it. The following year, he learned that his first and only horror story had been nominated for a Bram Stoker Award, which the Horror Writers Association of America gives to the best short story of the year. The eventual winner of the award was Harlan Ellison, a respected writer also known for more than genre work. "[Ellison] was in good company," an interviewer said a few years later, complimenting Harry on the story. "No, he was not good company," Harry said. "It was a piece of shit."

The new, cheerier outlook that was evident in *Scar Lover* may have had something to do with the addition of a love interest into Harry's own story. Since he'd split with Maggie in the mid-1980s, Harry had been without a long-term partner. Though his relationships with women were always rocky, there had usually been a woman around to take care of him through most of his adult life. Now he had been sober and single, home alone in his three-bedroom house, for several years.

The house gained one more resident in the early 1990s. Harry met George Kingson, an attractive, thirtysomething teacher and aspiring writer from Gainesville, and in short order they were a couple. George assumed the role that Maggie, and before her Charné, had played in Harry's life — typing, proofreading, and managing his affairs and finances. She read Harry's pages hot off the typewriter and offered low-key opinions, opinions that Harry began to give much more weight than those he received from some of his current editors at Simon & Schuster. Harry thought George to be a talented writer herself and encouraged her to submit one of her pieces to Hawkins, which she did. Hawkins's lack of response would be one of the main reasons that Harry's relationship with his longtime agent would begin to deteriorate.

When Harry's next novel reached bookstores in 1995, it came with a dedication to George. Because of his feelings about the new book, *The Mulching of America*, he soon began to promise her another dedication in a book that was more worthy of her name. *Mulching* was Harry's take on the corporatization of the country, his disgust with business and advertising. To satirize the soul-deadening powers of the American corporation, Harry invented Soaps for Life, a company ruled by a grotesquely harelipped dictator known as "the boss," a bullying sexist who pits his salesmen—all of whom are men—against each other while employing an all-female, all-blonde team of secretaries to do their paperwork. To suffocate under the weight of the monolithic company, Harry invented a host of characters—a dirty-mouthed prostitute who lives in a van with her bulldog, an arthritic old lady soap customer whose breath smells of death, a three-hundred-pound salesman with a head the size of a cue ball, his "eyes, nose and mouth pushed tightly together and buried so deeply in thick red fat that they were hardly distinguishable from one another," and many others from the Crews pantheon who would suffer for the sins of their superiors.

The corporate excesses of 1990s American business were a new target for Harry. *Mulching* contained broad humor and comic situations, more so than his previous books, as well as sharp satire of the workplace. More than much of his previous work, however, the scenes and characters within *Mulching* had a cartoonish feel to them, especially those involving the lisping boss. In one scene, the boss races his hapless chauffeur up three flights of stairs and then reaps his own self-created rewards:

> The Boss turned to his chauffeur. "Drop 'em nan grab ne nodnam table. Winner kicks."
>
> The chauffeur dropped his trousers and his shorts to his ankles, bent over, and put his hands on the massage table.
>
> The Boss stepped behind him, set himself, and kicked him soccer style squarely in the ass. The chauffeur went flying over the table, and, turning in the air, landed on the other side on his back. As the chauffeur got slowly to his feet, the masseur started enthusiastically applauding.

The Boss whirled and slapped the huge masseur. The surprise and force
of the blow collapsed the masseur onto a straight-back chair. The print
of most of the boss's hand was outlined in red on the masseur's face and
blood was running from both nostrils.

"Who nold nu to clap, nasshole?"

The plot of the book veered wildly from its conception, a point made
to Harry by editors at Simon & Schuster. Even as he was promoting the
book, Harry had his own misgivings. "If I've got any reservations about
this book, or any deep concern, it's that the reader doesn't follow me
where I want to take him, because it makes a couple of leaps," he told the
Gainesville Sun. "This story couldn't have happened, which may say all
kind of things about it, about me. I wrote it, and I ain't gonna apologize
for it."

Most critics didn't see the problem. The book earned an early rave from
the *New York Times*. "Harry Crews is a writer who bears down on American enterprise with fierce eyes and a cackle," novelist Valerie Sayers wrote
in the *Times*, which chose *Mulching* as a notable book of 1995. Newspaper
reviewers around the country followed suit. The *Los Angeles Times* said
it was "the sort of satire that makes Swift look slow." *Publishers Weekly*
saw it as "a vision of America as a land of hucksters run amok" that was
"as black-humored and bilious as anything" Crews had written.

In its conclusion, *The Mulching of America* departs from reality to a
greater degree than anything Harry had written, even more than the little horror story he had dashed off on a bet. Employees at Soaps for Life
are used as mulch around the pristinely landscaped grounds of company
headquarters. Harry's metaphor for the evil powers of corporate America
had bled over into his story. No amount of positive press could reconcile
what Harry felt had been an error of the highest magnitude. "*Mulching of
America* just got away from me," Harry said two years later. "It has about
it, certainly in the end and in other places, the cardinal sin of any drama
or novel; it is just totally unbelievable. It's painful to say these things, but
if it's the truth. . . . So the truth is, I wish I had that *Mulching* book back,
and I would burn it."

CHAPTER THIRTY-FOUR ASSAULT FROM WITHIN

> And I could see from there that Luke's mother was the strong,
> enduring breed of woman that you find in those mountains.
> She was getting old and she was tired but she still had that
> expression of determination, of suffering long ago accepted
> without question.
> —Donn Pearce, *Cool Hand Luke*

The comfortable existence brought about by sobriety and domesticity was shattered in the summer of 1995. Harry's mother, Myrtice, suffered a massive stroke, at age eighty-three, which left her brain damaged, unconscious in the hospital. Doctors said she would not recover her faculties and was unlikely to live much longer.

The inevitable death of his mother, whom he had idealized his entire life, was a deep emotional trauma. But the circumstances surrounding her death, and the effect it had to enflame his already antagonistic relationship with his brother Hoyett, would add another layer of conflict and serve to isolate Harry further from those closest to him.

The years of hardship that Myrtice, Hoyett, and Harry had suffered together during the 1930s and 1940s had been the most desperate of each of their lives. They had left their wounds on each of them in different ways. Apart, they had each gone about their lives attempting to heal those wounds.

Myrtice married Alfred Turner, a hardworking farmer with a gentle disposition, in the early 1950s and had moved with him to Ashburn, Georgia, where the two had maintained a stable existence for three decades. After Korea, Hoyett had lived in Jacksonville, married, had a son named Ray, divorced, and lived single for years. In 1974 he married his high school sweetheart, Ann McDonald, whose first husband had died. Hoyett had farmed, worked as a fireman in Atlanta, and eventually settled in Rome, Georgia, a small city thirty miles northwest of Atlanta. By 1995, he and Ann were retired and ran a kennel where they raised thoroughbred American bulldogs.

Hoyett and Harry each had extremely close relationships with Myrtice but virtually no relationship with each other. Hoyett was a born-again Christian with deeply held religious beliefs, one of which was that Harry's writing was immoral, although, Harry claimed, Hoyett refused to actually read any of it. The brothers had rarely spoken in twenty years and could barely manage civil interactions when thrown together at family functions. "My brother is convinced I'm sending a lot of people to hell," Harry said.

The animus between the two had its origins on the farm in early childhood, when Hoyett wielded his power (he was four and a half years Harry's senior) over his younger, weaker brother. Harry viewed himself as the victor in the brothers' battle for their mother's affection, and Hoyett took out his anger on Harry. "Did Mama's favoritism, in part, make him the bitter man he had become today?" Harry wrote. "Was it mostly responsible for his unthinkably brutal behavior toward me as a child when Mama or nobody else was around to protect me? . . . Looking back, I cannot forgive him for marking me with memories that still jerk me from my sleep, startled and shaking in the middle of the night."

In adulthood, the schism grew and hardened as the years went by. Hoyett viewed Harry's writing with disgust and saw his little brother as a godless drunk. Harry thought Hoyett to be a mindless Bible thumper who forced his own beliefs on others and could see only from his own point of view. The circumstances of their mother's death brought their hostility, usually in the shadows, right out into the open.

Harry would write the following account of Myrtice's death a few years after the fact. He acknowledged within that the story, if told from Hoyett's point of view, would be markedly different. But Hoyett had the misfortune of having a writer for a brother, and "the hand that holds the pen leaves the record that will last." Harry drove up to Ashburn upon hearing the news of Myrtice's stroke. There, he found Hoyett, praying "aggressively" by his mother's side. The two had a series of tense exchanges, and eventually they decided that Harry would go home to Gainesville, rest, and return the following day to relieve Hoyett, who would stay to watch over Myrtice. When Harry arrived back in Ashburn at the hospital the following day, Hoyett had arranged, without consulting Harry, to have Myrtice removed from the hospital, taken off oxygen, and brought back to her home to die, essentially without medical care.

The decision, and the lack of consultation, was an affront to Harry of the highest magnitude. The life of a "noble woman" should not end in such a "sorry fashion," with intense suffering, "her ruined body collapsing upon itself," because her family had denied her food, water, and care. Harry hated himself for standing by and watching it happen. His rage settled on a familiar target. "I blamed my brother for ignoring me in the last decision of my mother's dying with an intensity that went beyond criminality," he wrote.

Harry held his tongue and participated in the vigil with Myrtice's extended family, as they waited through her final days and hours of life. While family members came in and out of Myrtice's house, Harry, each day, would sit in a recliner in the corner of the living room and slowly turn the pages of Myrtice's Bible.

Myrtice died soon thereafter. Harry would never speak to Hoyett again. He spent the summer grieving for his mother and soon began to contemplate another memoir. Such a project would be sure to reopen old wounds, he told a reporter while promoting *The Mulching of America*. "You gotta be honest. You can't just write that you loved your mother and she was sweet and she made these marvelous dumplings. Some bones have got to break, some teeth have got to grind," he said.

The following year, Hoyett sent Harry a letter outlining some minor details in the settling of Myrtice's estate. A checking account in her name had five hundred dollars that belonged to Harry, and Hoyett had some of Myrtice's belongings—a sewing machine, some silverware, a car—that were left for Harry in Myrtice's will. Hoyett was requesting instructions as to how the items should be shipped to Harry or Byron. Hoyett signed the letter, "My love and best wishes, always, Hoyett."

Harry's response a week later still dripped with anger from the previous summer. He would not be taking any of their mother's belongings, he wrote. The items should be given to charity. He and Byron were both to be left alone. In the future, Hoyett should refrain from contacting him, and anything Hoyett sent would be returned unopened. "I wish I could undo everything that has happened but I cannot," Harry wrote to his brother.

By the time he mailed the letter to Hoyett, he had resolved to delve back into his personal history and bring it to the page one final time. His row with his brother, and all the memories it had unleashed, now dominated his thoughts and left a permanent knot in his stomach. In April 1996 he and George drove up to Bacon County, ostensibly to visit relatives, but, in fact, to conduct more research for the new project. He interviewed his aunt Eva, Myrtice's sister-in-law, then ninety-four years of age, for hours, asking, one more time, all the old questions that still kept him up nights, the ones he thought he had excised when he wrote *Childhood* and again when he wrote *Blood Issue*. How was it that his mother and uncle were married so soon after the death of his father? Whose blood was running through his veins? Who was Harry's father? There was one question he really wanted answered, the one that was truly behind all the others, the one he had been asking his entire life: Who is Harry Crews?

Simon & Schuster was in the process of readying Harry's next novel, *Celebration*, for publication. Harry went to New York to meet with Bob Mecoy, one of the editors on the Crews account. The two had been acquainted twenty years earlier, when Mecoy was a paperback editor for the publishing house Dell, but had not spoken since. Almost immediately, Harry brought up the subject of his brother. "The whole lunch . . . he's talking about the fact that he's had a huge physical fight with his brother about his nephew," Mecoy recalled. "Harry said he didn't want his nephew to turn into the same sort of redneck piece of shit that his brother was."

For the next few years, Mecoy and Harry spoke regularly about various projects. Each time they spoke, Harry would bring up the subject of Hoyett. He told Mecoy how Harry and Hoyett were both Marines and hated each other's guts. "It always came back to . . . his theory that 'if you can't eat it and you can't fuck it, you're going to fight it,' which is pretty much the way I remember him putting it," said Mecoy.

The new novel, *Celebration*, marked a return to a familiar subject for Harry: a nursing home, the same setting he had used in *This Thing Don't Lead to Heaven* twenty-five years before. The theme of impending death, as with *This Thing*, is the spine of the novel. This time, the action takes place in a South Florida retirement community, called Forever and Forever, run by a Korean War vet named Stump because he had lost most of his arm in a farming accident. Stump cynically profits off the death of his tenants. The story centers on the relationship between Stump and Too Much, a bikini-clad teenage beauty who takes up with Stump and fills the heads of the inhabitants of Forever and Forever with dreams of regaining their zest for life. (Harry had originally titled the book *Circus Act*, because of a sexual maneuver Too Much would perform, in which Stump's stump played a significant role.) Harry dedicated *Celebration* to the memory of his mother.

The book appeared in 1998. Once again, national reviewers heaped praise on the latest work of satirical magic from Harry Crews. Book buyers, however, were not as kind. By the late 1990s, sales of Harry's novels were trending steadily downward, and the people at Simon & Schuster who monitored such things had noticed.

The trend of media conglomeration that had begun in the 1980s had accelerated in the 1990s, and midlist authors of literary fiction like Harry were feeling the pinch. Publishers were looking for big returns, and now. Gone were the days where writers were respected for the art they produced when money didn't follow. The dreaded "stockholders" were now referenced, and, it seemed, stockholders didn't give a damn about literary fiction. Publishers seemed to be able to find $3 million to pay an advance to O. J. Simpson's former girlfriend but were unwilling to spend a few thousand on authors whose books sold fewer than ten thousand copies.

"If you were going to play the game, you really needed to do ten to fifteen thousand copies in hardcover, and you needed to do another seven in trade paper and have a continuing sale in trade paper," Mecoy said. "I mean, that was the literary play, and we were looking at twenty-five hundred to thirty-five hundred. And a very big piece of that were . . . libraries and lit circles, and that's just too small."

On top of that, Harry would no longer consider editing suggestions on his manuscripts. Nearly all of Mecoy's editing notes were summarily rejected. "A quick reading of your suggestions for changes strikes me as a long list of things readers will never notice, or for that matter care about," Harry wrote. "No offense, I hope. . . . After all, it is my name that will be on the book, and I will be the one who will have to take the heat for whatever lapses there are in the story."

Harry had another novel in the pipeline about an alligator farmer in Florida, now called *Bone Grinder*, which he had been writing off and on for several years. Reaction at Simon & Schuster was tepid at best. There was a feeling, Mecoy said, that the publishing world was leaving Harry behind. The "strange Southern man" of Harry's fiction had lost its intrigue and felt, to some at the company, like a tired subject. "The review media were becoming more PC, more multicultural, more things that moved further and further away from Harry," Mecoy said. "And he wasn't coming toward them. He wasn't even engaging them enough to make fun of him." Harry, it seemed, offered nothing new, no element of surprise.

It soon turned out that Harry had a few more surprises left for his publisher.

Harry and his editor, Mecoy, continued their discussion about Harry's relationship with Hoyett. Soon, Harry was dropping hints about a memoir, a companion volume to *Childhood*. It was something Harry had talked about, off and on, since the 1970s. Mecoy wasn't sure how serious Harry was, but the subject continued to arise. After they'd discussed it several times, Mecoy decided it was time to let the idea out of the nest. Simon & Schuster held a weekly acquisitions meeting, attended by the high-ranking executives and editors of all the imprints at the house. Editors would have a few minutes each to discuss manuscripts they'd read that week and make their pitch for what they believed might be the next Simon & Schuster best-seller. It was a long, intense meeting, and at the end, attendees were given one last chance to bring up ideas for the future.

Mecoy dropped his Harry Crews bomb, hoping for excitement, but bracing for yawns. A second *Childhood* was in the works, he said.

The room lit up. This was just what was needed to reignite the Crews brand, executives said. Everybody knew about *Childhood*, how it was the pinnacle for Harry. If he could produce something as revelatory as *Childhood*, interest in Crews would be revived, and the value of his back catalog would skyrocket, as would that of any future novels. There might just be some money for the stockholders at the end of the Crews rainbow.

Contracts were signed, and *Childhood, Volume 2* was added to the Simon & Schuster calendar.

In Gainesville, the mood was far less upbeat. Just as they had during the writing of volume 1, the subjects within frayed Harry's nerves. He titled the new project *Assault of Memory*. He dug in, spent as much time as he could stand back in that world, with those people, the ones he loved but who brought him such emotional pain. When he couldn't stand it, he'd switch back to revising *Bone Grinder*, to keep him from going insane and doing "something unseemly."

In New York, Mecoy waited patiently. He went back and forth with

Hawkins, who reengaged significantly with Harry for the first time in years, belatedly catching himself up on the situation. Hawkins prodded his client to complete his most anticipated project in years. Can you finish the memoir on time, he asked?

"I not only can write *Assault of Memory*, I have written it," Harry responded. It was complete by the summer of 1998, sitting on Harry's desk in northwest Gainesville.

And there it would stay. Harry spent long hours considering the reaction to what he'd written. Certain people, he resolved finally, could, and should, never read this book. He delivered the news to Hawkins first. "I have decided that a couple of people have to die before I can publish it," he said.

The news reached Mecoy in New York. After months of promises, he returned to the acquisitions meeting with one final Harry Crews update. "I had to walk into the meeting and say, 'Harry Crews will not be delivering a memoir this year or next year or ever, as far I can tell, because he'll probably die before the rest of these people die,'" he said. "I had to eat my crow with salt."

A $10,000 check was written to Simon & Schuster to return the advance on the project. Privately, Harry told people that the book was killed because Simon & Schuster viewed it as libelous and had asked him to fictionalize it.

Though he did not honor that request, Harry continued to revise *Assault of Memory* for the rest of his life. Shortly after the deal fell through with Simon & Schuster, Harry offered the first two chapters for publication to *The Southern Quarterly*, which was devoting an entire issue to criticism and analysis of Harry's writing. "I stood at the foot of the hospital bed watching my Mama die," reads the first line of *Assault*.

The chapters in *Southern Quarterly* revealed the structure of the book, with scenes alternating between Myrtice's death in Ashburn and Harry's recent conflict with Hoyett, and scenes dealing with Harry's life as a boy of ten, taking up where he had left off at the end of *Childhood*.

Those two chapters, and the promise of more to follow, were all that Harry offered the public of the project for years. Hoyett, it seemed, was the living person who prevented publication. If the book was published, Harry told his friend William Dulaney a few years later, "Hoyett's not going to sue me or anything. He'll just come down here and blow my head off with a shotgun."

When he eventually sold his archives to the University of Georgia in

2006, Harry locked the folders containing *Assault of Memory*. As part of the sale agreement, the library was forbidden from allowing anybody to view the folders without a letter signed by Harry. Editors from *The Georgia Review* were granted access, and in 2007 the journal planned to print another section of the manuscript. Harry objected.

"I looked at what they were going to print, and I said, 'Whoa. No. No. We can't do that,'" Harry said at the time. "Why hasn't it yet been published? Because it's not fit to be published, that's why. I didn't want it to be published. It's not right." Language in the contract, however, granted the *Review* publication rights. After some dialogue between Harry and the *Review*, he relented, a few sentences were excised, and publication moved forward.

The chapters were published in *The Georgia Review*'s Winter 2007 issue under the title "Leaving Home for Home." The section picks up from the point where the *Southern Quarterly* excerpts ended. Adult Harry argues with Hoyett, reviving memories of youth. Cut to Jacksonville, 1945. Myrtice puts young Harry on a bus to Bacon County. After being hounded by a frightening Greyhound passenger, Harry forces his way off the bus and makes his way back to Jacksonville, where he's taken in by the prostitute who lives next door to the Crewses' apartment.

The passage has undertones of sexual abuse throughout. Young Harry is forced to hitchhike and relates the consequences of getting into a car with the wrong kind of driver. He speaks directly to the reader, fending off imagined accusations that "Crews is a fag" for submitting to such abuse. "Go look down the barrel of a gun or feel a blade on your throat and then come back and talk to me about dying being better than getting your dick sucked." Later, in the scenes with the prostitute, Harry says he doesn't want to go back to the apartment with his brother. The prostitute threatens to have Hoyett killed, "the rotten bully." Hoyett, the prostitute says, is a lot like her daddy.

That would be the last the general public would see of *Assault of Memory*. Harry continued to work on the manuscript. As his capacity diminished, he grew more pessimistic that it would ever rise to his standards of publication. In one version, which includes a handwritten note that says it was completed in 2005, the story picks up at the end of the *Georgia Review* excerpt. A gang of tough street kids, with Harry as the leader, is introduced. Harry is now thirteen years old, though time does not appear to have moved forward. Harry uses violence against his friends to maintain control over the gang. The gang plans a crime. Before the crime is committed, Harry goes back to the prostitute and discusses Hoyett's sexual abuse. Harry then threatens to act out the abuse on the gang's crime victim, a drunk whom they are in the process of robbing. At the story's conclusion, Myrtice returns home, and the prostitute threatens to shoot Hoyett if he touches Harry again. The prostitute, who had become Harry's lover, then dies, either by murder or suicide, the following day.

The tone of the manuscript deviates wildly. The early sections, those that were published, are similar in style and structure to *Childhood*, seemingly clear, realistic depictions of actual events. The latter half of the book feels more like an amateur attempt at Crews fiction, with violent confrontations, graphic sexual images, and sudden death, all of it difficult to believe as memoir. Was it written this way because Harry found himself unable to write a realistic account of events that did not actually happen? Or was it written this way purposefully, to blunt the accusations against Hoyett? Was Harry's final literary act, his *Assault*, an attempt to reveal a secret or to settle a score?

The author repeatedly apologizes for the conclusion within the text, as if Harry knew he had not successfully ended the work. His lifelong declaration that a writer's most valuable resource was his time was now proving true; as the last grains of sand were running down his hourglass, and his abilities were slipping below his own standards, he had begun to realize his time had indeed run out. He acknowledged in 2008 that the project had become a race with death.

"Can I get it done before that? I don't know. I think not," he said. "But I can leave instructions: If there's not a note here saying it's fine to publish, then don't do it. Will they honor that? Well, they haven't honored anything else, so they probably won't honor that either. I don't know."

CHAPTER THIRTY-FIVE CURTAIN CALL

> You've just said what the whole race of beasts wants to say,
> scream for, beg for even: They want to be young again, with the
> blood pumping all over again the way it once pumped, pumping
> again that way and never stopping.
> —Too Much, in *Celebration*

When Harry pulled back *Assault of Memory*, he essentially killed his relationship with Simon & Schuster. The company still had the rights to *Bone Grinder*. Harry delivered a manuscript soon after he had reclaimed *Assault*. The pages came to the desk of a senior editor named Frederic Hills, who asked Harry for extensive revisions, including a change in the ending. Harry, perhaps sensing the tenuous relationship he now had with his publisher, reworked the manuscript to some degree, attempting to appease his editor. Most of the editor's suggestions, though, were ignored. Harry wrote to Hills to explain and to ridicule him a bit as well. "I don't think you could get a happy ending or a smooth closure from me with a whip," he wrote. "If you cannot buy into what I have done here, up to and including publishing the novel, for God's sake, don't feel bad. The people who do not want to publish me are legion."

Simon & Schuster would now be counted among the legion. The company passed on *Bone Grinder*. Another project, an anthology called *Glimpses Through the Keyhole*, was killed as well. America's major publishing houses were through with Harry Crews.

He may have been done as a productive, publishable writer, but his status as a legend had long been cemented. He was becoming, as someone had once eloquently phrased it, a "living statue." He was old enough that personal jealousy and critical analysis of his work by his contemporaries had given way to adulation and worship by those of younger generations. Despite his own protestations that there were books to come, awards and honors came from organizations that wanted to put a cap on his life and career.

In 1998 he learned that he had won the Conch Republic Prize for Literature and would be the guest of honor at the annual Hemingway Days Festival in Key West. The award was given to authors whose "careers have reflected a devotion to the art and craft of literature, a willingness to take creative risks and the maverick spirit of Key West."

Harry had long been a Hemingway devotee himself. He remembered breaking down upon hearing the news, as an undergraduate in 1961, that Hemingway had killed himself. As a teacher, a standard lecture of his, one he'd given hundreds of times, revolved around Hemingway's short story "The Killers." Hemingway's *The Old Man and the Sea* was assigned each year that Harry taught his "Forms of Literature" class. So, despite his growing reluctance to leave Gainesville, George made the arrangements, and the couple traveled downstate to receive the honor.

The Key West trip went smoothly, but that wasn't always the case. As Harry's health continued to deteriorate, leaving the safety of home became more and more stressful. Unable to get to the gym, his weight had ballooned. And his legs had essentially failed him. He now needed a cane to get around at all times. The basic, daily chores of life now were rife with challenges.

George managed his affairs, made arrangements, and helped get him to and from appointments as best she could. His French publisher, Gallimard, invited him to Paris as an honoree at another writers' festival. This time, the stress of travel, and of a much greater distance, proved to be too much. Harry slipped off the wagon. At the home of an editor from Gallimard, he found his way into a wine cellar, locked the door, and downed bottle after bottle before he was finally discovered by his host.

Life was more manageable in Gainesville. Harry and George stayed home most nights. Occasionally they would leave the nest to socialize with friends. Huntley Johnson and his wife, Melissa Miller, hosted the couple regularly for dinner. Johnson found George "very nice but also a little distant," yet he acknowledged that George was the reason Harry remained functional.

The arrangement worked for Harry, but, at a certain point, it was no longer acceptable to George. Marriage was discussed, and Harry expressed interest in the topic but would go no further than that. Eventually, it became apparent to George that Harry was unwilling to marry. He'd long said that he'd been married to one woman, Sally, and that was his full share. Sally was still a presence in his life, always had been. Despite the divorce, they were, in Harry's view of the universe, still man and wife.

So George packed up her things and left Harry for good. Years later, a friend asked about the end of Harry's relationship with George. The friend asked: Why did she leave? Because I wouldn't marry her, Harry told him. And why wouldn't you marry her?

"Because it would hurt Sally's feelings," Harry said.

Harry would wrestle with the decision after it was made. He was profoundly saddened when George left his life, and the feeling would reverberate. He marked the relationship with a dedication a few years after the breakup: "For George Kingson—Your exquisite cradle of body, mind and spirit has rocked me to a place where only angels know. You gave me back my life. Lovely lady, my heart will forever beat with your heart."

With George gone, Harry had lost his liaison with the public at large. To a portion of the public, though, Harry was still in demand. In 2000 the University of Georgia's Hargrett Rare Book and Manuscript Library hatched the idea of creating a Georgia Writers Hall of Fame to honor the state's most famous authors. Its team of literary experts chose an inaugural class that featured Flannery O'Connor, Margaret Mitchell, Erskine Caldwell, and several others who constituted an extended Georgia literary Mount Rushmore. The following year, Harry was chosen for induction.

Skip Hulett, a librarian and researcher at UGA's Hargrett Library, was tasked with bringing Harry to Athens for the ceremony. Harry initially said he would make an appearance. Hulett told him the list of current inductees, and it was a list Harry wanted to be on. But with George gone, he had become even more reluctant to travel. He called his cousin, Jeannie Gaskins, in Bacon County and asked her to accompany him.

"He said, 'Jeannie, you know, I'm so debilitated,'" Gaskins recalled. "He said, 'If I accept that invitation and go, the only way I'd go is if you'll go with me.' I told him, 'Harry, I'll have to really think about that.' Because sometimes Harry gets so irate . . . I didn't think I could handle him."

Hulett told Harry the library would take care of all the travel arrangements and make sure somebody was with him for the duration of the visit. Still, Harry turned him down. No amount of coaxing would convince him. Without George, Harry now felt uncomfortable traveling more than a few miles from the safety of his home. Instead, Hulett came to Gainesville and conducted a short on-camera interview that would eventually be played at the induction ceremony.

Harry was the one living member on the list of hall of fame inductees in 2002. At the gala event, sons and cousins and editors and friends of Georgia's legendary writers walked to the stage, one by one, to collect the awards. When it was Harry's turn, a television was wheeled in. The room grew quiet, and in the video, a tired-looking yet contemplative Harry Crews looked into the camera and shared a sixty-year-old story of how, when his stepdad came up lame one morning and could not work in the field, fourteen teams of farmers and mules showed up and plowed his family's tenant farm. No plea for help had been made; the farmers just arrived and, without a word, went to work. "It may not mean anything at all, but it made a tremendous impression on me," he said.

If interest in the writing of Harry Crews had dried up in the publishing industry, the film industry was moving in the opposite direction. Movie projects that had been slow to boil for years were heating up, and one would finally bubble over in 2004.

It had now been more than three decades since Hollywood first took notice of Harry, and still, none of his novels had been turned into a movie. In addition, he had written dozens of screenplays, some based on his own books, some original, and none of those had made it to the screen either. Harry had, for years, employed a Hollywood agent who worked to ensure that options on his novels remained live. Producers continued to pay for the right to film future movies based on Harry Crews novels but did not film those movies. Hundreds of thousands of dollars had gone from movie producers to Harry, but cameras had yet to roll.

Acclaimed directors or novices, it did not seem to matter. None could conquer a Crews tale, or Crews himself. Robert Altman, director of *M*A*S*H* and *Nashville*, signed on to direct the film version of *Car*, one of many such directors attached to that novel. Francis Ford Coppola wanted

Harry to write a screenplay for Kerouac's *On the Road*. He offered to pay for a Winnebago and driver and told Harry he would be chauffeured across North America, following Kerouac's path, in order to write the script for a Coppola film of the Kerouac book. Harry turned him down.

He was more receptive to director Michael Cimino, who had an Oscar for *Deer Hunter*. Harry went to Giddings, Texas, to write a screenplay about ore mining called *Boomtown*, and accepted an assignment to write one about New York Yankees player and manager Billy Martin. In each case, checks were cashed, but films were not made. More recently, Sean Penn had spent years struggling, unsuccessfully, with *The Knockout Artist*.

Early on in his career, Harry had waited with anticipation for the projects to materialize. After the endless string of failures, he resigned himself to the cycle yet appreciated the income. Maybe his material just wasn't right for the movies. "You put most of anything I write on the screen, blow it up that big, people are going to bolt the theater, their popcorn flying," he said.

There had been one movie, though, to which Harry contributed that was actually shown in theaters. The director Sean Cunningham had gotten rich and famous in 1980 for *Friday the 13th*, a horror movie that came early in the explosion of the genre ignited by John Carpenter's *Halloween* in 1978. Years before, Cunningham's wife, Judith, had read *The Gypsy's Curse*, and the couple decided it should be a movie. They went down to Gainesville to pitch the idea to Harry. Nothing came of it, but Cunningham kept in touch with Harry through the years.

In 1985, Cunningham began production on a film called *The New Kids*. The story was set in rural Florida. It wasn't much of a script, Cunningham said, a violent tale of teenage revenge. He called Harry. "I think I told him, here is the script we're shooting in three weeks. Can you think of anything that would be cool, or make it better, or anything?" Cunningham asked.

Harry did his best. He worked on the dialogue, trying to help make the lines sound authentic. The actor James Spader, then a twenty-five-year-old unknown, played the lead villain, a hillbilly tough who terrorized the protagonists. Spader, a Boston native, couldn't grasp a southern accent. Harry tutored Spader for two straight days, but Spader, Harry said, never got any better.

Mostly, Harry hung around the set and entertained. "He would sprawl around the living room and just come up with ideas and tell stories," Cunningham said. "I think, as much as anything, he was just telling stories about teaching, or writing, or those fuckers that were trying to screw him."

In the end, Harry's contributions couldn't save *The New Kids*. The film made no impact, financially or critically. One reviewer called it "mindless carnage and moral primitivism." Cunningham exempted Harry from blame. "We started with original material and brought him in just to try to add some of his special stuff," he said. "You know, you can't really come in and add special sauce at the end, though. It really has to work from the ground up."

Cunningham was happy to write Harry a paycheck and hoped it would revive his attempts to bring *The Gypsy's Curse* to the screen. He continued to fiddle with script ideas and put together a fantasy cast for the parts of Marvin Molar, Al, Hester, and the rest of the inhabitants of the Fireman's Gym.

The rights to *The Gypsy's Curse* changed hands several times over the years, eventually falling to a French company, Davis Films. By early 2004, the company had firmed up a director and cast. Philippe Decouflé, a choreographer who had successfully orchestrated the opening ceremonies of the 1992 Albertville Winter Olympics, was set to make his directorial debut. Harvey Keitel, famous for his work in Martin Scorsese films, would play gym-owner Al Molarski, French actress Vanessa Paradis signed to portray the femme fatale role of Hester, and, in the casting coup of the century, the producers had found a legless British dancer named David Toole to play Marvin Molar, perhaps Harry's most inspired fictional creation, the deaf-mute hand dancer. Johnny Depp, boyfriend of Paradis, would have a cameo. Filming was set to begin in the summer in Britain and Portugal.

The casting coup ultimately became the undoing of the project. It turned out to be very difficult—impossible, in fact—to secure insurance when your star has only one kidney, as was the case with Toole. It was to be just one more failure. Just a few months later, the filmmakers wrote to Harry to tell him they had no insurance, no financers, and now no money to renew the option. "We would respectfully ask you to hold (the rights) for us for 18 months to give us the chance to make this film a reality," the producers wrote desperately to Harry a few months after the project had fallen through.

It would not be until a big check appeared in his bank account, Harry had long ago concluded, that he would know that a Crews movie would actually be made. The money arrived in early 2004. The check had come from Antidote Films, an independent production company with a string of festival-circuit hits, the current owners of the rights to *The Hawk Is*

Dying. Harry's contract with the producers called for an initial payment, once cameras rolled, of $75,000 or 2.5 percent of the total budget (not to exceed $250,000). It would be his largest paycheck, and it signaled that there would indeed be a movie this time.

A young director and fan of Harry Crews named Julian Goldberger had written a screenplay for *Hawk* in 2001, before acquiring the rights to the book. He had earned some cachet with his feature debut in 1998, *Trans*, which had won several film festival awards. That and the script was enough to win him the job to direct *Hawk*. The producers also had had some recent success with independent films filled with actors from the indie A-list, such as *Laurel Canyon* and *Thirteen*. Once again, they packed the cast with names of actors on the rise. The lead role, the pseudo–Harry Crews part, would be played by Paul Giamatti, a talented actor with a non-leading-man face who was the independent it-guy of the moment, with a recent critical hit in *American Splendor*. Up-and-comers Michelle Williams and Michael Pitt were on board, too.

The filmmakers came to town early in the year to scout locations. It was to be a true Gainesville production, three and a half weeks of filming, all on location in North Florida. *Hawk* had been Harry's most personal book, set in and around the places he frequented in town, and the producers, in independent film fashion, wished to be true to his vision. "We definitely want it to feel like Gainesville," said Mary-Jane Skalski, a coproducer. "The characters say they're from Gainesville, and we're not shooting here and wanting people to think it's any place, or no place. We want people to know it's Gainesville, Florida."

Location scouts planned scenes at Gainesville landmarks. Shooting would take place at Rainbow Springs State Park and Paynes Prairie Preserve, where Harry had done his actual hawk training in the early 1970s. Local residents and business owners were promised parts as extras in exchange for the use of their stores and homes.

Three African auger buzzards were brought to town to play the titular hawk, which the character of George Gattling attempts to train as his life falls apart around him. Giamatti would spend much of the production with one of the buzzards on his arm.

Goldberger went to Harry's house to discuss plans. Harry was cordial and supportive. He would not be visiting the set, he said, though he was told often it would be just a few miles from his house. He would only be a nuisance, he told Goldberger. Mainly, he expressed concern about the training and feeding of the birds.

Filming wrapped on schedule in December. Prior to *Hawk*, Giamatti had acted in a movie called *Sideways*, an intellectual buddy comedy set in California's wine country. *Sideways* was a critical and financial hit; Giamatti was on all the Oscar lists. Antidote Films had his next movie in their pockets, and once the movie was edited and ready for audiences, they packed it up for a debut at the Sundance Film Festival in Utah with extremely high expectations.

The Hawk Is Dying was given a prime-time slot at Sundance, an eight p.m. showing in the 550-seat Racquet Club Theatre in the tiny ski town of Park City, where the festival was held. Press releases touted the film as the next surefire hit to come out of Sundance. The curtain was raised to a packed house, film buffs, industry types, and Giamatti fans, all ready for a laugh-out-loud experience in front of what one attendee called "*Sideways* with feathers."

Instead, they got a dark, meandering drama, filled with despair, tears, extended monologues, and, as one reviewer would write, "a barrage of falconry facts." And it was dark in the literal sense too, bathed in shadow, making it difficult to understand the action on screen in multiple scenes. What had been a loud, supercharged Sundance theater became a mausoleum in a hurry. Walkouts followed shortly thereafter. Better to get to the parties early than to stick it out and watch Giamatti pour his heart out to the bird.

For the filmmakers, it was a disappointment. Distributors with big pocketbooks took their money elsewhere. One would pay $10 million for *Little Miss Sunshine*, a crowd-pleasing comedy in the vein of *Sideways*. Checkbooks remained closed for *Hawk*.

Reviewers generally followed the crowd out of the theater. The trade papers panned it immediately, driving away the distributors. "Loaded with obtuse symbolism, the film is not only hard to understand, it isn't much fun trying to figure it out," said the *Hollywood Reporter*. A "self-conscious exercise in narrative obfuscation," said *Variety*. Newspaper reviewers would mostly follow suit when the film was made widely available. Even the few positive reviews managed to damn the film. Nathan Lee of the *Village Voice*, one of the few who liked the director's work, wrote, "Goldberger is less concerned with storytelling than sculpting an immersive, essentially non-narrative space—a sinkhole for the viewer to fall into and suffocate."

What Goldberger had done was fall into the trap that dozens of filmmakers had avoided over the years by balling up their napkins and calling for the check. As they had all discovered at some point along the way, Harry's stories didn't really add up in a literal sense. There was an element of the ludicrous at the heart of each and every one of them. Harry brought his reader along slowly, so that the bizarre would eventually seem conceivable. But on the screen, it was a different trick. Even somebody as gifted an actor as Paul Giamatti, who was exempted from the criticism of the film, couldn't make movie magic out of a desperate loner engaged in the two-hour, methodical death by starvation of a red-tailed hawk.

Of course, Harry understood the problem and was sympathetic to Goldberger. Antidote had sent him a copy of *Hawk* days before the Sundance premiere. He agreed it was a little slow, and he could have written a better screenplay, he said. But ultimately, he was glad they had made it and pleased to finally see what his work looked like on-screen. If it happened again, great; if it didn't, he could live with that, too. "There are other books of mine that are in the works, and maybe they'll do a job that will please me more," he said. "But because it pleases me more, doesn't mean it will necessarily be a better film. I'm not a film critic, and don't pretend to be one."

The saga of the *Hawk* movie was a nice diversion and some easy cash. Harry was still emotionally invested, however, in publishing fiction. Alone and homebound, he maintained his writing schedule. And now, without a publisher and with an inattentive agent, he cast about for a new outlet for his work. He continued to revise *Grinder* and wrote a new novel, *Baby*, about a community college professor who faces humiliation after humiliation brought about by his estranged wife and others in his life. It had several of the ingredients of a Crews novel—violence, dogfighting, even a crazed former novelist who hangs himself over the dinner table:

> "Got good reviews, but didn't sell for spit. His was Southern Gothic, don't you know."
>
> "I'm sure I do not know," said Nicky, "and I'm equally sure I do not want to know. Do you think someone could cut the gentleman down from over the table before dessert is served?"

It also repeated themes, even lines, from earlier Crews novels. The new book, in total, was barely twenty thousand words.

He urged Hawkins to sell the new book, at the same time fretting about its length. He was shocked by how short it was, but he could list a hundred others that are shorter, he wrote. "For God's sake, John, let's hope that we don't get an editor who weighs the ms. rather than reads it."

Even before the severing of his association with Simon & Schuster, Harry had been open to other avenues for his work when unable to find a major buyer. In 1971 he had started a novella called *Where Does One Go When There Is No Place Left to Go?* In it, a fictional Harry Crews is kidnapped by characters from other Crews novels. It was the most inward-looking piece of fiction he'd ever written, and he'd been tinkering with it for years. In 1995 a London publishing house, Gorse, published it along with a reissue of *The Gospel Singer*.

In 1998 Harry met Craig Graham, the owner of a small publishing house called Blood & Guts Press in Los Angeles. Soon, Graham had agreed to publish *Where Does One Go?* Graham commissioned Ralph Steadman, the artist known for his association with Hunter Thompson, to draw the cover art. The limited edition consisted of four hundred copies, each with Harry's signature.

After Harry had heard nothing from Hawkins about *Baby*, he packed it up and sent it to Graham in California. It had now been eight years since a new Harry Crews novel had been released by anybody.

Graham signed on happily. This time, he would go all out to capitalize on what was an original work by a literary legend. There would be three editions: twenty-six lettered and signed copies hand-bound in goatskin, three hundred signed and numbered copies, and two thousand hardbacks. On the cover of the thin volume was a black noose silhouetted against a blood-red background. Graham went about trying to remind the public that Harry Crews was still alive and writing.

The publicity effort would have to go on without him, Harry said. Publishing again after a long absence had not warmed him to the reading public. "I don't want to go all over the fucking country. Talk to these dull-ass people who have absolutely no idea," he said. "They haven't even read a fucking book. Man, it's a waste of everybody's time. It's a waste of money, damn sure of that."

Graham shipped five hundred copies, mostly to Florida, and hoped for the best. Word eventually made it to the *New York Times*, where editors saw Harry as an interesting What-Ever-Happened-To story. The subsequent feature article reminded readers of the Crews bio, which now firmly cemented him as a "literary wild man" and a representative of "a gruff Southern reality." The newspaper sent a photographer to Gainesville to see what had become of him. He was, they found, "a large and physically imposing figure, with a pallid face, close-cropped gray hair and crystalline blue eyes that make him look like an apparition."

The idea, of course, was to take one final look at another crazy writer, before he fades into the sunset. Harry did his part, signing off on cue. "Now I just keep wondering how this life's going to wind down. It's time to die, but I don't feel like dying. I feel good all the time," he told the *Times*. "Except when I don't."

CHAPTER THIRTY-SIX   LAST STOP

> That's how it works. That's how it's always worked. The big oaks
> have to fall down so the little oaks can grow up. And now it's my
> turn to go down.
>   —Harry Crews, interview with author

The days were long and lonely and painful. Harry's ailments progressed, and month by month, his physical condition worsened. Getting from one room of the house to another was a chore. He relied on friends or acquaintances for help when he had to venture out of the house. On the table next to his recliner in the living room, by his cigarettes and ashtray, he kept a small address book with phone numbers of those who were willing to assist him with daily needs. The book became his lifeline.

His legs were the main source of his discomfort. Each step could be an inferno of pain. When he did walk, he leaned on a cane, the furniture, the wall, emitting cries of pain with each step, as if he were walking across a bed of burning coal.

The diagnoses varied. Doctors had told him he had a condition called peripheral neuropathy, which caused the nerves in his feet to work improperly. Neuropathy has many causes, one being extended abuse of alcohol. His deterioration was also, at times, attributed to postpolio syndrome, which causes those who suffered polio in their youth to experience muscle weakening and atrophy in old age. Harry also blamed a botched knee operation he'd had in his late sixties.

Whatever the root of his condition, doctors were unable to provide a cure. Instead, he was prescribed Oxycodone to deal with the pain. Oxycodone is a powerful narcotic, highly addictive even to those without Harry's history of drug abuse. Soon, his reliance on the drug was complete. Doctors would prescribe a monthly supply; Harry's calendar revolved around securing the refill at the beginning of each month. Usually, he would go through his supply well before the month was over. On occasion, alcohol would provide a bridge to the end of the month.

Most of his friends had drifted out of his life by now. When he completed his last class at the University of Florida in 1997, his association with the university was severed, closing a channel of interaction that had been his main connection with the outside world. Sometimes, former students, old acquaintances, or hard-core Crews fans would show up on his doorstep. Harry would make time for his visitors and invite them in, offer stories and counseling, grateful for the company. "Nobody has ever been turned away," he said. "Why would I turn them away? Everyone has terrible and wonderful mysteries just dripping off of them."

From time to time, visits such as these would lead to extended relationships. William Dulaney was a retiree living in Jacksonville who had become an aficionado of Harry's writing. In his younger days, he had been a reporter for the *Atlanta Journal-Constitution* and the *Arlington Heights Herald* in Illinois, then had spent thirty years as a journalism professor at Penn State. Dulaney wrote Harry a fan letter and was soon invited to Gainesville. Similar in age and outlook, the two soon became "very tight."

Dulaney and Harry spoke on the phone two or three times a week. Dulaney began to travel to Gainesville regularly. Harry would ready a room for his new friend, and the two would discuss books, authors, and life as senior citizens. Often, Harry would grow serious and delve into his deepest fears and regrets.

Once, Dulaney was awakened by a phone call from Harry at two a.m. "Do you have any money?" Harry asked, with desperation in his voice. Somehow, he had become convinced that he was unable to pay his taxes and that he was going to lose his house. Dulaney called Sally, who was able to talk Harry off the ledge.

Another time, Dulaney received a late-night call from Sally. She told him Harry was in trouble. Dulaney called Harry to find out the cause of the emergency. Harry, audibly upset, told his friend that he had lost his address book.

Dulaney was troubled by the fact that Harry didn't own any copies of his books. By the 2000s, most of Harry's early novels were long out of print, and copies were valuable to collectors, often $500 or $1,000 for a volume in good condition. Dulaney sent Harry books and told him to put them somewhere safe, where they wouldn't be stolen. According to Dulaney, people from Harry's past who knew of his condition would come over, get Harry drunk, and steal from him. "They found out he was an easy touch," Dulaney said.

Harry's loneliness was readily apparent, Dulaney said. After they'd known each other for a while, Harry called with a request. He wanted to come and live with Dulaney in Jacksonville. You're the only person in my life who's never stolen from me or wanted anything from me, Harry told him.

His nuclear family members, Sally and Byron, maintained a presence in Harry's life. Sally continued to monitor Harry's well-being, cooking for him, looking after his finances. Byron was more removed, emotionally and geographically. He had left Florida and settled in Dayton, Ohio, earning bachelor's and master's degrees in English literature at Wright State University, then moving into the professor ranks. He got married and had a son named Henry.

An incident when Henry was only two caused a rift in the relationship between Harry and his son and daughter-in-law. Harry was drunk during a visit, and Henry's parents were no longer comfortable bringing Henry near his grandfather. Harry told Dulaney that Byron's wife was embarrassed by him and wouldn't allow him around Henry. "The fact that Harry never got to see his grandson was one of his greatest sorrows," Dulaney said.

According to Sally, Byron's bond with his father remained strong despite family conflict. On one of Harry's birthdays when Henry was a toddler, Byron wrote his father a card that expressed those sentiments. "When I have my back against the wall, I just look over my shoulder and see you running down a rutted dirt lane in a rubber suit in late August," he wrote to his father. "I know who I came from: chicken thieves, dreamers and hard core ass-kickers. We are together always, dad. There never was a time when this was not so."

Skip Hulett, at the University of Georgia libraries in Athens, kept in touch with Harry after his induction into the Georgia Writers Hall of Fame. The two discussed, over a period of years, the sale of Harry's archives. Harry had been saving his manuscripts and letters for fifty years, starting before he had even published a novel, and had accumulated numerous filing cabinets full of material. "I knew from the get-go, you save everything you write, all the letters, and all the drafts, everything," Harry said. "I made it my business to save stuff."

A series of hurricanes in central Florida in 2004, along with Harry's deteriorating health, spurred negotiations to move the collection to a safer location. Harry told Hulett that he had given much of the collection to the University of Florida years before, only to return later and find them in virtually the same condition he'd left them. He told Hulett he reclaimed them, and they had been in his study ever since. That neglect, plus Harry's resentment toward his old employer—hardened through his years of retirement—led him to choose UGA as the final curator of his works.

A deal was soon struck. Harry said at the time it was strictly a financial decision, and he planned to use the money to put his grandson, Henry, through college. Hulett and a few others from UGA drove down to Gainesville in the fall of 2006 to collect the materials. They found that Sally had meticulously organized the file cabinets that documented Harry's life on paper. Manuscripts from every novel, published and unpublished, more than six hundred letters, reporting notes, family photos, contracts, and hundreds of articles and reviews about Harry had been arranged in folders, chronologically ordered, and readied for the transaction. Aside from the inclusion of a few cigarette packs here and there, Hulett said, the collection was in remarkably good shape.

The following spring, UGA unveiled its new collection with an exhibit called "The Faith of Harry Crews: Put Your Ass on the Chair," after his favorite motivational axiom, the one he'd stared at day after day while writing *The Knockout Artist* in the backwoods of Louisiana. Harry said he was planning a trip to Athens to see for himself but did not follow through. The collection, he said, was there for posterity, so those interested in his work could peer back into the past and try to imagine exactly how he'd done it, how he'd conceived of and written all those novels.

Of course, he added, they'd probably be wrong.

Day by day, he tried to manage with his continually deteriorating physical condition. Much of the time, life was lived in isolation. Friends who did spend time with him noticed that his moods fluctuated. In the morning, when he was writing or felt he had made progress, hitting his mark of five hundred words a day, he might be cheerful and optimistic. Later in the day, when his medication would wear off, he could slip into dark depressions.

His college roommate Ed Nagel spent a lot of time with Harry during this period. One afternoon, Nagel was driving Harry around, trying to cheer him up. Harry would not be cheered. He complained, as he did regularly, about his ailments and the sorry state of affairs that was his life. They stopped for ice cream. I feel like I could commit suicide, Harry said. "I'm tired of hearing this shit," Nagel told him. "I know you're in pain, but we've all got pain." Harry was appeased that day, but the subject would arise more and more in conversation.

Despite his dire condition, another woman entered Harry's life and brought much-needed companionship during this period of hardship. Melissa Bass, a former Auburn University athlete and an employee at the University of Florida's College of Veterinary Medicine, answered an ad Harry had placed for in-home assistance. Soon, Bass was preparing Harry's meals, doing his shopping, and adding a woman's presence to his life. The relationship progressed. Bass would come over after work and help Harry out of some of his bleakest moods. She said she found him to be a soft-hearted man, much different than the reputation that preceded him.

In 2005 Tallahassee documentary filmmaker Tyler Turkle approached Harry with the idea of making a film. Turkle had chatted with Harry at a book signing in the early 1980s, been impressed, and pocketed the idea of putting him on film. Now, twenty-five years later, he drove to Gainesville and knocked on Harry's door with his proposal. A voice called to him from behind the closed door, telling him to enter. Once inside, Turkle was shocked by what had become of his subject.

"It was just sad. [In 1982] I'd seen a really stand-up, strong, big man, who you knew could probably wrestle an alligator and win. And then the next time I saw him, he was broken," he said. "He was sort of faking it, but you could tell."

Harry agreed to participate in Turkle's film, and, on and off for the better part of two years, Turkle filmed Harry and documented his life. Harry's condition dictated the narrative, he said. "It was evident that the only thing we could do was make the movie about Harry's pain and suffering."

Turkle dealt with Harry's mood swings the best he could. "He went from high to low almost every day. One time, he'd seem strong as an ox, the next, weak as a kitten," he said. Harry had developed an obsession with orange soda of all types and would often be willing to go before the camera only after Turkle placed a six-pack of his latest drink of choice in the fridge.

Filming progressed. Turkle traveled to Bacon County, interviewing a few of Harry's relatives and getting footage from the area. He spoke to a group of VIPs at the Alma Exchange Bank, publicizing his project and introducing the idea of a Harry Crews Day, which he envisioned as the Bacon County version of the Faulkner Day held annually in Oxford, Mississippi, Faulkner's birthplace. Harry's name was in the air in Bacon County again. Turkle asked Harry if he would be willing to go with him on a return trip, to see the place of his birth one final time, all to be recorded on film. Harry was enticed by the idea and, once Turkle told him how it could be accomplished, agreed to take the trip.

It was to be an expensive proposition. Turkle rented a wheelchair-equipped van and enough people to meet Harry's needs. "He really couldn't do anything for himself. He needed a staff, so I hired a staff," Turkle said. It took two months of planning for the three-day excursion.

On the day of the trip, Turkle called Harry with final details. Harry informed him that he wasn't going. It was off indefinitely. No reason was offered.

Turkle pleaded his case. Do you realize, Harry, he asked, that we've invested time and money and have a crew assembled, all ready to pick you up tomorrow at eight o'clock? I'm not going, Harry reiterated.

Turkle and his crew made the trip to Georgia without their subject. Harry's cousin Jeannie took the filmmakers from place to place to film the scenes of Harry's childhood. She showed Turkle the site where the blood of Ray Crews was buried in 1937, where the family's hound dog Sam had lain, howling for three straight days and nights.

While on site, one of the members of the film party discovered the body of a freshly killed hawk under a tree about fifteen yards away. The corpse of the bird had been placed on a concrete block, next to an empty bottle of vodka. Turkle called and related the story to Harry.

"What kind of fucking omen is that?" Harry asked. "What the fuck do you think that could mean?"

The awards for Harry continued to roll in, all to be presented in absentia. He was declared a Literary Legend by the Florida Heritage Book Festival in St. Augustine. He would be honored at a high-class affair at the St. Augustine Hyatt, along with historian Michael Gannon and perhaps Harry's most successful former student, Michael Connelly, author of a series of best-selling detective novels.

Harry declined the invitation and asked Dulaney to accept for him. Dulaney obliged. He called Harry afterward. "I've got a nice piece of glass here for you," he said.

"Did they give you any money?" Harry asked.

"Nobody got any money," Dulaney said.

"Well then fuck them, I don't want it," Harry retorted. Sally called later to claim the trophy.

Turkle nominated Harry to be inducted into the Florida Artists Hall of Fame, operated by the State of Florida's Division of Cultural Affairs. The organization picks two artists a year, and inductees have included Hemingway, Burt Reynolds, and Ray Charles. Harry would be honored in 2008 with country singer Mel Tillis.

Again, Harry declined to attend, despite the offer of a paid trip with transportation arrangements. Bass drove up to Tallahassee for the induction dinner and spoke on Harry's behalf. Turkle was left to handle the details, about which Harry showed extreme interest. He had become increasingly concerned with his legacy. Soon, he was proposing the idea of a biography to Dulaney. It would be called "The Final Chapter." Dulaney agreed to take the idea under consideration.

In his own writing he was focused on fiction, and he continued to haul himself into the study in the wee hours of the morning. He was hard at work on another novel, he told people, "the best book I've ever written," called *The Wrong Affair*. A "midget" figured prominently in the story.

The despair became too much one afternoon in the early summer of 2008. Harry picked up a hunting knife and plunged it into his stomach, dragging it upward toward his heart.

He was discovered in a pool of blood and rushed to the hospital, where he would remain for several months. He told people that he had been stabbed in a late-night fight by a longtime rival.

Friends questioned whether Harry wanted to die or whether the act was a plea for attention. Other attempts had preceded it, though with less devastating consequences.

Dulaney called him and Harry admitted the truth about the incident, how he'd stabbed himself, somehow missing all the vital organs.

"You're the most inept person I've ever met at killing yourself," Dulaney told him.

Byron came down from Ohio for Harry's convalescence, and Sally took an even more active role in Harry's life, hiring a full-time nurse to provide round-the-clock care, controlling his finances, and checking on him more regularly.

Physically, his decline continued steadily. He rarely left the house and got from room to room in a wheelchair. Lucidity was fleeting. In the early morning, he'd be sharp and communicative; later in the day, he could become confused or check out entirely.

Still, if he was physically able, he made time for visitors who found their way to his door. A young writer named Jason Hodges called asking for an interview in 2010. He was initially turned down, but Hodges had Bacon County connections and managed to sway Harry. He nervously arrived twenty minutes early and approached the door. Harry lectured him that he ought to know to wait in the car until one minute prior to the scheduled time before ringing the doorbell. But then Harry softened and gave the young writer what he'd come for, as he'd done with so many others who harbored the dreams he himself had held half a century before. He shared the old stories of *Playboy*, and *Childhood*, the motorcycle trip. On his way out the door, Hodges was given something to take home, to be used during all those hours at the keyboard in his future: "Okay, buddy," Harry told him. "From one writer to another, I hope you find something that helps you get over the hump."

People from his past seemed to find their way back into Harry's life, sensing the end was near. Pat Waters, his college classmate and close confidant through the 1960s, got back in touch and visited, sharing a long memorable night at a Gainesville hospital. Charné and Maggie, who both had maintained intermittent contact, were in touch and paid visits to his house. In *Karate Is a Thing of the Spirit*, Harry's dedication had been a call into the wind to find his traveling buddies from his cross-country journey: "Remember the motorcycle, and that bloody Sunday? . . . Remember, Ben Roark? Remember, Keith Shaver? I do. Wherever you are, I remember, with affection." Now, Ben Roark finally tracked him down and called to share a lifetime of stories. Harry told him he'd fallen on hard times because of too much whiskey. Then you've followed in the footsteps of the greatest artists, Roark told him.

His student Jay Atkinson, who had likely gone down in the University of Florida record books by taking Harry's classes eight straight semesters in the early 1980s, came through Gainesville while researching a book about Jack Kerouac in 2010. He hadn't seen his old professor in twenty-eight years. Atkinson came to the house in the afternoon with one of his UF rugby teammates who was also a friend of Harry in the 1980s. Harry was heavily medicated and in pain, unable to enjoy the reunion. Atkinson returned the following morning, however, and the Harry he remembered had returned. They shared stories from the old days, Atkinson and his friend acting out memorable moments, and Harry chiming in. At one point, Harry called Bass to tell her to come meet his visitors, describing them as if they were just back from rugby practice in 1980. "You'd know these boys just walkin' down the street, 'cause just seein' 'em walkin' down the street says they're jocks," Harry said into the receiver.

A loose confederation of those remaining in Harry's life would pop in and out, escorted into the living room by his nurse, Darleen, if he was well enough for visitors. He watched the Super Bowl in 2011 with Gary Lippman, a fan he'd met at a reading in Miami twenty years before and become close with through two decades of monthly phone calls and annual visits. To enhance the game, Harry let Lippman and a few other visitors share some of his Oxycodone. Lippman came to Gainesville the following year and gave Harry an early-twentieth-century Sears Roebuck catalog. Harry, though clearly suffering, was visibly moved by the gift.

Hulett, the UGA librarian, arranged a visit to Gainesville in the fall of 2011. He brought Harry some boxing videos and cigars. He found the number of hours in the day that Harry could communicate had decreased drastically. By the early afternoon, now, he was in the grips of his medication. He could barely get himself from the bed to the wheelchair to move through the house.

Despite his condition, Harry was still determined to get to his keyboard and try to make progress on his novel. One night, his wheelchair had been left in the other room. While the house was dark in the wee hours of the early morning, Harry somehow managed to lower himself to the floor, and, his legs now worthless appendages, dragged himself across the carpet, through the hall, and into the next room. He couldn't have helped but be reminded of a similar physical motion he'd used when, as a six-year-old boy in the grips of polio, he'd pulled himself by his arms across the dirt floors of the tiny wooden house of his youth.

Hulett awoke around seven a.m. that morning, after Harry had been up and writing for hours. Harry was sitting in the wheelchair, smiling, smoking one of the cigars Hulett had brought him.

"Jesus, chief," he exclaimed. "You're a late riser, aren't you?"

A urinary tract infection had him back in the hospital for an extended stay in late 2011, followed by a trip to a rehab clinic. His quality of life was now near zero. Often, he was not sure if he was at his home, in the hospital, or in rehab.

During one lucid moment, Sally was explaining to him his remaining medical options. Doctors were recommending more time in the rehab center until his condition improved and he could function with less care. Harry raised his hand and stopped her.

"I want to get off this train," he said.

He died at his home just days later, on March 28, 2012. The cause of death, doctors said, was postpolio syndrome, a series of infections, and neuropathy.

The major American and British news organizations devoted considerable ink to Harry's passing. He was hailed as the voice of the South for his generation of writers, a final epitaph he likely would have scoffed at but, deep down, appreciated. He was "a writer whose unflinching novels about life, death, and hope in the dark corners of the South made him a revered figure among a devoted band of readers," said the *Washington Post*. He was "a rough-hewn Southerner who drew a keen following with novels that describe a Hieronymus Bosch landscape of grotesques," said the *Los Angeles Times*. In the *New York Times*, he was declared a writer whose "novels out-Gothic Southern Gothic by conjuring a world of hard-drinking, punch-throwing, snake-oil-selling characters whose physical, mental, social and sexual deviations render them somehow entirely normal and eminently sympathetic."

Former students, writers, and friends also took to the keyboard to eulogize, offering more personal memories. Journalist Steve Oney wrote a tribute for the *Los Angeles Times*, telling of a night long ago when Harry, revived by a few swigs of whiskey Oney had provided, grabbed him by the back of the neck and proclaimed, "Men such as us should never die!"

Harry's student Maud Newton wrote a eulogy, recalling her introduction to Harry in the classroom: "Sitting there in my chair on the first day, I was terrified and awed and more than slightly defiant, but I intuited as he stood at the chalkboard, drawing an incomprehensible diagram and shouting, 'Fiction is an action!' that I did not have to shrink from darkness and horror in my writing, that he would welcome it."

Hilma Wolitzer, whom Harry had mentored at Bread Loaf, fondly remembered the experience. "I have total recall of sitting on the sun-warmed steps of Maple, the house where faculty resided for the conference, alongside this incredibly dynamic and sexy man who appeared to take my stories, with their landscape of supermarkets and schoolyards and frequent mention of Jell-O molds, seriously and consider them worthy of constructive criticism," she wrote.

Per his wishes, no memorial of any type was held for Harry. A short time after his father's death, Byron received a package in the mail, fourth class/ book rate, containing his father's ashes and a book.

As Harry's will instructed, Byron took the container of ashes, drove north from Gainesville, got out of his car, and placed his feet on Bacon County soil. He took the container to the shore of Big Hurricane Creek, the waterway that serves as the border between Bacon County and Appling County, Georgia, where Harry, during the happiest moments of his youth, had swum and cast for fish. Byron opened the container, emptied it, and watched as Harry's ashes hit the water and then slipped below the surface, slowly drifting out of sight.

EPILOGUE

The morning excursions went on for a year or so. I moved away in 2008 and spoke with Harry a few times after that. Soon, he didn't answer the phone by barking his name anymore, as he had all his life. Instead, a nurse picked up, sometimes with the news that he was unable to talk on the phone, laid low by ailment or medicine. If he could talk, though, he usually sounded like the same old Harry, going over his litany of physical problems, then asking, "What's on your mind, coach?"

I drove down to see him in 2010. It had been two years. His skin was pale, his cheeks and eyes more sunken, and he seemed like a patient in his own home.

At least on that day, though, his spirit was not broken. He showed me his new motorized wheelchair, proudly pointing out the dent he'd made in the wall while learning how to steer it. "This thing can go sixty on the highway," he declared.

When I told him I wanted to write his biography, he was agreeable. I'd said I'd like to start coming by regularly again, asking him questions, digging back into some of those difficult subjects. Would he be willing?

"Ask me anything you want, bud," he said. "But you better do it quick."

Harry was true to his word. His condition deteriorated further with each visit, and often he needed several respites to get through a story, but he fought through it. The satisfaction of telling a tale that elicited a reaction was worth the pain, it seemed.

A few months before he died, I went down to see him again for what turned out to be the last time. (I'd make the trip a few more times, but he was either unconscious or, if conscious, not communicative, fading in and out of delusions, not sure of who I was, or why I was asking him questions.) On this day, his mind was sharp, and he wanted to talk.

His nurse, Darleen, ushered me into his bedroom. The room was dark, save for a few rays of sunlight sneaking in from the one open window. Harry was sitting up, legs hanging over the side of the bed, smoking a cigarette and staring into the light.

"Not feeling too good today, coach," he said. He asked me to check his nightstand for his pain pills.

I looked. "All I see here is your cigarettes and an apple," I said.

"That's a peach, man."

"You're right, it is a peach."

"Let me see the peach," he said. "Do you like peaches?"

"Sure."

"This one was washed before it was put there. Eat it if you want it, put it back if you don't. I don't like 'em peeled, I like to eat 'em skin and all. One unwashed fruit a day will keep you alive. I've got a book that says that," he said.

Though it was a struggle just to talk, he was in a passionate mood. I brought up the name of one of his old friends, and Harry, perceiving a slight from the friend, launched into a diatribe against him. The gist of it was that the friend had committed the ultimate sin against the craft of writing—he'd stopped writing.

"There is no quit in this," he said. "There is no finish line. You don't quit. That's the one thing you can't entertain. To quit lets you off the hook, takes the hook out of your gut, is what it does. You don't have to wake up every morning and say, 'Oh god, I've got to go in there and try to finish that fucking thing.'"

It was the one rule Harry had managed to live by on his entire ride. His faith in the importance of writing, the power of it to give meaning to his life, never wavered. The obsession sprouted deep within him, before he could understand it. *When people see me walking down the street, I want them to say, "There goes a writer."*

He hung onto it like a life preserver in a storm when tragedy struck. And it always did. As a child unsure about his next meal, he turned to books as an escape. While the other Marines in his platoon goofed off in their free time, he snuck away to the library to read Shakespeare, to teach himself how to write. As a young father coping with the unimaginable pain from the loss of his son, his treatment was to place himself in front of his typewriter and write another novel. Rejections piled up; he continued to write.

Success, which softens many, only intensified Harry's drive. He wrote faster, set the bar higher. When he was at his lowest point, drunk and addicted, barely able to function as a member of society, falling apart personally and professionally, he would still find a way to write. And in his decline, when the culture had passed him by, forgotten him, he still woke up in darkness and dragged himself to the chair and placed his fingers on the keyboard. *I have found nothing in this life that can match the feeling of writing something I'm proud of.*

Being a writer, to Harry, meant being an outsider. A freak. The two were intertwined. And he was both. This, too, had been thrust upon him early, as a youngster laid up in bed with a vicious disease, relatives, neighbors, strangers stopping by to catch a glimpse, to gawk. The characters he would create took on the same qualities, abnormalities on the outside, and within.

He held onto that view of himself for the rest of his life. Acceptance would not be granted, and if it were, it would not be acknowledged. He saw himself as an outsider in the military, at the university, even, eventually, among those he admired and respected the most, his kin, the community from which he had risen. And he did whatever he felt necessary to maintain his outsider status—tattoos, Mohawks, all manner of bizarre behavior. *Now I can feel the hate dripping off them like sweat.* He'd used that worldview to create his characters, to invent a new kind of fiction.

We were talking about the early days, before Harry Crews the wild man came into being. Harry was a little shaky on some details, so he asked for the phone and dialed Sally's number. She still lived in the house he had bought for her when they were a young married couple and was still, despite everything, the love of his life. Sally picked up the phone, and the two began to talk with the warmth and familiarity born from a lifetime of shared experience.

"Hey, baby. You asleep?"

"I'm in bed," Sally said. "It's okay though, I'm just lying here."

"Are you warm?"

"Yeah, I'm nice and warm. How about you? How are you holding up today?"

"I'm having a dreadful time today, baby, but I'm trying."

They went on like that for a while in a kind of timeless patter. Harry talked to her in the same way he must have when he saw her in Spanish class in 1958. Then Harry remembered their old friend, the one who had quit writing fifty years ago.

"He's an unadulterated fucking asshole," he said matter-of-factly.

"I didn't realize you thought of him in that way," Sally said.

"Well, I didn't, until he started being an asshole. Then I started thinking of him as an asshole."

It was a funny line, meant for me, and Sally let it slip by. Harry told her the point of his call, that he was being interviewed, and he wanted her to participate. Sally agreed. Why don't we do it together? she asked.

"We could play off each other—I'll remember something and then you'll remember something," she said. "I would never say anything you don't want me to say."

"Okay, darling."

"And then we could make it a happy story," Sally said.

"Yeah, we'll make it happy," Harry said. And then he paused for a few seconds and gave the idea a second thought:

"Or maybe we'll just make it whatever it is."

We talked through the morning, pausing regularly for Harry to fight through the pain, which was increasing as the morning drugs wore off. Several times I thought I had overstayed my welcome, only to have him assure me he wanted to keep talking and urge me to ask more questions. We struggled to get him from the bed to the wheelchair, to the toilet, and back again, a thirty-minute process that left him exhausted. He lay back on the bed, naked and covered only by a sheet, lit another cigarette, and kept talking.

Soon, the discussion turned back to Bacon County. His mood grew wistful. He talked about his aunt, his uncle, and some of the other ghosts of his childhood. It wasn't good enough to describe it, he decided, and he started offering directions.

"You just go east on Williams Road," he said. "Ask somebody from Alma and they'll tell you." And then he came up with another plan.

"We'll go over there," he said. "I've got a pretty good car. A Ford Taurus. It's a nice big car. Think we could do that?"

"I'd love to," I said.

"We'll go over there. Yeah, we'll go over there, and I'll show you all the places. I'll take you around to all the places I was raised." His attention seemed to be elsewhere now, somewhere far beyond the walls of his bedroom.

"We could do that," he repeated, taking another drag and peering off into the window, the few rays of light reflecting off the smoke rising from his cigarette. "We'll plan it all out and go up there real soon. Yeah, yeah, we should do that. We should do it. This time, we'll do it right . . ."

AUTHOR'S NOTE

A few years back, I was perusing the shelves in Collector's Corner at the semiannual Gainesville Friends of the Library Used Book Sale, when I came across a first-edition paperback copy of *The Gospel Singer*, priced at fifty dollars. I was a few years into researching this book and already keenly aware that to buy an early edition of most of Harry's books, it usually costs five to ten times that amount. Most items at that book sale are a dollar or less, so I only allowed myself to bring twenty dollars, lest I return home with several boxes of old books.

I jumped in the car, drove to the nearest ATM, and hustled back to the sale. No *Gospel Singer*. I punched myself for leaving it on the shelf and then asked the volunteers at the checkout desk who bought it. "A gray-haired gentleman," she said. "I think it was Mr. Crews's lawyer."

A few days later, I got Huntley Johnson on the phone. I had no luck getting the book back, but he was a little more receptive to being interviewed. At first, he would only speak with another lawyer present, "to keep him from saying anything that would get him in trouble." But eventually he relented, invited me to his home, and showed me his library, where I saw my lost copy of *Gospel Singer*, resting comfortably alongside at least five hundred other volumes of Crews titles.

It turns out Huntley is a book collector. He's got Fitzgerald and Faulkner and O'Connor in the collection, but, by far, Crews takes up the most wall space in the library. Another shelf is full of manuscripts and other Crews papers. Later I would learn that Harry spent many hours in that very room, talking about books and authors and literature with Huntley. When the mood struck, Harry would pick up a book that interested him at that moment and inscribe it with his own brand of literary insight. Some authors were praised, others were ridiculed in the pages of their own book. Depending on the author, they might or might not consider that an honor.

On Steinbeck's *Of Mice and Men:* "This book was on Faulkner's desk when he died . . . and it deserved to be."

On Thomas Wolfe's *Of Time and the River:* "This damn thing is 1,000 pages. *Nothing* needs 1,000 pages to tell."

On Flannery O'Connor's collection *A Good Man Is Hard to Find:* "Dearly Beloved, Here is the real thing, of which the rest of us are only a cheap imitation."

I went back to Huntley, for this or that, many more times in the last few years, and after several rounds of begging, he usually granted my wish. As I write this, he's still holding onto some cassettes that I've been requesting for a year and a half, which he promised to hand over on Monday.

The fun of a project like this is getting the chance to meet people like Huntley, even if it means you lose out on a cheap book in the process. During the course of my research, dozens of people have moved me closer to the goal line by providing me with anecdotes, letters, leads, photos, or just the right words of encouragement at the right time. (Many others, of course, did not want to be found, and if they were, chose not to participate, such as one of Harry's old students, who told me, "We raised some bodacious hell . . . with copious amounts of cocaine and booze . . . but I'm in my sixties now, with grandchildren, and I don't want them to know the crazy shit we did.")

Many people along the journey have gone out of their way to help. I first called Jay Atkinson more than a decade ago, when I was writing newspaper articles about Harry. He told me stories about as well as Harry could have told them and has been doing so ever since. Ed Nagel has been a friend and mentor since the day he saw one of those articles and mailed me a letter. One particularly pleasurable afternoon was spent on the Nagel tour of Gainesville and its environs, when Ed showed me where and how aspiring UF writers lived and played sixty years ago. Skip Hulett at the University of Georgia was instrumental in getting Harry's papers safely out of his house and has helped me navigate those papers ever since. Tyler Turkle has been on my source list for years as well and is always ready with details and encouragement. More than anyone, Ward Scott helped me understand the literary codes and rituals that emerged from Andrew Lytle's musty classroom. Ward was also one of many people who dug up materials for me that haven't yet found their way into a library.

My gratitude goes out to all who shared their time and knowledge, including Mark and Rob Chiappini, Pat Craddock, Sally Crews, Sean Cunningham, Tom Davis, Grady Drake, Rod and Debbie Elrod, John and James Feiber, Michael Garcia, Jeannie Gaskins, Laurence Gonzalez,

Robert Gottlieb, Tom Graves, Joe Haldeman, Melvin Harrelson, David Jeffrey, David Johansson, Brandy Kershner, Maxine Kumin, Jim Landis, William Logan, Charles Loyless, Lydia Lunch, Bill Luse, Bob Mecoy, Susan Mickelberry, Willie Mickelberry, John Morefield, Marilyn Moriarity, Buck Nall, Barbara Nellis, Melvyn New, Maud Newton, Geoffrey Norman, Ann Patty, Donn Pearce, Charné Porter, Maggie Powell, Ben Roark, Marie Speed, Dan Wakefield, Pat Waters, Hilma Wolitzer, Larry Hetrick, Teresa Burns, Brock Brower, Steve Oney, William Dulaney, Gary Jones, Tom Lavin, Gary Hogle, Don Haselden, Julian Goldberger, Paul Giamatti, Merrill Joan Gerber, and many more.

Thanks to my good friends Pat and Evie Reakes, who are always willing to serve as my library experts. Thanks also to Mary Linnemann at the University of Georgia, Andrew Dutka at Broward College, Ann Harvey at the Bacon County Historical Society, Danielle Rougeau at Middlebury College, Phil Nagy at the Jean and Alexander Heard Library, Vanderbilt University, Harry Ebeling at the Oakwood Historical Society, Susannah Chase at Andrew Jackson High School, Peggy McBride and Janine Sikes at the University of Florida archives, and many others.

In Valdosta, Stuart Taylor, another proud Bacon County product, was a tremendous asset in cleaning up and improving this manuscript. Tiffany Conley, Nick Palombo, Rene Alligood, Kiley Thompson, Kent Pettit, Phillip Hamner, and Kaci West provided much needed research and copyediting help. Thanks also to Mark Smith, Pat Miller, Becky Gaskins, Jeff Vasseur, and Crews scholar Dave Buehrer. The assistance of Denise Montgomery and Emily Rogers at vsu's Odum Library was invaluable.

I've relied on the work of many journalists and researchers to put this story together, and I want to specifically acknowledge two such individuals: Erik Bledsoe, whose two outstanding books on Crews were an immeasurable aid, and Crews student Damon Suave, whose thoroughly researched website offered a perfect roadmap to Harry's career.

Back to the beginning: thanks to the Feature Department staff at the *Gainesville Sun*, circa 2004: Dave Schlenker, Sarah Sain, Alisson Clarke, Julie Garrett, Erik Lindstrom, Gary Kirkland, Sarah Stewart, Kate Storey, Travis Atria, everybody's favorite editor, Jeff Tudeen, and all other full- and part-time inhabitants. Great thanks to Bill Dean at the current-day *Sun* for tips and Rolodex questions. Wink Weinberg is always willing to explain and translate medical issues. Many people listened or pretended to listen while I droned on about this book and provided useful or ridiculous advice along the way, including John Westerman, Keith Saliba, Boaz Dvir, Lisa and Mike Miller, Marcel Geltner, Jason Cristy, Richard and Annette Anguiano, Andy Edelstein, Burt Gundelson, Scott Dudley, and many, many more.

Thanks to Walter Biggins, John Joerschke, David Desjardines, Bethany Sneed, and everybody at the University of Georgia Press for taking an interest in this project and for all the work it took to see it through, and to Daniel Simon for his careful copyediting. Linda Murray Hofmans was instrumental in getting me started as a biographer and for that will always have my great appreciation. Without John Brenner taking a chance on my last book, this one would probably never have gotten past page one.

For both literary and legal advice, and, more importantly, lifelong support and guidance, I want to thank Jane and Mike Geltner.

Most importantly, I want to thank my wife, Jill, who is always willing to listen to me babble on about the triumphs and tragedies of my latest obsession and, when the mood strikes her, provide her own unique perspective. And Cassie, Bethany, Luke, and Lainey, my favorite people in the world, who, someday, when they're much, much older, might be allowed to read this book.

NOTES

Chapter One. Bacon County

5 "it would be forever impossible": Crews, *A Childhood*, 170.
6 *There is an entry:* Baker, *History of Alma*, 131.
7 *Attitudes toward Crews:* Tom Davis, interview with author, May 12, 2012.
7 *Those who can actually:* Tom Davis, email exchange with author, April 21, 2012.
8 *One of Bacon County's:* "Pot of Gold: The Role Marijuana Already Plays in American Life, Especially the Economy," narrated by Peter Jennings, ABC News, originally aired April 18, 1998.
8 *The outlaw posture:* Crews, *A Childhood*, 26.
9 *Bacon County lies:* Baker, *History of Alma*, 4, 9–11.
9 *The British came:* Lane, *People of Georgia*, 108.
9 *Bacon County wouldn't:* Baker, *History of Alma*, 18–21.
10 *The area remained:* Coleman, *History of Georgia*, 270.
10 *In 1906:* This theory discounts Savannah, which was actually Georgia's first capital, 1777–1778.
10 *Two industrious fellows:* Baker, *History of Alma*, 25, 29, 119, 138–39.
10 *Harry's grandfather:* Jeannie Gaskins, interview with author, January 24, 2012.
11 *The Haseldens:* Harry Crews, *Take 38*, unpublished memoir, Harry Crews Papers (abbreviated HCP hereafter), 133.
11 *Around this time:* "The Tamiami Trail," *St. Petersburg Times*, www.sptimes.com/2003/webspecials03/trail/intro.shtml (accessed June 21, 2012).
11 *Work crews:* Garrett, "Blasting Through Paradise," in Davis and Arsenault, *Paradise Lost?* 270.
11 *Violence was rampant:* Crews, *A Childhood*, 20–25.
11 *Ray enjoyed:* Crews, *Take 38*, HCP.
12 *In 1932:* Crews, *A Childhood*, 40–49.

Chapter Two. Dreams and Nightmares

13 Birth of Crews: Crews, *A Childhood*, 49.
14 *The baby arrived:* Myrtice Crews, undated, untitled manuscript, HCP.
14 *"hundreds of thousands":* Henry Wallace, "Wallace Maps a Farm Pro-

gram: Balance within Agriculture and Industry, and Between the Two Groups, Is His Objective, *New York Times*, January 3, 1937. The *Times* will be abbreviated *NYT* hereafter.

14   *"delighted to live":* Julian Harris, "Starvation Near for Many in South, *NYT*, June 17, 1934.

14   *Governor Talmadge:* "The Nation," *NYT*, October 13, 1935, E1.

15   *He did his best:* Taylor, *American Made*, 130–32.

15   *And the mechanized:* Kyvig, *Daily Life*, 42–46, 66–70.

15   *"You live off the land":* Buck Nall, interview with author, May 25, 2012.

16   *That was the life they knew:* Crews, *A Childhood*, 50–51.

16   *The work was never-ending:* Myrtice Crews, undated, untitled manuscript, HCP.

16   *There were signs:* Crews, *A Childhood*, 53–55.

16   *"Daddy won't wake up":* Crews, *Take 38*, unpublished manuscript, HCP, 22–24.

17   *Burial of Ray Crews:* Crews, *A Childhood*, 56–57.

17   *Ray and Paschal:* Jeannie Gaskins, interview with author, January 24, 2012.

18   *The questions did not evaporate:* "Harry Interviewing Aunt Eva," interview transcript, unpublished manuscript, HCP.

18   *Discussion of polio:* Oshinsky, *Polio*, 1–11, 19–22, 80–82, 287–88.

19   *Crews and polio:* Crews, *A Childhood*, 82, 91, 99–113.

20   *It was February 1941:* Crews, *A Childhood*, 114–16.

20   *The vats:* Jeannie Gaskins, interview with author, January 24, 2012.

21   *The children screamed:* Lorenzo Carcaterra, "Writing on the Edge," *Gallery*, August 1982, 45–47, 70.

21   *There was an old:* Ford began producing the Model T in 1908 and stopped in the late 1920s. By 1941, automobile technology had advanced considerably beyond the original mass-produced passenger car.

21   *Myrtice wrapped Harry:* Crews, *A Childhood*, 117–20.

21   *Harry's life had bottomed out:* Gaskins interview.

22   *Life on the farm:* Crews, *A Childhood*, 69–71.

23   *Sears catalog discussion:* Crews, *Take 38*, HCP.

24   *"Since where we lived":* Crews, *A Childhood*, 64–67.

24   *Harry didn't need:* Gaskins interview.

Chapter Three. Jacksonville

The epigraph is from Harry Crews, "Leaving Home for Home," *Georgia Review* 61, no. 4 (winter 2007): 741.

26   *To Bacon County:* Crews, "Assault of Memory," in Bledsoe, *Perspectives on Harry Crews*, 179.

26   *King Edward:* "An Urban Jacksonville Legend: Swisher International," www.metrojacksonville.com/article/2010-sep-an-urban-jacksonville -legend-swisher-international (accessed May 10, 2013).

27   *Hundreds of women:* Crews, "What Mama Knows," *Southern Magazine*, May 1987, 49–51, 66–67.

27   *Baby Ruth bar:* Joann Biondi, "Clean and Sober, But Still Crazy After All These Years: Harry Crews," *Sunshine: The Magazine of South Florida*, June 9, 1991.

27   *Paper boy:* Crews, "What Mama Knows," *Southern Magazine*, May 1987, 49–51, 66–67.

28   *But often:* Myrtice Crews, undated, untitled manuscript, HCP.

28   *"Harry was a good friend":* Charles Loyless, interview with author, June 28, 2012.

29   *But Harry never:* Crews, "Assault of Memory," in Bledsoe, *Perspectives*, 180–87.

30   *In the summers:* Don Haselden, interview with author, March 6, 2015.

30   *By the time:* Loyless interview.

31   *First attempt at fiction:* Jason Hodges, "Harry Crews," April 2, 2012, jasonehodges.blogspot.com/2012/04/harry-crews.html (accessed July 9, 2014).

31   *Hoyett had joined:* Bledsoe, *Getting Naked*, 341.

31   *Grades:* Bledsoe, *Getting Naked*, 366.

31   *Background on Slaughter:* Paul Lewis, "Frank Slaughter, Novelist of Medicine, Is Dead at 93," *NYT*, May 23, 2001. Slaughter published more than fifty-six books and sold 60 million copies during his lifetime. He was known as a gifted storyteller who relied on plot and action to drive his narrative, rather than descriptive writing, a characteristic he shares with Crews. Slaughter began writing in 1935 while practicing medicine. His first book, *That None Should Die*, was published in 1941, after six re-writes and numerous rejections. He died May 17, 2001.

31   *Contacting Slaughter:* Kay Bonetti, "An Interview with Harry Crews," *Missouri Review* 6.2 (1983), 145–64.

Chapter Four. The Marines

33   Less than four weeks: Kay Bonetti, "An Interview with Harry Crews," in Bledsoe, *Getting Naked*, 167.

33   *"Going to the Marine Corps":* Rodney Elrod, "The Freedom to Act: An Interview with Harry Crews," in Bledsoe, *Getting Naked*, 187.

34   *The U.S. Marine Corps:* O'Connell, *Underdogs*, 1–5.

34   *Harry travels to S.C.:* Crews, "Building Men the Marine Corps Way," *Esquire*, September 1976, 22.

35   *Red-haired boy:* Ibid.

35   *Boot camp:* O'Connell, *Underdogs*, 35.

35   *Their new overlords:* da Cruz, *Boot*, 16.

36   *"You goddam black bastard":* The practice of using profane language or degrading recruits based on race, religion, or national origin was eventually phased out of boot-camp training. Today's Marine Corps drill in-

structors use the same techniques but use words such as "dag-gone" and "friggin" to pepper their verbal assaults.

36   *Drill instructor behavior:* Crews, *Building Men,* 22.

36   *Physical punishment:* O'Connell, *Underdogs,* 35–36.

36   *Physical combat:* Bledsoe, *Getting Naked,* 340.

36   *His best friend:* Crews, *Building Men,* 50.

37   *About forty-five of the sixty:* Harry Crews, interview with author, November 2, 2011.

38   *Choosing a specialty:* Melvin Harrelson, interview with author, September 26, 2013.

38   *Discussion of base:* Tom Lavin, interview with author, August 1, 2013.

38   *Once a month:* Harrelson interview.

39   *Incident in Puerto Rico:* Harrelson interview.

39   *Plane engine incident:* Larry Shealy, "Crews Sure Can Pin a Tale on a Story," *Atlanta Journal,* date unknown.

40   *Base library:* Bledsoe, *Getting Naked,* 341.

40   *His education:* Terry Gross, "Harry Crews on Writing and Feeling Like a 'Freak,'" *Fresh Air,* WHYY, National Public Radio, May 23, 1988.

40   *Tammy Lytal and Richard R. Russell, "Some of Us Do It Anyway," Georgia Review 48, no. 3 (Fall 1994), 539.*

40   *Discharge:* United States Marine Corps, Report of Separation from the Armed Forces of the United States, Form DD214, Leonard W. Thomas, Clerk, HCP.

40   *Boxing career:* John Williams, "Harry Crews: An American Tragicomedy," October, 2, 1989, sites.google.com/site/fivepubs/harrycrews (accessed May 28, 2013). This is a self-reported career record; no documentation exist.

41   *"What it put into me":* Hank Nuwar, "Harry Crews Plays with Pain: He Writes the Way He Feels, So Be Forewarned," *The Dynamic Years,* September/October 1984.

Chapter Five. King of the Road

42   Back in Bacon County: Crews, *A Childhood,* 169–70.

43   *Discussion of GI Bill:* Mettler, *Soldiers to Citizens,* 20–21, 230.

43   *He arrived:* Bledsoe, *Getting Naked,* 341.

44   *Small apartment:* Nancy Beth Jackson, "Just an Ole' Georgia Boy Tryin' to Write a Novel," *Miami Herald,* November 2, 1967.

44   *He secured a job:* David Lord Shelley, "One of UF's Own: Harry Crews Telling the Truth," *Independent Florida Alligator,* February 24, 1978.

44   *Harry fared better:* Bledsoe, *Getting Naked,* 341.

44   *"granite men riding granite horses":* Harry Crews, "We Are All of Us Passing Through," *Georgia Review* 65, no. 4 (Winter 2011), 723.

45   *Fight over eggs:* Harry Crews, "The Violence That Finds Us," *Playboy*, April 1984.

45   *The fall before: On the Road* was published in the summer of 1957. It was reviewed positively in the *New York Times* on September 5, 1957. Within a few weeks, it was a top seller, and Kerouac was receiving offers from Hollywood and appearing regularly on television and in magazines as the voice of the Beat Generation.

45   *Discussion of On the Road:* Douglas Brinkley, "The American Journey of Jack Kerouac," in Warren, *The Rolling Stone Book of the Beats*, 112–16.

46   *Kerouac's Odyssey:* Bisbort, *Beatniks*, 1, 14–15.

46   *It was generous:* Harry Crews, interview with author, November 2, 2011.

47   *On off days:* Ben Roark, interview with author, June 3, 2013.

48   *Once the tomato season:* Ben Roark, interview with author, December 21, 2014.

48   *Boys go their separate ways:* Harry had no contact with either of his travel companions from the summer of 1958 until shortly before his death, when Roark contacted him. Harry dedicated his 1972 novel *Karate Is a Thing of the Spirit* to Roark and Shaver, hoping they would find it and respond. Roark eventually graduated from college in Arkansas, became a stock trader, moved to Bentonville, Arkansas, and became an associate of Sam Walton.

49   *Harry purchased:* Crews, "We Are All of Us." Here, the recollections of Crews and Roark diverge, relative to transportation. Roark remembers Crews being without a vehicle through the summer of 1958, purchasing his motorcycle only after the group's employment at Hunt Foods. Crews, when he discussed his western excursion, would usually include the motorcycle as being his transportation for the entire trip. It's possible that Crews had an older motorcycle that did not make it to Yellowstone, and he replaced it with the Triumph purchased in California.

49   *He also continued:* Harry Crews, "Cadillac's Ghetto," unpublished manuscript, HCP. The piece was originally written as a column for *Esquire*. The black dancer and the "Georgia in my mouth" quote are also mentioned in the dedication to Crews's novel *Karate Is a Thing of the Spirit*.

50   *Incident in the YMCA:* Crews, *We Are All of Us*, 729–35.

51   *The trip still:* Harry held onto this journal for years, but he told the author that he eventually destroyed it, an act that he would later regret.

52   *Final trek:* Crews, "We Are All of Us," 735.

52   *Woman on bike:* John M. Bogert, "Modesty Is Not His Cup of Tea," *Independent Florida Alligator*, October 13, 1973.

52   *Crash with eighteen-wheeler:* Mary Voboril, "Harry Goes Cruising for a Bruising," *Miami Herald*, June 28, 1987.

52   *Crash in Gainesville:* Larry Shealy, "Crews Sure Can Pin a Tale on a Story," *Atlanta Journal*, date unknown.

Chapter Six. Mr. Lytle

53   Harry and Sally meet: Sally Crews, interview with author, November 11, 2011.

54   *Prior to his trip:* The name "Twelve Oaks Bath and Tennis Club" was introduced to the house members by Crews. It had been used as a name for a hideout he and his friends played in as an adolescent in Jacksonville.

54   *"There was no tennis":* Pat Waters, interview with author, October 28, 2011.

54   *Ed Nagel was:* Ed Nagel, "Sleeping with Harry Crews," unpublished manuscript, 2006.

54   *The leader of:* Crews, "Twelve Oak Bath and Tennis Club," unpublished, undated manuscript, HCP.

55   *Along with Harry:* Ed Nagel, interview with author, May 9, 2012.

55   *Mateen passes test:* Crews, "Twelve Oak."

55   *Harry's education:* Nagel interview.

56   *Though Harry Crews:* Biographical Note, the Andrew Nelson Lytle Papers, Special Collections, Jean and Alexander Heard Library, Vanderbilt University.

56   *From Vanderbilt:* Blotner, *Robert Penn Warren,* 36.

57   *Poetry was not:* Flora, *Fifty Southern Writers,* 290–91.

57   *The Fugitives had morphed:* Conklin, *The Southern Agrarians,* 57–88.

57   *Lytle remained:* Lucas, *Andrew Lytle,* 293–94.

57   *It was in Iowa:* Jean W. Cash, "The Flannery O'Connor–Andrew Lytle Connection," *The Flannery O'Connor Bulletin* 25 (1996–97), 183–92. The relationship between Lytle and O'Connor would continue until her death in 1964 at age thirty-nine. In the year of her death, she submitted the story "Revelation," her last story to see print before she died, to Lytle at the *Sewanee Review,* where he was editor. She could have sold it to *Esquire* for $1,500, she said at the time, but sent it to Lytle because "there should be some folks that some things mean more to them than money."

58   *In the fall of 1948:* Lawrence Hetrick, *The University of Florida Writing Program, 1948–1980,* www.english.ufl.edu/crw/history.html (retrieved June 4, 2013).

58   *James Dickey incident:* Hart, *James Dickey,* 176–201.

58   *"That was the first glimmer":* William Walsh, "Harry Crews," in Bledsoe, *Getting Naked,* 237.

59   *When Harry began:* Charlie Rose, "Remembering Andrew Lytle," *Alabama Literary Review.*

60   *Lytle was in:* Lawrence Hetrick, "Last Class," *The Chattahoochee Review* 8, no. 4 (Summer 1988): 5–13.

60   *Mr. Lytle visits Harry:* Eric Hedegaard, "Mentors: Students Who Made It and Teachers Who Made the Difference," *Rolling Stone,* April 15, 1982.

60   *Harry and Mr. Lytle in restaurant:* Jay Atkinson, "A Nasty, Bloody Business: Learning to Write with Harry Crews," *Poets & Writers,* March/April 2003, 35.

61   *Lytle became:* Waters interview.

61   *The game was:* Walsh, "Harry Crews," 237.

61   *Often, he and Nagel:* Nagel interview.

61   *Harry's own work:* Lawrence Hetrick, interview with author, March 10, 2014.

61   *Many of the mantras:* Waters interview.

62   *"There are only two subjects":* Rick Barnett, "A Recollection of Smith Kirkpatrick," *The Christendom Review* 1, no. 1 (2008/2009).

63   *On another occasion:* Nagel interview.

Chapter Seven. Married Life

64   The complication: Ed Nagel, interview with author, May 9, 2012.

64   *The couple began planning:* Harry and Sally Crews, interview with author, November 11, 2011.

65   *Being married:* Harry Crews, interview with author, November 2, 2011.

65   *Pat Waters had become:* Pat Waters, interview with author, November 28, 2011.

65   *Waters's degree track:* Crews interview.

66   *Harry took Sally's:* Waters interview.

66   *Meanwhile, Sally's:* Harry and Sally Crews interview.

66   *Harry soon conquered:* Harry Crews, "Fathers, Sons, Blood," *Playboy,* January 1985.

67   *Harry moved:* Waters, interview with author.

67   *Waters made:* Harry and Sally Crews interview.

67   *The upheaval:* Allen Pierleoni, "The Sideshow Mind of Harry Crews," *Tropic: The Miami Herald Sunday Magazine* 5, no. 24 (June 13, 1971).

67   *In late 1960:* Biographical Note, the Andrew Nelson Lytle Papers, Special Collections, Jean and Alexander Heard Library, Vanderbilt University. Lytle would edit the journal for thirteen years and eventually rise to the position of full professor at the University of the South. He was awarded an honorary Doctor of Letters degree by the University of Florida in 1970.

67   *Lytle would remain:* Lawrence Hetrick, "Working with Kirk," 1961, *The Christendom Review* 1, no. 1 (2008/2009).

68   *Smith Kirkpatrick:* Smith Kirkpatrick, *The Sun's Gold,* inside front cover, book jacket.

68   *He came of age:* Barnett, "Recollection."

68   *In his mid-thirties:* Hetrick, "Working with Kirk."

69   *Harry loses fellowship:* William Logan, interview with author, September 22, 2011.

69   *Without a fellowship:* Harry and Sally Crews interview.

70   *Harry urged to spank:* Crews interview.

70   *Harry himself was looking:* Pierleoni, "The Sideshow Mind."

70   *Staying in Jacksonville:* Harry and Sally Crews interview.

71   *All was corrected:* Pierleoni, "The Sideshow Mind."

71   *The master's in education:* Bledsoe, *Getting Naked*, 344.
71   *Harry was still:* Crews interview.
71   *There was little:* Harry and Sally Crews interview.

Chapter Eight. A Self-Education

73   When Harry arrived: Florida State Department of Education, *Five Years of Progress*, ii.
73   *Broward County was:* "History of Broward College," Broward College, www.broward.edu/discover/Pages/History-of-BC.aspx (retrieved June 12, 2013).
73   *Broward Junior College:* The school was originally called Junior College of Broward County, but the state changed the nomenclature in the mid-1960s and it was renamed Broward Junior College.
74   *Drake was the fourth:* Grady Drake, interview with author, February 20, 2012.
75   *He integrated:* Gary Hogle, interview with author, February 14, 2014.
75   *Patrick looks through keyhole:* Sally and Harry Crews, interview with author, November 11, 2011.
76   *In the early 1960s:* Wynne-Davies, *Bloomsbury Guide to English Literature*, 574–75.
76   *Greene was the rare writer:* Cassis, *Graham Greene*, xxv–xxvii.
76   *Thompson comparison:* McKeen, *Outlaw Journalist*, 41.
76   *End of the Affair synopsis:* Sharrock, *Saints, Sinners, and Comedians*, 157–60.
77   *It wasn't the themes:* Sterling Watson, "Arguments Over an Open Wound: An Interview with Harry Crews," in Bledsoe, *Getting Naked*, 52.
77   *The months added up:* Steve Oney, "The Making of a Writer," *NYT*, December 24, 1978.
77   *The adjustment to teaching:* Watson, "Arguments," 60.
78   *Harry First:* Andrew Lytle to Harry Crews, June 27, 1962, HCP.
79   *I never want to say:* Harry Crews to Andrew Lytle, July 3, 1962, HCP.
79   *Two weeks later:* Andrew Lytle to Harry Crews, July 23, 1962, HCP. Lytle later moved the story back to the spring issue, which was devoted entirely to fiction and included a story called "The Aftermath" by Kirkpatrick, about his experiences in the Pacific theater during World War II.
79   *Even before:* Smith Kirkpatrick to Harry Crews, November 16, 1962, HCP.
80   *Harry was not convinced:* Ward Scott, interview with author, August 19, 2011.
80   *The old man:* Harry E. Crews, "The Long Wail," *Georgia Review* 18, no. 2 (Summer 1964): 222.
80   *After the acceptance:* Andrew Lytle to Harry Crews, November 14, 1962, HCP.

81   *Once Lytle:* Andrew Lytle to Harry Crews, November 21, 1962, HCP.
81   *"I read your story":* Hiram Haydn to Harry Crews, April 29, 1963; David
       Segal to Harry Crews, April 18, 1963, HCP.
82   *"Your stories seem to me:* Andrew Lytle to Harry Crews, December 1,
       1962, HCP.

Chapter Nine. Hope Fades

83   Tragic events: Crews, "Fathers, Sons, Blood," *Playboy*, January 1985.
83   *On a Thursday morning:* Hank Nuwer, "The Writer Who Plays with
       Pain," in Bledsoe, *Getting Naked*, 214–15.
83   *The Lee house:* "Boy Dies in Pool Near Home," *Fort Lauderdale News*,
       July 31, 1964.
83   *A group of neighborhood kids:* Crews, "Fathers, Sons, Blood."
84   *As his playmates:* "Man, 69, Found in Canal," *Fort Lauderdale News*,
       August 1, 1964, B1.
84   *The photograph:* "Hope Fades," *Miami Herald*, July 31, 1964.
85   *Patrick was pronounced:* Crews, "Fathers, Sons, Blood."
85   *Fort Lauderdale police:* "Man, 69, Found in Canal."
85   *Grady Drake heard:* Grady Drake, interview with author, February 20,
       2012.
85   *In the first hours:* Tammy Lytal and Richard R. Russell, "Some of Us Do
       It Anyway," *Georgia Review* 48, no. 3 (Fall 1994), 544.
85   *"In those nightmare days":* Crews, "Assault of Memory," in Bledsoe, *Per-
       spectives on Harry Crews*, 194.
85   *The funeral for Patrick:* Sally and Harry Crews, interview with author,
       November 11, 2011.
86   *Discussion with Alton:* Crews, "Fathers, Sons, Blood."
86   *Harry and Sally:* Sally and Harry Crews interview.
86   *Harry concurred:* Crews, "Fathers, Sons, Blood.
87   *Alton's advice:* Drake interview.
87   *Friends detected:* Ward Scott, interview with author, August 19, 2011.

Chapter Ten. Broward Blues

The epigraph is from Benjamin Alsup, "This Was a Man," *Esquire*, October 1,
2005, 138.
88   *Following the publication:* Bledsoe, *Getting Naked*, 332.
88   *Another novel:* There is no copy of the novel *Don't Sing My Name* in the
       Harry Crews Papers at the University of Georgia. The only reference to
       the novel is in several rejection letters from publishers.
89   *It also opened doors:* John Morefield, interview with author, September 6,
       2013.

89   *Drake had become:* Grady Drake, interview with author, February 20, 2012.

89   *His friends were:* Kirkpatrick Smith to Harry Crews, February 1964, HCP.

89   *"You're too far away":* Andrew Lytle to Harry Crews, January 30, 1964, HCP.

89   *Virginia Quarterly and FDU rejections:* Charlotte Kohler to Harry Crews, February 25, 1964; Ruth D. Buist to Harry Crews, May 7, 1964, HCP.

90   *Rejection letters:* HCP.

90   *"Three of us have now read":* David I. Segal to Harry Crews, January 15, 1964, HCP.

90   *"I think the trouble":* Ivan Von Auw Jr. to Harry Crews, February 27, 1964, HCP.

91   *Adviser to P'an Ku:* Collection Finding Aid, ed. Skip Hulett and Rebecca Winfrey, HCP.

91   *"I really enjoy":* "Campus Spotlite: Author Advocated Teaching Career," *The Venetian Crier*, Junior College of Broward County, Fort Lauderdale, Florida, 1963.

91   *Harry wrestled:* Martha Davis, "Author Advises Profs: Students Must 'Rewrite,'" *Waycross Journal-Herald*, May 10, 1986.

91   *The coalescing:* Harry Crews, "Blue Collage Badge of Self-Esteem, Too: Some Students Don't Belong in College," *The Surplus Record*, November 1965. The article first appeared in the *Fort Lauderdale News and Sun-Sentinel* on Sunday, April 4, 1965.

92   *The article ran:* Thomas P. Scanlan to Harry Crews, October 19, 1965, HCP. The editor and publisher of the *Surplus Record* appreciated Harry's views on higher education. "Believe me, we need more men like you on faculties of colleges throughout the country," he wrote.

92   *The conflict:* Drake interview.

92   *To add a little:* Ralph Thomas Clark, "Bureaucratic Snarls and Political Embellishments: The Blee Crisis, an Educational Cul-de-Sac," unpublished manuscript, circa 1985.

92   *With Drake's:* Nancy Beth Jackson, "Just an Ole' Georgia Boy Tryin' to Write a Novel," *Miami Herald*, November 2, 1967, B1.

92   *The faculty was divided:* Drake interview.

93   *"I might as well":* Harry Crews to Smith Kirkpatrick, undated correspondence, private collection.

93   *Before Blee:* "Board Reaffirms Blee Firing," *St. Petersburg Times*, May 27, 1967.

93   *Blee lasted:* Blee eventually was given a $17,000 settlement in exchange for ending his legal battles ("Acting School Chief to Be Named Today," *St. Petersburg Times*, April 9, 1968). He returned to work soon thereafter for the state board of education.

93   *In the wake of:* Clark, "Bureaucratic Snarls."

94   *Pearce had been toiling:* Donn Pearce, interview with author, August 4, 2011.

94   *At fifteen, Pearce lied his way:* Alsup, "This Was a Man."

95   *"We got drunk a lot":* Pearce interview.

95   *While Pearce's misdeeds:* Gerard John Schaefer to Harry Crews, October 18, 1974, Box 5, HCP.

96   *Racquetball:* John Williams, "Harry Crews: An American Tragicomedy," October, 2, 1989, sites.google.com/site/fivepubs/harrycrews (accessed May 28, 2013).

96   *Eventually, his writing:* "How 'Killer Fiction' Helped Convict G. J. Schaefer of Murder," Jimgoad.net, www.jimgoad.net/index.shtml?pulpfact (retrieved August 26, 2014).

96   *Schaefer soon:* "Crime: Bluebeard on the Beach," *Time,* May 28, 1973.

96   *"Best wishes":* Dorothy E. Willenborg to Harry Crews, August 9, 1966, HCP.

97   *Harry meets Gospel Singer:* Kay Bonetti, "An Interview with Harry Crews, *Missouri Review* 6, no. 2 (1983): 145–64. Crews did not name the singer.

Chapter Eleven. Gold from a Coal Mine

The epigraph comes from Harry Crews, "Teaching and Learning Creative Writing," *The DeKalb Literary Arts Journal* 3, no. 2 (1969): 1.

98   *It didn't take long:* Al Burt, "Harry Crews: Working the Kinks Out," *Miami Herald,* June 30, 1974.

99   *Jack Daniels deal:* Harry Crews, interview with author, November 2, 2011.

99   *Since graduate school:* Pat Waters, interview with author, October 28, 2011.

99   *"I will be a frightened man":* Pat Waters to Harry Crews, May 11, 1966, HCP.

99   *The response from:* Waters interview.

100   *Harry enters contest:* Crews, *Take 38,* unpublished manuscript, HCP, 108.

101   *"I will reiterate":* David C. Nelson to Harry Crews, October 5, 1966, HCP.

101   *On another excursion:* Burt, "Working the Kinks Out."

101   *"I had a mason fruit jar":* Bledsoe, *Getting Naked,* 342.

101   *Incredibly:* Ibid., 332.

102   *"Write me about anything":* Bert Cochran to Harry Crews, March 20, 1967, HCP.

102   *The show of support:* Bert Cochran to Harry Crews, March 28, 1967, HCP.

102   *Still, Harry fought:* Crews, *Take 38,* unpublished manuscript, HCP, 110.

102   *"I have both books":* Bert Cochran to Harry Crews, April 10, 1967, HCP.

102   *Five days later:* Bledsoe, *Getting Naked,* 333.

103   *"I've thought of you":* Andrew Lytle to Harry Crews, July 16, 1967, HCP.

103   *"You were doing fine":* Andrew Lytle to Harry Crews, September 26, 1967, HCP.

103   *"I've never expected":* Harry Crews to Smith Kirkpatrick, undated correspondence, private collection.

104   *Advance check:* Bert Cochran to Harry Crews, October 14, 1967, HCP.

104   *"a remarkable first novel":* Richard E. Kim to James Landis, September 17, 1967, HCP.

104   *Around the same time:* Bert Cochran to Harry Crews, September 28, 1967, HCP.

104   *Among the strokes:* Jim Landis, interview with author, October 4, 2011.

105   *"I happen to feel":* Jim Landis to Harry Crews, December 19, 1967, HCP.

106   *The Miami Herald received:* Nancy Beth Jackson, "Just an Ole' Georgia Boy Tryin' to Write a Novel," *Miami Herald,* November 2, 1967.

106   *"This thoroughly modern":* Virginia Kirkus Service, January 1968.

106   *"While such a judgment":* Jim Landis to Harry Crews, December 20, 1967, HCP.

107   *"They know I'm available":* Harry Crews to Smith Kirkpatrick, undated correspondence, private collection.

107   *He contacted Lytle:* Andrew Lytle to Harry Crews, October 17, 1967, HCP.

107   *And he began pursuing:* Edmund J. Robins to Harry Crews, December 14, 1967, HCP.

107   *Harry tells Myrtice:* Kay Bonetti, "An Interview with Harry Crews," *Missouri Review* 6, no. 2 (Winter 1983).

Chapter Twelve. Arrival

113   *On the cover:* Ernest J. Simmons, "Eight Plans for a Masterpiece," *NYT,* February 18, 1968.

113   *"Mr. Crews' novel":* Martin Levin, "Readers Report," *NYT,* February 18, 1968.

114   *Synopsis, quotes:* Crews, *The Gospel Singer,* 9, 11, 67–68.

116   *Gospel Singer reviews:* "Florida Books," by Ed Hirschberg, *Fort Lauderdale News,* February 25, 1968; "Powerful First Novel in Grotesque Tradition," by Howell Pearre, *Nashville Banner;* "Allegorical Novel Centers on Self-Ordained Healer," by Robert P. Hilldrup, *Richmond News-Leader.*

116   *Book party:* Grady Drake, interview with author, February 20, 2012.

116   *"Oh, how devious":* Smith Kirkpatrick to Harry Crews, February 15, 1968, private collection.

117   *The official word:* James Hodges to Harry Crews, March 26, 1968, HCP.

117   *The title was significant:* Smith Kirkpatrick to Harry Crews, February 15, 1968, private collection.

118   *"Well, the only way":* Harry Crews to Myrtice Crews, undated correspondence, HCP.

118   *The movie contract:* James Landis to Harry Crews, March 12, 1968, HCP. Landis told Harry that most paperback advances fall in the $2,000 to $2,500 range, so Harry's advance from Dell was extraordinary.

118   *"The flaw is real":* Andrew Lytle to Harry Crews, May 15, 1968, HCP.

118   *Before he settled:* Edward Martin to Harry Crews, May 22, 1968, HCP.

119   *The family made:* Harry and Sally Crews, interview with author, November 11, 2011.

Chapter Thirteen. Second Time Around

121   Dueling typewriters: Ward Scott, interview with author, August 19, 2011.

122   *"They're really raunchy":* Johnny Feiber, interview with author, July 25, 2013.

122   *He knew he didn't:* Lawrence Hetrick, interview with author, March 10, 2014.

122   *Cleaning pool:* Scott interview.

124   *Harper Lee praise:* Jim Landis to Harry Crews, November 22, 1968, HCP.

124   *"I will tell you":* Andrew Lytle to Harry Crews, February 10, 1969, HCP.

124   *"The only person":* Scott interview.

125   *"It may be you need":* Andrew Lytle to Harry Crews, September 6, 1969, HCP.

125   *The disagreements:* Harry Crews, interview with author, November 2, 2011.

125   James Martin, "Madness Down Around the Magnolias," *Los Angeles Times,* July 27, 1969, P50.

125   *Stafford review:* Jean Stafford, "Fat Man and Jester Have Sad Fun," *NYT,* April 13, 1969.

126   *Sally continued:* Bob Summer, "PW Interviews: Harry Crews," *Publishers Weekly,* April 15, 1988.

126   *"If you have a withered":* Sterling Watson, "Arguments Over an Open Wound: An Interview with Harry Crews," *Prairie Schooner* 48, no. 1 (1974): 60–74.

126   *The manuscript:* Jim Landis to Harry Crews, March 11, 1969, HCP.

126   *"I don't mean for you":* Jim Landis to Harry Crews, March 24, 1969, HCP.

Chapter Fourteen. A New Form of Combat

128   Mushroom hunt: Maxine Kumin, interview with author, February 7, 2012.

128   *"He took over":* Jim Landis, interview with author, October 4, 2011.

129   *"Harry was talking":* Dan Wakefield, interview with author, February 7, 2012.

129   *"What we ought to do":* ibid.

129   *The Good Guys:* Hilma Wolitzer, interview with author, March 12, 2012.

130   *Kumin remembered:* Kumin interview.

130   *Harry's entertainment value:* Wakefield interview.

130   *"Harry was just so accessible:* Wolitzer interview.

131   *"It's not wise to talk":* Andrew Lytle to Harry Crews, September 6, 1969, HCP.

131   *Though he'd been:* Harry Crews to Mr. Wendt, undated correspondence, HCP.

132   *To those he respected:* Harry Crews to Guy Davenport, December 22, 1969, HCP.

132   *Whether because:* Anne Foata, "Interview with Harry Crews," in Bledsoe, *Getting Naked,* 44.

132   *The sport had begun:* "Sport: Violent Repose," *Time,* March 3, 1961.

133   *Harry won a few:* Sally Crews, interview with author, November 11, 2011.

134   *"It's a preposterous novel":* James Boatwright, "A Regular Old Sunday in the Senior Club," *NYT,* April 26, 1970.

134   *"Not only does this":* James Martin, "Monstrosities Neath the Magnolias," *Los Angeles Times,* October 4, 1970.

135   *"If you know or ever see":* Harry Crews to Mel McKee, May 6, 1970, HCP.

135   *Despite the defiance:* Harry Crews to Henry Van Dyke, May 7, 1970, HCP.

135   *For years after:* Bledsoe, *Getting Naked,* 344–45.

136   *Reynolds agency:* Edwin McDowell, "Paul R. Reynolds, Literary Agent for Many Top Writers, Dies at 83," *NYT,* June 11, 1988.

136   *Morrow did a lot:* Landis interview.

136   *The decision was made:* Harry Crews to Bert Cochran, April 3, 1970; Bert Cochran to Harry Crews, April 9, 1970; Harry Crews to Bert Cochran, April 12, 1970, HCP.

136   *The details remained:* Jim Landis to Harry Crews, April 13, 1970, and April 27, 1970, HCP.

Chapter Fifteen. Berkeley of the South

138   It might not have been: Randy Bellows and Prem Datt, "Prof. Released After Arrest for Obscenity," *Florida Alligator,* September 25, 1970. The university eventually walked back the firing and Canney was allowed to continue his studies at UF.

139   *Inept bomb:* Harry Crews to John Hawkins, September 24, 1970, HCP.

139   *UF's administration:* Dave Mankin and Cathy Roberts, "Draft Counseling Called Beneficial," *Florida Alligator,* October 8, 1970; Joseph Margetanski, "The May 1972 Protests in Gainesville," *The Gainesville Iguana,*

May 2, 2002, www.afn.org/~iguana/archives/2002_05/20020509.html (retrieved September 21, 2014).

139   *Culturally Gainesville:* Carlos Licea, "It's Easy to Get Drugs in Gainesville," *Florida Alligator*, September 23, 1970.

139   *Gainesville itself:* Cindy Swirko, "Gainesville Was Once Well-Known for Its Marijuana," *Gainesville Sun*, July 15, 2013.

140   *Feiber often:* Marie Speed, interview with author, July 31, 2013.

141   *Kirkpatrick had yet: The Sun Is Gold*, Kirkpatrick's only published novel, would be released in 1974. During this era, he would read from his work-in-progress regularly during class.

141   *Harry could play a big room:* Marilyn Moriarity, interview with author, December 13, 2011.

142   *The advanced writing:* William Mickelberry, interview with author, June 24, 2013.

142   *Whatever the reason:* Ward Scott, interview with author, August 19, 2011.

143   *Harry prided:* Ward Scott, interview with author, September 24, 2011.

143   *Harry was generous:* Several publishers were interested in Scott's novel, *Stadium*, and he signed multiple contracts on the book. It was never published. Around the same time, Harry persuaded Landis to consider a novel by his friend Pat Waters. Landis praised it but did not want to publish the novel, so Harry gave it to Hawkins, who represented the book but was unable to sell it to a publisher.

143   *Vase incident:* William Luse, email to author, August 2, 2013; Ned Crabb, "Occupation: Novelist," *Floridian Magazine, St. Petersburg Times,* April 28, 1974; Scott interview.

144   *A similar situation:* Scott interview.

145   *"Are you crazy?":* Ed Nagel, interview with author, July 12, 2013.

145   *Perry was an established:* McKeen, *Mile Marker Zero*, 139–40.

145   *He called Pearce:* Donn Pearce to Harry Crews, undated correspondence, HCP.

146   *With Pearce's glossary:* Crowder, *Writing in the Southern Tradition.*

Chapter Sixteen. The Hawk Flies

The epigraph is from Frederick II of Hohenstaufen, *The Art of Falconry*, 4.

147   *Jefferson Davis:* Throughout the writing of *Karate Is a Thing of the Spirit,* the novel was titled *Jefferson Davis Is Alive and Well and Living in Atlanta.* Landis convinced Harry to change to the eventual title after consulting with peers at Morrow.

148   *Karate disclaimer:* Harry Crews to Jim Landis, August 13, 1970, HCP.

148   *Karate ranking:* Allen Pierleoni, "The Sideshow Mind of Harry Crews," *Tropic: The Miami Herald Sunday Magazine*, June 13, 1971.

148   *"Crews writes with a hand":* John Deck, "Gaye Nell Odell Is a Brown Belt," *NYT*, April 25, 1971.

148   *The reaction was a relief:* Harry Crews to Robert Overstreet, May 20, 1971, HCP.

148   *Harry's graduation:* John Feiber, interview with author, July 24, 2013.

149   *And the dates:* Ward Scott interview, interview with author, September 24, 2011.

149   *Harry's descent:* Jim Knipfel, "Stories Told in Blood: Listening to Harry Crews," *New York Press*, April 22, 1998.

149   *The Mercury proved:* Harry Crews, "The Car," *Esquire*, December 1975.

150   *"I hate the stifling presence":* Harry Crews, *Classic Crews*, 16.

150   *The writing of Car:* John Hawkins to Harry Crews, September 24, 1970, and November 25, 1970, HCP.

151   Donn Pearce to Harry Crews, undated correspondence, HCP. Pearce was referring to two iconic scenes in *Cool Hand Luke*. The prisoners on Luke's chain gang watch as a woman provocatively washes a car. Later, on a bet, Luke eats fifty hard-boiled eggs.

151   *"tormented Burt Reynolds":* Pierleoni, "The Sideshow Mind."

151   *One regular running partner:* Sterling Watson, "Arguments Over an Open Wound: An Interview with Harry Crews," *Prairie Schooner* 48, no. 1 (1974).

152   *Grandmother's biddies:* Harry Crews, "Pages from the Life of a Georgia Innocent," *Esquire*, July 1976.

152   *"A bird that drinks blood":* Harry Crews, "The Hawk Is Flying," *Esquire*, June 1977.

152   *Hawk argument:* Leil Cook, "Harry Crews: A Candid Interview," *New Look*, October 15, 1975.

153   *Hawk argument fictionalized:* Crews, *The Hawk Is Dying*, 70–71.

153   *Though he was dedicated:* Feiber interview.

153   *Research for his latest:* John Bogert, "Modesty Is Not His Cup of Tea," *The Florida Alligator*, October 13, 1971.

154   *"They had a charming":* Susan Mickelberry, interview with author, July 18, 2013.

154   *"Harry was extremely":* Willie Mickelberry, interview with author, June 24, 2013.

154   *"I just finished a novel":* Harry Crews to Bob Heilman, May 12, 1970, HCP.

155   *"If I hadn't been a writer":* Michelle Green, "Life-Scarred and Weary of Battle, a Literary Guerrilla Calls Truce," *People*, June 8, 1987.

155   *Monogamy was:* Harry Crews, interview with author, November 2, 2011.

155   *He began renting:* William Luse, interview with author, August 2, 2013.

155   *Most of these relationships:* Crews, *Take 38*, Box 56, HCP.

155   *To what extent:* Feiber interview.

156   *Gattling similarities:* The passage describing the death of George Gattling's father in *The Hawk Is Dying* is nearly exactly the same as the description of the discovery of Harry's father's death in *A Childhood: The Biography of a Place*, Harry's memoir of Bacon County.

156   *Sally's brother:* Harry and Sally Crews, interview with author, November 11, 2011.
156   *"something dangerously":* Crews, *The Hawk Is Dying,* 80, 70, 221–22.
158   *Sally felt strongly:* Sally Crews interview.
158   *"Anyone who tells you":* Harry Crews interview.

Chapter Seventeen. Melrose

159   *"He came strolling":* Mark Chiappini, interview with author, July 10, 2013.
160   *While he was waiting:* Marie Speed, interview with author, July 31, 2013.
161   *"I got so disgusted":* John Feiber, interview with author, July 25, 2013.
161   *He applied the same:* Ned Crabb, "Occupation: Novelist," *Floridian Magazine, St. Petersburg Times,* April 28, 1974.
162   *Beginning Enthusiast:* Note on *Enthusiast* typescript: "Book begun at 11:15, Sunday, Sept. 17. 1972" (HCP).
162   *Begins play:* In an author's note on the manuscript, Crews wrote that he had never written a play before and wanted to try it.
162   *Though he yearned for it:* Chiappini interview.
162   *Drugs were so readily:* John Feiber, interview with author, July 25, 2013.
164   *Charné Porter was a regular:* Charné Porter, interview with author, December 5, 2013.
164   *As time went on:* The party was originally called The Goat, in Harry's honor. The Olympics tag was added when Ron "Spider" Jourdan, a University of Florida athlete who was on the 1972 U.S. Olympic team as a high jumper, began to participate.
164   *Killing goat:* Feiber interview.
164   *Goat Day became:* Harry Crews, "The Goat Day Olympics," *Esquire,* July 1977.
165   *The idea of writing:* Upon hearing of the plans, Edward Martin, director of Bread Loaf, told Harry "to be sure to make a left turn when you get to southern Vermont, on to the Long Trail which goes across Bread Loaf Mountain. Otherwise, you'll end up in Maine." Edward Martin to Harry Crews, April 2, 1973, HCP.
165   *Tape recorder:* Harry Crews, *Take 38,* unpublished manuscript, HCP.
165   *Adventures on trail:* Crews, "A Walk in the Country," *Playboy,* April 1975; *Blood and Grit,* 31–44; "The Wonderful World of Winnebagos," *Esquire,* August 1976.
166   *Mostly, though:* Porter interview.
166   Crews, "Take 38," unpublished manuscript, HCP.

Chapter Eighteen. Free Agent

167   *If his personal life:* "Harry Crews Wins Literary Award," *Alma Times,* May 18, 1972.

167   *To accept:* The Arts and Letters Award has been presented since 1941 to artists, writers, architects, and composers by the organization as a way of encouraging the arts. American Academy of Arts and Letters, www .artsandletters.org/awards2.php (accessed September 6, 2013). Welty received the Gold Medal for novel writing. Barthelme was given the Morton Dauwen Zabel Award for fiction. McGuane received the Rosenthal Foundation Award for his novel *The Bushwhacked Piano.*

168   *"I didn't learn":* Crews, *Take 38,* unpublished manuscript, HCP.

168   *"I'd never heard":* Jim Landis, interview with author, October 4, 2011.

168   *Shortly after he got:* Al Burt, "The Troubles with Harry," *Miami Herald,* December 31, 1978. John Feiber, who was with Crews that night, remembers it differently: Crews was confronted by police while urinating in the parking lot, arrested, and released later that night.

169   *Crews's salary:* University of Florida, Notice of Appointment, November 16, 1972. From Harry Crews employment file, University of Florida, Gainesville.

169   *Contracts:* HCP.

169   *For screenplay work:* Willie Mickelberry, interview with author, June 24, 2013.

169   *"This was written":* *Car* screenplay, dated May 30, 1972, private collection.

170   *"I am horribly":* John Hawkins to Harry Crews, May 26, 1971, HCP.

170   *Landis and Harry:* Jim Landis to Harry Crews, September 9, 1970; Harry Crews to Jim Landis, September 12, 1970, HCP.

170   *Along with feelings:* Landis interview.

171   *"I want what's best":* Jim Landis to John Hawkins, March 24, 1972, HCP.

171   *As the negotiations:* Landis interview.

171   *Knopf offer:* Paul Reynolds to Harry Crews, April 21, 1972, HCP.

172   *Landis expressed:* Landis interview.

172   *"Now dig this":* Harry Crews to Jim Landis, April 1972, HCP.

172   *"I have told":* Jim Landis to Harry Crews, April 24, 1972, HCP.

173   *"Hardcover book publishing":* Lawrence Hughes to Harry Crews, May 8, 1972, HCP.

173   *The contentiousness:* Bledsoe, *Getting Naked,* 336.

Chapter Nineteen. No Man's Land

174   Robert Gottlieb: Eric Pace, "At Knopf, Avid Reader Rises to Top: The Gottlieb Strategy," *NYT,* August 16, 1973.

174   *He had precisely:* Josh Greenfeld, "22 Was Funnier Than 14," *NYT,* March 3, 1968. The book was originally titled *Catch-18* but was changed when *Mila-18* by Leon Uris, an established author, was scheduled to be released around the same time. Heller offered the new title *Catch-14,* but Gottlieb substituted the eventual title.

175   *Lured to Knopf:* Henry Raymont, "Knopf Hires 3 Top Aides of Simon and Schuster," *NYT*, January 6, 1968.

175   *His modus operandi:* Larissa MacFarquhar, "Robert Gottlieb: The Art of Editing No. 1," *The Paris Review*, Fall 1994.

175   *thirty-page letter:* Jim Landis, interview with author, October 4, 2011.

175   *Still, when Harry:* Crews, "Television's Junkyard Dog," *Esquire*, October 1976.

176   *Writer and editor:* Robert Gottlieb, interview with author, August 2, 2013.

176   *"I leaned forward":* Crews, "Television's Junkyard Dog."

176   *"I leaned back":* Chuck Eisman to Harry Crews, March 26, 1994, HCP. This is a transcription of an interview Eisman conducted for publication in *Quixote Quarterly.*

176   *After many years:* MacFarquhar, "Robert Gottlieb."

177   *In fact:* Robert Gottlieb to Harry Crews, March 22, 1973, Box 5, Folder 3, Harry Crews Papers, Hargrett Rare Book and Manuscript Library, University of Georgia.

177   *"His books as I remember them":* Gottlieb interview.

177   *Meets deaf-mute:* Eric Estrin, "Tropic Conversation: Harry Crews," *Miami Herald*, February 27, 1977, 15. Harry said in the interview that he did not get to know the hand balancer well at all.

177   *"We are your normal":* Crews, *The Gypsy's Curse*, 5–6.

177   *The novel's titular curse:* "I had the Gypsy's Curse. ¡Que encuentres un coño a tu medida! I can still spell it out although I'm not a spick and never have been one. May you find the cunt that fits you." Crews, *The Gypsy's Curse*, 64.

178   *The book employed:* Robert Gottlieb to Harry Crews, August 13, 1973, HCP.

178   *Heller comment:* Robert Gottlieb to Harry Crews, May 29, 1974, HCP.

178   *His next effort:* Harry was thirty-eight years old at the time he was writing this manuscript, hence the name. An earlier version was titled *Halflife: An Autobiography*, a prescient title, since he would eventually live to the age of seventy-six.

178   *The exact nature:* Harry Crews to R. H. Green, September 19, 1973, HCP.

179   *"I don't care much":* Harry Crews, *Take 38*, unpublished manuscript, HCP.

179   *"It isn't an autobiography":* Robert Gottlieb to Harry Crews, March 13, 1974, HCP.

180   *Award:* Nancy Hanks to Harry Crews, May 14, 1974, HCP.

180   *Willie Mickelberry was:* Willie Mickelberry, interview with author, June 24, 2013.

Chapter Twenty. Playboy Journalist

182   "It's a little choppy": Crews, "Going Down in Valdeez," in *Blood and Grits*, 52.

183   *"I just read":* Laurence Gonzales to Harry Crews, May 3, 1974, HCP.

183 *"I had absolutely"*: Laurence Gonzales, interview by author, October 28, 2007.

183 *Hugh Hefner had:* William E. Farrell, "Hefner Sees Bright Future for Playboy Empire Despite Critics," *NYT*, March 11, 1974.

184 *Sports Illustrated offer:* Pat Ryan to Harry Crews, April 5, 1973; Pat Ryan to Harry Crews, December 30, 1973, Box 5, Folder 11, Harry Crews Papers, Hargrett Rare Book and Manuscript Library, University of Georgia.

184 *"The wanted me"*: Eric Estrin, "Tropic Conversation: Harry Crews," *Miami Herald*, February 27, 1977.

185 *Playboy rejection:* Form postcard from *Playboy* editors, undated, HCP.

185 *Indeed, the meeting:* Gonzales interview.

185 William D. Smith, "Work Is Finally Starting on Trans-Alaskan Pipeline," *NYT*, August 23, 1974, 45.

185 *Valdez residents:* Wallace Turner, "Oil Pipe Town Girds for Rush of Workers," *Los Angeles Times*, June 26, 1974.

186 *"The mob is"*: Daryl Lembke, "Pipeline May Bring Alaska More Than Oil," *Los Angeles Times*, July 14, 1974.

186 *The pipeline Crews,* "Going Down," *57, 66.*

187 *"I would be the"*: Crews, "The Knuckles of St. Bronson," in *Blood and Grits,* 106.

188 *At the fish fry:* Crews, "Going Down," 70–77.

189 *Back in Florida:* Laurence Gonzales to Harry Crews, September 24, 1974, HCP.

190 *A few days later:* *Playboy*'s editors added the extra "e" to "Valdeez" in the headline in reference to Crews's discussion of the local pronunciation of the name of the town.

190 *"The legless man"*: Crews, "Going Down," 51–52.

191 *"It was no doubt"*: Crews, "Going Down," 77.

191 *The article was:* "Going Down in Valdeez" was honored as *Playboy*'s best nonfiction piece of 1975.

191 *Notebook entry:* Geoffrey Norman, interview with author, December 4, 2007.

Chapter Twenty-One. Grit Journalism

192 *"resident weirdo"*: Steve Oney, "Harry Crews Is a Stomp-Down Hard-Core Moralist," *Atlanta Journal and Constitution Magazine*, May 15, 1977.

193 *"There's an award in there"*: David Johansson, interview with author, August 8, 2011.

193 *He had started:* Laurence Gonzales to Harry Crews, January 9, 1975, HCP.

193 *For the next two years:* Mark Chiappini, interview with author, July 10, 2013.

193 *He traded in his:* Harry Crews to Laurence Gonzales, 1975, private collection.

194 *Bronson background:* Wayne Warga, "For Bronson, Piecework Is a Virtue," *Los Angeles Times,* November 2, 1975.

194 *"Somebody said Charlie":* Laurence Gonzales, interview by author, October 28, 2007.

194 *Brakeheart Pass:* The plot of *Brakeheart Pass* followed a train ride in which Bronson's character, a federal prisoner who is actually an undercover agent, is transported across the mountains to an army outpost overrun by a diphtheria epidemic. The cast included Ben Johnson, Richard Crenna, Charles Durning, former NFL quarterback Joe Kapp, and boxer Archie Moore. The movie was, as one writer described it, "a machismo Charles Bronson western which calls for guys to hang off moving trains, fight on train roofs, and bust up barroom mirrors."

194 *"I got a little frantic":* Crowder, *Writing in the Southern Tradition.*

194 *In his notebook:* Crews, notes taken on movie set, 1975, HCP.

194 *After a few aborted:* Harry Crews, "Charles Bronson Ain't No Pussycat," *Playboy,* October 1975, 114.

196 *Headline:* Harry had submitted the title "The Knuckles of Saint Bronson." When the article was anthologized in *Blood and Grits* in 1979, the original title was restored.

196 *Harry was more:* Hank Nuwer, "The Writer Who Plays with Pain," in Bledsoe, *Getting Naked,* 211–12.

196 *Joan Little:* Wayne King, "Joan Little Acquitted in Jailer's Slaying," *NYT,* August 16, 1975, 49.

197 *Robert Mitchum:* Reva Fredrick to Laurence Gonzales, November 14, 1975, private collection.

197 *The next successful:* Laurence Gonzales to Geoffrey Norman, September 2, 1975, private collection.

197 *"I woke up one day":* Crews, "Carny," *Playboy,* September 1976.

198 *Soon after he had begun:* "Crime: Bluebeard on the Beach," *Time,* May 28, 1973.

198 *He was in jail:* Jayne Ellison, "Schaefer Sentenced to Life," *Palm Beach Post,* September 28, 1973.

199 *Schaefer's rambling:* Gerard John Schaefer to Harry Crews, October 18, 1974, and December 3, 1974, HCP.

199 *Harry pitched it:* Harry Crews to Gerard Schaefer, December 4, 1974, HCP.

199 *Killing the story:* John Williams, "Harry Crews: An American Tragicomedy," *John Williams Crime Fiction Resource,* sites.google.com/site/fivepubs (accessed September 2, 2014).

199 *In the end:* "How 'Killer Fiction' Helped Convict G. J. Schaefer of Murder," Jimgoad.net, www.jimgoad.net/index.shtml?pulpfact (retrieved August 26, 2014).

199 *Birth of Esquire:* Baker, *Ernest Hemingway,* 240, 244.

200 *In 1976:* Geoffrey Norman, interview with author, December 4, 2007.

200 *"We want the most":* Geoffrey Norman to Harry Crews, March 13, 1976, HCP.

200 *The column was christened:* Geoffrey Norman, "Pages from the Life of a Georgia Innocent" (editor's note), *Esquire,* July 1976. Crews wrote fourteen installments of the "Grits" column between July 1976 and October 1977.

201 *It was now entirely:* Nuwer, "The Writer Who Plays with Pain," 211.

201 *Luckily, he had a secret:* The articles described were published in *Esquire,* July, August, and September of 1976.

202 *"Harry realized":* Ward Scott, interview with author, September 24, 2011.

202 *"After he got":* Donn Pearce, interview with author, August 4, 2011. Pearce published a nonfiction book called *Dying in the Sun* in 1974 and continued to write magazine journalism for a few years, before essentially retiring from writing. He worked as a private investigator and a bail bondsman for most of the 1980s and 1990s. He began writing again in the 1990s and published a World War II novel called *Nobody Comes Back* in 2005.

202 *Somehow, each month:* Norman interview.

202 *The editors at Esquire:* Crews, "Television's Junkyard Dog," *Esquire,* October 1976.

204 *When he signed:* Frazier Moore, "Harry Crews Bares Life, and Himself," *Fort Myers News-Press,* date unknown.

204 *During the year:* Deirdre Carmody, "Esquire Magazine Aiming to Cut Losses," *NYT,* April 12, 1976.

204 *"Those were the beginning":* Norman interview. The first edition of *People* was published in March 1974.

204 *Esquire sold:* Grace Lichtenstein, "*Esquire* Magazine Sold to Felker with the Help of British Publisher," *NYT,* August 27, 1977, 27.

205 *Whitman incident:* On August 1, 1966, Charles Whitman, an ex-Marine and University of Texas student, killed his wife and mother, then proceeded to shoot people at random from the top of the tower located in the middle of campus. He killed sixteen people and wounded thirty-two before being killed by a police officer.

205 *"If I believe anything":* Crews, "Climbing the Tower," *Esquire,* August 1977.

205 *It was a dark:* Moore, "Harry Crews Bares Life."

205 *Though he would continue:* Jeffrey, *A Grit's Triumph,* 140–51.

205 *"Crews had this wonderful":* Norman interview.

Chapter Twenty-Two. End of the Feast

206 The first time: Maggie Powell, interview with author, March 7, 2012.

207 *Underwood typewriter:* When the Underwood was returned to Harry af-

ter repair, it had been repainted, without Harry's permission. The removal of the scars it had acquired during his career threw Harry into a rage.

207   *The performances:* Ward Scott, interview with author, September 24, 2011.

208   *"Writers scare the hell":* Harry Crews to Bob Heilman, May 12, 1970, HCP. This view on PhD's was shared by Smith Kirkpatrick, who would often say "The PhD program is the graveyard of the creative writer."

208   *"Harry was not an academic":* Melvyn New, interview with author, September 30, 2011.

208   *Bigelow incident:* This incident was described by New as well as another colleague, Brandy Kershner, in a subsequent interview, March 21, 2012.

208   *At another memorable:* Bledsoe, *Perspectives on Harry Crews*, xiii.

209   *Tennessee Williams incident:* Bledsoe, *Getting Naked*, 355–56. This account of Harry's introduction of Tennessee Williams comes from this and other interviews with Crews. The *Independent Florida Alligator* account of the speech notes that Crews gave the introduction and quotes him as saying "despair and hate and love and anxiety, people like Tennessee Williams make these emotions come alive." Robert McClure, "Award-winning Playwright Pleases UF Audience," November 1, 1976.

209   *Trips back into:* Al Burt, "Harry Crews: Working the Kinks Out," *Miami Herald*, June 30, 1974. In 2012, after years of efforts by environmentalists, the Claxton Rattlesnake Roundup became the Claxton Georgia Rattlesnake and Wildlife Festival, an event in which snakes were to be celebrated instead of mutilated.

210   *Corn background:* Stacy Finn, "Charles Corn, Historian, Writer and ex-Marine," *San Francisco Chronicle*, March 20, 2001.

210   *Corn edits Snakes:* Charles P. Corn to Harry Crews, May 2, 1974; Charles Corn to Harry Crews, March 3, 1975; John Hawkins to Harry Crews, March 3, 1975; Charles Corn to Harry Crews, May 16, 1975, HCP.

211   *"I'm going to rewrite it":* Harry Crews to Laurence Gonzales, undated, private collection.

211   *He spent six weeks:* John Hawkins to Laurence Gonzales, March 1976, HCP.

211   *Banned in South Africa:* Harry Crews, "Climbing the Tower," *Esquire*, August 1977.

211   *"the kind of novel":* John Hawkins to Harry Crews, May 17, 1976, Box 6, Folder 5, HCP.

211   *Feast reviews:* Lloyd Zimpel, "Macabre Doings at Snake Hunt," *Los Angeles Times*, November 14, 1976; Christopher Lehman-Haupt, "Gratuitous Grotesqueries," *NYT*, July 12, 1976.

212   *Heller quotes:* Joseph Heller to Harry Crews, April 11, 1976, HCP.

Chapter Twenty-Three. A Sense of Place

213   One Saturday morning: John Feiber, interview with author, June 25, 2013.
213   *It was in the tradition:* Crews, "A Small Boy on the Floor, Listening," *Esquire*, December 1976.
214   *With the help of:* Steve Oney, "The Making of the Writer," *NYT*, December 24, 1978.
214   *Byron joined him:* Rodney Elrod, "The Freedom to Act: An Interview with Harry Crews," Bledsoe, *Getting Naked*, 175.
214   *Harry felt an even deeper:* Al Burt, "The Troubles with Harry," *Miami Herald*, December 31, 1978.
215   *The disconnect:* Don Haselden, interview with author, March 6, 2015.
215   *As he got further:* Crews, *Classic Crews*, 15.
215   *The difficulty was reflected:* Dinty W. Moore, "An Interview with Harry Crews," in Bledsoe, *Getting Naked*, 256.
216   *"a surreal scene":* Steve Oney, interview with author, July 11, 2013.
216   *The Childhood project:* Charné Porter, interview with author, December 5, 2013.
217   *"I hope that we":* Harvey Ginsberg to Harry Crews, February 10, 1978, HCP. Ginsberg was an experienced editor who had begun his career with Doubleday in 1957. He went on to edit the work of Saul Bellow and John Irving. Bruce Weber, "Harvey Ginsberg, Editor of John Irving and Saul Bellow, Dies at 78," *NYT*, January 12, 2009.
217   *"No, son":* Glenn Abel and Johnny McLean, "The World According to Crews: Blood, Grits and Conversation with Gainesville's Leading Writer," *New Look*, May 1, 1979.
217   *Opening sentence:* Crews, *Classic Crews*, 19.
217   *"I can quote that sentence":* Bledsoe, *Getting Naked*, 356.
217   *He had initially:* Crews, *Classic Crews*, 22, 95.
219   *Childhood reviews:* Hank Reidelberger, "'A Childhood': Crews Takes Us South to a Very Old Place," *Gainesville Sun*, November 5, 1978; "Year's Best," *Time*, January 1, 1979; Michael Mewshaw, "The Facts of Imagination," *The Nation*, February 3, 1979; Betty Lukas, "Harry Crews on an Identity Trip," *Los Angeles Times*, November 19, 1978; John Leonard, "Books of the Times," *NYT*, December 11, 1978.
219   *Once again, however:* John Hawkins to Harvey Ginsberg, December 28, 1978, HCP. Linda Goodman was an astrologer whose book *Linda Goodman's Love Signs* was a best-seller in 1978. Alex Haley's novel told the story of his family's history through slavery and the American South. It won the Pulitzer Prize in 1977 and was made into a television miniseries that same year.
220   *In his imagining:* Crews, *Classic Crews*, 15–16.
220   *"After I'd written it":* John Williams, "Harry Crews: An American Tragicomedy," *John Williams Crime Fiction Resource*, sites.google.com/site/fivepubs (accessed November 11, 2011).

Chapter Twenty-Four. Hard Work

224   The audience was steadily: Robert Ely, "Harry Crews Painfully Climbs the Tower," *St. Petersburg Times*, March 5, 1979.

225   *When the room quieted:* Jeff Calder, "Harry Crews," *Jeff Calder's Personal Archive*, theswimmingpoolqs.squarespace.com/display /ShowGallery?moduleId=200172&galleryId=14751 (accessed November 25, 2013).

225   *Eventually, Harry:* Ely, "Harry Crews."

225   *It was how each night:* Harry Crews, "Harry Interviewing Aunt Eva in 4/96," unpublished transcript of interview, HCP.

225   *And each morning:* Mary T. Schmich, "Still in the Game: On the Straight and Narrow with Writer Harry Crews," *Atlanta Journal-Constitution*, January 27, 1985.

226   *Visit to Agnes Scott:* Steve Oney, interview with author, July 11, 2013; Michelle Green, "A Writer Driven to the Edge," *Atlanta Journal-Constitution*, April 16, 1979.

226   *Checking card catalog:* Harry Crews, "Climbing the Tower," *Esquire*, August 1977; John L. Parker, "Wild about Harry: The Author as Victim," *Miami Magazine*, July 1979.

226   *Visit to Anderson University:* David Johansson, interview with author, August 8, 2011.

227   *After such an aborted:* Melvyn New, interview with author, September 30, 2011.

227   *"It's my boss!":* Brandy Kershner, interview with author, March 21, 2012.

227   *Gainesville restaurants:* John Feiber, interview with author, July 25, 2013.

228   *Part of the problem:* Charné Porter, interview with author, December 8, 2013.

228   *Feiber recognized: Harry Crews: Guilty as Charged,* directed by Tom Thurman and Chris Iovenko, Noir Films, 1993.

228   *Drinking all the wine:* Huntley Johnson, interview with author, December 1, 2012.

229   *The problem, Harry said:* Johansson interview.

229   *Doctors prescribed:* Anabuse is regularly prescribed as part of a treatment for severe alcoholism.

229   *It would work for a while:* Joe Haldeman, interview with author, March 28, 2012.

229   *He did his best:* Lawrence Hetrick, interview with author, March 10, 2013.

230   *Such behavior:* Bob Mecoy, interview with author, April 30, 2014.

230   *A call from Harry:* Steve Oney, "Harry Crews and Getting Naked," *Los Angeles Times*, April 4, 2012.

230   *Emmett Kelly:* Kelly achieved fame for his clown character "Weary Willy," who sported a painted frown on his face and was based on Depression-era hobos. The screenplay *Clown* was never produced.

231   *Harry signed:* Crowder, *Writing in the Southern Tradition*, 106; Rod El-
       rod, interview with author, November 12, 2011.

231   *Those who encountered:* University of North Dakota Writers Conference,
       "Writers Conference Summary," www.undwritersconference.org/wc-past.
       html (accessed December 12, 2013); Bruccoli and Baughman, *Crux*, 414.

231   *Those who had known:* Lawrence Jordan to Smith Kirkpatrick, March 6,
       1978, private collection.

231   *"I spoke with Harry today":* June 6, 1979, private collection.

232   *"hard work":* Guilty as Charged, Thurman.

232   *"Alas, can't drink":* Harry Crews to Laurence Gonzales, April 21, 1981,
       private collection.

232   *Publicly, however:* Rodney Elrod, "The Freedom to Act: An Interview
       with Harry Crews," in Bledsoe, *Getting Naked*, 187.

Chapter Twenty-Five. Muscle Memory

233   Building D: Turlington Hall opened in 1977.

233   *"He was a testament":* Susan Mickelberry, interview with author, July 18,
       2013.

233   *Harry's binging:* David Johansson, interview with author, August 8, 2011.

235   *Harry had been living:* Maggie Powell, interview with author, March 7,
       2012.

235   *Bodybuilding background:* Tom Hamilton, "Is She a Model, or a Body-
       builder?" *Los Angeles Times*, October 31, 1980; Alan Multan, "Woman
       Body Builder High on Lifting," *Los Angeles Times*, September 2, 1979.

235   *By now, Harry:* John Williams, "Harry Crews: An American Tragicom-
       edy," *John Williams Crime Fiction Resource*, sites.google.com/site
       /fivepubs (accessed November 11, 2011).

235   *After she won:* Powell interview.

236   *In the few years:* John Duka, "When a Woman Pumps Iron," *NYT*, Febru-
       ary 5, 1984.

236   *Another addition:* Powell interview.

237   *The relationship bottomed out: Harry Crews: Guilty as Charged*, directed
       by Tom Thurman and Chris Iovenko, Noir Films, 1993.

237   *"I'd get to a point":* Powell interview.

237   *It was natural:* William Walsh, "Harry Crews," in Bledsoe, *Getting Na-
       ked*, 243.

237   *"I'm the easiest":* Rodney Elrod, "The Freedom to Act: An Interview with
       Harry Crews," in Bledsoe, *Getting Naked*, 184.

237   *"Nobody could be":* John Morefield, interview with author, September
       12, 2013.

237   *Harry had little:* Harry Crews, interview with David Jeffrey, December 10,
       1978, private collection.

238   *Age was no barrier:* Teresa Burns, interview with author, September 14,
       2011.

238 *"It was no deep dark":* Marie Speed, interview with author, July 31, 2013.

238 *"You got to be holding":* Damon Sauve, "Everything Is Optimism, Beautiful, and Painless: A Conversation with Harry Crews," *A Large and Startling Figure: The Harry Crews Online Bibliography,* www.harrycrews.org/Features/Interviews/SauveD-Interview.html (accessed December 16, 2013).

238 *Burns said Harry:* Burns interview.

239 *Even in the anything-goes:* Harry received tenure when he was promoted to associate professor in 1973 and was promoted to full professor a few years later. "Notice of Appointment," University of Florida, signed by C. A. Vanderwerf, Dean, October 1, 1973.

239 *"I find it rather":* Burns interview. After receiving her master's from the University of Florida, Burns studied with Donald Barthelme at the University of Houston, earning a doctoral degree. She later became chair of the Humanities Department at the University of Wisconsin–Platteville.

240 *The fiction writing:* William Logan, interview with author, September 22, 2011.

240 *Burns recalls:* Burns interview.

240 *Sometimes, the young women:* Johansson interview.

Chapter Twenty-Six. Violence Finds Us

The epigraph comes from Crews, "The Violence That Finds Us," *Playboy*, April 1984.

243 *"I don't remember him":* Willie Mickelberry, interview with author, June 24, 2013.

243 *The results of combat:* Mary Voboril, "Harry Goes Cruising for a Bruising," *Miami Herald*, June 28, 1987.

243 *He bruised easily:* John Morefield, interview with author, September 12, 2013.

243 *Many of the incidents:* Crews, "The Violence That Finds Us."

244 *Trips to Texas:* John L. Parker Jr., "Wild about Harry: The Author as Victim," *Miami Magazine*, June 1979, 31. Fear of Texas authorities followed Harry around. One memorable evening, when he was being escorted from a speaking engagement in Tampa, he began yelling that the cops were going to get him. A friend who was helping Harry to his car tried to calm him. "Don't worry, Harry, you're safe," he said. "We're not in Texas."

244 *Vic Morrow incident:* Harry Crews, "Leaving Pasadena: Resume Safe Speed," *Esquire*, January 1977.

244 *Dogfight incident:* Harry Crews, "A Day at the Dogfights," *Esquire*, February, 1979.

244 *Airport incident:* Steve Oney, "Harry Crews and Getting Naked," *Los Angeles Times*, April 4, 2012,

244 *Drunk biking:* William Logan, interview with author, September 22, 2011.

244 *If Harry's wounds:* Mark Chiappini, interview with author, July 10, 2013.

245   *"They chain-whipped me, Larry":* Lawrence Hetrick, interview with author, March 10, 2014.

245   *His combatants:* Michael Garcia, interview with author, October 29, 2013.

246   *"He could get angry":* John Feiber, interview with author, July 25, 2013.

246   *The wrong move:* Atkinson, *Memoirs of a Rugby Playing Man*, 33–35, 54–57.

248   *On another night:* Al Burt, "The Troubles with Harry," *Miami Herald*, December 31, 1978.

248   *"As menacing as Harry was":* Feiber interview.

248   *Alcohol didn't always:* Burt, "The Troubles with Harry."

249   *Those were the types:* Crews, "The Violence That Finds Us."

250   *"More people are more interested":* Bledsoe, *Getting Naked*, 361–62.

Chapter Twenty-Seven. The Racist Gene

251   "So me and Hoyett": Crews, *A Childhood*, 58–59.

252   *In his youth:* Crews, "Leaving Home for Home," *Georgia Review* 61, no. 4 (Winter 2007): 709; Crews, interview with author, November 11, 2011.

252   *In his writing:* Crews, *The Gospel Singer*, 11.

252   *Race took center stage:* Karlyn Barker, "A Resurgence by the Klan: Symbol of Racism Exploits New Tensions," *Washington Post*, June 2, 1980.

252   *The trend caught:* James Morgan to Harry Crews, July 16, 1979, HCP.

253   *"ultimate gray flannel racist":* Wayne King, "The Violent Rebirth of the Klan," *NYT*, December 7, 1980.

253   *Unlike the shadowy:* "Klan Leader Debates Racial Bias with Ralph Abernathy at Campus," *NYT*, October 5, 1979, A26. The debate took place at Alfred University in Alfred, New York. Duke first ran for the Louisiana State Senate in 1975, receiving almost eleven thousand votes in the election, nearly a third of the vote total. He was eventually elected to the state senate in 1988.

253   *Harry took the assignment:* Crews, "The Buttondown Terror of David Duke." In the article, Harry wrote about the variations on the rhetorical arguments made to people he encountered in the course of his publicity tour. "He was possessed of many favorite phrases, one of which was 'busing a little blonde, blue-eyed girl into a black ghetto or vice versa.' I never told him that the vice versa of that phrase would be busing a black ghetto into a little blonde, blue-eyed girl."

255   *The rally:* Crews, "Buttondown Terror."

255   *In his response:* James Morgan to Harry Crews, July 12, 1979, Box 6, Folder 32, HCP.

255   *Harry sent:* James Morgan to Harry Crews, July 12, 1979; Harry Crews to James Morgan, October 1979, HCP.

255   *"Not one single instance":* Crews, "Buttondown Terror."

255   *The piece proved prescient:* Robin Toner, "Duke Takes His Anger into

1992 Race: An Ex-Klansman Accuses Bush of Selling Out the G.O.P.,"
NYT, December 5, 1991.

256   *Duke career:* Peter Applebome, "Klan Figure's Bill Approved by the Lou-
isiana House," *NYT*, May 31, 1990; Roberto Suro, "Louisiana Puts Ex-
Klan Leader in Runoff Race," *NYT*, October 21, 1991; Michael R. Kagay,
"Hidden Vote for Duke Never Materialized," *NYT*, November 18, 1991.

256   *"How did I manage":* Crews, "Leaving Home," 709–11.

256   *Last article:* Harry Crews, "Why I Live Where I Live," *Esquire*, September
1980. In the article, Harry discussed the advantages of living in Gainesville and its effect on his writing.

256   *Falwell article:* Crews, "Jerry Falwell: Reverend of the New Right," *Playgirl*, July 1982. On the comparison between Duke and Falwell, Harry
wrote: "The Wizard is young, extremely handsome, charismatic, and full
of fire. The Reverend Falwell, in contrast, is about as exciting as a sack of
laundry. . . . The views of both men are diametrically opposed to my own,
but the preacher's capacity to give more grief to more people, it seems to
me, is infinitely greater than the Wizard's."

256   *Steenburgen article:* Crews, "Mary Steenburgen: Born with the Gift,"
Playgirl, September 1983, 12–13.

257   *This assignment led:* Maggie Powell, interview with author, March 7,
2012.

257   *"I'm like an old whore":* Harry Crews to James Morgan, undated, HCP.

257   *Maggie returned:* Powell interview.

257   *Harry drops money:* Jay Atkinson, interview with author, April 7, 2012.

258   *Larry Shealy, "Crews Sure Can Pin the Tale on a Story," Atlanta Journal,
date unknown.*

258   *"I've been carrying":* Hank Nuwer, "Harry Crews Plays with Pain," *Dynamic Years*, September–October 1984.

258   *"Excellent choice":* Ed Nagel, interview with author, May 9, 2012.

258   *Sally remained:* Atkinson interview.

259   *"Sometimes, it was like":* Charné Porter, interview with author, December
5, 2013.

259   *By that time:* Harry Crews, "Fathers, Sons, Blood," *Playboy*, January 1985.

259   *Waxing poetic:* Shealy, "Pin the Tale."

260   *There was no alternate: Guilty as Charged*, directed by Tom Thurman and
Chris Iovenko, Noir Films, 1993.

260   *"I've never hidden":* Frazier Moore, "Harry Crews Bares Life, and Himself," *Fort Myers News-Press*.

260   *The strategy:* John L. Parker, "Wild about Harry: The Author as Victim,"
Miami Magazine, June 1979.

260   *Music became:* Michael Garcia, interview with author, October 29, 2013.

260   *After high school:* Teresa Burns, interview with author, September 14,
2011.

260   *When Byron decided: Guilty as Charged*, directed by Tom Thurman and
Chris Iovenko, Noir Films, 1993.

Chapter Twenty-Eight. A Messy Business

261   The world might have: Rod Elrod, interview with author, November, 12, 2011.

262   *You didn't have to:* Marilyn Moriarity, interview with author, December 13, 2011.

263   *He was a demanding:* Elrod interview.

263   *Harry's classroom:* Moriarity interview.

264   *"who are ready to eat nails":* Jay Atkinson, "A Nasty, Bloody Business: Learning to Write with Harry Crews," *Poets & Writers*, March/April 2003.

264   *Male or female:* Crews, "Teaching and Writing."

264   *Those who bought:* Crews, "Teaching and Learning Creative Writing," *The DeKalb Literary Arts Journal* 3, no. 2 (1969).

264   *An anecdote he told:* Atkinson, "Nasty, Bloody Business."

264   *"to climb to the mountaintop":* Crews, "Teaching and Learning."

264   *"After a class":* Marie Speed, interview with author, July 31, 2013.

264   *Rod Elrod studied:* Elrod interview.

265   *Not all of Harry's:* "Teaching Means Learning for Author Sterling Watson," *Orlando Sentinel*, May 4, 1986 (retrieved February 2, 2014, articles.orlandosentinel.com/1986-05-04/lifestyle/0220100239_1_university-of-florida-florida-gas-harry-crews).

266   *"It was a cheap shot":* Thomas B. Harrison, "The Write Stuff: Sterling Watson Speaks Volumes about His Craft," *St. Petersburg Times*, August 2, 1989, 1D.

266   *He told friends:* Ed Nagel, interview with author.

266   *"blood offense":* John Williams, "Harry Crews: An American Tragicomedy," *John Williams Crime Fiction Resource*, sites.google.com/site /fivepubs (accessed November 11, 2011).

266   *The book was:* Sherie Posesorski, "Finding Folly in Seeking Out Master Writer," *Fort Lauderdale Sun-Sentinel*, May 11, 1986; Nancy Pate, "Watson Puts Heart Into Calling," Orlando Sentinel, May 4, 1986, articles .orlandosentinel.com/1986–05–04/lifestyle/0220100240_1_toad-odom -watson (retrieved February 3, 2014).

267   *"He has shown":* Harrison, "The Write Stuff."

267   *He made no attempt:* Bledsoe, *Getting Naked*, 360

267   *"We had Smith":* Melvyn New, interview with author, September 30, 2011.

268   *Powell background:* Andrea Stevens, "Chemist, Roofer, Writer," *NYT*, April 15, 1984; Dan Halpern, "Southern Discomfort," *NYT*, October 18, 2009; Ron Loewinsohn, "Age 12 and Burning with Questions," *NYT*, April 15, 1984.

268   *Crews-Powell comparison:* Christopher Lehmann-Haupt, "Books of the Times," *NYT*, May 4, 1984.

269   *Powell-Crews dinner:* David Johansson, interview with author, August 8, 2011; Maggie Powell, interview with author, January 31, 2014.

269   *He'd begun work:* The first thirty-one pages of *The Enthusiast* were published as a limited edition in 1981 by Palaemon Press, and again as an excerpt in *Florida Frenzy*, a collection of Crews journalism and fiction published by the University Press of Florida in 1983.

269   *Duffy Deeter:* The Deeter character had first appeared in *Feast of Snakes*.

270   *In 1986:* William Logan, interview with author, September 22, 2011.

Chapter Twenty-Nine. The Worm Farm

271   "New Orleans": Rod Elrod, interview with author, November 12, 2011.

272   *Harry's longtime:* Maggie Powell, interview with author, March 7, 2012.

272   *The plan went bad quickly:* Harry Crews, "The Poison Within," *Gallery,* May 1987.

275   *"It was just a little barn":* Elrod interview.

275   *To visitors:* Michelle Green, "Life-Scarred and Weary of Battle, a Literary Guerrilla Calls Truce," *People,* June 8, 1987.

275   *jerry can:* Damon Sauve, "Everything Is Optimism, Beautiful, and Painless: A Conversation with Harry Crews," in Bledsoe, *Getting Naked,* 318–19.

275   *Once sober:* Elrod interview.

275   *He had his old truck:* Sauve, "Everything Is Optimism," 318.

275   *The subject was boxing:* Harry was set to cover the Muhammad Ali–George Foreman fight in Zaire in 1974, only to be replaced at the last minute when Norman Mailer took the assignment.

276   *On Sundays:* "Harry Crews on Writing and Feeling Like a 'Freak,'" *Fresh Air,* March 30, 2012 (originally aired March 23, 1988).

276   *Needless to say:* Herbert Mitgang, "The 'Screwy' World of the Novelist Harry Crews," *NYT,* February 19, 1987.

277   *But even before:* Crews, *The Knockout Artist,* 13–14.

278   *"compulsion":* Green, "Life Scarred and Weary."

278   *All We Need sales:* Mary Voboril, "Harry Goes Cruising for a Bruising," *Miami Herald,* June 28, 1987.

279   *Harry's final binge:* Debbie Elrod, interview with author, May 31, 2012.

279   *Knockout reviews:* Chauncey Mabe, "Crews Performs Like Champ in Ring Novel," *South Florida Sun Sentinel,* June 5, 1988; Charles Nicol, "Thinking Gives Eugene a Headache," *NYT,* May 1, 1988; Christopher Lehman-Haupt, "A Pugilist's Descent into a Self-Inflicted Hell," *NYT,* April 18, 1988.

Chapter Thirty. An Acquired Taste

283   It took very little: Mary Voboril, "Harry Goes Cruising for a Bruising," *Miami Herald,* June 28, 1987.

284   *"Tell 'em I'm sleeping":* David Johansson, interview with author, August 11, 2011.

285   *Mailer mention:* Mailer had been a fan of Harry's work since at least the mid-1970s, when he gave a favorable comment for *Feast of Snakes.* In 1985 he chaired the PEN American Center's 48th International Congress of Writers and personally invited Harry as a special guest (Norman Mailer to Harry Crews, September 25, 1985, HCP). Mailer's biographer, Barry Leeds, asked Mailer about the Crews reference in *Tough Guys Don't Dance.* "I think he's very funny and very tough and kind of incorruptible," Mailer said. "Like he's set his course and if storms came across, then they come, it's all right, but he's staying on that course. He knows what he knows and he's going to write about it. He has a clarity of purpose that I like" (Lennon, *Conversations with Norman Mailer,* 377).

285   *Lunch background:* Ada Calhoun, "Finding Inner Peace with the Angriest Punk of '70s New York," *NYT,* December 20, 2013.

286   *"We wanted to do":* Lydia Lunch, interview with author, February 24, 2012.

286   *"But I knew":* Johansson interview.

286   *"People really liked":* Lunch interview.

286   *Gordon invited:* Johansson interview.

287   *"I wish the band well":* Tom Nordlie, "Harry Crews: Naked in Garden Hills," review, *Spin,* September 1990, 76–77. A few years later, the Canadian new wave band Men Without Hats also took an interest in the work of Crews, including a song titled "Harry Crews" on its album *Sideways,* released in 1991. The band's lead singer, Ivan Doroshuck, said he was inspired by a line from *The Hawk Is Dying:* "Find what was real in the world and touch it, that was what a man ought to do" ("A Brief History, Men Without Hats," menwithouthats.com/info.html, retrieved February 24, 2014).

287   *"a true warrior":* Pat Putnam, "The Big Showdown: After a Soap-Opera Prelude, Mike Tyson and Michael Spinks Meet at Last," *Sports Illustrated,* June 27, 1988.

288   *The two met:* Mary Louise Oats and John Voland, "Madonna, Penn—It's a Glitzy Wedding," *Los Angeles Times,* August 17, 1985.

288   *She had passed:* Kelly, *Sean Penn,* 216.

289   *"I ain't a fan of hers":* Johansson interview.

289   *Arrangements were made:* Kelly, *Sean Penn,* 216.

289   *"My first thought":* Harry Crews, "Madonna Goes the Distance," *Fame,* December 1988.

289   *The fight was:* "Cameraman: Sean Penn Took Some Shots, Too," *Los Angeles Times,* January 28, 1988.

289   *The limousine shuttling:* Crews, "Madonna Goes the Distance."

290   *"Cameraman," Los Angeles Times.*

290   *Inexplicably:* Crews, "Madonna Goes the Distance."

290   *The tension grew:* Earl Gustkey, "Tyson Does a Minute-and-a-Half Waltz: It Takes 1:31 to Make Spinks a Lightweight," *Los Angeles Times*, June 28, 1988.

291   *"with no socks":* Jim Murray, "This Fight Wasn't a Mismatch, It Was Really a Non-Match," *Los Angeles Times*, June 28, 1988.

291   *The Madonna entourage:* Crews, "Madonna," 94.

291   *It was an awkward:* Johansson interview.

291   *Two days after:* Madonna to Harry Crews, June 30, 1988, telephone message, HCP.

292   *Wedding gift:* Huntley Johnson, interview with author, December 11, 2012.

292   *Television gift:* Johansson interview; Ed Nagel, interview with author, July 12, 2013.

292   *"I hope you keep writing":* Madonna to Harry Crews, July 1, 1988, postcard, HCP.

292   *Circumstances would:* The *Fame* article, along with three other Crews magazine pieces, were published in book form by Lord John Press of Northridge, California, under the title *Madonna at Ringside* in 1991.

293   *Madonna-Penn divorce:* Kelly, *Sean Penn*, 223.

293   *In the subsequent:* Johnson interview.

293   *On January 2, 1990:* Kelly, *Sean Penn*, 251; Rick Shultz, "Crews Control," *Village View*, March 6–12, 1992.

294   *The script was inspired:* Kristine McKenna, "New Directions for Sean Penn," *Los Angeles Times*, August 18, 1991.

294   *Harry left Malibu:* Screenplay notes, *Pickin' and the Payback*, HCP.

294   *If the trip:* Harry Crews to Sean Penn, September 3, 1990, HCP.

294   *"well paid":* Damon Sauve, "Everything Is Optimism, Beautiful, and Painless: A Conversation with Harry Crews," in Bledsoe, *Getting Naked*, 316.

294   *Penn, however:* Kelly, *Sean Penn*, 259.

295   *old silent acquaintance:* In *The Indian Runner*, Penn would make of Bronson two notable requests: he must shave his mustache and must cry onscreen. Bronson agreed to both.

295   *Harry Spent:* Crews, "Sean Penn Lives to Tell," *Fame*, November 1990.

295   *"What with casting":* Kenneth Turan, "'Runner': Penn Bows as Writer-Director," *Los Angeles Times*, September 20, 1991.

Chapter Thirty-One. Stage Craft

297   House shopping: Huntley Johnson, interview with author, December 11, 2012.

298   *An opportunity:* Michael Bigelow Dixon to Harry Crews, May 1, 1987, HCP. The initial offer was for $12,500. Crews later said he was paid $15,000 for the play.

298   *Mabel Boatwright:* For the surname of the family in *Blood Issue*, Crews

chose the same surname of *New York Times* critic James Boatwright, who had trashed several of his books earlier in his career. Boatwright is also a common name in Bacon County.

299 *"Damn you and Alaska both":* Crews, *Blood Issue*, script dated January 25, 1989, with revisions inserted, HCP.

299 *"I've got blood":* Crews, *Blood Issue*, 112.

299 *"People will say":* Dan Hulbert, "Bad Familial 'Blood' Flows in Harry Crews's First Play," *Atlanta Journal-Constitution*, April 9, 1989.

300 *Packing for trip:* David Johansson, interview with author, August 8, 2011.

300 *In Louisville:* Hulbert, "Bad Familial 'Blood.'"

300 *Jory's strategy:* Mel Gussow, "New Plays in Louisville Provide Glorious Moments," *Lakeland Ledger*, April 9, 1989.

301 *"the biggest thing":* Dave Hunter, "Harry Crews' Writing Has Reached a New Stage," *Gainesville Sun*, January 2, 1989.

301 *As was now his habit:* Johansson interview.

302 *"In two hours":* Crews, *Body*, 13.

302 *Still, the positive:* Ann Patty to Harry Crews, October 17, 1989, HCP.

302 *Through their limited:* Two years later, Crews called Patty his favorite editor (after Simon & Schuster shuttered Poseidon Press). Bill DeYoung, "Novelist Harry Crews, a Reluctant Classic," *Lakeland Ledger*, December 12, 1993.

302 *"I have done the very":* Harry Crews to Ann Patty, January 18, 1990, HCP.

303 *"Not for a moment":* Faye Weldon, "A Single, Shining Muscle of a Girl," *NYT*, September 9, 1990.

303 *"You have made":* Crews, *Body*, 179–80.

303 *Maggie was proud:* Maggie Powell, interview with author, March 7, 2012.

Chapter Thirty-Two. Out of the Bottle

The epigraph is from the documentary *Guilty as Charged*, directed by Tom Thurman and Chris Iovenko (Fly by Noir Films, 1993).

305 *Gary Hawkins was:* Gary Hawkins, "Reconstructing Harry Crews," *The Paris Review Daily*, posted May 24, 2012, www.theparisreview.org /blog/2012/05/24/reconstructing-harry-crews (accessed April 5, 2014). Hawkins's film, *The Rough South of Harry Crews*, was released in 1992.

306 *He was invited:* Huntley Johnson, interview with author, December 1, 2012.

306 *Hours later:* John Morefield, interview with author, September 12, 2013.

306 *At another book festival:* Maxine Kumin, interview with author, February 7, 2012.

307 *"with malice and forethought":* Ruth Ellen Rasche, "Blue-Eyed Boy," *University of Florida Today*, November 1992.

307   *Miller appearance: The Dennis Miller Show*, NBC, February 4, 1992. Crews appeared on the short-lived talk show to promote the release of *Scar Lover*.

307   *Arm tattoo:* From the Cummings poem "Buffalo Bill's," 1923. Crews told David Aronson, writing for University of Florida's alumni magazine in 1992, "Cummings just wrote it down on paper, but I got it on my body, and I'm going to take it to the grave with me."

307   *"When folks see me":* Hawkins, *Deconstructing Harry Crews.*

307   *Jeffrey began:* Another writer, Tom Graves, interviewed Crews for *The Paris Review* in 1979. George Plimpton, editor of *The Paris Review*, rejected the piece after it was written. As an explanation, he told Graves he felt Crews's work was "gutter writing." "I don't consider Harry Crews quite in the front rank of American writers," he said. The piece was eventually published in *The Chouteau Review.*

308   *After the interview:* David Jeffrey, interview with author, November 11, 2011.

308   *"Tell the chairman":* Barry Hannah to Harry Crews, undated, HCP.

308   *McLaurin background:* Carpenter and Franklin, *Grit Lit*, 34.

309   *He stopped in Gainesville:* Tim McLaurin, "Is Your Novel Worth a Damn," in Bledsoe, *Perspectives on Harry Crews*, 11–13. McLaurin was also the focus of a documentary by Gary Hawkins, *The Rough South of Tim McLaurin*, released in 1990.

309   *"I read the book":* Crews, "Perfectly Shaped Stones," *Los Angeles Times*, October 21, 1990.

309   *Brown-Crews correspondence:* Larry Brown to Harry Crews, December 5, 1990; Harry Crews to Larry Brown, January 2, 1991; Larry Brown to Harry Crews, May 7, 1991, HCP.

310   *Brown recommendation:* Harry Crews to Mary Ann Workman, June 14, 1991, HCP.

310   *Harry arranged:* Larry Brown, "Harry Crews, Mentor and Friend," in Bledsoe, *Perspectives on Harry Crews*, 6–9.

310   *Harry brought:* Johnson interview.

311   *"The incredible amount":* Brown, "Harry Crews."

311   *"Alcohol whipped me":* Mary T. Schmich, "Still in the Game: On the Straight and Narrow with Writer Harry Crews, *Atlanta Journal-Constitution*, January 27, 1985.

311   *It was an empty:* Johnson interview.

312   *He tried acupuncture:* Harry Crews to Philip K. Springer, April 15, 2002, HCP.

312   *"They all tell":* John Williams, "Harry Crews: An American Tragicomedy," sites.google.com/site/fivepubs/harrycrews (retrieved November 16, 2011).

312   *It would be his last:* Roger Bull, "Everyone's Wild About Harry: Gaines-

ville Author Taking a Sober Look at the Future," *Florida Times-Union*,
April 5, 1992.

312   *He found a therapist:* Williams, "An American Tragicomedy."

312   *Another documentarian:* Thurman, *Guilty as Charged*.

313   *Though everybody:* Huntley Johnson, interview with author, April 18, 2014.

313   *It may have been:* Bill DeYoung, "Long Road from Hell: Once He Climbed Out of the Bottle, Harry Crews Became a Writer Again," *Gainesville Sun*, October 10, 1995.

313   *The solitary existence:* Crews, *Blood Issue*, script dated January 25, 1989, with revisions inserted, HCP.

Chapter Thirty-Three. Scarred Over

314   *In the spring of 1992:* Harry Crews to Pat Craddock, March 26, 1992, courtesy University of Florida.

314   *He had twenty-five years in:* Pat Craddock, interview with author, November 16, 2011.

314   *Salary:* Employment contract, 1991–92, courtesy University of Florida.

314   *Gone were the days:* Maud Newton, interview with author, November 20, 2011.

314   *"My only consolation":* Maud Newton, "Recalling Harry Crews' Fiction Class," maudnewton.com, October 14, 2004.

314   *"weirdly encouraged":* Newton interview.

314   *Harry hated:* Newton, "Recalling."

314   *"He would sometimes":* Newton interview.

314   *His diminishing role:* Bill DeYoung, "Novelist Harry Crews, A Reluctant Classic," *Lakeland Ledger*, December 12, 1993. Crews changed the title of *Circus Act* to *Celebration of Death* and eventually to *Celebration*, the title under which it was published. *Soap* became *Soap for Life*, then *Saippuakivikauppias* (the world's longest palindrome, meaning soap salesman), and finally *The Mulching of America*.

316   *Under the direction:* Ann Patty, interview with author, April 6, 2014.

316   *The shift wasn't:* Rick Schultz, "Crews Control," *Village View*, March 6–12, 1992.

316   *On the promotional tour:* *The Dennis Miller Show*, NBC, February 4, 1992.

317   *Patty, at Simon & Schuster:* Patty interview.

317   *Harry hated the title:* DeYoung, "Novelist." Earlier in the publishing process, the book had been titled *The Harry Crews Reader: Two Sides of Harry Crews* (Ken Siman to Harry Crews, September 29, 1992, HCP).

317   *For decades:* From the syllabus for Creative Writing—Fiction, instructor: H. Crews, University of Florida, 1995, HCP.

318   *Soon after:* Damon Sauve, "Everything Is Optimism, Beautiful, and Pain-

less: A Conversation with Harry Crews," from *A Large and Startling Figure: The Harry Crews Online Bibliography*, www.harrycrews.org /Features/Interviews/SauveD-Interview.html (retrieved May 12, 2014). Crews would not reveal the name of the writer but told Sauve it was a name he would recognize.

318   *The house gained:* Bledsoe, *Perspectives on Harry Crews*, 148.

319   *Harry thought George:* Harry Crews to Elinor B. Sidel, June 15, 1997, HCP.

319   *When Harry's next novel:* Harry Crews, *The Mulching of America* (New York: Simon & Schuster, 1995), 47.

319   *The Boss turned:* Crews, *The Mulching of America*, 47, 77–78.

320   *"If I've got any reservations":* Bill DeYoung, "Long Road from Hell," *Gainesville Sun*, October 10, 1995.

320   *Mulching reviews:* Valerie Sayers, "Pants of a Salesman: The Hero of Harry Crews' Novel Is Thrust into a Trouserless World," *NYT*, November 4, 1995; Dick Roraback, "The Birth of a Salesman: Harry Crews Deals Hyperbole Like a Card Shark," *Los Angeles Times*, January 14, 1996; "Mulching of America," *Publishers Weekly*, October 2, 1995.

320   *In its conclusion:* Bledsoe, *Perspectives*, 162.

Chapter Thirty-Four. Assault from Within

321   The comfortable existence: Harry Crews, "Assault of Memory," in Bledsoe, *Perspectives on Harry Crews*, 189.

321   *Myrtice married:* Crews, "What Mama Knows: A Son's Tribute to the Tough Little Lady Who Taught Him to Stand and Fight," *Southern Magazine*, May 1987.

322   *After Korea:* Jeannie Gaskins, interview with author, January 24, 2012.

322   *By 1995:* Crews, in Bledsoe, *Perspectives*, 192.

322   *Hoyett and Harry:* Chuck Eisman to Harry Crews, draft of "Singing His Own Song: An Interview with Harry Crews," *Quixote Quarterly*, March 26, 1994, HCP.

322   *The animus between:* Crews, in Bledsoe, *Perspectives*, 177, 192, 196.

323   *Harry held his tongue:* Gaskins interview.

323   *Myrtice died soon:* Jeffrey Good, "The South and Harry Crews Shall Rise Again," *St. Petersburg Times*, October 15, 1995.

324   *The following year:* Hoyett Crews to Harry Crews, July 11, 1996; Harry Crews to Hoyett and Ann Crews, July 18, 1996, HCP.

324   *By the time he mailed:* "Interview with Aunt Eva (Eva Haselden)," recorded April 1996, HCP.

324   *"The whole lunch":* Bob Mecoy, interview with author, April 30, 2014.

325   *The trend of media:* Doreen Carvajal, "Middling (and Unloved) in Publishing Land: Authors with Less Than Stellar Sales Are Unwanted by Big Houses," *NYT*, August 18, 1997.

325   *"If you were going"*: Mecoy interview.

325   *On top of that:* "A Writer's Face: The Letters of Harry Crews," commentary by Douglass Carlson, *Georgia Review*, Winter 2007.

325   *Harry had:* This book was originally titled *Horse-Hog-Gator Connection*, then changed to *Things That Swim in the Night*, and eventually *Grinder*.

326   *It soon turned out:* Mecoy interview.

326   *He titled the new project:* Earlier versions of the manuscript were titled *Mama Is Dead, Long Live Love and Hard Times,* and *The Death of a Lady.*

326   *In Gainesville:* Harry Crews to John Hawkins, July 16, 1998, HCP.

327   *"I had to walk into the meeting"*: Mecoy interview.

327   *A $10,000 check:* William Dulaney, interview with author, June 19, 2012.

327   *Though he did not:* Crews, in Bledsoe, *Perspectives*, 175, 187.

327   *Those two chapters:* Dulaney interview.

328   *"I looked at what"*: Ted Geltner, "Literary 'Assault,'" *Gainesville Sun*, March 16, 2008.

328   *The chapters were published:* Harry Crews, "Leaving Home for Home," *Georgia Review*, Winter 2007.

328   *That would be the last:* Harry Crews, *Assault of Memory*, dated 2005, private collection.

329   *"Can I get it done"*: Geltner, "Literary 'Assault.'"

Chapter Thirty-Five. Curtain Call

330   When Harry pulled back: "A Writer's Face: The Letters of Harry Crews," commentary by Douglass Carlson, *Georgia Review*, Winter 2007.

331   *Hemingway prize:* "Florida Writer Wins Literature Award," *Sarasota Herald Tribune*, July 20, 1998, 2A.

331   *Harry had long:* David Jeffrey, interview of Harry Crews, 1978, private collection.

331   *His French publisher:* Huntley Johnson, interview with author, April 19, 2014.

332   *"Because it would hurt"*: William Dulaney, interview with author, June 19, 2012.

332   *To George:* Harry Crews, *An American Family*, dedication.

332   *Georgia Hall of Fame:* Joan Stroer, "Hall of Fame to Recognize State's Writers," *Athens Banner-Herald*, July 10, 2000, onlineathens.com /stories/071000/new_0710000008.shtml (retrieved May 27, 2014); Georgia Writers Hall of Fame, 2001–2002 Induction Ceremony, www .georgiawritershalloffame.org/photo-gallery/2001-2002/index.php (retrieved May 27, 2014). The inaugural class of the Georgia Writers Hall of Fame also included Martin Luther King Jr., James Dickey, W. E. B. Du Bois, Joel Chandler Harris, John Oliver Killens, Sidney Lanier, Augustus Baldwin Longstreet, Carson McCullers, and Lillian Smith.

332   *"I'm so debilitated"*: Jeannie Gaskins, interview with author, January 24, 2012.

333   *Harry was the one*: Harry Crews, interviewed by Skip Hulett, 2002, HCP.

333   *Altman to direct Car*: Robert Altman to Joel Freedman, November 13, 1985, HCP.

334   *On the Road script*: Bledsoe, *Getting Naked*, 346.

334   *Cimino scripts*: Crowder, *Writing in the Southern Tradition*, 106–8. Unproduced scripts for *Boomtown* and *Clown* are in the Harry Crews Papers at the University of Georgia.

334   *"You put most"*: Chuck Eisman to Harry Crews, draft of "Singing His Own Song: An Interview with Harry Crews," *Quixote Quarterly*, March 26, 1994, HCP.

334   *In 1985*: Sean Cunningham, interview with author, July 5, 2012.

335   *"mindless carnage"*: Michael Wilmington, "New Kids But the Same Old Violence," *Los Angeles Times*, March 20, 1985.

335   *Cunningham exempted*: Cunningham interview.

335   *The rights to*: Charles Masters, "France's Davis Puts 'Curse' on Keitel, Paradis," *Hollywood Reporter*, 2004.

335   *"We would respectfully"*: Pierre-François and Philippe Decouflé to Harry Crews, December 27, 2005, HCP. Earlier in 2005, another film production based on a Crews novel, *The Knockout Artist*, died after scheduling had begun. Filming was set for the fall of 2005 in New Orleans. Hurricane Katrina struck the city on August 30.

336   *Hawk contract*: HCP.

336   *A young director*: Ted Geltner, "Other Crews Novels Headed for Films, Too," *Gainesville Sun*, November 20, 2004.

337   *"a barrage"*: Noel Murray, "Review: *The Hawk Is Dying*," March 29, 2007, 37www.avclub.com/review/the-hawk-is-dying-3533 (retrieved May 28, 2014).

337   *For the filmmakers*: Ted Geltner, "So-So at Sundance," *Gainesville Sun*, Friday, January 27, 2006. The following year, Goldberger re-edited the film and brought it to the Cannes Film Festival, where it was part of the Director's Fortnight, which showcases avant-garde material. It received a much better reception in France than it had in Utah. Shortly thereafter, Antidote Films found a distributor, Strand Releasing. It premiered in New York and Los Angeles in early 2007 and was released on home video later that year.

337   *Hawk reviews*: David Rooney, "Review: *The Hawk Is Dying*," *Variety*, January 22, 2006, variety.com/2006/film/reviews/the-hawk-is-dying-1200519185 (retrieved May 28, 2014); Nathan Lee, "Bye-Bye, Birdie," *Village Voice*, March 27, 2007, www.villagevoice.com/2007-03-20/film/bye-bye-birdie (retrieved May 28, 2014).

337   *What Goldberger*: Long after the film had been forgotten, Giamatti contended that it was an undiscovered masterpiece. Asked what movie he's

most proud of that never gets mentioned, he told a reporter in 2013, "There's a very small movie I did called *The Hawk Is Dying*. . . . Nobody has ever seen it. It's a really, really small budget movie. We shot it in two weeks. The original cut of it, I think, was brilliant. It got cut down for distribution, though. It's a good movie now, but it's really weird. I really, really have a strange affection for that movie ten people have seen" (Jack Giroux, "Why Paul Giamatti Never Gets to Play Nice Guys," *FilmSchoolRejects.com*, October 4, 2014).

338   *"There are other books":* Ted Geltner, "'I'm Glad They Made It,' Crews Says of the Film," *Gainesville Sun*, January 27, 2006.

338   *"Got good reviews":* Crews, *An American Family*, 80.

338   *"He urged Hawkins":* Harry Crews to John Hawkins, January 18, 2005, HCP.

339   *Three editions:* Crews, *An American Family*.

339   *The publicity efforts:* Ted Geltner, "Crews at 70: Still Fully Charged," *Gainesville Sun*, May 7, 2006.

339   *Word eventually:* David Shaftel, "Harry Crews, Aging Wild Man, Publishes Again, Quietly," *NYT*, August 22, 2006, www.nytimes.com/2006/08/22/books/22crew.html?ref=books&_r=0 (retrieved May 28, 2014).

Chapter Thirty-Six. Last Stop

341   Diagnoses background: Medical information from the National Institute of Neurological Disorders and Stroke, National Institutes of Health, www.ninds.nih.gov (retrieved May 30, 2014).

342   *"Nobody has ever":* David Shaftel, "Harry Crews, Aging Wild Man, Publishes Again, Quietly," *NYT*, August 22, 2006, www.nytimes.com/2006/08/22/books/22crew.html?ref=books&_r=0 (retrieved May 28, 2014).

342   *From time to time:* William L. Dulaney, interview with author, June 19, 2012.

343   *An incident:* Charné Porter, interview with author, December 5, 2013.

343   *Harry told:* Dulaney interview.

343   *According to Sally:* Sally Crews, interview with author, November 11, 2011.

343   *"When I have my back":* Byron Crews to Harry Crews, June 10, 2002, HCP.

344   *A series of hurricanes:* In 2007 John Ingram, deputy director of University Libraries and director of collections at UF, said that the UF library had had discussions with Crews in the late 1990s about housing his collection, but nothing concrete ever developed (interview with author, May 2006).

344   *That, plus Harry's:* Ted Geltner, "Diction-Harry," *Gainesville Sun*, May 11, 2007, 1D.

345   *His college roommate:* Ed Nagel, interview with author, May 9, 2012.

345   *"It was just sad":* Tyler Turkle, interview with author, May 21, 2014.

346   *Filming progressed:* Michael Thompson, "Lights, Camera, Action . . . Maybe," *The Alma News Courier*, April 13, 2006.

346   *While on site:* Mark Hinson, "The Last of a Kind: Two Filmmakers with Tallahassee Connections Work to Capture the Essence of Writer Harry Crews," *Tallahassee Democrat*, March 19, 2006.

346   *The awards:* "A Novel Opportunity at Event," *St. Augustine Record*, August 25, 2009, staugustine.com/stories/082509/community_1874941 .shtml (retrieved June 3, 2014).

347   *Harry declined:* Dulaney interview.

347   *Again, Harry:* Turkle interview.

347   *Soon, he was:* Dulaney interview.

347   *In his own:* Hinson, "The Last of a Kind."

347   *The despair:* Huntley Johnson, interview with author, December 1, 2012.

348   *"You're the most inept":* Dulaney interview.

348   *Byron came down:* Johnson interview.

348   *A young writer:* Jason Hodges, "Harry Crews," *The Dirt Workers Journal*, Monday, April 2, 2012, jasonehodges.blogspot.com/2012/04 /harry-crews.html (retrieved June 3, 2014).

348   *People from his past:* Pat Waters, interview with author, October 28, 2011.

348   *Karate dedication:* Harry Crews, *Karate Is a Thing of the Spirit*, 9.

348   *Now, Ben Roark:* Ben Roark, interview with author, June 3, 2013.

349   *Atkinson visit:* Jay Atkinson, interview with author, April 7, 2012.

349   *A loose confederation:* Gary Lippman, "A Singular Southern Gentleman Goes Out 'Biting,'" *The Paris Review Daily*, April 25, 2012, www .theparisreview.org/blog/2012/04/25/a-singular-southern-gentleman-goes -out-"biting" (retrieved June 3, 2014).

349   *Despite his condition:* Skip Hulett, interview with author, May 22, 2012.

350   *During one lucid:* Sally Crews, interview with author, March 29, 2012.

350   *Obituaries:* Matt Schudel, "Harry Crews, Novelist of Hard Lives and Dark Corners of the South," *Washington Post*, March 29, 2012; Elaine Woo, "Harry Crews Dies at 76; Southern Writer with Darkly Comic Vision," *Los Angeles Times,* April 1, 2012; Margalit Fox, "Harry Crews, Writer of Dark Fiction, Is Dead at 76," *NYT*, March 30, 2012.

351   *Remembrances:* Steve Oney, "Harry Crews and 'Getting Naked,'" *Los Angeles Times*, April 4, 2012; Maud Newton, "And Now He's Dead: Remembering Harry Crews," March 30, 2012, *The Awl*, www.theawl .com/2012/03/remembering-harry-crews (retrieved June 3, 2014); Hilma Wolitzer, "Remembering Harry Crews," *Reuters*, April 5, 2012, blogs.reuters.com/great-debate/2012/04/05/remembering-harry-crews (retrieved June 3, 2014).

REFERENCES

Primary Sources

The Gospel Singer. New York: Morrow, 1968. Reprint, London: Gorse, 1995.
Naked in Garden Hills. New York: Morrow, 1969.
This Thing Don't Lead to Heaven. New York: Morrow, 1970.
Karate Is a Thing of the Spirit. New York: Morrow, 1971.
Car. New York: Morrow, 1972.
The Hawk Is Dying. New York: Knopf, 1973. London: Secker & Warburg, 1974.
The Gypsy's Curse. New York: Knopf, 1974.
A Feast of Snakes. New York: Atheneum, 1976.
A Childhood: The Biography of a Place. New York: Harper & Row, 1978.
Blood and Grits. New York: Harper & Row, 1979.
The Enthusiast. n.p.: Palaemon Press, 1981.
All We Need of Hell. New York: Harper & Row, 1987.
The Knockout Artist. New York: Harper & Row, 1988.
Body. New York: Poseidon Press, 1990.
Scar Lover. New York: Poseidon Press, 1992.
Classic Crews: A Harry Crews Reader. New York: Poseidon Press, 1993.
The Mulching of America. New York: Simon & Schuster, 1995.
Celebration. New York: Simon & Schuster, 1998.
Where Does One Go When There's No Place Left to Go? Los Angeles: Blood & Guts Press, 1998.
An American Family: The Baby with the Curious Markings. Los Angeles: Blood & Guts Press, 2006.
Harry Crews Papers (HCP), Hargrett Rare Book and Manuscript Library, University of Georgia, Athens.

Secondary Sources

Atkinson, Jay. *Memoirs of a Rugby-Playing Man: Guts, Glory, and Blood in the World's Greatest Game.* New York: St. Martin's Press, 2012.
Bain, David Haward, and Mary Smyth Duffy, eds. *Whose Woods These Are: A History of the Bread Loaf Writers' Conference, 1926–1992.* New York: Ecco Press, 1993.
Baker, Bonnie Taylor. *The History of Alma and Bacon County, Georgia.* Privately published, 1984.

Beatty, Richmond, et al., eds. *The Literature of the South*. Chicago: Scott, Foresman, 1952.

Beck, Charlotte H. *The Fugitive Legacy: A Critical History*. Baton Rouge: Louisiana State University Press, 2001.

Bisbort, Alan. *Beatniks: A Guide to American Subculture*. Santa Barbara, Calif.: Greenwood Press, 2010.

Bledsoe, Erik, ed. *Getting Naked with Harry Crews: Interviews*. Gainesville: University Press of Florida, 1999.

————. *Perspectives on Harry Crews*. Jackson: University Press of Mississippi, 2001.

Blotner, Joseph. *Robert Penn Warren: A Biography*. New York: Random House, 1997.

Brown, Larry. *Billy Ray's Farm: Essays*. Chapel Hill, N.C.: Algonquin Books, 2001.

Bruccoli, Matthew J., and Judith S. Baughman, eds. *Crux: The Letters of James Dickey*. New York: Alfred A. Knopf, 1999.

Buehrer, David. *The Psychology of Social Class in the Fiction of Russell Banks, Denis Johnson and Harry Crews: Neo-Realism, Naturalism, and Humanism in Contemporary Fiction*. Lewiston, N.Y.: Edwin Mellen Press, 2014.

Caldwell, Erskine. *Tobacco Road*. New York: Modern Library, 1960.

Calhoun, Richard J., and Robert W. Hill. *James Dickey*. Boston: Twayne, 1983.

Carpenter, Brian, and Tom Franklin, eds. *Grit Lit: A Rough South Reader*. Columbia, S.C.: University of South Carolina Press, 2012.

Cassis, A. F., ed. *Graham Greene: Man of Paradox*. Chicago: Loyola University Press, 1994.

Coleman, Kenneth, ed. *A History of Georgia*. 2nd ed. Athens: University of Georgia Press, 1991.

Conklin, Paul. *The Southern Agrarians*. Knoxville: University of Tennessee Press, 1988.

Crowder, A. B. *Writing in the Southern Tradition: Interviews with Five Contemporary Authors*. Atlanta: Rodopi, 1990.

Cummings, Bruce. *The Korean War: A History*. New York: The Modern Library, 2010.

da Cruz, Daniel. *Boot: The Inside Story of How a Few Good Men Became Today's Marines*. New York: St. Martin's Press, 1987.

Datlow, Ellen, ed. *Little Deaths: Twenty-four Tales of Sex and Horror*. London: Millennium, 1994.

Daugherty, Tracy. *Hiding Man: A Biography of Donald Barthelme*. New York: St. Martin's Press, 2009.

Davis, Jack E., and Raymond Arsenault, eds. *Paradise Lost? The Environmental History of Florida*. Gainesville: University Press of Florida, 2005.

Flora, Joseph M., and Robert Bain, eds. *Fifty Southern Writers after 1900: A Bibliographic Sourcebook*. New York: Greenwood Press, 1987.

Florida State Department of Education. *Five Years of Progress: Florida's Junior Colleges, Their Contributions and Their Future: A Report to the State Board of Education by the State Junior College Advisory Board.* Tallahassee: State Department of Education, 1963.

Frederick II of Hohenstaufen. *The Art of Falconry: Being the De Arte Venandi Cum Avibus of Frederick II of Hohenstaufen.* Trans. and ed. Casey A. Wood and F. Marjorie Fyfe. Stanford, Calif.: Stanford University Press, 1961.

George-Warren, Holly. *The Rolling Stone Book of the Beats: The Beat Generation and American Culture.* New York: Hyperion, 1999.

Gould, Tony. *A Summer Plague: Polio and Its Survivors.* New Haven, Conn.: Yale University Press, 1995.

Greene, Graham. *The End of the Affair.* New York: Penguin Books, 1979.

Halliwell, Martin. *American Culture in the 1950s.* Edinburgh, Scotland: Edinburgh University Press, 2007.

Hart, Henry. *James Dickey: The World as a Lie.* New York: Picador USA, 2000.

Hunt, Tim. *Kerouac's Crooked Road: Development of a Fiction.* Berkeley: University of California Press, 1996.

Jeffrey, David K. *A Grit's Triumph: Essays on the Works of Harry Crews.* Port Washington, N.Y.: Associated Faculty Press, 1983.

Johansson, David. *Skin of Sunset.* Melbourne, Fla.: Squire Press, 2009.

Kelly, Richard T. *Sean Penn: His Life and Times.* New York: Canongate U.S., 2004.

Kerouac, Jack. *On the Road.* New York: Viking, 1997.

Kirkpatrick, Smith. *The Sun's Gold.* Boston: Houghton Mifflin, 1974.

Klevar, Harvey L. *Erskine Caldwell: A Biography.* Knoxville: University of Tennessee Press, 1993.

Kyvig, David. *Daily Life in the United States, 1920–1940: How Americans Lived through the "Roaring Twenties" and the Great Depression.* Chicago: Ivan R. Dee, 2004.

Lane, Mills. *The People of Georgia: An Illustrated Social History.* Savannah, Ga.: The Beehive Press, 1975.

Lemon, J. Michael, ed. *Conversations with Norman Mailer.* Jackson: University Press of Mississippi, 1988.

Lytle, Andrew. *The Hero with the Private Parts: Essays by Andrew Lytle.* Baton Rouge: Louisiana State University Press, 1966.

Mailer, Norman. *Tough Guys Don't Dance.* New York: Random House, 1984.

McCarthy, Kevin M., and Murray D. Laurie. *Guide to the University of Florida and Gainesville.* Sarasota, Fla.: Pineapple Press, 1997.

McKeen, William. *Mile Marker Zero: The Moveable Feast of Key West.* New York: Crown, 2011.

————. *Outlaw Journalist: The Life and Times of Hunter S. Thompson.* New York: W.W. Norton, 2008.

Mettler, Suzanne. *Soldiers to Citizens: The G.I. Bill and the Making of the Greatest Generation.* New York: Oxford University Press, 2005.

O'Connell, Aaron B. *Underdogs: The Making of the Modern Marine Corps.* Cambridge, Mass.: Harvard University Press, 2012.

Oshinsky, David M. *Polio: An American Story*. New York: Oxford University Press, 2005.

Pearce, Donn. *Cool Hand Luke*. New York: Scribner's, 1965.

———. *Pier Head Jump*. Indianapolis: Bobbs-Merrill, 1972.

Pleasants, Julian. *Gator Tales: An Oral History of the University of Florida*. Gainesville: University Press of Florida, 2006.

Polsgrove, Carol. *It Wasn't Pretty, Folks, but Didn't We Have Fun? Esquire in the Sixties*. New York: W.W. Norton, 1995.

Proctor, Samuel, and Wright Langley. *Gator History: A Pictorial History of the University of Florida*. Gainesville: South Star Publishing, 1986.

Sharrock, Roger. *Saints, Sinners, and Comedians: The Novels of Graham Greene*. Notre Dame, Ind.: University of Notre Dame Press, 1984.

Sumner, David E. *The Magazine Century: American Magazines Since 1900*. New York: Peter Lang, 2010.

Taylor, Nick. *American Made: The Enduring Legacy of the WPA, When FDR Put the Nation to Work*. New York: Bantam Books, 2008.

Tolles, Zonira Hunter. *Shadows on the Sand: A History of the Land and the People in the Vicinity of Melrose, Florida*. Keystone Heights, Fla.: Privately published, 1976.

Van Ness, Gordon, ed. *The One Voice of James Dickey: His Letters and Life, 1942–1969*. Columbia: University of Missouri Press, 2003.

Warren, George, ed. *The Rolling Stone Book of the Beats: The Beat Generation and American Culture*. New York: Hyperion, 1999.

Watson, Sterling. *The Calling*. New York: Dell, 1986.

Wynne-Davies, Marion, ed. *Bloomsbury Guide to English Literature*. London: Bloomsbury, 1989.

Zollo, Paul. *Conversations with Tom Petty*. New York: Omnibus Press, 2005.

INDEX

Turner, Alfred, 321–22
Tuttle, Lyle, 188
Tyson, Mike, 287–89, 291, 293

"Unattached Smile, The" (Crews), 39, 90,
   91; writing of, 78–79
Updike, John, 183, 309
Uris, Leon, 113
U.S. Marine Corps, 41, 44, 54; basic training, 33–36; Marine Air Corps Station,
   38–41

Van Dyke, Henry, 135
Variety, 337
Velvet Horn, The (Lytle), 58, 60
Venetian Crier, 93
Village Voice, 337
Voboril, Mary, 283–84
Vonnegut, Kurt, 212, 303

Wagner, Minerva, 84
Wakefield, Dan, 128–30
Wallace, Henry, 14
War and Peace (Tolstoy), 68
Warren, Robert Penn, 3, 56
Washington Post, 350

Waters, Pat, 54, 61, 65, 66, 307, 348; cri-
   tique of *Gospel Singer*, 99–100
Watson, Sterling, 265–67
Weep No More, My Brother (Watson), 265
Weldon, Faye, 303
Welty, Eudora, 140, 167
*Where Does One Go When There Is No
   Place Left to Go?* (Crews), 271, 339
Whitman, Charles, 205
Willey, John, 136
Williams, Aubrey, 68
Williams, Michelle, 336
Williams, Tennessee, 116, 209
Winningham, Mare, 293
Wolfe, Tom, 184, 200
Wolitzer, Hilma, 130–31, 351
Wright, Piers, 55
Wright, Robin, 295
Wyatt, Lawrence, 155

X, Malcolm, 136

Yearling, The (Rawlings), 62
Yellowstone Red, 46

Zimpel, Lloyd, 211